THE COMPLETE ELVENOMICON

Thank you for supporting independent publishing.

20TH ANNIVERSARY DELUXE EDITION

THE COMPLETE ELVENOMICON

A TREASURY OF ELVEN MAGICK, FAERIE SPELLS and DRUID LORE

Collected Works by Joshua Free

© 2024, JOSHUA FREE

ISBN : 978-1-961509-58-0

All Rights Reserved. No part of this publication may be reproduced in any form or by any means, electronic or mechanical, including copying/scanning, or any information storage or artificial intelligence system, without permission from the publisher. This book is a religious artifact. It is not intended to substitute medical treatment or professional advice.

A MARDUKITE ACADEMY PUBLICATION
Mardukite Esoteric Research Library Reference
Mardukite Academy Grade-I Educational Textbook
cum superiorum privilegio veniaque
20TH ANNIVERSARY EDITION
Deluxe Edition—September 2024

Published from
The Joshua Free Imprint – JFI Publications
Mardukite Borsippa HQ, San Luis Valley, Colorado
Representing Mardukite Truth Seeker Press
Mardukite Academy of Systemology
and Founding Church of Mardukite Zuism

mardukite.com

AN UNDERGROUND FAVORITE FOR TWO DECADES!
THE ORIGINAL CLASSIC GUIDE TO THE ELVEN WAY, NOW EXPANDED!

Come and enter the Enchanted Forest, deep in the heart of the Green World, and discover the greatest secrets of the Ancient Mystery Tradition—a hidden legacy of long-forgotten "druidic magick" maintained by real Elves and Faerie in history.

This revised oversized deluxe edition commemorates the 20th Anniversary of the underground release of "*Book of Elven-Faerie*." This tome is expanded to combine the original material (*The Secret Book of Elven-Faerie*, *The Elven-Faerie Grimoire*, and *The Enchanted Forest*) along with three recently released never-before-published companion volumes (*A Secret Legacy of Elves and Fairies*, *Elven-Faerie Spellbook*, and *The Book of Ogham*)—providing six-books-in-one.

Make your passage into Faerie as you unveil the mysteries contained within this revolutionary and controversial classic by Joshua Free, which has revealed for the first time to the mortal world: a uniquely beautiful, authentic and complete guide to this ancient Elven-Faerie Celtic-Druid Tradition.

The shinning path of the Elven Way grants any *Seeker* the key to unlock forbidden truths of esoteric archaeology including:

- How traditions of the Ancient Near East evolved into mythical, mystical and societal systems in Europe.
- How the forgotten arcane legacies of Elven-Faerie and even "Dragon" races on Earth have shaped the Western world and "Western magical tradition."
- How modern folk-magic and "New Age" revivals may be traced back to coincide with evolutions in Human civilization marked by specific ancient migrations.

"*The Complete Elvenomicon*" by Joshua Free offers an entire exploration into the Elven Way, Celtic Faerie Tradition and Danubian Druidism as never seen before. Drawing from hundreds of sources and underground groups, the "Elven-Faerie" tradition and system of magic is presented in its candid entirety, as applicable and alive today as it was thousands of years ago—and critically needed for our times, and in our current environmental conditions.

Expanded to now include several complete "grimoires" that add an entirely new dimension of everyday enchantment to the "New Age," allowing all truly dedicated initiates an opportunity to:

- Tap a vast otherworldly network of Elemental Power only alluded to elsewhere in "Fairy" or "Druid" lore.
- Experience the vibrant energy of "Faerie Magic" and "Fairy Spells" with many unique solitary rites and group liturgies.
- Access deep "Earth wisdom" known only to trees, with a complete system of Elvish-Ogham "Forest Magick."

These long-lost teachings and techniques may even provide new historical foundations and credibility for modern magical revivals, resulting from *one seeker's* pursuits for the unspeakable origins of ancient Celtic Druidism... and the discovery of a complete tradition.

THE COMPLETE ELVENOMICON

Introduction to the 20th Anniversary Deluxe Edition . . . 11
Foreword to the 15th Anniversary Edition (reprinted) . . . 15

THE SECRET BOOK OF ELVEN-FAERIE

Ancient Eurasia: The Genesis of the Elven-Faerie . . . 21
Age of Faerie: A Legacy of the Children of the Stars . . . 35
Dark Ages of Earth-History:
    The Thousand-Year Elven-Faerie Holocaust . . . 45
Elves and Druids: The Secret World of Faerie . . . 58

A SECRET LEGACY OF ELVES AND FAIRIES

Mortals and Elves: The Secret Legacy of Robert Kirk . . . 75
The Quest for the Otherworld . . . 78
Mardukite Master Course:
    "Otherworld Tech" (Academy Lecture) . . . 81
Secret Commonwealth of Elves, Fauns, and Fairies . . . 89
On the Subterranean Inhabitants . . . 91
Of the Predictions Made by Seers . . . 104

THE ELVEN-FAERIE GRIMOIRE

The Elven Way: Elements of the Tradition . . . 113
Casting the Circle of Power (at the Nemeton) . . . 117
Extinguishing the Circle of Power . . . 124
"Gifts of Faeire" (Consecrating Symbols of Power) . . . 126
Basic Rites of Faerie-Calling . . . 129

An Introduction to Elven-Faerie Spellcraft . . . 132
The Elven Wizardry of Healing and Protection . . . 136
Self-Dedication Rite (Elven-Faerie Tradition) . . . 139
Circle-Initiation Rite (Elven-Faerie Tradition) . . . 143
The "Eisteddfodd" (Festival Liturgy) . . . 147
The "Alardana" (Festivals and Seasonal Rites) . . . 153
Samhain (Alardan Festival) . . . 154
Alban Arthuann (Alardan Festival) . . . 156
Imbolc (Alardan Festival) . . . 158
Alban Eiler (Alardan Festival) . . . 161
Belteine (Alardan Festival) . . . 163
Alban Heruin (Alardan Festival) . . . 165
Lughnassadh (Alardan Festival) . . . 166
Alban Elved (Alardan Festival) . . . 170
The "Cor Anar" (Annual Wheel of the Year)
    De'ea Canayen Istari Elandra . . . 172

THE ELVEN-FAERIE SPELLBOOK

The Elven-Faerie Celtic-Druid Magical Tradition . . . 177
Mardukite Master Course:
    "Danubian Druidism" (Academy Lecture) . . . 180
Mardukite Master Course:
    "Elven-Faerie Tradition" (Academy Lecture) . . . 188
Enchantment of the Faerie Realm . . . 199
Inviting the Nature Spirits Into Your Realm . . . 200
Natural Magic: The Ancient Craft of Elven Wizards . . . 205
Natural Magic: Tuning Into Nature . . . 207
Natural Magic: Herbcraft and Earth Power . . . 209
Faerie Magic: Herbs and Plants . . . 212
Alchemical Herbcraft: High Arts of Natural Magic . . . 215
An Elven-Faerie Celtic-Druid Herbal Grimoire . . . 217
Emmenagogic Herbs & Fertility (Women's Wisdom) . . . 218
The Faerie Gem . . . 220
Elven-Faerie Language Dictionary (abridged) . . . 221

THE ENCHANTED FOREST

The Magic of the Enchanted Forest . . . 233
Elven High Magick: The Basics . . . 236
Enchanting Trees, Forests and Groves . . . 241
Elven Magic: Rays of Light and Energy-Play . . . 245
Elven Magic: Communing With Nature . . . 252
Elven Magic: The "Great Tree Rite" . . . 260
By Wand, Ward and Staff (Magical Tools) . . . 264
The Alder Tree (sylva druieachd) . . . 269
The Apple Tree (sylva druieachd) . . . 270
The Ash Tree (sylva druieachd) . . . 271
The Aspen Tree (sylva druieachd) . . . 272
The Beech Tree (sylva druieachd) . . . 273
The Birch Tree (sylva druieachd) . . . 273
The Blackthorn Tree (sylva druieachd) . . . 274
The Ceder Tree (sylva druieachd) . . . 275
The Cherry Tree (sylva druieachd) . . . 276
The Elder Tree (sylva druieachd) . . . 276
The Fir/Pine/Elm Current (sylva druieachd) . . . 277
The Furze/Gorse Current (sylva druieachd) . . . 278
The Hawthorn/Whitethorn Tree (sylva druieachd) . . . 279
The Hazel Tree (sylva druieachd) . . . 280
The Heather/Mistletoe Current (sylva druieachd) . . . 280
The Holly Tree (sylva druieachd) . . . 281
The Ivy Current (sylva druieachd) . . . 282
The Maple Tree (sylva druieachd) . . . 282
The Oak Tree (sylva druieachd) . . . 283
The Reed/Broom Current (sylva druieachd) . . . 284
The Rowen Tree (sylva druieachd) . . . 285
The Vine Current (sylva druieachd) . . . 285
The Willow Tree (sylva druieachd) . . . 286
The Yew Tree (sylva druieachd) . . . 286

THE BOOK OF OGHAM

A Brief History of the "Ogham" ... 293
Mardukite Master Course:
    "The Ogham Paths" (Academy Lecture) ... 298
The Ogham Description Key ... 311
The Birch Tree / Beith ogham ... 313
The Rowen Tree / Luis ogham ... 315
The Alder Tree / Fearn ogham ... 317
The Willow Tree / Saille ogham ... 319
The Ash Tree / Nuin ogham ... 321
The Hawthorn Tree / Huathe ogham ... 323
The Oak Tree / Duir ogham ... 325
The Holly Tree / Tinne ogham ... 327
The Hazel Tree / Coll ogham ... 329
The Apple Tree / Quert ogham ... 331
The Vine / Muin ogham ... 333
The Ivy / Gort ogham ... 335
The Reed / Ngetal ogham ... 337
The Blackthorn Tree / Straif ogham ... 339
The Elder Tree / Ruis ogham ... 341
The Fir Tree / Ailim ogham ... 343
The Furze / Ohn ogham ... 345
The Heather / Ur ogham ... 347
The Aspen Tree / Eadha ogham ... 349
The Yew Tree / Ioho ogham ... 351
Divination in the Elven-Druid Tradition ... 355
Oghamancy: The Art of Casting the Ogham Fews ... 358
The Forfedha ("Fifths") Spread ... 359
A Celtic Tree Oracle Quick-Start ... 362

APPENDIX

Introducing the Original "Mardukite Master Course" ... 367
Suggested Reading and Additional Materials ... 377

20TH ANNIVERSARY INTRODUCTION TO THE "ELVENOMICON" DELUXE EDITION

by Joshua Free

My participation in the legacy behind 'The Complete Elvenomicon' began in the mid-1990's amidst a critical resurgence of 'New Age' interests—and foremost among these popular revivals: the *Celts* and *Druids.* Each of its parts is an integral of a greater body of work pertaining to my personal involvement with *Pheryllt* and *Elven-Faerie* traditions of Druidism for thirty years. This material was imparted to me through personal 'apprenticeship' directly by its modern developers —as reflected in the original *Elvenomicon* series (and my work concerning the *Draconomicon*).

The original '*Elvenomicon*' volume contained a trilogy. It first circulated in the underground as "*The Book of Elven-Faerie,*" but I later renamed it "*Elvenomicon*" to avoid confusing the total collection of work with the title of the first discourse it contained: *Book of Elven-Faerie—* now retitled *Secret Book of Elven-Faerie* for the 20th Anniversary reissue. It is really a separate discourse from the other two parts in the trilogy: *Greenwood Forest Grimoire* (now reissued as "*The Enchanted Forest*") and *The Elven-Faerie Grimoire.* Collectively, this trilogy comprises *Elvenomicon* 'Series-1' and contains my own original presentation of this specific Elven-Faerie Druidic Tradition, now standing for 20 years past.

The subject of 'Faery-Faiths in Celtic Countries' frequently occupies the attention of Druids throughout the ages, but also practitioners of modern Elven-Faerie magical traditions. The influence on 'New Age' revivals of 'Faery Wicca' and 'Celtic Witchcraft' are equally significant. Many customs and 'sabbats' observed today—and quite often taken for granted—very much owe their foundations to the ancient 'Celtic-Faerie Tradition' and what is better known today as "*Druidism.*"

Materials for the *Elvenomicon* first resulted from many years of research, deliberation and contemplation spent in personal dedication to the Elven Tradition before attempting to set this version of it in down in print. It is only now in this new deluxe edition that the first trilogy is joined with other parts that were not originally included— and of which have only recently been released as a companion 'Series-2' trilogy.

The original presentation was edited to specific "commercial specifications" prior to founding the Mardukite movement (and its Truth Seeker Press) in 2008. Such limiting considerations are no longer relevant for this large deluxe 20th Anniversary edition.

The "Elven Way" and "Faerie Tradition" are a part of nearly all relevant 21st century 'new consciousness', 'new thought' or otherwise earth-oriented forms of 'nature mysticism'. My own notebooks that *this* work is based on—as a *"living testament"*—have now been reevaluated numerous times before presenting this publication. It is quite difficult to solidify Elven lore and "words of light" to the printed page —for they are fluidly dynamic, shimmering etherically in the waves of the *Astral Sea.*

In many ways, only "Druidry" and indigenous shamanism reflect the same type of spiritual "pathway" for Human Ascension that is alluded to in Elven Tradition. And if supplemented with our latest spiritual developments for a new standard "Systemology," an Elven-Faerie Druid Tradition can also be an effective stepping stone on a truer Pathway to a Spiritual Ascension. This is how we present such gradients at the Mardukite Academy.

Although most New Age texts equate Elves and other elemental faerie beings exclusively with the Otherworld or Astral Plane, more experienced *Seekers* and practitioners understand the connection between these races and a "very real" legacy of Elven-Dragon traditions and the *Tuatha d'Anu* migrating westward across Europe from Mesopotamia and Anatolia, carrying with them a vast tradition and repository of knowledge essentially predating any "Ancient Mystery School."

The term "Elven magic" ("Elven magick") is used to distinguish this specific "Elven-Ffayrie" system—also called the *"Edaphic Tradition"*— from others in the 'New Age'. However, to the Elves themselves, magic *is* simply "magic" and it comes from an innate faculty—not some "supernatural" facet of life or intellectual study. Once again: Magic is *not* a "supernatural" power. On the contrary, real magick is quite "natural"—and, in this universe, it must also follow principles of "natural law" or "cosmic law" (various reality-agreements established for this universe) even if not commonly and clearly understood as such.

When Humans refer to "magick," they are simply referring to an esoteric study and a creative use of forces in the universe—the same principles that manifest reality on a moment-to-moment basis. It is a practical application of the true knowledge and lore in everyday life. It should always be enacted *towards* one's own Ascension and in acts to manifest a more harmonious world for all Life in existence.

True "magick" in the Elven Tradition is innate. These beings do not require years of arcane study and training that the Wizard Schools of Humans and "Fey-Touched" might resort to. Elven-Ffayrie simply do not see "magick" as something "outside" of themselves. It is developed and refined as part of their everyday natural life—over a period of progressive self-discovery—just as a Human might choose to refine their own personal tastes and skills, affecting muscle memory or some other artificial *automaticity* for experiencing (and creating) reality.

Wisdom of experience—and I mean "Self-Honest" experiences from a point of true actualized Awareness—develops with time, and this is something that Elven-Ffayrie races are not short on while residing in the 'Lands Beyond'. Elves and faerie folk also view magick as a part of art. When something created or changed becomes *charged* or imbued with energy as a result of *intention*, it becomes *art*—and the Fey learned to use this art to shape the natural world we see all around us as our "reality." And magick—in all of its forms—will create, transform or even destroy some reflection of our global "reality."

"Magickal feats"—as conceived and purported by Humans—are accomplished via the activation of the mind's subconscious faculties—which becomes "potential power." It may be activated with specific use of symbolism and imagery or focal aids that help an individual direct or channel energy.

We are always actively participating in this *game*—but it is only with our *conscious* participation that we have the power to truly and knowingly be creative.

Many customs and methods of raising energy for this very purpose exist—ritual movements, breathing exercises, ceremonial dances—all of which entice the *awareness* and *presence* of the total *Self* to become actively involved in bringing about desired results. All intentional acts are "magical"—even when it is cyclic self-talk of defeatism—and we consistently feed our awareness and attention-energies into wherever our focus lies.

All acts, whether mundane or esoteric—are magical when they are movements of energy that create change—in accordance with true will—and following natural laws and cosmic principles that may or may not be widely understood. The Human Condition is easily distracted—and so rituals and ceremonial drama; use of music and vocalized intentions; alternative attire and altar dressings; fragrance of sweet and musty incense and flickering firelight—all are effectively used to bring the *Self* into full awareness and control of the *Self* alone.

It is important to realize—especially if you desire a true understanding of "Elven Magick"—that it is not the rituals and incantations themselves that hold the "power" in magic. A catalyst only represents potential until properly used—and that use is based on ability. "Magickal abilities" come from within—first and foremost—from the part of the "individual" that is not "separated" from the All—but is interconnected and linked absolutely to the fundamental Oneness of reality.

—Joshua Free
Summer Solstice 2024
San Luis Valley, Colorado

FOREWORD TO THE 15TH ANNIVERSARY "ELVENOMICON"

An Introduction by David Zibert

"The normal world reflects a black magic spell designed to convince us that we are not Faerie Folk and that, in fact, Faerie does not exist. Once you see through the spell, a world of wonder unfolds before you."—The Silver Elves, *Elf-Quotes*.

Introducing the subject of the elves is always tricky business. Most, if not all, believe it impossible for such beings to actually exist, that they are contained only within the domain of imagination and fantasy. And yet, what is an "Elf" if not merely a word, a name? And names merely are *semantic* tools used for understanding an object (physical) or an idea (abstract). "Semantics" are a language system, and like all systems it was created (programmed) and is gauged (updated) with some purpose or agenda in mind, not only by its original developer, but by those who eventually took control of said system through time, as it is written: "Reality belongs to whomever holds the largest paradigm."* This is made particularly evident when looking up roots of the word "reality," as expressed in Joshua Free's major publication, *The Complete Anunnaki Bible*:

> *"This whole question of what is 'real' or 'not real' is a philosophical problem that affects not only the magickal world and metaphysics but all of science, religion and really any personal perception of 'truth.' The word 'reality' comes from an Indo-European root 'reg,' (as in 'regal,' 'region,' 'regular') which is related to a 'measuring device' or 'ruler' (and also as a 'ruler' as in 'king'). The word 'sane' relates to what is 'clean,' 'sanitary' or 'healthy' and functionally it was the purpose of the king or 'ruler' of the 'real world' or 'realm' to set boundaries for what is 'real' and 'not real'—and by which 'sanity' might be judged."‡*

It may be legitimately asked: who are these "Reality Engineers" behind our systems of perceptions and languages and, more importantly, what is their agenda concerning humanity—and everything else? Whatever the case might be, as per the "Hermetic teachings," everything in the universe follows the same course, coming from what might be called a singular, "divine breath." It thus logically foll-

---

* Phil Brucato. *Mage: The Ascnesion (2ⁿᵈ Ed)*. White Wolf, 1995. (p. 42)
‡ Joshua Free. *The Complete Anunnaki Bible*.

ows that man-made systems—such as those of machines and computers—are based upon the same precept as the ordainment of the universe. This analogy offers great help when analyzing the reality program of the human life-wave.

Most human-made machines are programmed to think only in binary language—"1" and "0"—that computes as either of the terms "white" or "black," meaning "yes" or "no"—*Lux* or *Nox*. Humans, being some sort of "gods-made" machines,§ are seemingly different. Indeed, we rather think through some kind of "grey zone," where lies notions such as 'maybe' or 'doubt', so that any "absolute" will appear "relative" from the perspective of the human program-paradigm. More appropriately, this zone is not "grey" but rather "rainbow," and it is within this zone that the games of semantic manipulation are played out as the "Reality Experiment." Names are used as a tool to define what lies in said grey zone (*i.e., reality*) with a common denominator so that humans may refer to them from a dualistic "I-not-I" perspective—shaping "agreed upon reality," the wording themselves having no actual relation to what is named from a fundamental or "*Self-Honest*" perspective. Thus, names are applied to concepts defining reality, and it appears that an elite somewhere is controlling and tweaking which concepts and ideas are part of what is "real" and what is not, since what is created must always be somehow maintained, in one form or another—by some 'keepers,' or 'guardians'—or else disappear.

A clear demonstration of this erupted from a conversation I recently had with my circle—doing some translation work, I was looking for the French equivalent to the word "mind." Finding no satisfactory answer, I asked the opinion of friends and fellows—and while several alternatives were proposed—they each already possessed a more direct equivalent in English: i.e. "*esprit*" = "spirit"; "*conscience*" = "consciousness" or "*pensée*" = "thought," &tc; all of which are not the "mind." We concluded—although fully aware of what the "mind" is—that no exact word exists in French to express the idea. This is something very curious, since the "mind" is a rather important concept for humanity. Shouldn't an important concept, such as the mind, be readily and easily expressed in every tongue? What other important concepts are out there that have no word to express them? How purposefully so? What does this reveal about reality—and our perception thereof?

---

§ Ref. *The Complete Anunnaki Bible* by Joshua Free.

Elven tribes of yore fell victim not only to physical persecutions but also to the psychological semantic warfare methods previously alluded to in what can only be termed a *'holocaust.'* This happened not only to the elves themselves but to all associated beings as well, now often relegated to fairy tales and fantasy role-playing games—beings such as *gnomes, faeries, dwarves, giants, trolls, &tc.*—we salute them!

Extending to the entire mythology of Pagan Europe—Elven Æurope—after the rise of Christianity: Indeed, the ancient gods and their tales are now seen as an integral of myths, which imply some kind of epic imagination, often interpreted through psychological lenses, as metaphors—more literal interpretations are seen as 'nonsense' or 'insane.' This process is, of course, not limited to Europe, but extends to all native spirituality, worldwide. It is also of interest to look upon the term "magic" in a similar light, also implying an act defying the rational—what is considered to be part of reality, being an act of the impossible or the miraculous. The word also refers to prestidigitation, or stage magic, which points to the use of 'deception,' or something 'false'—something that is "not real"—where true magic is actually concerned with practical applications for manipulating the "grey zone," allowing for a holistic, *Self-Honest*, reality experience.

As yet, the Elven Way is still well alive today, in some form or another, firmly rooted in our subconscious, for it is directly linked to our genetics. Elves not only marginally resurfaced, they are very popular today in pop culture—thanks to the work of fantasy pioneer J.R.R. Tolkien and role-playing games such as the ever-popular *Dungeons & Dragons*. Tolkien's influence regarding elves is now well known, and yet, while he is largely and rightfully recognized as the forefather of the fantasy genre, many believe that he created his world from scratch—when he actually "borrowed" much of it directly from ancient European pagan folklore. It thus happens that his work is, in some respects, a "revival"—or at least "survival"—of these lost traditions. Whether or not this reemergence occurred consciously seems irrelevant.

In *Dr. Leonid Korablev's* essay *"The True Elves of Europe"* he indicates that:

> *"Although Tolkien never made a secret of his sources, it is quite astounding how many of the folk and place-names in the 'Lord of the Rings' and 'Silmarillion' correspond precisely to ancient Norse-Icelandic, Anglo-Saxon and other ones that were actually used for things asso-*

ciated with elves. This seems to corroborate our hypothesis that in creating his elves, Tolkien might have been thinking of reconstructing the 'original' image that, should such an original exist, was reflected in various Elves of North-Western European mythologies."

In a manner similar to what has been remarked concerning the work of renowned author H.P. Lovecraft,[*] it appears that the forces behind Tolkien's inspiration—akin to the Greek "*dæmons*"—are using a human agent as a channel to resurface today. And we see this repeatedly in numerous instances at this dawn of a New Aeon.

Interesting parallels may also be drawn between the survival of the Elven Tradition through fantasy and that of the more commonly recognized Celtic Tradition and "Druidism," which stems from the same source and was kept preserved in the surviving writings of medieval Irish monks. This is demonstrated in another of Joshua Free's masterpieces, "*Merlyn's Complete Book of Pheryllt.*" It is curious to note how the Celtic Tradition and "Druidism" was absorbed by Christianity—thus any surviving texts are often viewed in the Neo-druid underground community as unauthentic, or else "corrupted," and yet it is this very commitment to writing which kept the tradition alive for us today.

Wherever we turn in the ancient world, we discover incredible testimonies that support the powerful ability of these archetypes to survive and adapt—an ability to adopt differing guises, often hidden in plain sight or else veiled as fantasy in the deceitful game of semantics. This is unsurprisingly quite typical of the Jovian-Mardukite energy current—the driving force behind all of the previously-mentioned aspects—accumulating and storing energy unnoticed, beneath the surface, only to bloom in full force when the conditions are gathered: just as a seed from a lone tree containing the potential of an eternal forest, waiting for millennia if necessary...

...finally to bloom against all odds when the stars are right.

—David Zibert, Patesi of Canada
Mardukite Council of Nabu-Tutu
Summer 2019
Blue Room Office, Canada

---

[*] Ref. *Necronomicon Revelations* or *Novem Portis* by Joshua Free.

The Secret Book of Elven-Faerie

ancient eurasia:
the genesis of elves and faerie

Origins of the true "Elven-Ffayrie" legacy are prehistoric—relating back to distant roots in the *Ancient Near East*, lands of *Mesopotamia* and "beings" that Sumerians and Babylonians refer to as the "*Anunnaki*." The legacy is directly linked to the development of "agriculture"—a gift from "high minds" to nomadic cultures, and a means to domesticate and systematize evolving societies. We see this present at the inception of our most recent "cradle of civilization"—and evidence of its migration as diverse "Elven," "Faerie" and "Druidic" traditions across ancient Eurasia—spanning from Anatolia (Turkey) to Ireland.

Some readers will find this material shocking. Others will oppose the terminology used throughout this tome and even the stoic sincerity of its presentation—believing perhaps that this is an elaborate intellectual joke. However, the true esoteric legacy and lore of this subject not only compliments existing historical and anthropological data but also satisfactorily resolves many unanswered questions about origins of 'humanity', development of a cultural "systemology" and perhaps even the "human role" in the universe.

The legacy and lore explored herein is "occult" or "esoteric" for the fact that it remains hidden from public mainstream view—though hidden in plain sight—yet ever in the shadows. This process of bringing "what is hidden to light" may result in what some have called "enlightenment." Humans would seem to have lost a feeling, or a memory, linking them to the "Earth Ways," that perhaps was once "second nature" or "innate." Or, perhaps humans have not simply forgotten but have chosen—albeit subconsciously conditioned to choose by society—to ignore this inner calling; to deny it to the point where it is no longer heard and to even think about it is to be deemed "insane."

This series of books seeks to accomplish the impossible—for it contains a secret tradition in a concrete printed form that is not otherwise ever relayed as such by "Elves" themselves, those which do not actually record their histories and lore in this static manner. There is an innate reserve or cultural taboo regarding *fixed* writing of 'sacred things'—called "light things" or "bright things"—including all history, "magic" and lore. The Druids later carried this in their tradition, believing that if one was no longer responsible to commit things to personal memory, then *"genetic memory"* attached to this legacy would become tainted or recessive and ultimately forgotten...

Cultural language and variegated regional semantics are all that separates the wisdom stream of the "Ancient Mystery School" as it evolved across time, alongside the systemology of the human condition. Spread of bloodlines, infiltration and development of diverse nations and their interpretations of a celestial-planetary religious pantheon all contributed toward further fragmentation of the original knowledge base.

Once we move away from an evolving Egypto-Babylonian paradigm in the *"Ancient Near East"* paradigms, we can trace evolutions of its tradition by the "Light Folk" or "Star Folk" described elsewhere in Western Europe—generally as either of the High Elf (or "Dragon") "Sidhe Elves" of the "Faerie Courts," or else the Wood Elf or "Sylvan" varieties we find most often revived in modern "Neodruidism" and "Faerie Traditions."

According to the most ancient traditions, these "Elves" are the "firstborn" of Europe—separate and yet interconnected to the later "human" developments in the same region—and also direct descendants of the Anunnaki of E.DIN, or else the fertile cradle of systematized civilization and agriculture in Mesopotamia. Their existence is intermediary between what we classify as an "ancient god race" and "modern humans."

To those unfamiliar with this wide-angle scope of lore and the "generative" practices of the ancient Anunnaki, this data is in some ways misleading. When we examine the Anunnaki texts closely, we note that the "Elves" are indeed a part of the genetic "Eden experiments" but are not the same as what the same tablets refer to as the "first generation" of "human" life—or else *"Adamu"*—on these tablets. The "Elves" are created, and evolve, separately from the specific species, breed or "race" evolving as modern humans. Although lore suggests it is possible for them to interbreed, the "Elves" are specifically distinguishes as the "Ninth Star Race" (or "generation") of hybridized "half-gods" seeded on the Earth planet.

A popular modern derivative of this paradigm has become a mainstream household concept over the past few decades, thanks to the wide revival interest in J.R.R. Tolkein's "Middle Earth." While it is easy to disregard all concepts related to a work of fiction—for the fact that it is relayed as "fiction"—an investigative seeker discovers inspiration is actually drawn from an author's own considerable interests or research into some aspect of history, esoterica or mythology. In Tolkein's version, the "Elves" are also the "first-born" race of "Middle Earth." He translates their name to link their genetic "star" ancestry as the *"Children of Eru"*—with striking similarity to Celtic-Druid lore regarding the same as the *"Children of D'Anu."*

"Eru" is *"Eurasian-Elvish"*—a feminine form of the name "Anu" in the earliest human language. Tolkein combined aspects of ancient language to base a "fictional" one for his own "Elves" and called it *"Quenya."* It bares a resemblance in many ways to Mesopotamian, Nordic-Germanic, Irish and Gaelic-Welsh—elements of languages that are all attributed to "Elves" in their own respective historical mythologies.

The ancient 'Elven Way' recognizes the name "Anu" or "Eru" as the Creative Force or "Source of All Being and Creation"—or essentially "God" in the most general 'supreme' or 'progenitive' sense. When we look to the Mesopotamian source traditions of the Babylonian 'Mardukite' paradigm, the name "Eru" or "Erua" is given to "Sarpanit" (or "Zarpanitu")—the "hyridized-Elvish"* consort-wife of Marduk, the Anunnaki god of Babylon proper.

By choosing an earthling spouse—and not the betrothed Inanna-Ishtar of the Anunnaki pantheon—Marduk relinquished "official rights" to reign in "Heaven." Babylon, in turn, became his medium to reign on "Earth" with assistance from his herald- heir-messenger-son "Nabu," who led a cult of cuneiform scribes and priest-magicians.

Even when the representative language and cultural icons change with time and geography, *"Elven Histories"* are aligned heavily with Sumerian and Babylonian lore—otherwise prehistoric and unrecorded—concerning an Anunnaki-governed Mesopotamia, from even a time before the "Flood." It alludes to a time "before humans"—something their 'loremasters' insist is correctly interpreted. This memory does not, however, attempt to reconstruct fantastic stories by which to explain natural forces or even the cosmic genesis of the solar-system. For this knowledge is not maintained in memory by direct experience but was instead taught to them by the "stars."

---

* *"Part-divine"*—of the seventh generation of Adapa, the original upgraded human, whose father was the Anunnaki god Enki and whose mother was a human. More details on the specifically Mesopotamian paradigm is found in modern "Mardukite" literature by Joshua Free.

Although it might seem more convenient to reflect only on the most recent examples of "Elves" and "Faerie" surviving in Western Europe, the truth is that this legacy is more wide-encompassing than the most familiar or popular stereotypes. It may be quite difficult for modern psyches to even grasp the existence of other terrestrial forms of evolved life in our past, interrelated yet separate from how we classify *homo sapiens*. Higher "forms" of life systematized and cross-bred new forms of life in our distant histories; and while only fragmented knowledge remains of these events, it is an undeniable unanimous universal theme present in the backwaters of all lore regarding "Elven-Faerie" *and* "human" origins.

If we take ancient lore at face value, a "higher class" of being essentially seeded this entire planet, then "Ascended," leaving the "Elves" and "Faerie" as Guardians responsible for it. Other "star-races" have since descended to the Earth, but we possess no reason to believe that all of these later appearances—or modern interactions with various interstellar or astral intelligences—are all directly linked to the same Anunnaki and Elven-Faerie races of our distant origins and/or of current relevance for this text.

The faction or legacy we are presently concerned with relates specifically to the "Ancient Mystery School" and its genetic representation in the ancient world—primarily bloodlines of kingship and "royal families" that protected this genetic memory of the "Elven Courts" and "Fairy Princess" sort of archetypes in their DNA. Over time, the secret lore integrated more strongly with a "priest class," which shared in the same legacy, even if only intellectually. But, the secrets protected themselves as a myriad of cultural interpretations and diverse languages mutated the original form.

The following is one interpretation of the "Anunnaki genesis of the Elven-Faerie on Earth" derived from one tradition's "*Sylva D'Terrestai*"—roughly meaning "*Book of the Everlasting Forest*"—that bares a remarkable resemblance to the human version of the "Urantia Book"[*]:

> *The 'first generation' of Gaea is nameless. We know that it consisted of two people, twins, brought or sent here to be sure that Middle Earth was inhabitable in its physical form. Their lifespan was purposely short-lived, reaching full maturity with the passing of only 12 solar years. They were of such a nature that they were innately aware of the*

---

[*] "Urantia Book"—A literary contribution regarding higher spirituality, published in the 1950's of unknown "channeled" origins.

> *need to live for and with each other. Though sexual gender is not mentioned, an aspect often obscure in matters of Elven-Ffayrie, "aliens" or any other interdimensional beings, we can be sure that they had the ability to reproduce. Thus, the planet was officially inhabited. [The vegetation and animals were here already, active and operating on their own 'genetic programs.']*
>
> *At Eleven (Elven) years old, the 'Twins', as they are referred to, parented the firstborn of the 'second generation,' but truly it was the first Earth-born generation. In the act of love resulting in this conception (lust was not a part of the psyche yet) the genetic material really bloomed. With the birth of Andon and Fonta, it was clear that the abilities and genetic potential had actually increased as a result of the loving union of the "Twins." Yes, the whole is greater than the sum of the parts alone; and for whatever reason this evolution did happen and has never happened again. The cup, being as full as possible with Andon and Fonta, could now only be emptied. For this reason there was a stress or pressure to maintain or preserve the purity and integrity of the Elven genetics and bloodline as time bore on...*

As humans understand the social concepts, "genetics" and "race" are most frequently expressed in terms of skin color or pigment called "melanin." But this is not the strongest genetic indicator by itself—there are other cues, such as eye shape and color, hair type and color, skeletal structure and other facets anthropologists frequently use. According to the previous example, the descendents of Andon and Fonta are charged with possession of the true or original melanin of the "People of Earth," but they seem to have quickly relocated away from the "cradle of civilization."

According to lore, the Andonites resembled closely to what we identify as Inuit Indians or "Eskimos" of "Elvish" decent that preserved a distinct genetics—as does another obscure evolving Elven race, the "Yezidi," which remained near Mesopotamia. But those "Elves" that left the "cradle" survived to evolve by first becoming "arboreal," else "living in the trees," using the forests for safety and shelter while honing their agricultural skills and herbal knowledge with the retreat of the last "Ice Age."

To continue from the previous text:—

> *Following the dispersion of Andonites across Europe, further generations and tribes emerged seemingly independent of one another. They continued first with the 'Foxhall Clan,' or 'Heidelberg Race,' that not*

only maintained some of their original Andonite genetics, but were also privileged to instruction of Onagar, the first 'Wise One.' With the ending of the Ice Age, folk culture emerged. Humans are adaptive, and modern day Hyperborean Inuits and Scandinavians seem to have mastered arctic living, yet have also had profound effects on the ecosystem of the North. With a focus shifting from keeping alive (or preservation) into expansion, more primitive and combative generations (races and factions) emerged. These others—such as the Badonan and Neanderthal—were not descendents from the Elves and did not survive...

For those races that did survive, a rainbow of genetic Melanin separated them by color. Each cousin race moved farther and farther from Mesopotamia but remained connected. The "red folk" became the Native American aboriginal shamans. The "orange folk" went to Africa for a while, but were later overrun by the "green folk." "Yellow folk" left Eurasia for East Asia. The "green folk" and "indigo folk" remained around North Africa, in Egypt and in their Mesopotamian homelands, which left the "blue folk" (or "light folk") who—according to this lore—represent the original strain back to the Source and are later known as the *"Fair Folk"* or *"Faerie."* From this point it is sometimes difficult to distinguish varying characteristics of "Faerie races"—*"dragons," "elves"* and *"fae"*—still present in some human genetics today, but it *is* there.

The Celtic-Druid "Dragons" were eventually driven to Ireland, as were any surviving vestiges of a "Dragon Priest-King" legacy that once even extended as far as the prehistoric Chinese empire. The Dragon-race carried very ancient and distinctive recessive traits: red hair, green eyes and fair or orange skin. It is the "Blue Race" of "Faerie," once residing in the Hyperborean Germanic and Norse regions, that carry the more commonly attributed "Elven" traits we conjure to mind of them: blonde hair, blue eyes and fair or "albinic" complexion.

In addition to the "high" or "northern" Elven races that migrated throughout Eurasia, an additional Faerie emigration from the Ancient Near East stuck closer to Anatolia (Turkey), the Mediterranean and Danubian River Valley, spreading its prehistoric tradition from there. This included what evolved into the proto-Celtic and *La Tene* cultures; the "gypsy clans" throughout Black Forests of Europe; ancient Etruscan kingdom; Tartaria or Transylvania; even extending its reach to the Albigensian/Merovingian legacy of France.

Ancient tablets record all of the "wood elf" races as "dark headed"—marking them nearly indistinguishable from surrounding "human" populations. Much of our knowledge over time is an extension of our understanding—or rather, misunderstanding—of the ancient Anunnaki cuneiform tablets and other teachings from the "Ancient Mystery School."

This information is fragmented and wholly disguised in the common "bedtime story" versions and reduced to fanciful religious "scriptures" that are little more than allegories in usefulness. They lead us to believe that all *homonids* on the planet are derived from a singular origin—Adam and Eve. While this would seem convenient in cataloging the descendants of a particular dynastic succession, it really leaves many questions.

The death of Abel—by Cain—alone would almost give reason to believe that everyone on the planet is the Son of Cain: of a lineage from Adam. The early Semitic *"Bible"* makes reference to other offspring begot by Adam and Eve, but these become mere background in the *Book of Genesis*. The *"Holy* Bible" omits Rabbinical lore of Adam taking a "wife" before Eve, named Lilith—lore mutated from early Sumerian *"lilitu"* demonology. The Vatican has removed these references believing that they know a "higher truth"—when in fact their own religion and "Bible" is completely based on Semitic texts.

We cannot tax the biblical Moses too heavily with fault—for he was roaming an endless desert charged with leading an up and coming nation of people. The story needed to start somewhere—and the Abrahamic tradition which first began in ancient Sumer (Mesopotamia) was no longer 'clear'. It all had to be simplified—reduced to something that the masses could remember, and simultaneously find motivation in. This legacy provided fuel sufficient to drive his people forward through their plight, resulting in an independent religion and Semitic race of "Hebrews."

The "Hebrews" and "Akkadians" (Babylonians) were once a part of the same Semitic cultural religion in Mesopotamia. It is only afterward that diverse peoples and languages spread out across the Ancient Near East—from Persia to Canaan. And while there is some scholarly debate about which early Anunnaki figure—or figures—is actually "Lord God Yahweh" of the *Old Testament*, there is little doubt that beneath the disguise of language and culture, the original ancient people once all shared a singular understanding of the "Celestial pantheon." And certainly this "Yahweh" or "Jehovah" of the *Old Testament* is a strikingly different persona than the "distant loving all-father" that Jesus is alluding to as "God" in the *New Testament*—a description which better fits the position and title of "Anu"—the "*Heavenly King of the Anunnaki.*"

As you reach for your handy copy of the "*Holy Bible*" to verify these things, a more intensive fifteen minutes of reading will also reveal to you that after Cain kills Abel, he leaves to lead a group of people occupying the land of Nod, even marrying a "cousin"—someone who is apparently born of something outside the *Eden Experiment.* Interestingly, Semitic texts reveal the strong possibly that Cain was not even Adam's son and was instead the result of an encounter between Eve and the "Serpent"—whoever or whatever that might be. It also seems clear that the Nodites did not originate in the Garden of Eden—so there was obviously something happening beyond what commoners are told in the standard "*Bible*" dilution.

Another example of the near-Eastern Elven legacy is the *Yezidi* people—a Mesopotamian sect found in northern Iraq that possess uniquely ancient genetics and culture that resembles a famous "lost tribe" that the Elves refer to. These folk are named for "God" in their language: who is *Yazdan*. According to their lore, this being is credited with creating (or naming) the Seven Chief Emissaries that we might best recognize in lore of the "Seven Anunnaki Zonei Gates." Most specifically for our purposes, the *Yezidi* claim to be descendants of "Adam but not Eve" and that the remainder of the world population exists independently of their own genetic legacy—a fact that is actually supported well with modern scientific DNA testing.

The biblical name Adam is derived from the "*Adamu*"—the class of Primitive Workers fashioned by the Anunnaki to ease the working toil of the ancient Igigi-Watchers, those developing the earliest prehistoric infrastructure in a time "before the Flood." If using the oldest writings as a base, the character we know as "Adam" is best related to "Adapa"—a name given to the "first man" of the newest race born of the "Eden Experiment" conducted by and personally begot by the Anunnaki god Enki—a son of Anu, and the father of Marduk.

Adapa's existence begins a new class of human being on Earth that is more advanced and intelligent than the original *Adamu* race. One tradition of the Elven Way is actually named for "Adam-Adapa" which is also spelled "Edapa" and hence the "*Edaphic*" tradition. It emphasizes tending or "stewardship" of the ground or *Earth*. It is thought that Adam's long lifespan—as alluded to even in the "*Holy Bible*"—is the result of his purest genetic faculties, something lost with the breeding of later generations. At a later juncture, the Anunnaki instill a "program" into human DNA that restricts the "life-program" to 120 years. As suggested in my original recension of the *Sylva D'Terrestai*:—

> *Outside the walls of Eden where things are not so sacred, the people began to get jealous about the 'supremacy' of those that resided within. Eve shared herself with one from the 'other races' because he had explained to her that it would 'help to spread the goodness and power' to the outland chaos. She had already been warned of this [by God]—not to mix the polarities of 'good' and 'bad.' The very moment Ffayrie mixed with Human, both Adam and Eve became aware of their mortality (prior they knew not death or suffering) because Eve's energy affected Adam when she shared herself with him thereafter. Adam and Eve lost their supreme graces. A new generation of Eve's offspring emerged that were quarter-breeds...*
>
> *The man, Cain, was not the son of Adam. Cano,[*] the 'Serpent in the Garden' was responsible for the Degradation of Eden and jealousy between half-brothers (as Adam would clearly have had favoritism towards his own blood son.) After being tainted with the energy of lust, Eve laid with Adam and they shared the 'apple' and realized that now they were both impure and for the rest of their days. Cain went on to the Nodites and quarter-breeds, leaving Eves other children to carry the blood of Adam...*

The "apple" or "cherry" remains an epitome of life and death as "decreed by the gods," or else divine fate or destiny. In the physical sense, it may even represent "life" via sexual union, or carry occult connotations to "blood." The "*Holy Bible*" even acknowledges the concept of two distinct opposing bloodlines quite frequently. Beginning with *Genesis 3:15*, we are told that there will be perpetual discord between the offspring of Cano ("the Serpent") against the remainder of Eve's children—presumably the "Sons of Adam." Then, Cain kills Abel from his jealousy of Abel being "so close" to Adam and leaves them all to pursue his own life. He does not actually carry the Adamic blood away with him; that all Humans have thought themselves to have been a part of since this story first spread.

---

* Sometimes written as *Kano*.

Some translate the name "*Adapa*" as "found," and his wife—the biblical Eve—is found on ancient cuneiform tablets by the name "*Titi*" meaning "alive"—actually the compound double of the Sumerian word "TI" meaning "life." After being inspected by the Assembly of Anunnaki, Adapa returns to Earth to lead the life of a farmer-shepherd. The names KA.IN and AB.AEL actually appear on Mesopotamian tablets as siblings. Ninurta—an emissary of the Anunnaki—instructs KA.IN in agriculture; while Marduk—another Anunnaki—is charged to teach AB.AEL in shepherding. In this version, KA.IN also kills AB.AEL and is exiled, requiring the Blessed Dynasty to be carried by further offspring of *Adapa* and *Titi*.

These archetypal themes reoccur throughout history: the rivaling brothers; positions of royalty and supremacy; genetic integrity of a bloodline, &tc.—these are all very ancient and without a clear source or explanation without considering the mythic and prehistoric lore alluded to in Elven tradition. The same divisions and schisms of our ancestors are present with our own brothers and sisters—in family and community. We see the schismatic division in ancient Mesopotamian religions and followings split between legacies of Enlil and Enki. These two Anunnaki gods are also brothers—And in this instance, Enki represents the shepherd and Enlil is depicted as the farmer. Later in Babylon, Marduk assumes roles of both.

The Hebrew-Rabbinical *Book of Genesis*—and *Book of Enoch*—do contain some details regarding Anunnaki or Igigi "*Watchers*"/ "*Nephilim*"—referred to as "*Sons of God*"—those who took "*Daughters of Men*" as wives and begot children. Nearly all of these references—and remaining ones at the foundation of the entire Judeo-Christian paradigm—are dilutions from far more antiquated and complete cuneiform records, those we have since found and translated and others undoubtedly still waiting to be unearthed and added to our understanding.

According to ancient Anunnaki tablets, Enki was technically Adapa's father. And by successfully blending his "essence," he genetically advanced humanity and ensured his distinctive bloodline could be carried on Earth apart from himself. After having several daughters, *Adapa* and *Titi* beget a child named SA.TI—the biblical "Seth." *Sati* and *Azura* have EN.SHI—the biblical "Enosh." *Enshi* and his sister-wife NO.AM beget KU.NIN—the biblical "Kenan." And on and on the generations go, the tablets closely matching common biblical scriptures—until we arrive at a special case: ENKI.ME, whose name means "By Enki, Understanding." This is the biblical "Enoch" that so greatly inspires mystic and occult lore. *Enkime*, of the seventh generation of *Adapa*, spent time with Enki and Marduk in "E.RI.DU"—the original proto-Sumerian home of Enki on the Mesopotamian coast of the Persian Gulf. *Sarpanit*, a daughter of *Enkime*, was raised to goddess-status in Babylon after her marriage to Marduk, thereby launching a Mardukite legacy as an extension of Enki's original one.

It is important to remember that there are many semantic discrepancies between the stream of ancient esoteric lore and the Judeo-Christian or Gnostic interpretations that are more commonly known or simplified. To these scriptural scholars, the Anunnaki and Igigi are "angelic forces of God manifest on Earth." In another reference they might be considered "emissaries" or "intermediaries between man and God." Whatever their nature, it is clear that these beings resided on the Earth in prehistoric times before present-day humans and this lore suggests that the rising human population (and its handling) caused—or continues to cause, depending on your beliefs—considerable conflict even among these "enlightened beings."

One commonly found primary facet of this ancient Elven lore relates back to the ability of these "ethereal," "godly," "angelic" or otherwise "faerie" beings to share consummate love with "mortals." In every ancient reference, this ability—even the thought of its physical action—was taboo in all respects among Anunnaki, Igigi, Elven-Faerie, &tc. In every instance "higher minds" considered humanity as still evolving "pets."

Close examination of cuneiform tablets records reveals that Enki conducted "genetic experiments" on humans. If we were to take ancient accounts literally, Enki is, in effect, the first to break the "Taboo of the Gods" by blending his own genetics with the Primitive Workers—a human female—resulting in the birth of Adapa. In the beginning, he attempts to hide the identity of Adapa from the Anunnaki, saying that he found the "*Adamu child*" as a baby floating abandoned on a river in a reed basket—*always a plethora of bastardized royal children being found in reed baskets on rivers in ancient times, if you notice.*

As a result, Enki maintained his Anunnaki position—as did his spouse Ninki. Although Enki broke the code of merging Anunnaki genetics directly with humans—or any indigenous planetary species—it is Marduk that is actually the first of the Anunnaki to take an Earthling spouse. Marduk justified *his* actions by explaining that his chosen mate—*Sarpanit*—was not simply of any Earth-blood, but a daughter of

Enkime, and a descendant of Adapa—who was ultimately the son of Enki.

Rules of 'Kingship in Heaven' are very strict—Marduk was informed by both Enki and Ninki that he would forfeit all rights of "Kingship in Heaven" if he insisted on espousing any Earthling. As tablets record, Marduk is deliriously laughing when he responds that "such rights" have never been with his family and his time of rulership on Earth was already in danger of Enlilite usurpation.

Marduk espouses Sarpanit and constructs Babylon—meanwhile two-hundred of the *Igigi-Watchers* "descend to earth" and follow suit, taking females as wives. These are undoubtedly the same beings recorded as "*Nephilim*" in *Genesis 6*. Lore even suggests that the *200* is a sum of *two-thirds* the total of the ranks: *300 Igigi-Watchers*—which follows perfectly with later (more recent) derived Semitic Judeo-Hebrew interpretations.

References to this lore are not only found in occult, esoteric and mystical sources—but also forgotten lore of the Gnostics and earliest Judeo-Christians. Consider the Dead Sea Scrolls, particularly the portion entitled: *Tales of the Patriarchs*. Within those pages we are made privy to a dialogue between *Enoch* and *Methuselah* where the natures of the "*Sons of God*" are revealed as "from a *star* origin." Elsewhere it suggests Noah was warned by a "mighty Watcher"—meaning a chief Anunnaki figure, and we know that since this "scripture" is based on a much older Mesopotamian version, the "*Atra-Hasis*" epic, this figure is undoubtedly Enki.

The "*Books of Enoch*"—which just so happens to include a work titled "*Book of the Watchers*"—describes the ability of "Enoch" to literally walk with "God" after being taken to "Heaven." Its alleged author, Enoch, writes for posterity to preserve the "secrets of the Universe"—lore that was deemed too esoteric for acceptance by the orthodox Church. The "angels" instruct Enoch in the ways of magick and science, including a trip through the solar system—on his way to 'Heaven'—which is explicitly described in astronomical detail thousands of years ago, including a description of the earth as "round." In Gnostic and Semitic Judeo-Christian versions of this lore it is *Shamihaza* who leads "200 angels" down to earth—synchronous with older Mesopotamian sources mentioning *Shamgaz*, a leader among the "200 Igigi-Watchers" that did the same.

If we fast forward through the data, we arrive at a period of time after the initial corruption of Eden, when the "*Great Flood*" or "*Deluge*" occurred. Enlil held a strong inclination to allow the humans running rampant on Earth to simply perish unaided during a natural devastation. Out of all the Celestial pantheon, it was Enki and Marduk who sought to preserve their own legacy—and genetics—on earth: their personal domain. Some of this is described in contemporary versions of the Semitic "Noah," but far greater details are found on older cuneiform tablet writings—such as the *Atra-Asis* and *Epic of Gilgamesh*—predating the Hebrew scripture by thousands of years.

When we refer to specific races and bloodlines of a culture we are often singling out smaller sects from larger populations. Ancient Celtic culture is very Elven-Ffayrie oriented, but only the "Sidhe" and original "Drwyd" Wizards are considered a part of the actual "divine" bloodline or legacy themselves.

We find a similar situation again with the installation of the first "Dragon Kings" of 'dragonblood' appearing in ancient Sumerian and Babylonian society; the Pharaohs of Egypt; Scythians and original "Vampyres," the list goes on and on. Certain dynastic genealogies carry a long tradition of association with "royal sky-god lineages." It is is even likely that the Sidhe derived their name from Scythian ancestry. The word is actually pronounced "*sithian,*" and "sith" in Gaelic is "*sidth*" (singular) and "'*sidhe*" (plural) pronounced "shee."

It is not difficult to see how "Anunnaki" lineages evolved into lore of "Devas" and "Sidhe" when each of these three names are varying regional titles for the same "Shinning Ones." These "Shinning Ones" emerge in a variety of forms in "New Age" mystical doctrine—typically as energies sought or connected with in ritual magick. Other lore indicates that the Anunnaki were similar to the Greek "Fates," a word based on lore of the European "*fata*"—yet another label for "Ffayrie."

Many stereotypes associated with "Elven Courts" and "Druid Councils" are rooted in the ancient proto-Sumerian Dragon Priesthood from a culture anthropologist classify as "*Ubaid.*" Masses of these people expanded their civilization and knowledge beyond even the domain of Mesopotamia—they became known as Scythian and Dravidian folk that spread to Anatolia, India and Western Europe.

In a region referred to as the *Gangetic*, the Aryans and Dravidians discovered one another and merged to form a race later many call the "*Tuatha De Dannan*" (*D'Anu*, or *Anu*). This race—still considered Andite (or *Children of Andon*)—carried their culture along the Danube and Rhine Rivers, bringing Mediterranean and Mesopotamian systemology across mainland Europe, eventually reaching the British Isles. Along their travels they met the 'blue folk' who had continued to develop separately from the Eden project. These folk had developed the "*La Tene*" culture that we now call Celtic. Together this "Danubian" race established "Druidism," which dominated Europe until the rise of the Milesians and Roman populations—and the inception of "human history" as it is, more or less, known today.

the age of faerie and children of the stars

Elven History—and the languages that preserve it—links directly with the cosmos. When we examine the words used to describe Elven-Ffayrie beings as *"Shinning Ones"* in any language, we find that they are really a reference to "shinning stars," including the hereditary Elven names "Eru" and "Anu" —as well as the common roots "*En-*"; "*El-*"; and "*Er-*."

In some Elven traditions, the root *"Ela-"* is reserved exclusively to refer to "stars" specifically to avoid confusion. This then, by some interpretation, makes the Anunnaki (*"anu-nagi"* or *anu-naki*) the 'star-dragons'—based purely on "Elvish" semantics. And a synonym for the same in Elven language is *"elaynor"*—which can mean either "star-dragon" and "star-fire."

Using this logic, the later "Children of Anu" become "*Children of the Stars*," or "Star-born," which translates as *"elen"* and *"elan"* in Elven language. *"Eloya"* translates in human tongue as either "Elven-heart" or "Star-heart." Ubaid Enki'ite proto-Sumerians are then: the descendents of a "star." We may simply attribute various differences in the terminology and semantics—as opposed to "Watchers" and "Nephilim" &tc.—to shifts in Eurasian cultural language and its ability to preserve the knowledge stream clearly.

The "Watchers" appear in ancient times almost as intermediaries in form—between the physical plane of Gaea and the spiritual place of the Source. They are powerful when they appear in archaic lore, but are not "God," even when the names of the energies include: *En, Enlil, Enki, Ea, Yah, Iah, Jahovah, Iao,* and *Yahweh*. Traditional "scriptures" might have us believe that the whole lot of these earthborn intermediary beings were wiped away with the "Flood"—but they would be wrong.

Mesopotamian mythology mentions these intermediaries as "Dragon Kings"—humanoid, but not "human." These tablets give them names like Enlil and Enki—and refer to "Gaea" as Tiamat, their word for the *Primordial Dragon.** It is Enki who claimed the title "Lord of the Earth"—and he is credited with discovering and perfecting many bioengineering practices. When we consider the archaic *Near Eastern*

---

* See "*Draconomicon: The Book of Ancient Dragon Magick*" by Joshua Free; also reprinted in "*Merlyn's Complete Book of Pheryllt*."

lore of "fallen angels" and "genetic intervention," we better understand later Elven-attributed archetypes of "faerie lovers," "changelings" and even the idea of giving birth to "alien babies."

Contemporary society treats these subjects as "fantasy"—and nearly all humans hold the idea that the "Creatures of Faerie" are simply fictional beasties of "myth" and "legend." We are not only speaking of stereotypical Elven "fair-skinned forest dwelling gardeners"—but also the Sylphs, Sprytes, Dragons, Drakes, Dwarves, Gnomes, Merfolk (Undines), Nixes, Pixies and Leprechauns... among others. These are all "Children of Faerie"—misunderstood beings that now primarily exist only on the brink of Human imagination. And yet for those who dare to seek the underlying origins of this lore—we do find reason to "believe" that there is something very "real" here.

In our previous discourse [chapter] the idea of genetic intervention is approached—whether as a result of leading groups of humanoids on Earth, a Creator God, or some intermediary in between. Even "selective reproduction"—when used in the manner described in Elven-Ffayrie history—is a method of genetic intervention. Environmental adaptation also affects our genetics—and adaptation is necessary for the survival of any species. That means for a species to eventually overcome a barrier that affects its livelihood, it will have to change. This "genetic intervention" paradigm, at the very least, helps us resolve some unresolved issues regarding Human ancestry— since it is clear that all existence on earth is manipulated and controlled in some form or another of "authority."

As a science, *Anthropology* is unable to sufficiently answer the problems of Human origins. Originally, the field sought to find an answer that would correlate with the Judeo-Christian *"Genesis"*—but at the time these goals were established, religion and science were at war with one another. Instead of "God-creates-Man so man comes from a Supreme and beautiful being," it somehow developed into "Man is a primitive ape who just got lucky out of random chaos." Darwin and other evolutionary purists also failed to demonstrate how only some Cro-Magnon evolved into Human, when in fact, Cro-Magnons do not get "bred out" or "evolve" at all—they *go extinct*.

The real issue for our current purposes concerns the "star origins" of Elves and Faerie races. There is certainly enough literary support for this within a paradigm that allows for aliens, inter-dimensional or interstellar beings. If Humans were able to put aside pride long enough to see clearly, great wisdom might come from acceptance of an advanced civilization or aspects of prehistoric Man that exist beyond traditional knowledge of history.

Without accepting the possibility or consideration of a particular 'scientific paradigm' or "framework" you cannot expect to see it or prove it as a "postulate." Usually the expectations and rules of what we see and experience are programmed by the social culture to which we belong or are raised. Without looking beyond an existing boundary, achievements cannot be made.

The historical setting for the arrival of the "*Tuatha D'Anu*" is "officially confined" to the legacy of ancient Ireland—called "*Eire*," "*Erin*," and "*Eriu*." They arrived there on Beltane (May Day or May's Eve) "concealed within a magical fog or mist."

While the European mainland lay off to the East and South of Ireland, the Tuatha D'Anu arrived from the North and West of the Island, settling first in the mountains of Western Ireland. This led many to believe they were the "People of the North" or that they came from somewhere in the Atlantic Ocean. But, their ships, on the other hand, were said to be of a "sky-nature," which somehow caused an uncanny solar eclipse for the first three days of their arrival. This could otherwise be a reference to the thick fog that cloaked their ships—enveloping them as they reached harbor. In either case, the ancient Celtic manuscripts record that the Tuatha D'Anu intentionally destroyed their ships in flames upon landing.

When the Tuatha D'Anu arrived, Ireland was already inhabited by an Elven-Ffayrie race—another descendent from the "blue folk" called the "Nemed" or "Fir-Bolg," translated perhaps too literally as "Men of Bags." The Fir-Bolg race were forced to take shelter during the three days that smoke/fog/mist affected Ireland. Needless to say they interpreted the Danubian arrival as an invasion of hostility—and a war ensued between the two Faerie races.

If we are to give European topics and semantics a treatment in this current volume, we must, of course, lend an ear to the Celtic-specific sources for literary verification. Unfortunately, both medieval and modern writers have a habit of confusing membership in the Tuatha D'Anu with their adversaries, the Fir-Bolg. Why unschooled practitioners would call on both sides for reconstructionism or "magickal work" simultaneously in modern traditions is beyond the author's understanding. This occurs frequently in "New Age" interpretations of ancient mysteries—and is especially evident in revivals of Mesopotamian Neopaganism using the "Anunnaki" pantheon. More confusing still is the incorporation of the pre-Fir-Bolg Cthonic "Fomorian mythos." To be certain, we have compared our research for this volume with more antiquated cryptic Celtic manuscripts, especially: "*The Book of Invasions,*" "*The Book of Leinster,*" "*The Book of Dun Cow,*" the Oghamist's "*Book of Ballymote*" (and "*Scholar's Primer*") and *Pheryllt-Barddas* material of the Welsh-Drwyds.

Some scholars and metaphysical writers are confused by the common spelling of the tribe—'Tuatha De Dannan'—and mistakenly align the Elven-Ffayrie tradition (origins) to "*Dana,*" derived from "*Diana,*" the Roman forest-huntress. The present author emphasizes the "*D'Anu*" spelling that is factually more accurate; as in the "*D'anube River*" and "*Children of Anu.*" To call them "Dannan" confuses them further with the "Danes"—a separate Elven-Ffayrie legacy partly found among Scandinavians (Norse/Nordic), Vikings and "*Svei*" or "Swedes."

When the Romans encountered one Danubian clan in Scotland they called them "Picts" or "Pict-Sidhe"—or "pict-shees"—which is where one of the more popular titles developed. Where we are led to believe the word "pixie" means "small," its roots—"*Pict-*" and "*Pix-*"—relate specifically to etymology for the words "picture" and "pixels," which is why Elven lore refers to the same tribe as the "Painted Folk," those known for their use in tribal full-body art, reminiscent in many ways to certain "primitive" revivals today.

Tuatha D'Anu possessed a unique cultural magical tradition far surpassing any other ones they encountered—making a tremendous impression on the proto-Celts—or *La Tene* culture. With the arrival of the Tuatha D'Anu, ritual and ceremonial "magick" practices began—aligned to the elements of nature, or else "Elementalism." The original Danubian tribe of Elven-Ffayrie carried with them the "Gifts of Faerie"—four objects or artifacts that proved their skill in the "Arts of Civilization" and crafts of magic—in fact, they viewed both "art" and "magic" as one and the same, a belief carried by most Elven and Faerie traditions. As such, "Western Æurope" saw the birth what we call the "Western Magical Tradition."

As some readers are undoubtedly familiar: Western ritual and "ceremonial magic" is based primarily on a four-fold alignment with the "Four Elements" and equally the four cardinal directions—or "four winds" if your prefer. These are the representations or embodiments of the four "Gates" to Beyond—or else "four corners" of the Universe—that bind together the parts we call "space and time." Using a paradigm such as the "Gifts of Faerie" allows a greater experiential understanding and handling of these energies—in ritual and consciousness, since they are both the same.

Ceremonialists and modern Wizards of the O.T.O, Golden Dawn and such, have been unable to break away from the core and fundamental Elementalist paradigm for their ritualized magickal expressions. Though their 'higher' ceremonial and celestial practices are not the same as what you find among indigenous-type shamans, the same correspondence charts of magick are as useful to them as to any Elf, Druid or Elemental Wizard.

According to tradition, the *"Gifts of Faerie"*—also known as the *"Gifts of Faeire"*—were brought to Ireland each from a different elementally-aligned city, by a surviving representative from that city. Many have believed these legendary cities existed on "Atlantis" or some other lost continent, meaning the Elven-Ffayrie—and specifically the Tuatha D'Anu—were the survivors of "Atlantis" or similar. Other lore suggests that their cities were of an "Otherworld" nature—perhaps "astral" and therefore, by definition, "stellar" or "celestial," meaning literally of a "star" nature. Another possibility is that these semantics are only a cultural paradigm and that the *Atlantis* described is really Mesopotamia—or similar—but *before* the "Great Flood."

> **THE GIFTS OF FAEIRE**
>
> "The 'Stone of Fal,' of the Northern city of Falias, came to us from Morfessa, High Wizard of the North. This stone was set at Tara, the 'Seat of the Kings' (literally "Dragons") where it would scream out whenever a true king set foot on it. Irish Druid history tells us that the only kings in Ireland during Celtic times were those who were made so on the 'Stone of Fal,' also called the 'Stone of Scone.' The true nature of the Element of Stone is Earth, and to the direction of North, Wizards have attributed it.
>
> "The 'Spear of Lugh' emerged from the Eastern city of Gorias carried by Esras. Known also as the 'Spear of Destiny,' this tool never missed its target. Some say it was the implement used to pierce Christ's side at the Crucifixion and was also carried by Hitler's Nazi army. That the item never misses its target hints at the relationship between the Wizard and a tool. It is driven or activated by willpower (the art of directing

> energy to a target) and so it becomes the "wand" in the magickal tradition. Both the wand and the spear are attributed to the power and energies of Elemental Air, reserved to the direction of East.
>
> "From the city of Finias the 'Sword of Nuada' came, carried from the South by Uscias. Here is the archetypal 'magic sword' archetype, for this blade carried with it other great names through history like "Albion," "Caliburn," and more famously, "Excalibur." It is connected to the Elven-Ffayrie tradition as the 'Sword of Greenwood Kings', carried by both Arthur Pendragon and Robin Hood. It is imbued with the ability to deal fatal blows with each strike, representing the surety of will, and the cutting, flaming, searing edge of willpower being properly directed. The sword or blade is always a symbol of Fire, dedicated to the Southern direction.
>
> "The 'Cauldron of the Dagda,' or Kerridwen's 'Cauldron of Rebrith,' came to Ireland by Master Semias from the city of Murias to the West. In one legend, the cauldron acts as a 'horn o' plenty', refilling itself with an endless supply of food. Other lore suggests the artifact was used as a part of a healing ritual, reviving and curing the wounded. Some believe the 'Gundestrup Cauldron,' found in the swamps of Denmark is similar to the 'Cauldron of the Dagda.' As a symbol, the cauldron itself is a primary icon of magick and witchcraft. Most modern practitioners use a goblet or chalice, representing the 'Holy Grail,' as their representation of the Water Element. Ceremonially, the symbolism is almost identical. Some traditions incorporate both the cauldron and the chalice for different ritual purposes."

When Tuatha D'Anu overcame the Fir-Bolg, they offered the remaining surrendering race—approximately 300 Elven-Ffayrie in all—their own region of Ireland to live and thrive, provided they could share the island in peace. Tuatha D'Anu were clearly not as aggressive of a race as the Fir-Bolg or the Fomorians before them—or even their cousin-fey: the Danes, Scandinavian Vikings and Norse Wizards. The true Highborn-Elves enjoy long lifespans. They are not quick to throw that privilege away, nor is a scar or severe wound considered a battle trophy—since they would have to carry it with them perhaps hundreds of years. Yet, pacifist ideals of many Tuatha D'Anu members did not keep them from eventually winning the battle with the Fir-Bolg, their own distant relations.

Danubians never came to Ireland seeking a fight. We are in some ways led to believe they were running from something themselves—

had no doubt already seen countless battles and suffering and abandoned their ships on arrival to Ireland as if to say: "This is it! Here is our new home. We're sick of running." But the existing populations viewed this as a malignant act of invasion—and battle was inevitable. Their intellectualism and few numbers did, however, keep them from fighting off the Milesians—the *'Sons of Mil,'* or else, "mortal humans."

Around the year 500 BC—though some suggest earlier—the Milesian "Celts" invaded Ireland from Iberia—presumably Spain—intending to drive the Tuatha D'Anu out. They new invaders were "mortal Humans" using their usual strengths—overwhelming numbers and crude weapons—to take over Ireland. The Milesians possessed no "magical abilities" themselves and were immediately intrigued by the Tuatha D'Anu and their mysticism. Some of them thought to enslave the race and force them to use their magic for Humans. Of course, the Danubian Celts did not share this idea—so the Elven-Ffayrie simply *left*! A few remained—loving the land of *Eriu* so much that they somehow transitioned into its Underworld—and beneath the conscious surface of Human awareness. Invisible, they were later called "Daoine Sidhe"—dwellers of burial mounds or "fairy hills."

The Tuatha D'Anu that did not remain hidden in Ireland went on to become legendary '*Trooping Faerie-Sidhe*' of Scotland—the ones that Rev. Robert Kirk[*] encountered—those known elsewhere as the "*Seelie*" and "*Unseelie*" courts. Others went to Wales, joining their cousins— the "Pheryllt" Dragon Priests inhabiting mountainous regions there. In Wales, surviving members of the Tuatha D'Anu maintained their mystical ways and natural philosophy, called "*Druideachd*" or "*Derwyth*"—which is better known today as "Druidism." Those readers that may have previously believed that traditions of the Elven-Ffayrie have been handed down to European humans in the form of Celtic Druidry would be essentially correct. Yet, the largest misconception about Danubian Druidism and its later Celtic Faerie Tradition is that instead of a confinement to Ireland and the British Isles, it was actually once found throughout Æurope/Eurasia.

Before the world-wide destruction of the Drwyds by the Romans, Keltia extended from Ireland all the way to "Galatia,"—meaning Anatolia or modern day Turkey. In fact, Galatia was home to a "Drunemeton," a legendary and sacred place in Ancient Elven-Ffayrie Drwyd lore, where large convocations/gatherings took place annually.

---

[*] *Rev. Robert Kirk*—explained in greater detail in the "*Secret Legacy of Elves and Faeries*" section later in this anthology.

The Sidhe shared a name and legacy with the bloodline of Scythian Kings. What's more: there may or may not be a connection between the "Scythians,"/"Sithians"/ "Sidhe" and the iconic Scythe-Sickle blade of the Druids. This blade was used to cut sacred herbs—and is a symbol of the Fire Element. The "Golden Sickle" may actually be used in place of the sword or ritual blade as a tool of "Elemental Magick." Other traditions employ it specifically as an "herbalist dagger" or *boline.*

When we follow the trail of lore concerning the Sidhe, we can determine that they are the largest or rather the tallest descendents from the Tuatha D'Anu. With their adept mystical skill, it is difficult to judge size of full-blooded Elven-Ffayrie races because most of them have ability to alter it, "shape-shift," and "polymorph." The form that the Sidhe took after the coming of the Milesians is considered ethereal or akashic-astral. This allowed them to transition easily into the Otherworld—an alternate "dimension." It could only be in such a form—spirit-like or invisible—beneath the surface of Human perception, that they would be able to remain in the same Green World, but in the "Hollow Hills" and the "Lands Beneath." Due to their ethereal nature, the Elvish Wizards and Drwyds (remaining in the physical world) said that "twilight" *threshold*—either dawn or dusk—is the best natural condition of *time* to see their "spirit-forms."

"Druidism" was never truly a "religion" to the Drwyds in the way we look at "religion" today. They may have viewed their own craft of knowledge as a philosophical art-form—or as a basic expression of "life." But—much like Moses and his own Abrahamic religion—ancient Drwyds were charged to lead a people with their wisdom, mysticism and natural philosophy, all of which reflected true teachings of the "Ancient Mystery School" and the legacy of "Dragon Kings" and Elven-Ffayrie wizards and priestesses. Just as we are able to witness in the Ancient Near East—cultural tradition developed as a result of "higher minds" mixing with indigenous populations. Keltia was a vast land occupied by many diverse tribes and clans. It is for this reason, giving credit to these wise "systematizers," that classical writers and historians refer to "Druidism" as the "Religion of the Celtic people."

Religious customs included water-elemental baptismal rites, representing an "Underworld Initiation." Baptism rituals are not exclusive to Christianity. Funerary traditions involved a three-day wake, after which the actual funeral ceremony was observed. The *La Tene* culture apparently cremated their dead at first, whereas the Ancient Ones preferred burial in mounds and tombs. The very idea of Elven-Ffayrie residing in burial mounds and Dragon Kings living in pyramidal tombs may have contributed to related traditions of "Vampyre" lore —another greatly misunderstood and misrepresented faction of esoterica.

Pliny the Elder speaks of an Elvish Drwyd custom of "cutting the Mistletoe"—a subject of controversy among neodruid revivals. Everyone seems to have an opinion about how Mistletoe grows; the range of it in ancient times; and on what trees it can grow on (or not at all). It actually *does* grow on Oaks; just not often. Mistletoe is associated with the Druidic "*Alban Arthuann*" festival—Winter Solstice or Yule. Names for the Mistletoe in Gaelic languages translate to mean "all-heal" and "high branch." This sacred herb was considered the primary active ingredient in all herbal medicines and ritual incense—thus, it was incorporated in nearly all uses of "herbalism" and "tree magic" as the "supreme catalyst."

When the Milesian Celts finally equalized with the remaining Dragon heirs, Elvish Druids and Ffayrie Priestesses, they were no longer their own race isolated on a private island or mainland forest for the first time. To maintain and preserve their most sacred traditions, history and mystic rites—a part of which you hold in your hands right now—they had to form an "Order," "Mystery School" or "Secret Society." They reserved themselves to ancient and secret groves to learn and teach their way, independent of Human eyes. Yes, many of them were now a large part Human—but those still maintaining any part of this tradition remained separate from the 'herd.' The "Bardic College" and "Druid Order" were born—origins for a modern "Wizard School" archetype. And while some secret cabals had existed prior, the Druids maintained influence in the Celtic World ("Keltia") for one-thousand years.

Gaelic-Welsh was once an official language of Elven-Ffayrie of the British Isles—written publicly in Greek letters. Other characters, such as Ogham, were not used for common purposes. Today the 'Ogham' is primarily a divination tool in the "New Age," but its application to "High Forest Magick" is explored elsewhere in this book series. Ogham was once even used for construction of coded wooden and stone signs spread all throughout Keltia, readable only by Elven Drwyds and members of their secret society.

While it was forbidden to write many of the sacred teachings down, lore was still maintained at hundreds of "sylvan libraries" formed from leaves and bark of trees to form characters and letters of the Ogham alphabet. The Romans destroyed many of these and St. Patrick reportedly burned (or overseen the destruction of) more than two hundred of them in Ireland. In a flash, the Romans and Christians became cardinal enemies of the Elves, Dragons, Faerie races, and the preservation of their most ancient tradition.

dark ages of earth's history: the thousand-year elven holocaust

The "Elven Holocaust"* is a period in world history synonymous with what we generally call the "Dark Ages." The Church of Rome controlled all maters of religion, science and state government during this era. Its suppressive influence caused the great Secrets-of-the-Ages (the *"Great Magical Arcanum"*) to be all but lost to human civilization forever—and this superior wisdom is only recently being reintroduced to mainstream awareness as it creeps out slowly from the underground in our work.

Until the Dark Ages, the Dragon Kings were the noble class of Europe. Kingship or "Enlil-ship on Earth" is originally granted by "Divine Right" based on "royal blood" and "genetic integrity"—overseen by "dragon-priests," the true wizards of what is now considered "mythological history." In addition to Anunnaki-born, other related biblical figures carry this line, including Abraham and Moses—even the Davidic House of Judah. More seeded dynasties were maintained in Egypt and elsewhere throughout Europe, especially after the migration of the Tuatha D'Anu. Parts of this original tradition have seeped into many surviving systems of Hebrew mysticism, the Edaphic Tradition and preserved lore and histories of the Ancient Near Eastern *"Holy Lands"* held by secret societies.

The Judeo-Christian system forsakes Anunnaki lore for later Semitic visions of monotheism held where Enki is the "wrathful God" of the *Old Testament* who worked with his "angels" (or names eventually passed on to Marduk when he attempts succession for "Enlil-ship") on Earth to perform remarkable feats. Immediate descendents of Enki are primarily the Babylonian "Elder Gods" of Mesopotamian Tablets—the "Mardukite" Pantheon of Babylon—and cousin to the Nephilim or Watcher races—specifically dedicated to Anu and Enlil—as mentioned in some translations of accepted scripture. This same bloodline went on to manifest throughout Europe as Elf Kings and Faerie Queens of legendary renown.

The term "Elven Holocaust" refers specifically to the chaotic period of intellectual and spiritual "Dark Ages" on the Earth between 751 AD

---

* *"Thousand-Year Elven Holocaust"*—a term coined by the late Nicholas de Vere von Drakenberg (of the "Imperial Sovereign Dragon Court and Society") to describe the period of Dark Ages illustrated in this chapter.

and 1736 AD. After this point, Fraudulent Medium Laws & Anti-Witchcraft Acts still made participation and/or adherence to the esoteric legacy illegal.

In similar fashion to how Romans eradicated Druidry, the new Church now feared any remaining true remnants of the esoteric past that might threaten their own self-given totalitarian "divine right to rule." As a result, they moved to eliminate all traces of "magic," and anyone in possession of its knowledge could be punished by death—including those naturally of Elven and Faerie "witch" ancestry. We use the word "holocaust" to describe these events due its parallels with World War II. True "royal blood" maintained by Dragon Kings (until 751 AD) now ceased to reside in the royal households. The Roman Church began distributing conquered lands and rights of Kingship for their own political and administrative ends.

Curiously, up until the Dark Ages, the Dragon Kings and Elves were actually cooperatively coexisting with the Church. They even carried hidden truths about Jesus, the "Holy Lands" and the *Old Testament*—which they mistakenly shared with the Church. The Merovingian legacy descended directly from the knights of Solomon's Temple. Elements of their tradition and genetic memory is maintained later by some exclusive orders of Freemasons, Cathars and Templar Knights—all of which originally required a family lineage of membership to be considered for admission/initiation. Today we see a different kind of "accepted" involvement that is not nearly as strict in its membership criteria.

The "Merovingians" were "Knights of the Temple" protecting the mysteries of Rome until they were brutally "dispatched" in 751 AD—or even earlier, as some suggest that executions may have begun in the year 664 AD—and replaced by the group known as the Carolingians, those with no affiliation with the original Elves and Dragon Kings.

A document appeared in 751 AD allegedly signed during the 4th Century reign of Emperor Constantine. This is what made enforcement of an "Elven Holocaust" possible—and justifiable in the eyes of the Church. When Pope Sylvester cured him of leprosy, Constantine supposedly donated the entire wealth and power of the Roman Empire to the Church...and yet this was not invoked until several centuries later, leaving many to believe this document—"*The Donation of Constantine*"—is not even authentic, but a forgery used for political ends.

With activation of this "trust," the Roman Church assumed control over the "known world," thrusting civilization into the Dark Ages. Certainly this could not be the original and true vision of Jesus Christ for his "church."

Consequently, all of the Dragon Kings and earthly sovereignty were replaced by those crowned exclusively by the Vatican.

After the "Age of Faerie" was forgotten, Danubian Druids became mythological and legendary deities of the Celtic people: they believed the Sidhe always resided in the invisible world; and the era of "magic" ended, giving way to a false lineage ruling Æurope under the banner of "Holy Mother Church." Although Gnostic and Essene sects of early Christianity inspired the now "secret" gospels, as well as Christ himself, those in control during the Dark Ages ruled under the name of Jesus, but developed propaganda for a religion of genocide.

While surviving members of the Elven-Ffayrie may hold a lingering resentment against ignorant members of Christian Tradition in history, they do not find contradiction between Christ's actual teachings and their own.

The misuse of a "Religious Empire" by the Church, however, marked the beginning of the "Dark Ages," a time when even Christians were leaving Catholicism to start their own protestant religions. In breaking with the original Church, however, these new religions continued propagating fundamentalist misconceptions about the Bible and its history—and no longer connected to Rome, they also lost access to Vatican records—even if most of them remained off limits. During these Dark Ages, a new version of the "*Bible*" emerged eliminating all esoteric references to the Elven-Ffayrie Histories, mysticism, reincarnation, *Old Testament* interactions with the Anunnaki, and several full books. By this time, all of the former traditions and lore relating to the Elven-Ffayrie, Druids and Dragon folk were condemned as "demonology" and "devil-worship" by the Church, and were equally considered off-limits "for the safety of your soul."

It is clear the Church viewed Elven-Ffayrie as a threat. No longer would they be recorded in history as the true "Sons of God"—no longer would they be acknowledged as the true ruling class of Æurope. A time for "Elves, Magic and Gods" gave way to the "Time of Men" and their ways. In time, the Elven Histories were construed as little more than fictitious mythology or cultural embellishments of diverse pagan pantheons.

For example—in one myth "God" comes to Lilith while she is bathing her children and asks her to present them all to Him. Embarrassed by those who were already clean for God's arrival, she hid away the unwashed. Already knowing full well the truth, God asks her if she has presented all of them. She replies, saying, "Yes"—and those children hidden away from God's sight were then cursed to live out their lives as Elven-Ffayrie. Hidden from God's sight, they would live hidden and invisible from the eyes of Men.

Other disturbing Elven genesis lore may be found in the Nordic Elven-Ffayrie tradition. Their version describes all Elven-Ffayrie as emerging or born from maggots feeding on the corpse of an ancient Wizard and Giant—"Ymir." Many other legends from the Dark Ages depict Elven-Ffayrie as fallen angels; and regarding "pixies"—the Church clergy explained that they were human souls of children that died before receiving a "true" baptism.

History-keeping is a very dangerous business. Entire traditions, races and people have been threshed out of existence due to personal biases and retention errors. Once things are written, they are rewritten, re-recorded, then changed again. With each new discovery one must alter what was previously accepted as fact, or be a victim to ignorance. But nations take over one another and then rewrite history. This was the case when the Romans finally conquered the Celts and annihilated Elvish Druidism—forcing most survivors "underground," beneath the "exoteric" surface world and out of public sight.

Druids handled all matters of authentic kingship in ancient times. They designated specific rulers—and no Celtic King was completely "official" without a ceremony overseen by a Druid Elf, and one of their representatives to "advise him" during his reign. Coexisting with Celtic society, the "royal line" again preserved Elven-Ffayrie Tradition—they installed their own blood into that of Kings and Druids to ensure a continuation of the legacy, albeit separate from the general Celtic population. For this reason, modern practitioners must differentiate between what is general "Celtic" from what is purely "Druidic," "Alferic" or "Elven" if their intention is to maintain authenticity of any modern Elven-Faerie tradition.

Before the Dark Ages, all kings and mystic priests were Elven-Ffayrie. We might assume—given chronology—that the 5th Century King Arthur is essentially the last of the great Pagan Celtic Kings. Emerging new leadership thrust civilization into ignorance and "Dark Ages."

These were not the legendary mystic seers and sages of the prior age —now known to the people as "pagan" or "heathen."

All magic from the prior age was dubbed "evil" with few exceptions: the god-given powers employed by Moses and Jesus. Such were not classified within a domain of "magic" and were instead "miracles" conducted by "God's hand" alone.

Then, after the Roman Church starts governing coronation of Kings, all existing claims to former Dragon legacies and sovereignty are denounced and its Elven-Ffayrie bloodlines annihilated—and forced underground.

The original legacy of Dragon Kings spans many regions and eras following the development of human culture in Mesopotamia. Historical references to *dragons* often confuse many novice students, and potentially even the current reader. The Elves, faerie races and dragons we speak of here do not resemble the "stereotypical" fantasy appearances a person is likely to conjure to mind. Certainly there are many forms and types of energy manifesting all around us, but for our current purposes of historical analysis, we are restricting our view to the "humanoids" derived from a "star race"—whether we wish to attach other labels like "astral," "inter-dimensional" or "extra-terrestrial" to this is a matter of personal taste, because such details are only alluded to on the ancient tablets.

Despite common popular beliefs about all things "fairy," the noble Elves are actually "tall"—not dwarfed and some Anunnaki races may have had scaled skin, but they weren't little green men or "winged-serpents." Our descriptions of the Anunnaki demonstrate that they were also tall—in fact, in addition to being "Watchers," the biblical "Nephilim" are often translated by scholars to mean "giant." Where many Humans have rounded facial features, the Elves generally carry more narrow, angular, sharper traits and pale skin that tans very quickly in the sun—which can given them a very Near Eastern appearance.

Sumerian and Babylonian cuneiform tablets—and secret lore maintained by the Dragon King legacy—suggest that specific dynastic bloodlines were seeded by the Anunnaki in Mesopotamia—but also elsewhere, in Egypt, the Indus Valley and so forth. This spread across the planet in tow of a developing human systemology as a caste of "priests and kings." From the time of prehistory until the rising power of the Romans and later Church, priest-kings historically maintained global power for thousands of years. This "higher," "winged" class of "Sky Gods"—the "Elder Race"—found representations in the art, culture, religion and government of all of these ancient civilizations and the heavenly pantheons they observed.

Angelic lore—and battles between angels—originates here, specifically derived from the genetic memory of an ancient "War in Heaven," then extended in human consciousness to disputes between Enki (the "Lord of the Earth") and Enlil (the "Bull of Heaven") over the handling of human populations. Other commonly held angelic lore was later adopted from Persian Zoroastrianism, but the moral dualism reflecting in these "dogmas" is dependent on the idea of Lucifer or Satan.

In orthodox interpretations of ancient history, it is Enki—the Lord of this Earth—that is demonized as Satan or Lucifer. Some of these same properties even fell into our classic understanding of his heir-son Marduk. But, the image of the Dragon—as attached to this class of Anunnaki or Star-beings and their Elven-Faerie descendants—was demonized by the Church and used as a symbol of effigy for all evil in the world.

In one account, even Enlil refers to Marduk as "the evil serpent in Babylon that the world needs to be rid of." Among medieval secret societies this "angelic rogue" energy current materialized as "Baphomet"—a goat-headed swan-winged "dragon"—and another representation of the "devil" for the Church to demonize.

It is obvious that the true and faithful rendering of ancient history—and our clear understanding of it—became so convoluted over two millenniums of world governance outside of true Dragon sovereignty that it is now reduced to mythology, and even more recently as a subject of controversy and conspiracy in the "New Age" over the past several decades—and now we have many claims of dragon societies and courts in operation today.

Perhaps the most impressive and original modern institution of the "Dragon Court" links back to the late esoteric researcher, Nicholas de Vere, whose work went on to inspire many similar "copy-cat" organizations.

The concept of Dragon sovereignty is lost to modern systems—although we might like to think of it as a backbone to some current *Illuminati*, none of the current conspiracy theories comes close to the true realization that those in charge are not sovereign, nor have they been for a very long time, since the decision to ultimate destroy this planet, and its inhabitants, yet again. This is not happening all at once—but it *is* happening—and no true "Lords of the Earth" would be allowing this.

The fate charted for humanity is nothing short of utter self-destruction and self-annihilation in the crudest sense—for we have not truly evolved so far from our ignorant days of spiritual handicapping during the Dark Ages. You may interpret this message however you please, but these events—the suppression of the "Children of Faerie"—blatantly contributed to the continuing pollution and destruction of Planet Earth.

Today, remnants of the Anunnaki tradition and Faerie faith of Æurope are concentrated into such specific locations and elements of archaic culture that it is sometimes difficult for a modern *seeker* to truly relate to the wide scope and sweeping influences that our current study touches upon. It is very important to understand, especially as pertaining to the subject of Druidism, that this tradition was not always restricted to the westernmost tips of modern-day Europe.

The original "Danubian" cultural influence—of the Tuatha D'Anu—stretched all the way back to ancient Mesopotamia as we have seen, and even from those roots, had expanded in other directions as well, like a star-burst. When we consider, for example, the "Drunemeton" of Galatia (Anatolia/Turkey), it is a very peculiar location for the Arch Druids ("Arch Dragons") of Western Europe to share convocation, if indeed the tradition was only restricted to Western Europe.

Semantic connections between "Druids" and "oaks" are practically cliché—what is less known is the relationship between the "*drui*" or "*draoi*" and the serpent or dragon. This is why Arch-Drui and Ban-Draoi carry translated titles, like "Grand Dragon," "Imperial Dragon" or even "Pen-Dragons" in Keltia.

We are told St. Patrick drove the last "serpent-dragons" from Ireland and once removed from society, dragons were later associated with caves *they hid in*.* Since then, genetic integrity of the Dragon Kings and Elves is under constant scrutiny as "racism." This is not so surprising in a world of blind acceptance and diversity celebration. That is not to say ignorant people have not used this lore in the past to

---

* See "*Draconomicon: The Book of Ancient Dragon Magick*" by Joshua Free; also reprinted in "*Merlyn's Complete Book of Pheryllt.*"

support racism. This has unfortunately already occurred and will probably continue to—that cannot be helped. But this is not the focus of our present volume or book series.

We find an emphasis of concentration on specific genealogies and bloodlines everywhere we turn in the ancient world and in every culture—this is nothing new. Each emphasized this aspect specifically over the higher spiritual ideals—which is something the present author will not allow to run rampant in this text.

This concept of preserving royal bloodlines and dynastic traditions has a familiar presence in history—particularly concerning the descent of rulers, kings, monarchs, pharaohs and any other claims to "Enlil-ship" on this planet. One example: the 'Ancient Near Eastern' and Semitic "Chosen People" of "Yahweh"—a group that even to this day prefers to exercise a degree of genetic separatism in their marriage (sexual and breeding) practices, instinctively preserving their cultural genetic memory.

Overtly and visibly, the global legacy of the Dragon Kings fell during the Elven Holocaust. This was an effort—quite successful—by the Roman Church to exercise all religious and political control of the known world, ultimately throwing Western Civilization into the Dark Ages. With establishment of 'Anti-Witchcraft and Magick Acts', the Elves, faerie folk and Dragon Kings were considered witches by heredity—criminals of both state and religion. Such events forced any surviving "Elves" into the underground—and the "Dragons" to their caves. All occult interests from this point were confined to "secret societies."

In 751 AD, the last of the Elven Mergovians—the *"Keepers and Guardians of the Holy Temple"*—said to be descendents from Solomon's own ancient occult temple-builders, are disbanded and excommunicated from Rome and "separated from the blessing" of *"Holy Mother Church,"* to be replaced by a new group of Vatican-selected "Carologians." Up until the 6th and 7th centuries, Gnostic Wizards and Drwyds actually worked closely with the Catholic Church. They saw Jesus as a figure of each of their own traditions. This disturbed the later heirs of the Church that saw the Elven-Ffayrie as a threat to the "Seat of Rome" and the Vatican's new authority to select kings and rulers, where once this privilege rested with Drwyds and the Elven (and Dragon) lineages.

The Wheel of Time turns but the cycles of history repeat. Yet again, the *"Sons of Man"* feared the *"Sons of God"* would rebel and thus the "New Church" was formed independent of them, with only a shred of the original Gnostic vision remaining. The focus of the Church now: to take control of Æurope and eradicate "paganism." The church installed leaders that could be easily controlled by its own inclinations. Under religious pressure, royalty was coerced to uphold Church law above all—meaning also to outlaw all witchcraft and "magic."

Even as the Church openly borrowed many ancient customs in order to ease the conversion of pagans, the laws were put forth to quickly suppress any *real* folk practice of these traditions.

Pope Gregory IX launched the historically famous Inquisition in the 13th Century. This later received more fuel with the publication of a ridiculous text—the *"Malleus Maleficarum"* or *"Witches' Hammer"*—a completely useless witch-hunter's manual derived from superstition and intended to inspire hatred.

In England, King Henry VIII was among the first to outlaw witchcraft as a significant "state" offense, authorizing "burning at the stake" as capital punishment as early as 1542. Queen-Elizabeth-I increased strictness of these laws in 1563—a peculiar move by someone personally fascinated by the occult and who had, in her employment, a "royal court magician," the famous John Dee—co-founder of the *Enochian Magic* system. She obviously protected Dee from the same mandates she herself installed (or upheld), but referred to him often as her *"astrologer royale."* Throughout Europe, various laws were in place allowing persecution and capital punishment of witches until an English repeal in 1736—after the public revival of Freemasonry and neodruidism in 1717. Strict laws were replaced with "Fraudulent Mediums Acts," which *could* imprison those guilty of claims to witchcraft or performing spellcraft—but no longer authorized executions.

Magical spiritual traditions once constituted the entire systemology of life and government in the ancient world; then it was entirely demonized as Satanism by the Church. Once the original practices and practitioners were sufficiently "out of the picture" long enough to be nearly forgotten, both church and state finally dictated that witchcraft and "magic" was an illusion—was not real—as enforceable by the Fraudulent Mediums Acts (or similar). Even prior to the union of Rome and the Church, Rome had handled their politics this way, as seen in their encounters with early Celtic Druids and Elven races.

When the darker overloads of the Church finally left—or died out—they left not only the Church, but also all it had affected, in a shambles. Many practitioners became confused with conflicting aspects of Christianity's evolution, and those now left in charge had little more to offer than to say: "Have faith."

However, the Vatican still possessed the wealth and records of the Roman Empire and some of the Elven Kings it had usurped. Works once attributed to legend are now resurfacing—such as the *Dead Sea Scrolls*, the *Apocrypha*, the *Book of Enoch* and the *Gospel of Thomas*, just to name a few. Yet, only the initiates of the Inner Vatican Circle once knew anything of this lore. When we consider all of this in light of the Elven-Ffayrie specifically—as is the subject of our volume—the people of the Renaissance era, and even modern society today, can usually distinguish their beliefs regarding "Elves and Faeries" into one of the following four categories:

> 1. The Sidhe-Sylvans are a distant genetic relation to Mortal Humans.
>
> 2. Ffayrie beings are "Nature Spirits" which inhabit the Green World Forest—where "*magical*" things happen.
>
> 3. Elven-Ffayrie races are descendents from the "Fallen Angels" or are the "Children of Lilith"—but essentially "vampyres," "demons" or "devils" (of the Christian paradigm).
>
> 4. Fey creatures are ancient ancestral spirits (genetic relatives) —particularly Eurasian—who were so attached to the land that they remained after the rise of Humans, albeit beneath the surface—or "invisible"—upholding their pledge as "Gaea's Guardians" even in death.

During the Dark Ages, the persecution of "magic" drove its beliefs, practices and practitioners out of public sight. The remaining "wizarding blood"—its legacy and direct lineage—was split in two: one group went into the deep woods where Nature-oriented more shamanic-like traditions developed.

The Faerie legacy was also carried by another faction—an elitist group descending from the Dragon race that maintains a large chain of secret societies coexisting with mortal society even to this day—and of which does play an important role in our global events and affairs, while simultaneously operating almost independently and "above" society.

The "secret societies" and "Elven Councils" of the Dark Ages did not exist to the same social degree as in the Age of Faerie—just as modern Druids do not, by that trade alone, have a position in society today as they once did in ancient Keltia. The knowledge stream and lineage has also fallen along the way and continues to cycle out from our world and our consciousness—apart from a select few *Seekers.*

All branches of the "Ancient Mystery School" have endured their own evolution across time and space—all of its members today, are in effect, reconstructionists—distant descendants with "mystical inclinations." Many of the elitist organizations still existent today moved further and further away from the true legacy and lineages that once guarded these societies thousands of years ago—and many of these organizations are granting "outsiders" membership "on commitment," which only occurs when esoteric membership is on the decline—and as a result, we have witnessed a surge of interest in these matters in the new millennium. Between the Ancient Drwyds and neodruids of today, there stands a long lineage of Masonic, Rosicrucian and Illumiinati organizations—and each has its own claims to "secret knowledge" about human history, in addition to a flavor of practical metaphysical lore. Nearly all secret sects, mystical cabals and magical orders have at one time shared their roots with this legacy.

We might assume—from the Elven Histories—that after its prehistoric "star origins," the original root tradition mainly emerged in the Mediterranean/Mesopotamian region, forming a "delta" of Sumerian/ Babylonian, Greek and Egyptian wisdom traditions that now share the same umbrella: Hermetic. "Hermetic Tradition" is a later synthesis of the three, of which Mesopotamia is the oldest, but it is *here* that many modern occultists are successfully able to trace their varying "secret traditions" back to. Where the classical world is quite familiar and we have long experienced the colorful revival of Egyptology, only recently has the more antiquated Mesopotamian mythos received public attention. This foreign wider encompassing paradigm has brought with it a whole new set of cultural language and vocabulary semantics to consider in developing a true holistic understanding of our origins.

Elitist practitioners of Modern Hermetics trace some of their lore and tradition to the Gnostics. Gnosticism was the highest religion of the Hermetic-Delta until the arrival of the Roman Empire. In Æurope we find remnants of the same tradition as maintained by the Celtic

Druids and the La Tene culture until it too is finally pushed to the very shores of the ocean and its islands and northern most "Hyperborean" reaches before it is completely forced underground—but it is not obliterated. The tradition split in two: some mystics taking to the woods and others becoming Holy Knights, that surfaced during the Crusades—among them the "Cathars" and "Knights Templar" —"Knights of the Temple"—that pledged to uphold the legacy the "True Church," that was no longer present in Rome.

Something very curious occurred in the year 1717: both the Knight-Rangers and Mystics rose again—and in public view. The neodruids and neo-masons—or Freemasons—emerged in England. On paper, many current long-standing orders and lodges of the same may actually trace their origins to this event—taking place in England, at the Apple Tree Tavern.[*] Only after the end of the Dark Ages does both the "Ancient Order of Druids" and "Ancient Order of Freemasonry" enter society in plain sight. From there it spread across the world in some revival form or another. Many scholars and skeptics viewed—and continue to view—these reconstructions and revivals as completely without merit. This continued through most of the 1900s as well, and is only beginning to change as more and more people take interest in "alternative paths."

The "knight-ranger" lineage became the "Illuminoids" that inspired the modern Masonic Traditions today with their neodruidic ideals. The other arm—the Mystics—became the Rosicrucians—Mystics of the Rose-Cross and other similar branches of active esoteric practice. Illuminoid Masons and Rosicrucians with interests in more "magickal" aspects of the Hermetic tradition formed the "Hermetic Order of the Golden Dawn"—or "GD"—and other lesser known occult fraternities and underground groups. The Golden Dawn was originally a very elitist and secret organization up until the publication of a large portion of its "graded" materials as interpreted by Aleister Crowley for his version of the GD—called Argentium Astrum (or "A.A.")—the "Order of the Silver Star." This was later clarified officially by Israel Regardie, known famous for his presentation of a complete system of Golden Dawn magic in a more "authentic" form.

Clearly, Crowley was something of a protestant mystic and a bit of rogue—not unlike Edward Kelley, the assistant to Dr. John Dee during the development of *Enochian Magic*—a subject of serious interest to

---

[*] See "*The Druid's Handbook*" by Joshua Free; also reprinted in "*Merlyn's Complete Book of Magick*" and "*Merlyn's Complete Book of Druidism.*"

Crowley, as introduced among the highest grades of GD material. Another group—the "Ordo Templi Orientis" or "OTO"—also emerged and was even handed down to Crowley at one juncture, later contributed to heavily by his secretary, Kenneth Grant. Mystical forces that these organizations made contract with were—and continue to be—astral, inter-dimensional or extra-terrestrial in nature, and Anunnaki in origin—which is dealt with at more length in a subsequent Mardukite publication.*

The other more rural family, solitary mystic and folk traditions did not often share ties with larger organized revivals, both during the Dark Ages and after. Many of these "hereditary" and "country" traditions developed in isolation and so, it has been the past century of time where the two have been able to openly blend—which has certainly happened when we analyze the actual core roots of modern "Wicca" movements, which are the same. These "simplified" methodologies began rising in popularity toward the end of the 20th century and continue to attract a large following even today.

For the first time in over a thousand years, mystical Nature-oriented "religions" exist in the public eye. New versions of Keltoi-Norse Neopaganism and eclectic Faery Wicca seem to sprout up every day now. What's more: many of them earn some degree of actual "religious" validation. And while the "Ancient Mystery School" was once exclusive to a specific legacy of practitioners—either by mystic ability or lineage and heredity—access to the "secret traditions" is now accessible independent of an instructor, and from wherever books are sold, for the mere price of twenty dollars. For some, this could be interpreted as somewhat dangerous in itself.

---

* *"Necronomicon: The Complete Anunnaki Bible" (15th Anniversary)* by Joshua Free; also reissued as *"The Complete Anunnaki Bible: A Source Book of Esoteric Archaeology."*

elves and druids: the secret world of faerie

Long ago, in the far and distant past, the "gods" once roamed the Earth—figures of legendary renown—before passing "divine right to rule" or *"Enlil-ship"* to their chosen messengers, those intermediaries serving between "gods" and "men." As time bore on and human populations grew, the "gods" left Earth, leaving their systemology in the hands of "priest-kings," "priestesses" and "mystics" that brought the tradition into recorded history. The "blue race" of "Fair Folk" moved westward from the Ancient Near East. These "higher minds" carried influential lore of this "Ancient Mystery School" in their migrations across Æurope, and a new highborn priestly class of Dragon Courts, Elf Kings and Faerie Queens of legend emerged.

Previous chapters introduced a wide-spanning legacy of Elven royalty and Dragon courts that lend us their traditions for this present tome. But to summarize: The Elves—as "Children of Eru/Anu" or "Children of the Stars" inherited the planet as long-distant descendants of Enki—"Lord of the Earth."

Enki—an Anunnaki god residing in the proto-Sumerian capital of Eridu—was first to introduce traditions of magic and science on Earth —which directly sprung up as the original 'Ancient Mystery School' spreading throughout the ancient Mesopotamia and Mediterranean regions—a region referred to in some lore as (*yes, you've guessed it*) 'Middle Earth', the 'mid-branch' place of 'meetings' and 'crossings' between worlds—or between the heavens and the Earth. This Elven race descended from the "Shinning Ones," the "star race," "angels" or "Sons of God"—connected with all of the original global "religions." Eventually, they become avatars of "wizarding" blood, "Earth deities" and "Tuatha d'Anu" heroes of "Celtic Myth."

Following the rise of the Sons of Mil—the rise of human populations in Keltia—most mystically inclined members of Elven and Faerie races "transitioned" to what many refer to as the Otherworld; though the legacy of Druidism continued on in public forms until the time of Saint Patrick and the "Elven Holocaust" or Dark Ages. After focused persecution lifted and many diabolical laws were repealed, the possession of "wizarding blood" —and the practice of magic—no longer carried a death sentence. Yet, by this new era of "enlightenment," dilution of Elven lore and Faerie ancestry dissolved contemporary human understanding of the subject, reducing it to the best that remains from the Grimm family collection as "fable" and "fantasy."

The Elven Way and Faerie Faith were not altogether lost. As the world revival of druidry or "neodruidism" emerged, more remnants of the ancient way started receiving attention, and even documentation. The original of these pertain mainly to daily magical rural living—the traditions that earth-oriented and Nature-based druids and "neopagans" frequently follow today. And this "Edaphic" tradition is, indeed, an original and innate form of "practical magick" in honor of the Ancient and "Shinning Ones." Elves and Faerie races traditionally practice what we consider "green magic," however, the other type—called "ceremonial high magick"—is also present in the legacy of the Dragon Kings, those first in possession of grimoires like the "*Sacred Book of Magic of Abramelin the Magic*" and other Rosicrucian documents, or journals of *Enochian magic*, long before the inception of the Golden Dawn System.

In contemporary lore, and even in some New Age interpretations, the term "Elven" is applied as a catch-all category for a host of ancestral spirits, Nature-spirits and elemental spirits aligned to a combination of earth and air forces. Some types occur in cultural traditions including *Dark Elves* of the *Unseelie Court*, misunderstood "devas," the "*Sidhe*" or *High Elves* of the *Seelie Court*, the *Linchetto* of Etruscan-Italy, the *Quendi* of Sumerian *Eridu* and finally, *Silvani/Sylph* woodland inhabiting Nature guardians—sometimes called *Wood Elves*.

Modern ritual and "practical magick" systems are aligned to "elemental magick" and elemental currents of energy that share affinity with specific "elemental" types—meaning the spiritual forms taken by "transitioned" Elves and Faerie Folk. These entities—appropriated to the "astral plane"—are called in ceremonial and ritual magick at the appropriate corners of the nemeton or ritual circle.

In the Edaphic tradition influencing this current book, "Elves" usually replace the traditional gnomes as "guardians of the north." In a similar fashion, "Dragons" or "Fire-Drakes" may replace the djinn. There are other types of elemental entities that may be incorporated with ritual magic and/ or daily magical living, as described within this chapter.

Lore of "Changelings" appear frequently in connection to traditional Elven-Ffayrie history—and although we do not know its definitive source, it is carried in worldwide belief systems.

"Changelings" are fundamentally human replacements, often newborns, which are switched with an "elf-child." That the Faerie races share a "low reproductive rate" is one driving theory behind this lore —therefore maintaining their populations and/or evolving their genetic diversity by occasionally "stealing humans." It is also possible that this lore applies to phenomenon attributed to many "Otherworldly beings" even in alternative culture today, although we choose contemporary semantics reflecting our technological knowledge, such as:"alien babies," "cloning" and "DNA harvesting." However, throughout the Dark Ages of the Church, religious beliefs maintained that sickly children and infant deaths were all consequences of faerie—or demonic—assault.

"Changeling Theory" is not restricted only to newborns and children —although the archetype of the "stolen child" is the most iconic. Direct interactions between Elven-Ffayrie and Humans are not common —sexual unions between them even less so. The only reference to "fairy theft" in the current Edaphic tradition regards obscure lore of *transignation.* This is when someone may not be willing, or even aware, of themselves being used as a *simulacrum* "host" for a "walk-in" type of entity or "personality."

In the classic anthropological examinations of Elven-Ffayrie by *W.Y. Wentz,** another theory regarding "fairy theft" is put forth. It is possible—as he suggests—that after Milesian humans invade and attempt to entrap the Danubian race (before their flight for hills and caves), that the Fae occasionally kidnapped unattended off-spring of the people who had conquered them. It is also theoretically possible that the later historical Elvish Drwyds themselves, after being driven underground to hide in the dense forests and old groves, may have kidnapped potential apprentices to raise and pass down their knowledge and wisdom to, before returning them to Human society.

When we examine other more recent historical cases like that of *Rev. Robert Kirk*—and perhaps *Thomas Rhymer* and others— we know that select mortals (perhaps even of Elven-Ffayrie lineage) have been taken to the "Otherworld Faerieland." Our primary examples from Faerie-lore, when Otherworld beings interact with mortals, all take place in a surreal yet vividly tangible manner. We know that Elementals are capable of imbuing all types of life with their spirit. There is also lore regarding their ability to use simulacra from birth or "walk-in" at some point during the person's "more able" years, such as pub-

---

*   W.Y. Wentz *"Fairy-Faith in Celtic Countries."*

erty. Either of these abilities—'*transition*' or '*transignation*'—would require, what we would consider (at this level or gradient of understanding and vocabulary), incredibly powerful and advanced "magical abilities" to perform; especially to result in permanent effects.

Elves and Ffayrie have abilities to disorient wanderers that happen upon enchanted fey woods. This belief inspired an old saying: "*Faerie folk live in old oaks.*" Surviving superstition inspires warned travelers passing through such forests to wear their cloaks backwards, or inside out (reversed) to ward against enchantments and glamours that might get a person lost. It is even possible that doing such would "subconsciously" increase one's present "awareness."

Clouds, heavy mist and dense fog are all natural threshold conditions related to the Otherworld and Elven-Ffayrie. Just as many unsuspecting travelers might get lost, there is a long-standing magical tradition of using fog to aid physical access the Otherworld. Lore suggests that these 'twilight' misty conditions create a conduit of communication between worlds that may be employed from either side. And while misleading wanderers through a forest might at first seem malicious, it is possible that Elven-Ffayrie beings make efforts to keep people away from certain locales, powerful thresholds or even dimensional portals and "star-gates" between worlds.

Elven-Ffayrie beings are often described as peculiarly restless. This is historically displayed in their nomadic lifestyle, undoubtedly running deep in genetic memory from being "on the move" for thousands of years. However, the *Seelie* "Sidhe Court" of the ancient Danubian race does not constantly shift their living circumstances because of some mundane dissatisfaction. On the contrary, regular movement of the Court is traditional—e.g. "it has always been that way"—and partly to "normalize" underlying "compulsions," (for lack of finer terminology). While the tradition may not be recognized by more solitary Fae beings, the Danubian Sidhe essentially relocate to a new dwelling space at the beginning of each "quarter." These times of movement were marked by ceremonial observations by the Druids—the "*Four Albans*"—which is to say the annual equinoxes and solstices.

Dwelling places for Elven-Ffayrie are constructed in a manner unlike that of Humans. The Elvish style is "natural"—it is set into the land; built in harmony with the energies of the land; not standing apart from it. Homes of other woodland animals do not destructively disrupt the balance of Nature, yet Humans typically do not establish any harmonious equilibrium with their natural environment—existing almost as its direct *"antithesis."* As such, Humans carry a false sense of elitism on the planet—and unable to naturally survive in its environment, they operate as an exception to all other life on Earth, when they are, in fact, the more recent "guests" of this Green World.

According to the accounts of *Rev. Robert Kirk*, the Sidhe Court resided in a particular faerie "mound," "hill" or *"howe"* at that time. When describing the space/time of the Otherworld Faerieland, Kirk found that, in his experience of it, the Otherworld was far too vast to have been contained within a single hill—providing early examples of "hyperspace" or a "fourth spatial dimension." Interestingly, many of these "Hollowed Hills" were ancient burial sites of Elven-Ffayrie ancestors once residing on the surface world.

The *"Tuatha D'Anu"* and other royal-fey bloodlines would preserve the remains of their ancestors in "tomb-hills." And while not used for burial, funerary rites of the "Ancient Mystery School" were often practiced in "pyramids" and "ziggurats"—artificial "hills" or mountains with cave-like chambers built in places that did not have these naturally occurring landforms. This motif also lends some "Gothic" overtones, inspiring other related mystical traditions emphasizing the more "vampyric" themes and semantics.

Since Elven-Ffayrie dwellings are natural, many are intended only for temporary use as a result of their frequent migration and the fact that they spend little of their time actually home. Of course, when we speak of the nomadic life of the "Trooping Faerie" and the *Seelie Sidhe Court*, we are not including all solitary sylvan folk that do not participate in these *"Rades."*

These Rade-times are traditionally significant in Druidism because they are the most optimum annual threshold periods for mystics to actually see movement of nature-bound Otherworldly beings. These experiences provide us with cultural "memory" of elemental beings. Also—the *Unseelie Court* does not share in the *Seelie Court's* celebrations—like the solitaries—or *"Rades."* Solitaries and sylvan folk also represent more "earthy" types, giving rise to our idea of dressing in leaves and wearing acorn-shaped hats; whereas the Sidhe Court and "High Elves" actually dress in more grandiose attire.

Elven Tradition is revived in Druidism, but it is not the same as the magic practiced by Humans—which employs these other beings to lend their Otherworldly powers to Human ritual. It is from Human lore *about* Elves—based on Human perception and vocabulary of "other" worlds—that we find terms like "Middle Earth" ("M.E."), "Mid-branch," and "Middle-world"—all of which imply the third-dimensional plane.

Each "point" in Middle Earth (physical space) has a center, called *"midhe."* This center is connected to an ethereal "Recursive Spiral" of cosmic energy where space/ time ascends and descends, coiling into upper and lower frequencies/dimensions, ultimately unifying all things—but at different perceptual or semantic levels of understanding or classification. But they are connected *All-as-One*.

Make no mistakes here in thinking of the spiral-like Multiverse in absolute terms of "upper" and "lower" worlds. We use this terminology as only an abstract differentiation to describe the effect or relationship we perceive as one plane or level of existence with another—but they are all interconnected together. If we apply modern science vocabulary and hyper-geometry in our view of an "Infinite" Universe or Multiverse, than we must accept that there are infinite "smaller/ lower" or "larger/upper" levels of existence or dimensions. Elven lore even suggests a type of hyperspace existence that is subjective to experience—particularly in ways Humans typically define "time-space."

The "Lands Below"—as Robert Kirk experienced them—possessed its own moon, stars, and even a sun similar to Earth's. He explained that by appearance, everything seemed more vividly real than even the physical world. *So... the "Hollow Hills" have their own sky..?* Remember that the Otherworld—that which is unseen from our view of reality or has not collapsed or condensed into our reality—is indeed without limit.

While there is some perceived separation between the Middle World and the Otherworld, the iconic idea of Faerieland as some exclusively 'Subterranean' (or a literally 'Underground') realm is not clearly relayed in any of Kirk's experiences—or the lore of others—except as pertaining to portals and entrances. This generalization expresses a sentiment that they *exist*, again, beneath the surface of perceptions—as if simply behind a door or "gate" that we are unable to simply peer through in day-to-day life.

When we confine our semantics to the mortal view of reality, the limitlessness of existence is collapsed in "our" dimension as various natural conditions that we can observe within our range of "awareness." Some of these are considered "portals" or "thresholds" because they allow for a more fluid exchange of energies between worlds—or else, between degrees of 'perception' and 'reality' for the same singular "world."

Specific conditions promote specific types of inter-dimensional energetic activity, which affects both the "external" world we are experiencing and the "internal" mental set doing the experiencing—a further example that these "two" facets are really one and the same spectrum of energy: that our "internal" and "external" worlds are One.

Cross-quarter 'thresholds'—the 'equinoxes' and 'solstices'—share qualities from other "degrees" of reality-experience (semantics), such as 'astronomical' alignment, or 'electromagnetic fields' around earth, but they are most often distinguished in Druidic tradition as the "Four Albans"—or *Four Lights*—which compose at least half of the Celtic "Grove Festivals" revived in modern "neopaganism" today. Springtime—between the Spring Equinox and Summer Solstice—is traditionally the most active period of the year for elemental Nature-spirits. Beltane (May's Eve) and Midsummer's Eve are particularly famous times for "Faerie Rade." Note that *Beltane* (May's Eve) and *Samhain* (ancient "Halloween") also mark periods of peak inter-dimensional activity—times that correspond to the setting and rise of the Pleiades (respectively).

Another facet of inter-dimensional "fairy lore" is called the "fairy ring"—naturally occurring circles or rings found on the ground in Nature that are set apart from its natural surrounding. Often this manifests as a bit of grass that grows higher or darker, forming a ring—usually only a few feet in diameter—or it may be a ring of mushrooms. Traditionally, these "Faerie-Rings" are signs of not only Elven-Ffayrie activity in an area, but also places in which a transition into—or from—the "Otherworld" is likely or has already occurred. Other degrees of semantics may be applied to this phenomenon too.

Scientists that study this growth tell us that—at a physical and biological degree of understanding—"mycelium" or 'fungus' grows beneath the ground that can cause abnormal growth and/or mushrooms. Terrence McKenna—in *Archaic Revival*—suggests that the original 'psilocybin' spores are probably not even indigenous to planet Earth.

The physical appearance—and physical explanations—of "Faerie-Rings" (and other natural or observable phenomenon) does not eliminate the existence of energetic activity that may be "perturbing" what we can see, but from beneath the surface of our awareness and understanding. It is also curious to note that Humans have experienced "alien" and "fairy" encounters under psychoactive effects of mushrooms, DMT and other hallucinogenic substances. It is possible that some of the receptors activated in the brain as a result of their use do allow for a "wider range" of perceptual experience of reality—but there are no guarantees that these "external" methods will result in Self-Honest experiences.

Wizards have suggested that falling asleep in a Faerie-Ring, or on an Elven-Mound, will increase your chances of Otherworld contact—possibly due to a presence of spores, *who knows?* Other folklore suggests that if you run around one nine times you will do the same—*kicking up more spores?*

One of the main issues—for Humans—regarding physically transitioning into the Otherworld, relates to inept faculties to not only sense "portal frequencies," but also adjust personal vibrations to successfully "transition" into other existential states. Most Humans do not carry an awareness of the energetic matrix we occupy, then alone possess an understanding of its influence—such is, and always has been, the main focus of the "wizarding ways" and high mystical arts. In other instances and occult practices, similar results may be obtained using "astral projection" and other experimental practices—frequency shifts in consciousness where the physical body is not transported, yet we can mentally experience it because everything is connected—our consciousness is already connected to the ALL. Our sensory faculties are simply limited to a specific range of an infinite spectrum of energies.

The cosmic spectrum of infinite potentiality includes many possible frequencies in existence "above" and "below" what Humans are normally capable of sensing. While these various degrees might be perceived and classified as separate "levels" in exclusion to one another, the separation exists only in consciousness—there is no actual separation between a subject and the individual doing the observing; there is only one singular reality.

Each "degree" of vision—each magnification of the microscope—yields only one "degree" of awareness, data and knowledge, but it is not the only "degree" of possible understanding, nor is it likely to be the true holistic totality of a "thing"—since we are always going to classify "things" in exclusion to all other "things."

One degree of observation in 1925 led the British antiquarian, Alfred Watkins, to discover the existence of "Ley Lines" or "Dragon Lines"—naturally occurring lines running across the surface of the Earth Planet. These lines or "fields" vibrate a more significant magnitude of energy than its surrounding area—similar to the appearance of "Faerie Rings," but larger and in a "line."

These lines sometimes link ancient sacred sites and other energetic "thresholds" or "portals." Some have put forth theories regarding underground water sources or mineral veins contributing to the visible surface appearance, but modern science suggests that the core of the Earth produces an electromagnetic field that interacts with other environmental systems and conditions.

The Ley Lines are now a basic facet of modern Earth-oriented traditions. Even sensitive mystics have learned how to trace or follow the lines of power using dowsing techniques.* In our present Edaphic Tradition—and some neodruid systems—the lines are called "Dragon Lines," named for the "flight path" of "dragons" as they moved between sacred sites—places where higher concentrations of natural forces collect or condense, even forming significant notable "vortex" energy spots.

Wizards and mystics throughout the ages are renown for their abilities to recognize true powers of Nature—particularly when there is a large concentration of these energies in a particular area. Over time, these places become recognizably "magical" locales frequently visited for "magical work" by those sensitive enough to be aware.

When such locations are identified, practitioners may even intentionally consecrate a "grove" of trees or "henge" of stones to mark the "*nemeton*"—or "sacred space"—specifically for personal "magical work" or even gatherings. Specific types of energy tend to concentrate relative to the region or terrain involved—the water element is sparse in the desert, just as those same dry-heat energies are quite absent in the jungle. Energies may also be amplified by other neutral catalysts, such as a presence of quartz crystal or other conductive minerals beneath the ground. A person could just as cleverly bury ap-

---

* See "*Draconomicon: The Book of Ancient Dragon Magick*" by Joshua Free; also reprinted in "*Merlyn's Complete Book of Pheryllt*."

propriate crystal clusters beneath a sacred space to increase resonance within the "*nemeton.*"

Another energetic interaction taking place between worlds is called an "Elf-Shot." If someone—typically a Human—is hit by an arrowhead from an Elf or Faerie being, we call them "Elf-Shot." This lore is the subject of some controversy in the New Age and as a result is not frequently discussed. The tradition holds, however, that one of the consequences of being struck by such an arrow is some degree of "Faerie-Sight"—or, at the very least, the ability to see the fey that shot you.

Rarer, but more serious, consequences of "Elf-Shot" include permanent "transitions" to the Otherworld or "Faerieland"—which other Humans, in many instances, would only see as 'death', because the "body" often remains in the physical world. This may not even occur overnight and might first be recognized as an illness that purges impurities of the physical body so that its spirit can be free. Keep in mind: this is not something that may be self-induced. In fact, it usually only happens unintentionally—because Elven Courts seldom assist Humans in "seeing them" or "inviting" them to their world.

Sometimes an "Elf-Shot" occurs when a Human just happens to be in the line of fire between rivaling courts—such as the *Seelie* and *Unseelie*. It is also possible that an "Elf-Shot" victim is struck without knowing it has occurred—so if they are not perceptive, they may not see the fey that shot them. Even if it does not produce an illness, it has been known to inadvertently have other unpleasant side-effects—such as promoting discord between friends and neighbors.

"Foison" is a common game where members of the fey will "steal" Human food. This should not to be misinterpreted as an act of malevolence—it *is* a "game." Lore suggests that they only eat the essence of Human food and not the foods themselves—possibly lending to the "thin" "angelic" "ethereal" descriptions carried by many of the types. As a result, they will absorb only what is necessary from foodstuff—leaving the remains often without nutrients. There are reports from farmers in Celtic Countries where the insides of their stalks are carefully eaten while leaving outsides intact and whole. Modern folk might just think it is a result of some pests, but often it does not seem eaten, rotted, infested or touched.

According to lore, foods prepared in Faerieland are the most exquisite—pure natural and organic essences drawn from the sweetest life-giving nectar of the Green World. One popular belief is that if you eat any foods during your stay in the Otherworld, you may find yourself trapped there. Although *Rev. Robert Kirk* was eventually trapped in Faerieland, it was not a result of eating the food there. He had tasted it and still continued to "transition" back and forth between worlds several times. However, he reports to us that the "want" or "memory" of it lingered perpetually and could not be equaled in the physical world.

Cuneiform Tablets describe an exchange between Enki and Adapa—where Enki instructs Adapa on the dangers of eating the "Food of Death" when visiting the "Otherworld," though Anu eventually offers Adapa the "Food of Life" and it is refused because of Enki's instructions. Had he eaten of it, the Human race would have been "as like the gods."

Long-standing metaphysical connections exist between faerie beings and foodstuffs. Wizards and mystics traditionally use food offerings in their workings and ritual magic to entice the Elven-Ffayrie, other Elemental Beings and helpful energies to their magic circles. They will also leave milk and sweat-bread cookies out to invite them into their home—something retained in the modern "Santa Claus" mythology today. Often, energy currents of these Otherworld beings may be extended to a Druid—or anyone calling on them or another ancestral energy current—without a "physical apparition."

The "Geirt Coimitheth" or "Just-Halver" is an anomaly of the Otherworld. Its titles are references to its abilities and function—called a "joint-eater" or "marrow-eater"—a reference to it feeding on energy or essences of humans; possibly even a human Elven-Ffayrie Simulacra. Humans will "live-to-eat" or eat for pleasure, while the fey generally just eat-to-live and take only what essences and nutrients are necessary for survival. A "Geirt Coimitheth" is really a shadow—or the shadow of a person—a "co-walker" that feeds on what the host eats.

With a lack of substance in ethereal/astral planes, there is a shortage of food-stuff—but memory of such remains. Those who maintain food and drug addictions in the physical world find great difficulty satisfying these cravings in a spiritual dimension. Addictions conditioned on the mind and spirit can actually remain in tact after one's physical lifetime, but are not ever satisfied. While truly ethereal beings have no need to eat physical substances, Elven-Faerie beings are not indigenous to the Astral World and once ate regularly as we do.

"Co-walkers" are Elven-Ffayrie creatures that walk invisibly in the Middle World of humans in disguise. They take on human form —'*Simulacrum Transignation*'—or they can simply take the appearance of a human. Like all elementals, they reserve a right to remain invisible—yet present—or to mimic surrounding and camouflage themselves. These abilities may also be used to assume animal forms.

The "Giert Coimitheth" is just one example of a co-walker that shadows a human form. Others exist as well—some not so clearly classified —that simply shadow Elvish descendents or assume a full "transignation" or "walk-in" using physical simulacra. There is still a lot of debate about the semantics and vocabulary that should be used for this spiritual phenomenon. Other lore suggests that the co-walker may act as a "spirit-guide," guardian "*ang-elf*" or "co-magician." They may also be of any elemental type.

Elves of the Unseelie Court share many attributes with their relatives of the Light. Their appearance is tall and slender like the Sylvan Elves, with their long angular and hardened faces set in humorless stoic expressions. Their eyes appear small, squinted, and hollow—yet burning and piercing. They are used to residing in a Realm of Darkness and make habitats in larger underground subterranean labyrinths and caves. "Dark Elves" typically lead solitary lives, but there is large capital city for the Unseelie Court, as reported by *Rev. Robert Kirk* in his journals and secret writings.

"Dark Elves" are so-called because they are no longer one-to-one with the "Tribe of Starlight." They are set apart—exiled from the Seelie Court—taking their lives to even further "underground crevices." They are still "fey-folk," but submission to anger and brooding has left many of them blinded to pursuits of harmony and ascension.

There are modern references to Dark Elves, calling them "*Drow*"— rhymes with "cow"—yet this word does not appear in ancient Elvish languages. But, there is, however, the ancient word "*Daetenin*"— meaning "Dark-Dragon folk"—and the unseelie word "*Ishmaen*," which is an Elven slur towards Wizards and Druids that have perverted their magical birthright. "Dark Elves" are not inherently evil— they simply remain perpetually bitter about their conditions of existence as a result of the "Rise of Humans." It is this very subject that drew a dividing line between Seelie and Unseelie Courts—which were originally the same race before the Rise of Humans and the Underground "transition."

The Elven-Druid Histories studied in previous chapter-lessons have focused on varying lineages existent on the surface world, such as the migrating "royal bloodline" of the Sidhe or High Elves and Drwyds. There is another sect of Elven-Ffayrie that are forest-oriented—called the "Wood Elves." These are the 'Elven' spirits that make frequent contact during 'Green Magic' and other earth-oriented mystical systems. "Sylvanus Folk" actually resided in the Otherworld prior to the "transitioning" of the *Tuatha D'Anu-Sidhe* and were not a part of that lineage—though they could interbreed—but maintained their own distinct woodland tradition.

The "Sylves"/"Sylphs" or "Wood Elves" are also known as the "Keepers of the Trees," though not necessarily inhabitants of trees—which is recorded in lore as a *"Dryad."* The "Sylves," then, tend to the trees housing Dryads—and their cousins, the 'Sylphs', are "Keepers of Flowers and Herbs" and "Guardians of the Wind."

Sylvan Folk are essentially caretakers for the Green World of Nature. Traditionally, Sylves or Elves (masculine) are keepers of the "Elven Garden"—which is to say the forests. The Sylphs or Ffayrie (feminine) are the keepers of the "Ffayrie Garden" or ground flowers. By "keeping" we of course mean "tending to" the life from the perspective of another dimension, as a tree's living spirit is interdimensional—as is all life. The life of a tree—and its spirit—both exists and affects other planes of existence. Care-taking and stewardship is far from a mundane act—it is a conscious acknowledgment of a holistic interdimensional relationship with all life. *They don't do it just to make the yard "look nice."*

Sylphs and Sylves tend to their gardens as a parent would a child—imbuing and charging it with love and energy. This is an important practice in such magical traditions—as the code states: all intentional acts are "magical." For them, tending the Earth is not performed out of idleness or "passing the time"—they take great pride in their work and are able to move tremendous amounts of energy through it.

Sylvan Folk believe that their "life purpose"—or lesson of "dharma" required for their Ascension, or return to the Source-of-All—is to achieve a state of "Perfect Love." This is far from the same state experienced by Humans in carnal, lustful or purely procreative relationships—and better reflects the pure love that a "gardener" might feel toward the beautiful flowers planted and tended to. Maybe the term "gardener" is too passive in the English language, which is why J.R.R.

Tolkein probably chose the term "tree-herder"—implying a more active role.

Otherworldly Elves do not have facial, arm, hand, chest, back, pubic, leg, foot, toe or orifice hair. This also matches descriptions of other inter-dimensional beings—even the genetics of "aliens," particularly those described as "Grays." Modern Humans society has become increasingly interested in removing unnecessary body-hair—even if only for aesthetics. As for the other stereotypical "Elvish" appearances—they match the tall slender forms that we have spoken of previously.

Sylvanus Folk carry a strong dislike for hardened steel and iron. According to their ancient traditions—and those of the Watchers throughout history—these metals have only been associated with destructive ends. In fact, before the period of "Dark Ages" imposed by Romans and the Church, the ancient world had "fallen" once before, when at the apex of a new age of spiritual technology—c. 12th Century B.C.—these intellectual pursuits were stopped short by the Iron Age, leading to a cruder Dark Age and even more disgusting Industrial Age.

Elves and fey hold feelings against Humans that do not maintain the "Faerie-Code" or "*d'Sylva Forest Code*," particularly Human responsibilities of ecological planetary protection, land stewardship and animal care-taking. There is no denying that Humans have—as a collective species—utterly failed in properly upholding these responsibilities.

Forests and natural wilds are both the home and children of Elementals—and deserving of our respect. Many of these spiritual beings are exclusively found in the most remote woodland and virgin untouched soils—and even what some might consider desolate wastelands and deserts—where all physical and/or subconscious thresholds and veils between the surface world and the Elven Otherworld are thinnest and most accessible.

Those of the Seelie Court, along with the highborn Sidhe, are particularly civil towards mortals—except where the destruction of the environment, Nature and life is concerned. The mystical practices of both the Danubian Sidhe and the Wood Elves comprises the mystical tradition of "Elvish Wizardry"—what Humans have experienced as "Druidism"—which is explored at length in later portions of the current book.

True Elves are slow to make friends and even slower to allow disharmonic relationships or enemies. In their relationships with humans—human Druids and human Wizards—Elves are known to first test those who might be potential allies. As a general stereotype they may be whimsical, but they are also quite serious, stoic and carry a genetic knowledge that far surpasses Human book-learning. They carry a youthful charm and enthusiasm, yet reflect an old soul that is wise beyond their visible physical years.

Of the many elemental types, species, entities and spiritual forms throughout the history of magic, it is the Elves that are the closest in connectivity to Humans, bonded since an ancient crossings—ever changing the shape of history, lore, magic, tradition and wisdom on the planet Earth.

A Secret Legacy of Elves and Fairies

of mortals and elves:
the secret legacy of robert kirk

Previously in these books, we have mainly concerned ourselves with esoteric information and mystic lore regarding phenomenon of Elven-Faerie 'transitions' and encounters with Elemental Beings in the "physical world"—"surface world" or "Lands Above" —perceived by mortal Humans.

The secret legacy of Reverend Robert Kirk is amazing—and unique—because it chronicles Elven lore from the *other side*—from a man who physically entered the Otherworld, became an initiate of the Elven-Ffayrie Tradition and returned to *our side* able to share it—at least, for a time and in some guise or another. We are not referring here to "mental/astral travel" or the type of "guided meditations" that run rampant in "New Age" '*How-To*' books for "*entering the fairylands.*" Original journal records and accounts of Robert Kirk's experiences are unparalleled in recent history.

Robert Kirk gained admittance to the "Otherworld," accessing the "Elven Libraries" on repeated occasions—not simply by happenstance or coincidence. He was even all-owed to keep a sketch-diary journal to account for his experiences—which have now been widely circulated in various editions.

Elemental and/or mortal "transitions"—or any contact with "nature spirits"—requires appropriate conditions or natural circumstances in addition to skills in directing or channeling currents of energy. During appropriate times, Robert Kirk was able to return to the same "Faerie Howe," or Hollow Hill and gain entrance at will. We make mention of these things here to entice you—but the story of Robert Kirk truly should begin, well, at the beginning...

****

Born in the year 1644, Robert Kirk was the *seventh son* of an Episcopalian minister and later even became a minister himself, in his home parish of Aberfoyle—Perthshire, Scotland. Although notably a devout Christian, Kirk spent his life interested and influenced by Elven-Faerie lore—though his religion did not permit him to accept the "magical" and "occult" aspects of the actual tradition. He did, however, see the importance in preserving Celtic lore and ancient Irish-Gaelic language—even overseeing a Gaelic translation of the Judeo-Christian

Holy Bible, personally translating the *Psalms* and *Proverbs*. Kirk's missionary life reflected the *Bardic Culdee* of the distant past, those that once preserved authentic Celtic and Druidic symbolism in the *Book of Kells*, an "illuminated" manuscript copy of the Four Gospels written in the Gaelic language.

It is evident that Robert Kirk never intended on becoming a monumental "New Age" figure—or advocate for 'occultism' and active "mystery traditions" revived today in favor of the Elven Way. His writings do display some personal familiarity with archaic Hermetic-Gnostic lore and Rosicrucian doctrines—making a direct reference to several in his most popularly known treatise: "*The Secret Commonwealth of Elves, Fauns and Fairies*." The precise nature of Kirk's personal background remains unclear—but he likely had access to many obscure Celtic manuscripts and other esoteric documents as an esteemed member of the Christian Clergy. It is likely that his strict religious upbringing resulted in a reluctance to delve into metaphysical matters—and it comes as no surprise that his "pagan" interests were of noted concern to his father.

The infamous "Faerie Howe"—where Robert Kirk's body was eventually found—was a location that he visited frequently throughout his life. But, one day, Kirk actually discovered, or rather, had revealed to him, the entrance to the "Faerieland Otherworld." By means of a special knock at the right 'threshold' times of month and day, Kirk would be granted repeated access to an alternate dimension—called by many names throughout lore: the *Elflands*, the *Faerieland*, the *Faerieworld*, the *Otherworld*, just to name a few.

In his published accounts, Kirk does not always refer to these matters —especially concerning the Otherworld—in first person. He prefers instead to attribute the accounts, lore and traditions to those seers and mystics interviewed as part of his research. No doubt there were many political and esoteric reasons for such anonymity, especially during this time in history. Kirk based his literary work on journals dated from 1688-1692, implying four years of practical "Otherworld Initiation" that complimented his research in folklore—at a time when, just across the pond in newly founded puritan America, people were burned at the stake for even speaking of such things.

Robert Kirk's "*Secret Commonwealth of Elves*" was never published in its complete state—and never revealed to the public at all during Kirk's lifetime. Some scholars believe that all of the first person references concerning mysticism, the Otherworld Tradition and Elven-Ffayrie encounters, were replaced in the published version as second-hand accounts from "seers"—or edited out of the "official" manuscript altogether—before its eventually distribution to a 17th century predominantly Christian society as authored by a Christian minister.

In spite of this, Kirk emphasizes and insists that there is no real conflict between his own religious beliefs and what he learns concerning the Elven-Ffayrie tradition. The only real contradiction emerges from the minds of Fundamentalist Christians that see these beings only as the demons and devils of their own paradigm or worldview. Kirk even goes as far as to say that he feels that it is his God-given mission in life to clarify misconceptions concerning the fey among his human Christian brethren.

It may be that the Antiquarian writers of Robert Kirk's time—the Brothers' Grimm, John Aubrey, John Toland and Iolo Morganwg, just to mention a few—all felt that there was a very real part of folklore and Elven-Faerie Tradition hidden within the secret folds of Nature—and that it was quickly disappearing from the consciousness of contemporary society, and therefore required advocates supporting its preservation.

* * * * * * *

After one disturbing encounter in Faerieland—concerning a chance episode with a solitary *Dark Elf*—Robert Kirk took it upon himself to seek out the city of the *Unseelie Court* and attempt to apologize for the rise in tension resulting from his appearance in the Otherworld. Apparently, he had not yet realized that by even setting foot on the grounds of the *Dark Elves*, he was in violation of the most severe *Unseelie* laws. The *Unseelie Court* immediately sentenced him to death—but the *Seelie Court* intervened, altering their judgment, ultimately deciding that Kirk should remain forever a "prisoner" in the Otherworld, and this permanent "transition" would still leave his physical body dead in the "Middle World." He is then allowed only one night to return to the "Lands Above" to set his affairs in order—being allowed to leave in good faith—then during this time he leaves his journals behind for his son and returns to the "Lands Below" to serve out his sentence.

Some time after Kirk's death, he makes a spiritual appearance to a relative—claiming he will again appear at the Christening of her daughter. He states that at that time, her husband is to throw an iron dagger at his apparition—if he does so, then the enchantment of the Faerieland would be broken and he could return to the "Middle World."

According to the accounts that followed—when the Christening came and Kirk's spirit did appear, those who were present were so astounded that they did not move to throw a dagger and so Kirk remained in the Otherworld.

Years later, Kirk makes his second spiritual attempt to communicate—this time with a different family occupying the house Kirk once resided in. His apparition informs them that they are to baptize their child in his writing room and stab a dagger in the seat of the chair Kirk sat in to write—which apparently remained in the room. According to the apparition, if they were to do this, he would be free. But, again, this is not even attempted and Kirk is never freed. Although easy to dismiss, these accounts do reflect behaviors that we might actually expect from the population at that time—or it may be that an eternity in the Otherworld was Kirk's destiny.

the quest for the otherworld

Mortals seeking encounters with nature-bound spirits—such as the Elven-Ffayrie—should first start by immersing themselves in natural valleys, untouched woodlands and virgin forests. By this, we mean those places where Humans are not falling trees and houses are not being developed—or even in view. Also avoid places overrun by "electromagnetic" transmissions through power lines and satellite dishes which can cause mystic-interference.

While smaller and urban parks are nice for walks, picnics, or maybe even studying, meditation or working with a specific tree current—most of these have been planned, planted and are arranged and maintained with little left to grow wild. They are also usually host to too much Human foot traffic and activity to make for the best places to meditate or connect with Nature—and especially those spirits that inhabit it. Other titles in this series also provide numerous examples of inviting "Faerie" into your life.

Make certain your own foot traffic is light and quiet—walking slow and deliberately—being sure not to disturb the natural vibrations of the environment.

To achieve the desired results, your energy must be in alignment (meaning, resonant or synchronous) with Nature—so a practitioner of the Elven-Faerie tradition does well to take care that they are not disrupting the 'natural flow' of Nature, or disturbing wildlife with unnecessary fast movement, ruckus or chatter. If the visible "Green World" you *can* see is disrupted by your presence, then you can rest assure that the same sentiment is shared by the "Nature-spirits." They carry a disdain for Human noise—so stop, sit and *shut up* often—perhaps with your back against a tree. Be patient. You may wish to practice certain breathing exercises or any meditations that will calm your vibrations and put you in tune with frequencies matching your surroundings. Calm your body; still your mind—activate a 'light body' and 'light shield' if you are proficient in such esoterica from other titles of this series—but the key here, no matter the technique involved—is to *increase awareness*.

During the course of your personal journey—ventures, experiments and experiences—should you happen upon a natural physical entrance to the Otherworld, lore suggests that you should not disturb it, or do anything immediately at first. Stop and wait. Watch and be patient, again. If nothing changes, try encircling it nine times and then waiting some more at the "doorway." You might then try knocking three times—making certain it will not disturb anything loose. Another secret knock sequence that is applicable here is: 1-2-3 or */-//-///*.

If an initiate is not given a "portal key" by direct personal apprenticeship with Elven-Ffayrie folk, the only other available option is trial and error. Do not, however, be a menace—this will only work against your efforts. After three passive attempts, an alternative is to set up a "Circle of Power" to help meditate and calm your mind—and if you desire, practice Elemental magick rites—"opening portal thresholds" or "calling the quarters"—whatever your preferred means of summoning Elemental powers or currents of energy with ritual applications. Fey folk are commonly attracted to Elemental Magick because it specifically validates and acknowledges their existence, asks for their assistance and utilizes energy streams they are akin to.

While selecting areas of exploration in the forest, keep in mind that certain Elven-Ffayrie types are especially attracted to places where land meets water. These might be ponds, streams, waterfalls, or the archetypal "babbling brook." Lore suggests that these places carry intensive connectivity—links between the physical world and the astral plane or Otherworld—making them very common places of spiritual encounter.

The element of water is among the most sacred in Elven tradition—for its "life-giving" qualities—as is the 'air' we breathe. Running water is specifically related to irrigation—which is an essential aspect of agricultural work and gardening—a skill mastered famously in the Ancient Near East and carried across Europe as the populations transformed from nomadic hunter-gathers into settled farmers. "Nature-spirits" and agriculture carry a long-standing tradition together. Naturally, living closer to the natural Elemental world allowed early "pagan" cultures to experience more significant encounters with the Elemental beings and "Nature-spirits" sharing an affinity with the planet Earth.

Elemental Spirits and Nature-beings encountered in magical practices are typically neutral in polarity and crystalline in nature. This means that they are generally charged with an energy type that mirrors the polarity of willpower, intention and emotional energy discharged by a Mystic, Druid, or Wizard, &tc. This is essentially how power of thoughtforms operates and how the psyche divides oneness into polarities of "good" and "evil." Hence, rituals "of the light" will attract spirits of a like nature—and those dark sacrificial ceremonies of cult abuse, that we often hear about in horror stories, will generate intense emotional resonance with "evil" polarities. Energy—as the Wizard understands it—is basically a catalyst of "attraction" operating on the "principle of like-forces." A ritual, rite or meditation will attract the same type of energy that is radiated from its conductance—if successful.

Shamans often use sages and sweetgrass as an incense smoke to clear an area of unwanted, static or negatively charged energies. Another "Faerie" formula is ash, elder and hawthorne—burned in equal parts. This may even attract the Sylvanus Folk—if that is your desire.

The fey folk are attracted to small shiny objects, mirrors and trinkets. They are also partial to the colors: green, red, blue and yellow. Natural folk-style acoustic music is sure to entice them. Remember that the Elven-Ffayrie are traditionally interested in celebrations of life and love—so you must invite them to bright shinning places that are not somber or negative in any way. Only once you have made your own *life* a place that is fit to include such experiences, will it be possible to make it your *reality*.

MARDUKITE MASTER COURSE ACADEMY LECTURE #20[*]

"otherworld tech"

The "Route of Druidism and the Dragon Legacy" is actually of such richness and color that you really could formulate a "Druid School" exclusively from that—or at least, quite an extensive curriculum for your "Wizard School."

In fact, it's been designed in such a way; that, for example, *Merlyn's Complete Book of Druidism*[‡] and the Master materials that compose this, is actually a qualifying "Grade-I" access-point for those that seek it—for those that prefer this to the broader study of the "magical curriculum" and "ritual magick" and "ceremonial traditions" of all that in the Western Magical Tradition (that are explored in Route-A).

Honestly, this has been designed, and this Master Edition textbook here has been designed, so that if necessary, *this* can be someone's introduction to "Magick & Mysticism" in addition to the "Route of Druidism & Dragon Legacy" that all leads into Grade-II.

Now, *you* being a "Master Instructor" and this being the "Master Course" and to be "*Certified*" in being able to instruct all Grades is to *know* all Grades, but when it comes to individual Seekers and it comes to bringing those onto the *Pathway to Self-Honesty* or as those enter into Mardukite Zuism or even the Academy of Systemology or the Systemology Society, we don't actually require that an individual work through Route-A. It does make exceptional reference material and background and a core foundation for doing the rest—there is no substitute, single source substitute, for *The Great Magickal Arcanum* out there today.

But for those who end up—their introduction or their entry-point onto the *Pathway*—ends up being the "Nature Magic," "Druidism," the "Dragon Tradition," "Celtic Faerie," any of this... just go ahead and use this as the Grade-I work and emphasize that which they're showing the inclinations in.

---

[*] Transcript of a lecture given by Joshua Free on September 23, 2020; revised from "*Druids, Elves & Dragons: Mardukite Master Course Academy Lectures (Volume II)*"—also contained in "*The Complete Mardukite Master Course.*"

[‡] Mardukite Academy anthology (released in 2020) containing "*Draconomicon,*" "*Druid's Handbook*" and the original "*Elvenomicon*" trilogy.

"The Elven-Faerie Grimoire" of the *'Elvenomicon'* series is, by itself, essentially a complete "ritual guide" for an individual to follow their traditional use of "practical magick," "ritual magic"—the same kind of flavor of work that we were discussing previously in lectures a couple of days ago. It's essentially an entire "Book of Shadows, Light and Enchantment" or *grimoire* for practicing within "Elven-Faerie" or "Faerie-Druid" tradition.

"Druid Magic" and "Elven Magic" places a lot of emphasis on incorporating Nature in any 'magical work', or communing with Nature, spending time in Nature, observing Nature, in order to essentially be "grounded" as an individual. 'Grounding' being one of the core fundamentals of operating any other work. And any other work can be done from, you know, as an Actualized Alpha-Spirit.

All you need to be doing is making sure you're grounded and in complete communication, control and command of the body; and then be able to operate from the point-of-view of the Alpha-Spirit. And this could easily be done when working in Nature, free of a lot of the worldly distractions, free of any disturbances—being able to achieve the first core of any higher-level work, which is essentially *grounding* and *centeredness* and being able to move out from there. We see that emphasis within any of the ritual texts or the "magick" that's presented in the *'Elvenomicon'* series.

Now, in terms of any "Magic Tech," "Ritual Tech"—anything along those lines; practical applications—well, "Druidism" is a little bit more "intuitive" in its applications of the "mystical traditions." In fact, it's a little bit more of a "mystical" tradition than a "magical" tradition.

With proper application, we start to see a bridge to higher applications routed in the authority of the individual as Self and their empowerment, their understanding, realizations, and their ability to actually *be* in a state of *knowing* true knowledge, that enables and empowers their skills and abilities and what they do went they go about treating the natural world, okay? Which is a little bit different from the more traditional rigorous ritual ceremonial formulas and particular times of day and astrological signs, in which we see other traditions a little bit more fixed in what they are intending to do in their ritual texts or their "magick."

In this case, you're dealing with, really, not as much of a rigorous roll-call of "rules" and "requirements" and "steps" as you are establishing that personal relationship—personal communion—with Nature, with the natural Elements, with, basically the "Cosmos" in essence, as you move your way up. In that relationship—in that *knowingness*—being able to have a better mastery and control of the experience of the material world.

In terms of the "New Age" concept of accessing, you know, the "Faerieland" or so forth, what you'd find in most "New Age" '*How-To*' books —most of which involve some sort of mental or astral travel; but, it's really descriptive scripts—what they will refer to as "guided meditations."

I mean, you'll find books just *filled*, hundreds of pages, of guided meditations—almost just reads like a "novel" of stuff. I mean, I don't know what... if they intended to record them and have them played back or you're supposed to remember all this stuff or just read through them, because honestly, probably the biggest benefit you'd have in reading through them—or any use whatsoever—is that they might be actually "restimulative" to some kind of memory recall triggering, or past-life thing, or some experience that's been forgotten or filtered out.

But, you could just as soon get that same stuff reading anything else or just watching many of the shows or movies that are available out there—would almost yield the same effect; and that's basically just increasing the acceptance or Awareness or concept or possibility or parameter within the realm of mental imagery, or within the realm of reality—within the realm, grasp, hold and reach of what's considered possible, that someone may be able to have these, kinda, "Gates" or "access points" open up to them.

Because prior to that, until someone knows it's, again, possible or real or any actual aspect to it, then there is nothing to behold. Suddenly an individual begins to read novels or watch TV or play various fantasy-oriented games, all of which have certain themes, it very well may end up "restimulating" certain imprints, certain programming, various implants—even 'past-life' recall—concerning not only times here on this planet when such things were present or there was more mysticism or certain themes or icons were present, but also in other civilizations and times on this planet and even distant pasts and even *before* incarnations on *this* Earth and so on and so forth.

It's for those reasons that some people get... you've heard of some of the "dangers" or you've seen the propaganda about some of the "inherent dangers" to some of this; and that's really all it is. Those who aren't really able to *handle* some of the mental imagery or the triggers of the "restimulation" of who they are—sometimes really have, without guidance, and again this is where a Master would really come in handy, they begin to lose themselves in it; or they lose touch with what's really going on, because they "restimulate" something, which is very real to them, and it was probably very real when it happened, but it's not present right now, is it?

And so a lot of times individuals get kind of "keyed in" or "trapped" or "locked into" specific modes because they've been "turned on" and they're being handled as if it's happening *now*, because for whatever reason it wasn't handled at the time or it hasn't been managed or it's been suppressed to the point where it's—the pressures are just, it can't be ignored anymore.

But one way or another, "keyed-in" stuff has to be faced and handled. As we step back to view these various traditions and histories and then even going into Mesopotamia (in Grade-II) and where some of the implanting for *this* current civilization first occurred—you are definitely running into many elements that could be "restimulative," that could trigger various responses, reactions or complete 'phase-shifts' to where someone or some aspect is flipped on like a switch.

Now *you*, from a Grade-III perspective—as a Systemologist—is actually able to treat these circumstances and this phenomenon, you know, far better and more effective and valuable to a Seeker, than we have ever been able to do before when we were only working with these systems and traditions within what we consider the Grades they are in.

Being true to this idea that we're treating a Master-level understanding of anything that could be considered "practical tech" or "authentic tech" in this level (or in this area), really it would be impossible to sidestep at least one case study that *is* explored within *Elvenomicon* material—referring, of course, to the legacy and life of Robert Kirk.

****

Robert Kirk—or Reverend Robert Kirk—is a 17th Century "case study" that we use to explore the encounters between "mortals" and "Elves." Robert Kirk—he was born in 1644—he was the seventh son of an Episcopalian minister; he was born in Scotland. He also became a minister.

His work titled *"Secret Commonwealth of Elves, Fauns & Fairies"* is actually one of the few real reference points that an individual has when exploring any kind of historical background for revival of, for example, the 'Elven' or 'Faerie' tradition—because in that material we learn about such things as the Seelie Court and Unseelie Court, the Faerie Courts, Faerie Traditions, beliefs, practices, customs—all things regarding the "Faerie."

Much of this is actually synthesized in the material for the '*Elvenomicon*' series. It's *not* a baseless tradition that I sought to establish—much like we're doing in Mardukite Zuism in bringing 'Mesopotamian Tradition' and aspects and explorations of our most ancient literature on the planet into the "Neopagan" realm. What I did with the *Book of Elven-Faerie* and *Elvenomicon* material was essentially integrate a complete tradition of Elven and Faerie Druidism.

Concerning source-material we have from Robert Kirk—now, you got to remember: his public work is being presented as... Well, don't forget: he's a member of the clergy—and he's writing particularly for a nation or society that is predominantly Christianized. And so most of the explorations and any of his personal encounters or opinions are actually passed off as being those of, for a example, a "seer" or given "according to an account of interview" with someone else.

Best we can tell, from 1688 until 1692, Kirk experienced some kind of actual four-year long encounter—or initiation—into the Otherworld, this 'Faerieland'; and was able to actually record much of what he discovered. And the thing is: unlike what you might find today, in terms of 'fame' and 'fortune', this was not something he divulged openly, or even capitalized on. "*Secret Commonwealth*" was not even published during his lifetime. He certainly wasn't trying to delude anyone or make any personal claims.

Most of Robert Kirk's encounters are connected to what we know today as a "Faerie Mound" or "burial mound"—an ancient ancestral "burial mound"—in Scotland. Some of the locals referred to them as "Faerie Hills" and they had a long tradition—a long legacy—for example, the locals would tell children, "Don't get caught going to close to the Fairy Hills," you know, things of that nature. And these places already had... Well, people knew there was something about them; that there was something different about them or that they had some significance. Of course, the nature and semantics of these beliefs have shifted across time and various cultures.

The end result of Robert Kirk's recorded life is interesting, but in many ways, also disturbing. He ends up trespassing in Unseelie territory while in the Otherworld. As a result of his encounter with a Dark Elf, he's actually sentenced to 'death', so to speak—and instead is actually claimed by... he's vouched for by the Seelie Court; and so they eventually decide that he can remain alive as a prisoner, and thereafter forever inhabit what he referred to as the "Lands Below."

In *his* accounts, the Faerieland is referred to as the 'Lands Below', and the surface world—that which is the physical world of humanity and where things take place on the surface of the Earth—is called the 'Lands Above'. And that's the distinction. The term 'Otherworld' isn't actually used; that's just a word that I often apply. And, of course, "Faerieland" is simply, again, another one of the terms that we might use when we are describing this.

Kirk is sentenced to serve out his remaining existence in the 'Lands Below'. He's given time to set his affairs in order; he's given one night to return to the 'Lands Above' on good faith, of course, that he's going to come back to serve his sentence. And thus, he prepared his manuscripts and journals and sketchbooks for posterity—for his son. In fact, the original "*Secret Commonwealth*" publication ends with a 'note' directing a reader to "see the rest in a little manuscript belonging to Colin Kirk"—presumably the name of Kirk's son, as Andrew Lang states in the 1893 printing of "*Secret Commonwealth*" that he edited.

What we can be certain of, is that the following morning, Kirk's body was found next to the "Faerie Hill." We cannot be absolutely certain of the nature of the 'transitioning'—it's very possible that his encounters with the Otherworld (or the Lands Below or this particular Faerie Realm) were not altogether "terrestrial"; that is was not necessarily that a physical "doorway" opened up and he literally walked down beneath the "soil."

Because one of the things he does write, is that the "Lands Below" were actually very similar—if not more "vivid"—to the Lands Above; that it had its own sky; that it had its own skyscapes that changed with night and day and so forth. And so from that we would have to assume that it is perhaps a different dimension; and for all intents and purposes *probably* the "Magical Universe"—something that we only really just touch upon in the Master Course, but of which we're exploring much more deeply at higher Systemological levels and Grades of the Academy.

And so in terms of "*beings*" or "*entities*": we know that this "Other" existence… we know that it is possible to transition between existences and that *beings* have an ability to inhabit or take on physical bodies or genetic vehicles as needed. But, we don't know for certain that all individuals are equally Actualized for this ability. Because an "*entity*" or "*spirit*" is not permitted much true freedom without being to a point where an individual could pick up and set down the command of bodies and continue a spiritual existence and later pick up a body again and so on.

We don't know that these were literally physical transitions into an Otherworld as a "body" or that each time that Reverend Kirk was encountering—and later inhabiting this Faerieland during these encounters—that his "body" wasn't being left back here and that this wasn't just simply a very surrealistic use of "transference of the point-of-view." To accomplish this requires an ability to actually "exteriorize" from the "interior" perspective or Awareness of the Human Condition.

Most individuals entrapped in the Human Condition are only able to maintain a point-of-view or Awareness from a physical body. We consider alternate—"higher"—potential for a point-of-view in higher Grades of Systemology; but applying such an understanding certainly elevates the realizations accessible on these matters.

The ability to actually 'transition' consciousness—knowingly—to another level of '*Beingness*' is far more understandable when we consider the 'condensation' or 'descent' of "Universes." Any type of kabbalistic model or sequentially-layered cosmology—even the understanding of 'chakras'—all suggests that a "higher" order of operations ensues back of and behind the visible phenomenon perceived of the 'Lands Above' or *this* world.

Taking our esoteric knowledge base collectively into consideration, we can at least theorize that there is a bridge between the original and basic existential state of what we call the Alpha-Spirit in our Systemology—or the "I-AM" or "Self"—and "*physical existence.*" There are levels and gradients of perception or 'Spiritual Awareness' between the actual *Self* or "Alpha-Spirit" and the experiences of reality through these successive Universes. And our Systemology describes this certain 'trail' or 'track' or 'timeline' that has taken *effect* on the individual—on their *Knowingness* and *Beingness*, or at least the perceptions or considerations on the "reality" thereof.

This 'timeline' or 'track' is compulsively created and carried by us as Alpha-Spirits; and it provides an illusion of sequential time by storing particular incidents as imprinted information. The 'weight' and 'mass' of this 'line' accumulates each step of the way—tying us to lower and lower 'considerations'.

So, it's very possible then, that each and every one of us that's occupying a consideration of a point-of-view of the Human Condition in *this* existence, has formerly occupied considerations of *Beingness* in this 'other' existence. All of this, again, boiling down to the basic 'considerations' for what is *"reality."*

And for most individuals, the memory of this has been blotted out—and, of course, any actualized ability or responsibility and 'conscious control' over it; the ability to move between "Universes"; or to again occupy this other higher universe that we once occupied before descending to the reality agreements that has fixed our attentions to this lower one—forgetting that we 'made' that choice; that these are conscious decisions or consequences of considerations along the way.

And one of the keys—one of the higher level keys behind any of this work, when we consider what's possible or what's taken place—is that we are trying to move back to *that* point from *this* point. And to do so, we are very much mirroring what we consider the *Pathway to Self-Honesty* or the *Ladder of Ascension* in our Systemology. And so in that, we can see a mirror of us getting back to these roots—getting back to the heart of where we came from. In tracing back along this legacy and map that has been left behind, we might find our route back out; and even more than this—that we might have the certainty and courage to follow that *Pathway* and return to our truest spiritual source-point.

THE SECRET COMMONWEALTH

THE SECRET COMMONWEALTH
—or—
A Treatise displaying the Chief Curiosities
as they are in Use among the Diverse
People of Scotland to this day;
Singularities for the most Part peculiar
to that Nation.

BY MR. ROBERT KIRK, Minister at Aberfoyle

```
Here is provided an essay of the nature and
actions of the subterranean (and, for the
most part) invisible people, heretofore going
under the name of ELVES, FAUNES, and FAIRIES,
or the like, among the low-country Scots, as
they are described by those who have the
SECOND SIGHT; and now, to occasion further
inquiry, collected and compared, by a circum-
spect inquirer residing among the Scot-
tish-Irish in Scotland.
```

{ *facsimile of the original title page* }

of the subterranean inhabitants

These *siths* or fairies—they call *sleagh maith* or 'the good people', it would seem, to ward off their ill attempts (for the Irish 'bless' all they fear harm of) and are said to be of a middle nature between 'man' and 'angel', as we daemons thought to be of old, of intelligent studious spirits, and light, changeable bodies (like those called 'astral') similar to the nature of a condensed cloud and best seen in the twilight.

These bodies are so pliable via the subtlety of the 'spirits' that agitate them, that they can make them appear or disappear at will. Some have bodies or 'vehicles' so spongy, thin and pure, that they are fed only by some fine spiritous liquors that pierce like pure air or oil. Others feed more substantially on '*foison*' [what can be harvested from something] or by the essence of 'corn' or on the 'corn' itself that grows on the surface of the earth, which these fairies steal away—in part, invisibly, and partly preying on the 'grain' as do cows and mice.

In this same age, they are sometimes heard to bake bread, strike hammers—performing such services within the little hillocks they reside. In previous times, before the Gospel dispelled paganism, and in some barbarous places as yet, they enter houses after all are at rest and set the kitchens in order, cleaning all the vessels. Such drudges go under the name of "*Brownies.*" When we have plenty, they have scarcity at their homes, and on the contrary; their robberies notwithstanding, they often collect up great stacks of 'corn' for its owners.

Their bodies of congealed air are sometimes carried aloft, otherwise walking in different shapes, and may enter any cranny or cleft of the earth (where air enters)—to their ordinary dwellings, the earth being full of cavities and cells; all places being inhabited by some creature or animal, living in or upon, as there is no such thing as a "pure wilderness" in the whole universe.

We then (the more terrestrial kind), have now so numerously planted all countries, also do labors for those 'hidden people' as well as for ourselves. Albeit when several countries were uninhabited by us, these had their easy tillage in wide open fields, wood and forests.

They remove to other lodgings at the beginning of each quarter of the year, so transversing until doomsday—being impatient to stay in one place and finding some relief by sojourning and changing habitations. Their chameleon-like bodies swim in the air near the earth with bag and baggage. And at such revolution of time, "seers" (or those with 'second sight') have very terrifying encounters with them, even on the highways.

The Scottish-Irish usually shun to travel abroad at these four seasons of the year and thereby have made it a custom to this day to keep church duly every first Sunday of the quarter, to 'hallow' themselves —and their 'corns' and 'cattle'—from the shot and stealth of these wandering tribes. And many of these superstitious people will not be seen in church again till the next quarter begin, as if no duty were to be learned or done by them, but still they pursue the use of worship and sermons to save them from these arrows that fly in the dark.

The Fae are distributed in tribes and orders and have children, nurses, marriages, trials, deaths and burials, equal in appearance to our own (unless they do so for a mock-show or to prognosticate such things among us).

They are clearly seen by those with the Second Sight to eat at funerals and banquets. Hence many of the Scottish-Irish will not taste meat at these meetings, or they will have communion with, or be poisoned by, them. So are they seen to carry the bier or coffin with the corpse among the middle earth men [humans] to the grave.

Some of those with the Sight (whether by art or nature) have told me they have seen at these meetings a 'double-man' or the shape of some man in two places; that is to say, a superterranean and a subterranean inhabitant perfectly resembling one another in all points. They vouch that every element and different state of being have animals resembling those of another element, as there are fish sometimes at sea resembling monks of late order in all their hoods and dresses; just as the Roman invention of good and bad daemons and guardian angels particularly assigned, is called by them an ignorant mistake sprung from this original.

They call this reflex-man a 'Co-Walker', in every way like the man, as a twin-brother and companion, haunting him as his shadow, as is often seen and known among men (resembling the original) both before and after the original is dead, and was also often seen to enter a house, by which these people knew that the person of that likeness was to visit them within a few days.

This copy, echo, or living picture goes at last to his own herd. It accompanied that person so long and frequently for ends best known to itself, whether to guard him from the secret assaults of some of its own folks or only to counterfeit all his actions.

However, the stories of old witches prove that there are all sorts of people with spirits which assume light airy bodies, or "crazed" bodies co-acted upon by foreign spirits, all seem to have some pleasure (at least to relieve pain or melancholy) by striking and capering like satyrs, whistling and screeching (like unlucky birds) in their unhallowed 'synagogues' and '*sabboths*'.

If invited and earnestly required, these companions make themselves known and familiar to humans. Otherwise, being in a different state and element, they neither can nor will easily converse with them. It is said that a *heluo*—a great eater or glutton—has a voracious *Elf* to be his attender, called a '*Joint-Eater*' or '*Just-Halver*', feeding on the pith or quintessence of what the man eats, and therefore he continues to be lean.

Yet it would seem that they convey the food substance elsewhere, for the subterraneans eat little in their dwellings; their food being exactly clean and served up by pleasant children like enchanted puppets. What food they extract from us is conveyed to their homes by secret paths. Their houses are called large and fair and (unless at some odd occasions) unperceivable by vulgar eyes—like *Rachland** and other enchanted islands—having for lights continual lamps and fires, often seen without fuel to sustain them.

Women are still alive who tell they were taken away when in 'childbed' to nurse *Fairie* children, a lingering voracious image of theirs being left in their place (like their reflection in a mirror), which (as if it were some insatiable spirit in an assumed body) made first semblance to devour the meat that it cunningly carried by and then left the carcass as if it expired and departed thence by a natural and common death. The child and fire, with food and other necessities, are set before the nurse as soon as she enters, but she neither perceives any passage out, nor sees what those people do in other rooms of the lodging. When the child is weaned, the nurse dies, or is conveyed back, or gets the choice to stay there.

But if any superterraneans [surface-dwellers] be so subtle as to practice 'sleights' for procuring a privacy to any of the Fae mysteries (such as making use of their ointments, rings which make them invis-

---

* *Rathlin Island*—a small "L"-shaped island off the coast of Northern Ireland. [Presumed by editor.]

ible or nimble, or casts them into a trance, or alters their shape, or makes things appear at a vast distance, &tc.), they smite them without pain, as with a puff of wind, and relieve them of their natural and acquired 'sights' in the twinkling of an eye, or they strick them dumb.

The Northerners ['*tramontanes*'] to this day, put bread, the Bible, or a piece of iron, in a woman's bed while traveling to save them from being 'stolen'; and they commonly report that all uncouth unknown 'wights' are terrified by nothing earthly as much as cold iron. They suppose the reason to be that Hell lies betwixt the chill tempests and the firebrands of scalding metals and iron of the north (hence the loadstone causes a tendency to that point).

By an antipathy thereto, these odious far-seeing creatures shrug and fright at all that is perceived which relates to so abhorred a place—where their torment is either begun or feared to come hereafter.

Their apparel and speech is like that of the people and country under which they live; so are they seen to wear plaids and variegated garments in the Highlands of Scotland—and *suanochs* (garments made of *tartan*) in Ireland. They speak little, and that by way of whistling, clear, not rough. The very 'devils' conjured in any country do answer in the language of the place, yet sometimes the subterraneans speak more distinctly than at other times.

Their women are said to 'spin' very finely—to dye, to tissue, and embroider: but whether it is a manual operation of substantially refined 'stuffs' with apt and solid instruments, or only curious cobwebs, impalpable rainbows, and a fantastic imitation of the actions of more terrestrial mortals; since it transcended all the senses of the "seer" to discern whether, I leave it to conjecture as I found it.

Their men travel much abroad, either presaging or aping the dismal and tragical actions of some amongst us, and have also many disastrous doings of their own, as convocations, fighting, gashes, wounds, and burials, both in the earth and air. They live much longer than we, yet die at last, or at least vanish from that state.

It is one of their tenets that nothing perishes, but (as the sun and year) everything goes in a circle, lesser or greater, and is renewed and refreshed in its revolutions. It is another tenet that every "body" in creation moves (which is a sort of 'life'); and further that nothing moves but has another animal moving on it, and so on and on, to the utmost minutest corpuscle that is capable to be a receptacle of life.

They are said to have aristocratic rulers and laws, but no discernible religion, love or devotion towards 'God'. They disappear whenever they hear 'His' name invoked, or the name of 'Jesus' (at which all do bow willingly or by constraint that dwell above or beneath within the earth, *Philippians 2.10*) nor can they act ought at that time after hearing of that sacred name.

The *tabhaisver*, or seer, corresponding with these kinds of familiars, can bring them to appear with a spell, as readily as the Endor Witch to those of her kind. He says they are ever ready to go on hurtful errands, but seldom will be the messengers of great good to humans. He is not terrified by their sight when he calls them, but seeing them in a surprise (as does often happen) extremely frightens him. They do not do all the harm that they appear to have the power to do, nor are they perceived to be in great pain.

They are said to have many pleasant toyish books, but the operation of these pieces only appears in some '*paroxysms of antic corybantic jollity*' as if ravished and prompted by a new spirit entering into them at that instant, lighter and merrier than their own. Other books they have of '*esoterica*', as like the Rosicrucian style. They have nothing of the Bible except collected parcels for charms and counter-charms, not to defend themselves, but to operate on other animals, for they are a people invulnerable to our weapons.

Albeit werewolves' and witches' true bodies are (by union of the spirit of nature that runs through all, echoing and doubling the blow towards another) wounded at home when the astral assumed bodies are struck elsewhere—as the strings of a second harp tune to a unison sound though only one be struck; yet these Fae have not a second or so gross a body at all to be so pierced; but as air, which when divided unites again. Or, if they feel pain by a blow, they are better physicians than we are and quickly cure it. They are not subject to sore sickness, but dwindle and decay at about the same age.

They are usually silent and sullen. Some say their continual sadness is because of their pendulous state (like those men in *Luke 13.16*), as uncertain what, at the last revolution, will become of them when they are locked up in an unchangeable condition.

But other men of the 'Second Sight', being illiterate and unwary in their observations, learned from witnessing frolic fits of mirth, that are as acted upon a stage. Some believe the subterranean people to be departed souls attending awhile in this inferior state and clothed with bodies procured through their alms deeds in this life; fluid, active, ethereal "vehicles" to hold them, that they may not scatter, nor wander and be lost in the wholeness or their first nothingness; but if any were so impious as to have given no alms, they say when the souls of such do depart, they sleep in an unactive state until they resume the terrestrial bodies again.

Others, that what the low-country Scot calls a *wraith*—and the Irish, *taibshe*—or "death's messenger" sometimes appearing as a little rough dog, and if crossed or conjured in time, will be pacified by the death of any other creature instead of a sick man), is only exuvious fumes of the man approaching death, exhaled and congealed into various likenesses—as 'ships' and 'armies' are sometimes shaped in the air—and called 'astral bodies', agitated as wildfire with wind; and are neither 'souls', nor counterfeiting spirits. Surely these are a numerous people by themselves, having their own politics.

Their weapons are mostly solid earthly bodies—nothing of iron, but much of stone; similar to yellowish soft flint shaped like a barbed arrowhead, but flung like a "dart" with great force. These armaments (cut by art and tools beyond human) have somewhat of the nature of a thunderbolt, subtly and mortally wounding vital parts without breaking the skin—wounds I have observed in beasts and felt them with my hands. They are not as infallible *Benjamites*, hitting at a hairsbreadth, nor are they wholly unvanquishable, at least in appearance.

Those of that 'Second Sight' do not discover strange things when asked, but at fits and raptures, as if inspired with some genius at that instant, which prior did lurk within or about them. Thus, I have frequently spoke to one of them, who in his transport told he cut the body of one these people in who with his iron weapon and so escaped this onset, yet he saw nothing left behind of that appearing divided body; at other times he outwrestled some of them.

His neighbors often perceived this man to disappear at a certain place, and about one hour after to become visible and discover himself near a bowshot from the first place. It was in that place where he became invisible, said he, that the subterraneans did encounter and combat with him.

They who are unseen, unsanctified or called "fey-doomed" are said to be pierced or wounded with those people's weapons, which makes them do [act] somewhat unlike their former practice, causing a sudden alteration, yet the cause of such remains unperceivable. Nor have they power (either they cannot make use of their natural powers or ask not the heavenly aid) to escape the impending blow.

A man of the 'Second Sight' perceived a person standing by him (found to others' view) wholly gored in blood, and he bid him instantly flee. The man wholly laughed at his art and warning since there was no appearance of danger. He had barely contracted his lips from laughter when his enemy unexpectedly leaped to his side and stabbed him with their weapons.

They also pierce cows or other animals—usually said to be '*Elf-Shot*'—whose purest substance (if they die) these subterraneans take to live on, *viz.*, the aerial and ethereal parts—the most spiritous matter—for prolonging of life, such as *aquavitae* (if moderately taken) is among liquors, but leaving the terrestrial matter behind. The cure of such hurts is only for a human to seek out the "hole" with his finger, as if the spirits flowing from a man's warm hand were a sufficient antidote against their poisoned darts.

As birds and beasts—whose bodies are used to the changes in free and open air—foresee storms, so do those 'invisible people' have more sagacious (intellect) to understand by the "Books of Nature" about the things to come than we do; we are more pestered with the grosser dregs of all elementary mixtures and have our purer spirits choked by them.

The 'deer' scents out a man and (gun) powder (though a late invention) at a great distance; a hungry hunter, senses bread; and the raven, a carrion: their brains being long clarified by the high and subtle air and will detect a very small change. Thus, a man of 'Second Sight', perceiving the operations of these forecasting 'invisible people' among us (indulged through a stupendous providence to give warnings of some remarkable events, either in the air, earth, or waters), said he saw a winding-shroud creeping on a walking healthy person's legs until it came to the knee, and afterward it came up to the middle, then to shoulders, and at last over the head, which was not visible to anyone else. And by observing the spaces of time betwixt the several stages of is progression, he easily guessed how long the person was to live who wore the shroud—for when it finally approached the head, he said that such a person was ripe for the grave.

There are many places called '*Fairy-Hills*', which the 'mountain people' think impious and dangerous to peel or discover by taking earth or wood from them, superstitiously believing the "souls" of their predecessors dwell there. And for that end, they say, a mote or mount was dedicated beside every churchyard to receive the souls until their adjacent bodies arise, and so become as a '*Fairy-Hill*', since they use their bodies of air when called abroad. Their accounts affirm that creatures move invisibly in a house, and cast great stones, but do not cause hurt much because they are counterwrought by some more courteous and charitable spirits that are everywhere ready to defend humans (*Daniel 10.13*), to be souls that have not attained their rest through a vehement desire of revealing a murder or notable injury done or received, or a treasure that was forgot in their lifetime on earth, which when disclosed to the conjurer alone, the 'ghost' quite removes [itself].

In the next country to that of my former residence, around the year 1676, when there was some scarcity of grain, a marvelous vision struck the imagination of two women in one night, living at a good distance from one another, about a treasure hid in a hill called *sithbhruaich*, or *Fairy-Hill*. The appearance of a treasure was first represented to the fancy, and then an audible voice named the place where it was to their awoke senses. Whereupon both arose, and meeting accidentally at the place, learning of each others' purpose; and jointly digging, found a vessel as large as a Scottish pech, full of small pieces of good money, of ancient coin; which dividing betwixt them they sold in dish-fulls upon dish-fulls of meal to the country people.

But whether it was a 'good' or 'bad' angel, one of the subterranean people, or the restless soul of him who hid it that discovered it, and to what end it was done, I leave that to the examination of others.

These subterraneans have controversies, doubts, disputes, feuds, and party-sidings—there being some ignorance in all creatures and the vastest created intelligences not encompassing all things. As to vice and sin, whatever their own laws be, surely similar to ours, and equity, natural, civil, and revealed, they transgress and commit acts of injustice, and sin—by what is said prior as to their stealing of "nurses" to their children and other sorts of "kidnapping" or stealing our children away (who may heir to some estate in those invisible kingdoms), which never return. Surely, for the inconvenience of their *succubi*, who tryst with men, it is abominable. But, as for swearing and intemperance, they are not observed to be subject to those emotional irregularities of envy, spite, hypocrisy, lying and dissimulation.

Our religion obliges us not to make a preemptive and curious search into these abstrusenesses—so that the history of all ages gives as 'plain' of examples as possible of the extraordinary occurrences as make a modest inquiry not contemptible.

How much is written of pygmies, fairies, nymphs, sirens, apparitions, which though not the tenth part true, obviously could not spring from nothing?

Even English authors relate of '*Barry Island*', in Glamorganshire, that laying your ear into a cleft of the rocks, blowing of bellows, striking of hammers, clashing of armor, filing of irons will be heard distantly, ever since Merlin enchanted those subterranean *wights* to a solid manual forging of arms to *Aurelius Ambrosius* and his Britains until he returned—which Merlin being killed in a battle and not coming to loosen the knot, these active '*Vulcans*' are there tied to a perpetual labor.

But to dip no deeper into this well, I will next give some account on how the 'seer', my informer, comes to have this secret way of correspondence beyond other mortals.

There are odd solemnities at investing a man with the privileges of the whole mystery of this 'Second Sight'. He must run a tether of hair (which bound a corpse to the bier) in a helix about his middle from end to end; then bow his head downwards, as did Elijah (*1 Kings 18.42*), and look back through his legs until he see a funeral advance till the people cross two marches, or look thus back through a hole where was a knot of 'fir'. But if the wind changes points while the hair tether is tied about him, he is in peril of his life.

The usual method for a curious person to get a transient sight of this otherwise invisible crew of subterraneans (if impotently or over-rashly sought) is to put his left foot under the wizard's right foot, and the seer's hand is put on the inquirers head, who is to look over the wizard's right shoulder (which has an ill appearance, as if, by this ceremony an implicit surrender were made of all betwixt the wizard's foot and his hand ere the person can be admitted *a privado* [an initiate] to the art).

Then will he see a multitude of *wights*, like furious hardy men flocking to him hastily from all quarters as thick as atoms in the air, which are no non-entities or phantasms (creatures proceeding from an frightened apprehension, confused or crazed sense), but realities, appearing to a stable human in his awakened senses and enduring a rational trial of their being. Those through fear strike him breathless and speechless.

The wizard, defending the lawfulness of his skill, forbids such horror, and comforts his novice by telling of Zecharias, being struck speechless at seeing apparitions (*Luke 1.20*).

Then he further maintains his art by vouching that *Elisha* to have had the same and disclosed it thus unto his servant (*2 Kings 6.17*) when blinded the Syrians, and *Peter* (in *Acts 5.9*) foreseeing the death of *Saphira* by perceiving it as a winding-sheet about her beforehand, and *Pail* (in *2 Corinthians 12.4*), who got a vision and sight as should not, nor could, be told. *Elisha* also in his chamber saw *Gehazi*, his servant, at a great distance, taking a reward from *Naaman* (in *2 Kings 5.26*).

Hence were the 'prophets' frequently called "seers"—or men of a "second" or more exalted sight than others. He acts for his purpose—also *Matthew 4.8*, where the devil undertakes to given even *Jesus* a sight of all nations and the finest things in the world at one glance, though in their natural situations and stations, were at a vast distance from another.

And it is said expressly that he did let him see them—and not in a map it seems, nor by a fantastical magical juggling of the sight, which he could not impose upon so discovering of a person. It would appear then to have been a sight of real solid substance and things of worth, which intended as a bait for his purposes.

Whence it might seem (comparing this relation of *Matthew 4.8* with the former) that the extraordinary or 'Second Sight' can be given by the ministry of bad as well as good spirits to those that will embrace it. And the instance of *Balaam* and the 'pythoness' [an oracle] makes it nothing less than probable.

Thus also the '*seer*' trains scholar by telling of the gradations of Nature, ordered by wise providence. And that men of the 'Second Sight' (being designed to give warnings against 'secret trappings') surpass the ordinary vision of other humans, which is a native (innate) habit in some, descended from their ancestors, and acquired as an 'artificial' improvement of their natural sight in others, resembling in their own kind a sort of artificial assistance like as with optic glasses—as prospectives, telescopes and microscopes.

Only with such supplementary aids, humans are treated here with an ability to perceive things that for their smallness or subtlety and secrecy are invisible to others, though they are in communication with the scientist daily. They have such a beam continually about them—as that of the sun—which when it shines clear only lets common eyes see the atoms in the air that without those rays they could not otherwise discern. Some have the 'Second Sight' transmitted from [parents]—the whole family—without their consent or others teachings, proceeding only from a bounty of providence, it seems, or by some compact or a complex quality of the first acquirer.

The minor sort of *seers* prognosticate many future events, only for a month's space, from the shoulder-bone of a sheep on which a knife never came [and there is also something of this in the Ancient Near East]—for as before is said, *iron* hinders all the operations of those that travail in the intrigues of these hidden kingdoms. By looking into the bone, they will tell if whoredom be committed in the owner's house; what money the master of the sheep had; if any in that house will meet their death in that month; and if any cattle there will take ill. Then they will prescribe a preservative and prevention.

A woman singularly wise in these matters of foresight, living in *Colnasnach*, an isle of the *Hebrides* (in the time of the *Marquess of Montrose*, his wars with the states in Scotland), being notorious among many, and so examined by some that violently seized the isle, if she saw them coming or not, she said she saw them coming many hours before they came in view of the isle. But earnestly looking, she sometimes took them for enemies, sometimes for friends, and moreover they looked as if they went from the isle, not as men approaching it, which made her not put the inhabitants on their guard. The matter was that the barge wherein the enemy sailed was a little beforehand taken from the inhabitants of the same isle, and the men had their backs toward the isle when they were plying the oars towards it.

Thus this old scout and *Delphian Oracle* was at last deceived—and did deceive. Being asked who gave her such sights and such warnings, she said as soon as she set three "crosses" of straw upon the palm of her hand, a great ugly beast sprang up out of the earth near her and flew into the air. If what she inquired had success according to her wish, the beast would descend calmly and lick up the crosses. If it would not succeed, the beast would furiously thrust her and the crosses over on the ground and so vanish to his place.

Among other instances of undoubted verity proving in these the *beingness* of such aerial people or species of creatures not vulgarly known, I add the subsequent relations, some of which I have from my acquaintance with the actors and patients, and the rest from the eye-witnesses to the matter of fact.

The first whereof shall be of a woman taken out of her child-bed and having a lingering image of her substituted body in her room, which resemblance decayed, died and was buried—but the person stolen returning to her husband after two years' space, he being convinced by many undeniable tokens that she was his former wife, admitted her home and have diverse children by her.

Among other reports she gave her husband, this was one: that she perceived little what they did in the spacious house she lodged in until she anointed one of her eyes with a certain concoction that was by her; which they perceiving to have acquainted her with their actions, they fanned her blind in that eye with a puff of their breath. She found the place full of light, without any fountain or lamp from whence it did spring.

This person lived in the country next to that of my last residence and might furnish matter of dispute among *casuists* [*ethicists*], whether if her husband had been married in the interim of her two years' absence, he was obliged to divorce from the second spouse at the return of the first. There is an art, apparently without superstition, for recovering of such persons that are stolen, but think it superfluous to insert it.

I saw a woman of forty years of age and examined her (having another clergyman in my company) about a report that passed of her long fasting. It was told by them of the house, as well as herself, that she took very little or no food for several years past; that she tarried in the fields overnight, saw and conversed with a people she knew not, having wandered in seeking of her sheep and slept upon a hillock, and finding herself transported to another place before daybreak.

The woman had a child since that time and is still pretty melancholy and silent, hardly ever seen to laugh. Her natural heat and radical moisture seem to be equally balanced, like an unextinguished lamp, and going in a circle, not unlike the faint life of bees and some sort of birds that sleep all winter over and revive in the spring.

It is usual in all 'magical arts' to have the candidates prepossessed with the belief of their tutor's skill and ability to perform their feats and act their juggling pranks and 'slight of hand'—but a person called *Stewart* (possessed with a disbelief of the 'Second Sight' and living near my house), was so put it by a *seer* before many witnesses; he lost his speech, power of his legs and, breathing excessively as if expiring, because of many fearful *wights* that appeared to him, the company were forced to carry him home.

It is notorious spoken of about *Killin* within *Perthshire*, who fell tragically out with a yeoman [attendant of a noble household]—who coming into a company within an ale-house where a *seer* sat at the table, that at the sight of the entrant neighbor, the *seer*, startlingly rose to go out of the house; and being asked the reason of his haste, told that the entrant man would die within two days—at which news the named entrant stabbed the *seer* and was himself executed two days after for the fact.

A minister, very intelligent but misbelieving all such sights as were not ordinary, chancing to be in a narrow lane with a *seer*, who perceived a *wight* of a known visage furiously to encounter them, the *seer* desired the minister to turn out of the way, who scorning his reason and holding himself in the path with them when the *seer* was going hastily out of the way—they were both violently case aside to a good distance, and the fall made them lame for the rest of their life. A little after the minister was carried home, the 'death-toll' rang for the man whose representation had met them in the narrow path some half an hour before.

Another example is a *seer* in *Kintyre* in Scotland, sitting at a table with diverse others, suddenly did cast his head aside. The company asking him why he did it, he answered that such a friend of his, by name, then in Ireland, threatened immediately to cast a dish-full of butter in his face. The men wrote down the day and hour and sent to the gentleman to know the truth, which deed the gentleman declared he did at that very time, for he knew that his friend was a *seer* and would make sport with it. The men that were present and examined the matter exactly, told me this story and withal that a *seer* would, with all his optics, perceive no other object so readily as this at such a distance.

[*Kirk's primary manuscript ends here.*]

of the predictions made by seers[*]

My Lord, after narrow inquisition, have discovered many true and remarkable observations on the subject of the 'Second Sight'.

Firstly, that this sight is not criminal, since a man can come by it unawares and without his consent. But it is certain that he will see more fatal and fearful things than he will gladsome.

Secondly, the *seers* avouch that several who go to the *siths* (or people at rest, and, in respect to us, in peace) before the natural period of their lives expire, do frequently appear to them.

Thirdly, a vehement desire to attain this art is very helpful to the inquirer, and the species of an absent friend, which appears to the *seers* as clearly as if he had sent his lively picture to present itself before him, is no fantastic shadow of a sick apprehension, but a reality and a messenger coming for unknown reasons; not from the original similitude of itself, but from a more swift and pragmatic people that recreate themselves in offering secret intelligence to men, though generally they are unacquainted with that kind of correspondence, as if they had lived in a different element from them.

Fourthly, I presume to day that this sight can be no quality of air nor of the eyes, because: such as live in the same air and see all other things as far off and as clearly, yet have not the 'Second Sight'; a *seer* can give another person this sight transiently by putting his hand and foot in the posture he requires of him; the unsullied eyes of infants can naturally perceive no new unaccustomed objects but what appear to other men, unless exalted and clarified in some way, as Balaam's donkey[*] for a time (though in a witch's eye, the beholder cannot see his own image reflected, as is visible in the eyes of other people).

Fifthly, since the things seen by *seers* are real entities, the passages and predictions found true, but a few endowed with this sight and whose not of bad lives or addicted to malefices, the true solution of the phenomenon seems rather to be the courteous endeavors of our

---

[*] This discourse is attached to Kirk's manuscript, in regards to "a succinct account of My Lord Tarbett's relations in a letter to the Honorable Robert Boyle, Esquire" as given in the original edition.

[*] In *Numbers 22:21-39*, Balaam's donkey diverts from the trail, blocked by the 'Angel of the Lord' and Balaam beats the donkey, to which God says "if your donkey had not seen me and diverted, I would have killed you and spared the donkey."

fellow creatures in the invisible world to convince us (in opposition to *Sadduce's, Socinians*, and atheists) of a deity, of spirits, of a possible and harmless method of correspondence betwixt men and them even in this life, of their operations for our caution and warning, of the orders and degrees of angels, whereof one order with bodies of air condensed and curiously shaped may be next to a human, superior to them in understanding yet unconfirmed, and of their region, habitation and influence on man, greater than that of stars on inanimate bodies; a knowledge (belike) reserved for these last atheistic ages, wherein the profanity of human lives has debauched and blinded their understanding as to the prophets and regions of the dead.

Nor does the ceasing of the visions upon the *seer's* transmigration into foreign kingdoms confirms greatly my account of an invisible people, guardian over and careful of men, who have their different offices and abilities in distinct countries (as in *Daniel 10.13*), Israel's, Grecia's, and Persia's assistant princes, whereof who so prevails, give the dominion and ascendant to his pupils and vassals over the opposite armies and kingdom having their topical spirits or powers assisting and governing them, the Scottish *seer* banished to the Americas, being a stranger there as well to the invisible as to the visible inhabitants and wanting a familiarity of his former correspondents, he could not have the favor and warnings, by the several visions and predictions which were wont to be granted him by these acquaintances and favorites in his own country.

For if what he wanted to see were realities (as I have made appear), it would be too great an honor for Scotland to have such seldom-seen watchers and predominant powers over it alone, acting in it so expressly, and all other nations wholly destitute of the like; though without all peradventure, all other people wanted the right *key* of their *cabinet* and the exact method for corresponding with them, except the sagacious active Scots, as many of whom have retained it for a long, and by surprises and raptures do often foretell what in kindness is really represented to them at several occasions. To which purpose, the learned lynx-eyed Mr. Baxter (on *Revelation 12.7*), writing of the fight between Michael and the Dragon, gives a very pertinent note, *viz.* that he knows not but ere any great action (especially tragical) is done on earth, that first the battle and victory is acted and achieved in the air between the good and evil spirits.

It seems these were the human's guardians, and similar battles are oftentimes perceived aloft in the night time, the event of which might easily be represented by someone of the number correspondent on earth, as frequently the report of great actions have been more swiftly carried to other countries than all of the art of us mortals could possibly dispatch it.

Saint Augustine (on *Mark 9.4*) gives no small intonation of this truth, averring that *Elias* appeared with *Jesus* on the Mount in his proper body; but *Moses* in an aerial body, assumed like the angels who appeared, and had the ability to eat with *Abraham*, though no necessity on the account of their bodies, as likewise the late doctrine of the preexistence of "souls" living into aerial vehicles, gives a singular hint of the possibility of the thing, if not direct proof of the whole assertion; which moreover may be illuminated by diverse other instances of the like nature and as wonderful, besides what I said above.

Sixthly, the invisible *wights* which haunt houses seem rather to be some of our subterranean inhabitants (which appear often to those with the 'Second Sight'), rather than 'evil spirits' or 'devils', because they throw great stones, pieces of earth and wood at the inhabitants without hurting them, as if they acted not maliciously like 'devils' but in sport like buffoons.

All ages have afforded some obscure testimonies of it: as Pythagoras, his doctrine of transmigration; Socrates's *Daemon* that gave him warning of future dangers; Plato's classifying them into various vehiculated species of spirits; Dionysius Areopagitica's marshaling nine orders of spirits, superior and subordinate; the poets, their borrowing of the philosophers and adding their own fancies of fountain, river, and sea nymphs, wood, hill, and mountain inhabitants, and that every place and thing in cities and countries has special invisible regular gods and governors.

Cardano speaks of his father, his seeing the species of his friend in a moonshine night riding fiercely by his window on a white horse the very night his friend died at a vast distance from him, by which he understood that some alteration would suddenly ensue. Cornelius Agrippa and the learned Dr. More have several passages tending that way.

The noctambulos* themselves would appear to have some foreign joking spirit possessing and supporting them when they walk on deep waters and tops of houses without danger when asleep in the dark.

---

* Latin for 'night-walker'; a 'night owl' or someone that stays up late (into the nighttime hours). The reference here seems to be of *"sleep-walking."*

For it was no way probable that mere apprehension and strong imagination, setting the animal spirits at work to move the body, could preserve it from sinking in the deep or falling down headlong when asleep anymore than when awake, the body being then as ponderous as before; and it is hard to attribute it to a spirit flatly evil and enemy to man, because the *noctambulo* returns to his own place safe.

And the most furious tribe of the *daemons* are not permitted by providence to attack men so frequently either by night or by day: for in the Highlands, as there may be many fair ladies of this aerial order which do often tryst with lascivious young men in the quality of *succubi* or lightsome paramours and strumpets (called *leannain sith*, or familiar spirits in *Deuteronomy 18.11*), so do many of our Highlanders, as if astrangling by nightmare, pressed with a fearful dream, or rather possessed by one of our aerial neighbors rise up fierce in the night and apprehending the nearest weapons, do push and thrust at all person in the same room with them, sometimes even wounding their own comrades to death, the like whereof fell sadly out within a few miles of me at the writing hereof.

I add but one instance more of a very young maid who lived near to my last residence, that in one night learned a large piece of poesy by the frequent repetition of it from one of our nimble and courteous spirits, whereof a part was pious, the rest superstitious (for I have a copy of it), and no other person was ever heard to repeat it before, nor was the mail capable to compose it of herself.

Finally, having demonstrated and made evident to sense this extraordinary vision of our tramontane *seers* and what is seen by them by what is said above, many having seen this same *spectres* and apparitions at once, having their visive faculties entire; for *non est disputandum de gustu*, it now remains to show that it is not unsuitable to reason not the Holy Scriptures.

First, that it is not repugnant to reason: doth appear from this that it is no less strange for immortal sparks and souls to come and be immersed into gross terrestrial elemental bodies and be so propagated, so nourished, so fed, so clothed as they are, and breathe in such an air and world prepared for them, than for Hollanders, or hollow-cavern inhabitants, to live and traffic among us in another state of being without our knowledge.

For Raymond de Subinde, in his third book, chapter 12, argues quaintly that all sorts of living creatures have a happy rational polity of their own with great contentment, which government and mutual converse of theirs they all pride and plume themselves because it is as unknown to man, as man is to them. Much more, that the Son of the Highest Spirit should assume a body like ours convinces all the world that no other thing that is possible needs be much wondered at.

The *manucodiata*, or 'bird of paradise', living in the highest region of the air; common birds in the second region; flies and insects in the lowest; humans and beasts on the earth's surface; worms, otters, badgers, in waters; likewise, Hell is inhabited at the centre and Heaven in the circumference; can we then think the middle cavities of the earth empty?

Further, let us take up all that remains to us now—to answer the obvious objections against the reality and lawfulness of my speculations.

QUESTION 1: How do you salve the 'Second Sight' from compacts and witchcraft?

ANSWER: Though this correspondence with the intermediate unconfirmed people (betwixt man and angel) be not ordinary to all of us who are 'superterraineans', yet this sight falling to some persons by accident and its being connatural to others from their birth, the derivation of it cannot always be wicked. A too great curiosity indeed to acquire any unnecessary art may be blameworthy, but diverse of the secret commonwealth may be permission discover themselves as innocently to us, who are in another state, as some of us men do to fishes, which are in another element, when we plunge and dive into the bottom of the seas, their native region; and in process of time we may come to converse as familiarity with those nimble and agile clans (but with greater pleasure and profit) as we do now with the Chinese and Antipodes.

QUESTION 2: Are they subject to vice, lusts, passion, and injustice as we who live on the surface of the earth?

ANSWER: The *seer* tells us that these wandering aerial people have no such an impetus and fatal tendency to any vice as men, as not being drenched into so gross and dreggy bodies as we, but yet are in an imperfect state, and some of them making better essays for heroic actions than others, having the same measures of virtue and vice as we, and still expecting advancement to a higher more splendid state of life.

One of them is stronger than many humans, yet are not inclined to hurt mankind, except by commission for a gross misdemeanor, as the destroying angel of Egypt and the Assyrians (*Exodus 12.29, 2 Kings 19.35*). They haunt most where is most barbarity, and therefore our ignorant ancestor to prevent the insults of that strange people used as rude and coarse a remedy; such as exorcisms, donations and vows.

But how soon ever the true piety prevailed in any place, it did not put the inhabitants beyond the reach and authority of those subtle inferior co-inhabitants and colleagues of ours: the Father of all Spirits and the person himself having the only command of his soul and actions. A concurrence they may have to what is virtuously done, for upon committing of a foul deed, one will find a demur upon his soul, as if his cheerful colleague had deserted him.

QUESTION 3: Do these airy tribes procreate? If so, how are they nourished and at what period of time do they die?

ANSWER: Supposing all spirits to be created at once in the beginning, souls to preexist and to circle about into several states of probationship to make them either totally inexcusable or perfectly happy against the last day, solves at the difficulties.

But in every deed, and speaking suitable to the nature of things, there is no more absurdity for a spirit to inform an infantine in body of air than a body composed of dull and drowsy earth, the best of spirits have always delighted more to appear into aerial than into terrestrial bodies. They feed mostly on quintessences and ethereal essences.

Now the air being a body as well as earth, no reason can be given why there may not be particles of more vivific spirit formed of it for procreation than is possible to be of earth, which takes more time and pains to rarify and ripen it ere it can come to have a prolific virtue. And if our aping darlings did not thus procreate, their whole number would be exhausted after a considerable space of time.

For they are of more refined bodies and intellectuals than we, and of far less heavy and corruptive humours (which cause a dissolution), yet many of their lives being dissonant to right reason and their own laws and their vehicles not being wholly free of lust and passion, especially of the most spiritual and haughty sins, they pass (after a long healthy life) into an orb and receptacle fitted for their degree until they come under the general cognizance of the last day.

The Elven-Faerie Grimoire

elements of tradition and the elven way

Elven-Faerie tradition alludes to a singular unifying Oneness—an ALL interconnected with All life and energy in the Cosmos. However, the energy that manifests the world of forms that we experience within the parameters of physical reality (within a Human sensory range) is filtered down and condensed into a series of perceived 'levels' or 'degrees', 'vibrations' and 'frequencies' which are constantly in motion in accord with the Cosmic Law of ALL.

There are—in reality—no actual separations between these varying degrees although we experience them that way subjectively as individuals perceiving a "world around us"—not always realizing that it is *us* that projects the separation of "things" from other "things." This holistic type of *"systemology"* is "meta-thinking" for most Humans. Some elemental schema that follow in this chapter-lesson do relate directly to traditional more familiar Fourfold Elemental paradigms aligned to *Tuatha d'Anu* lore.

However, Elven-Ffayrie traditions often record their Elemental schema in other methods that are not restricted to cross-quarter symmetry many *Seekers* have undoubtedly encountered in other sources of western magical tradition. They more commonly appear as threefold, sixfold and even ninefold "aspects" or "elements"—called *"duile"* in Celtic fae traditions.

Neodruids and other New Age Wizards have also called the same: *"aires"*—so named after the "Four Winds." Sometimes the classification of elements are misunderstood—for example, because *"Nwyvre"* may be interpreted as both *"Akasha"* and *"Fire,"* but as you will see, Elvish Wizards interpret the traditional "Fire Element" a bit differently when experienced in the "Otherworld."

> **THE THREEFOLD ELEMENTAL SCHEMA**
>
> <u>Element of Land</u>: bone, tissue, muscle, skin, soil, ground, minerals, crystals, plant life, vegetation, and mainland ecosystem.
>
> <u>Element of Sky</u>: oxygen, lungs, voice, circulatory system, winds, upper atmosphere, clouds, vapor, and winged life.
>
> <u>Element of Sea</u>: blood, fluids, hormones, neurochemicals, natural bodies of water, running water and marine life.

THE SIXFOLD ELEMENTAL SCHEMA

<u>Element of Stone</u>: "brown magick"—animals, business, gems, metals and soil.

<u>Element of Earth</u>: "green magick"—agriculture, ecology, fertility, forests, herbalism and trees.

<u>Element of Vapor & Cloud</u>: "indigo magick"—quantum physics, Otherworld magick, psychic powers, spirits and time travel.

<u>Element of Wind</u>: "yellow magick"—alertness, books, communication, confidence, knowledge, study, reading and writing.

<u>Element of Sun</u>: "red magick" & "orange magick"—alchemy, art, courage, healing, love, passion, strength, success and attraction.

<u>Element of Sea</u>: "blue magick"—creativity, dreams, love, emotion, glamour, the moon, enchantment, mysticism, peace, tranquility, understanding and visions.

THE NINEFOLD ELEMENTAL SCHEMA

<u>Element of Salt</u>—Land: nighttime, northwest, white, consecration ceremonies and purification.

<u>Element of Earth</u>—Land: midnight, north, green, trees/forest growth magick and fertility.

<u>Element of Stone</u>—Land: evening, northeast, brown, crystal magick, charging and protection.

<u>Element of Wind</u>—Sky: morning twilight, east, yellow, new beginnings, insight and summoning.

<u>Element of Star(fire)</u>—Sky: dawn, southeast, white, dreams, wish magick and awareness.

<u>Element of Sun</u>—Sky: noon, south, gold, insight, willpower, strength and leadership.

<u>Element of Vapor & Cloud</u>—Sea: twilight, southwest, astral magick, Otherworld work and enchantments.

<u>Element of Sea</u>—Sea: sunset, west, blue, subconscious magick, dreams, healing and love.

<u>Element of Rain</u>—Sea: dust, west-northwest, purple, emotions, emotional healing, cleansing, love and beauty.

Practice of Elemental Magick in Elvish Wizardry is typically composed of three main levels of progression—or degrees of experience. They relate not only to the development of one's abilities, but are also the same steps taken for ritualized exercises in meditation for effective physical magick:—

1. Dedication: study and initiation.
2. Purification: grounding and creating sacred space.
3. Invocation: calling forth and dismissing Elementals.

When utilizing rites of "Elemental Magick," a Wizard gains astral, spiritual and subconscious experience with a specific element. While all normal ritual observations will employ the four Elemental Quarters of the Middle World, Elvish Wizards often focus on a single element during personal meditations—working intensely with a particular aspect of the Elemental Kingdoms.

By encountering each single element individually, an Apprentice Wizard to gains experience and "authority" with a each specific element before calling its powers directly in a ceremonial/ritual setting. However, when an affinity to a particular element emerges be warned that you will begin to assimilate attributes specific to that elemental type. For example—a Wizard who works with the Air Element most of the time may begin to develop a more *flighty*, *spacey* and *imaginative* personality. A "Fire Wizard" might develop an increased sense of personal *courage* and/or *passion*, but also *irritability* when untempered, &tc.

Elven Tradition observes four main styles or types of magickal practice. They are the ceremonial/ritualisitic (*Air*); energy and/or light work (*Fire*); use of astral or spirit vision to access the Otherworld (*Water*); and tree/forest magick (*Earth*). The "grimoires" within the current *Elvenomicon* series make a collective use of all these practices as specific to the observance of a modern "Elven-Druid Faerie Tradition."

This book does not, however, claim to substitute material of a full "magickal primer" for the novice.* In additional to elemental schema provided previously, the following are "Elemental Keys" of the four primary "*duile*" as more commonly used in Elemental Magick by various Wizards, Druids and Mystics of the "Lands Above." Elsewhere in Druidic lore, they are referred to as the "Elven Keys" or "Faerie

---

* For a general magick primer, see "*The Sorcerer's Handbook*" by Joshua Free (writing as Merlyn Stone in the 1990's); or the more recently composed omnibus anthology "*Arcanum: The Great Magical Arcanum*" (first published in 2008).

Keys"—relating quite succinctly with lore introduced in a previous volume of this series regarding the *"Gifts of Faeire"*—which inspired the original Elemental "magic" correspondences of the *Tuatha D'Anu*.

> **THE FOURFOLD ELEMENTAL SCHEMA**
>
> Element of Earth: Elven Key to foundation and fertility, Kingdom of Stone, North, midnight and winter, ruled by King Ghobas, pentacles and holed stones are indicative of the Stone of Fal.
>
> Element of Air: Elven Key to communication and intellect, Kingdom of Wind, East, dawn and spring, ruled by King Paraldas, wands and feathers represent the Spear of Lugh.
>
> Element of Fire: Elven Key to transformation and protection, Kingdom of Flame, South, noon and summer, ruled by King Djin, the blade, staff & 'golden sickle' are representations of the Sword of Nuada.
>
> Element of Water: Elven Key to inner wisdom and well-being, Kingdoms of Sea, West, dusk and autumn, ruled by King Niksas, the goblet, chalice, cup, mirrors and pools follow the tradition of the Cauldron of Dagda and Kerridwen.

casting the circle of power at the nemeton

Meditation is a common and effective practice, but there is a subconscious desire inherent in wizardry—and those called to its orders—that seeks a uniform physical ritualization or ceremony to represent energetic action of "Natural Law." For these reasons, all ritual and ceremonial observations should occur within the "Circle of Power." Here, the Elvish Wizard creates a microcosm—or fractal miniaturization—of the Universe. Currents of Elemental energy are represented in ritual with symbolic catalysts or tools.

The "Circle of Power" is really the atomic *sphere*—fractal in nature, duplicating itself in "smaller" and "larger" dimensions or degrees, "above" and "below" frequency vibrations of what Humans separate as the "physical world." It may help to envision it not as a circle, but as a multi-dimensional "sphere."

In eastern traditions, the 'magic circle' is called a "mandala," but in the Elven-Druid traditions, sacred space is frequently referred to as a "*nemeton*." This "Magick Sphere" is not only a *microcosm* of the cosmos but simultaneously a *macrocosm*—an expanded or enlarged view —of the subatomic and cellular worlds also existing "beyond" normative mortal perceptual vision. All these varying worlds or dimensions are connected in an "Absolute Reality" or unified encompassing field—what ancient Druids called "*Ceugent*," where exists only the Source of All Being and Creation.

Preliminary ceremonial methods for a rite of casting the "Circle of Power" or "Magick Sphere" vary between known systems of practical occultism. More variations probably exist in the "New Age" concerning "Rites of the Magick Circle" than any other aspect of practical metaphysics. The "Magick Sphere" or "*Nemeton*" is a sacred place of power. It is suggested that you should bring this "magic" to the wilderness and forests—find a clearing, or if possible, a "grove of trees." There you may even call on "Earth" and "Stone" as you erect your own "stone circle" or "henge of stones."

The size of your "*kirc*" or physical "sacred circle" will vary based on the location used and the number of participants expected to be present at a given time. Understand that when you bring magick to the same place repeatedly—especially when you are permitted to leave your circle in place—the woodlands will become reminiscent of an ancient archetypal "Enchanted Forest" as the land takes on an increased "charge" over time.*

According to classical accounts, the *"Nemeton"* is a "sacred space" when using terminology of ancient Druids and Elves—the same vocabulary appears regarding groves and henges. One of the famous *"Drunemetons"*—a place of annual gatherings for ancient Druids, Dragon-kind and Elven-Faerie—existed somewhere in ancient Anatolia/Galatia (modern-day Turkey), revealing to us the true extent of geographic expansion once maintained by the Druids. There is even an ancient Druidic deity named as a patron of sacred space, Nemetona —"Goddess of the Grove"—closely identifying (siimilar to 'Diana of the Forest') with a feminine form of the Dagda or Kernunnos as a male "Lord of the Forest" or Green Man. Stonehenge and Woodhenge are two basic examples in Britain of ancient structures built to mark a *"nemeton."* Groves and henges can easily be "artificially" planted or manufactured—and consecrated to this tradition—so long as they are "left open to the sky."

The "Nemeton"—sacred space—is a critical component of practical "ritual magick" energy-work. A wizard must be free of physical, emotional and mental restraints, or bonds to the "material" degrees of existence, during "magical" operations. Creating and distinguishing "sacred space" allows both the conscious and subconscious mind to synchronize salient beliefs that "something magical is about to happen."

In the past, Druids and Elves have followed energetic vibrations or currents ("*ley lines*") of Nature to reach certain "power spots" and distinguished locations—such that even an only partially sensitive Human might describe as "enchanted" or "magical." Modern Druids, Wizards and Mystics dedicated to "green magic" continue to do this today, seeking out places for personal and overt "Earth power" to work their magick from.

A *Seeker* is encouraged to research the vibrations and energetic currents of local trees and find natural representations that reflect the stream-current or ray that best reflects your own energies and/or the function of a ritual. Additional lore to assist this is provided in the *"The Enchanted Forest"* volume within this *Elvenomicon* series. New Age practitioners frequently consider the astrophysical qualities of celest-

---

* See also a later section in this anthology: *"The Enchanted Forest."*

ial bodies—such as the Sun and Moon—during selection of the ritual area and timing of ceremonies—especially those linked to annual seasonal cycles, such as the solstices and equinoxes.

A *"Nemeton"* for a solitary practitioner does not obviously carry the same space requirements as one intended for group (or even "coven") use. The center of the *Nemeton* is typically marked with an Altar. The same rules apply to the altar: the size and shape are dependent on your needs. Be sure to leave enough space to move around the altar within the circle without affecting *Nemeton* boundaries. For group magick—practitioners will require much more space to move around freely. Here, you might reflect on energetic tension differences between times when you are alone and when you are in a crowded room. If movement is restricted in close quarters, energy does not have the freedom to expand—and those gathered together will be more likely to draw their energies and auras *in* rather than properly project them *out*.

When you are ready to perform your magick, go to your "altar." For projective magick, it is customary to call forth and visualize a white field of light to surround yourself with—or another relevant ray-vibration of light—and ask your "Higher Self"—or interconnected consciousness—to guide and protect you in your magickal endeavors. After this, an Elvish Wizard asks for peace, grace and acknowledgment from the elemental spirits in the Universe—and then the ritual can begin.

CASTING THE CIRCLE OF POWER

Take a "goblet of water," holding it up to the west and say:

May the Spirits of Water bestow their blessing and remember.

Take up the "bowl of salt," hold it up to the northern direction and say:

May the Spirits of Earth bestow their blessing and remember.

Sprinkle a portion of the "salt" into the "water," hold it up, facing north and affirm:

By this alchemical expression do I transform and purify my being—consecrating my spirit to the Source of All Light and the Children of Light, the Ancient and Shinning Ones.

Take up the "incense resin" (or stick) and hold it up to the east, saying:

May the Spirits of Air bestow their blessing and remember.

Hold up the "incense burner" to the south and say:

May the Spirits of Fire bestow their blessing and remember.

If you are using an incense stick, light it—otherwise the coals you should be prepared within the burner. Then add some of the incense resin to it and affirm:

By this alchemical expression do I hereby transform and purify my being, stripping away old skin, leaving my mortal body, affirming my Elven (Ffayrie) soul, consecrated to the Source of All Light and Starfire.

Allow the incense to burn. Take the chalice of salt-water and go to the north, working clockwise around the circle, sprinkling the water lightly as you walk. Be sure to ration your use so that some remains.

Once you have moved about full circle, returning again to the north, go to your altar or 'work space' and take up the incense burner—adding some more if necessary—and go to the east, moving again around the entire boundary of the circle, slowly and deliberately. Your actions should express that you are walking or testing the boundaries of the "ends of the Universe"—represented by the Nemeton.

Go to the north with your "magick wand,"—carrying it in your projective hand (the one you write with) and begin to inscribe your circle, tracing or defining it on a metaphysical level—where before, you were only testing and sensing it. When using a wand in this way, your projective arm usually crosses the body as you walk clockwise in your initial conjuring of the "Circle of Power."

Empower and/or envision your arm as an extension of your will, and the "magick wand" as a further extension—representing where your will meets that of the external energies that your will has summoned and attracted. See bluish-white energy projecting from your wand and imprinting the horizon of your circle at waist height. You may wish, if you are adept in visualization, to see this band of energy extending both above and below to form a "sphere."

Once you circumnavigate the "*kirc*," return to the central altar and address the Universe:

Here I stand at the Entrance of the Golden Threshold. Between the Finite and Infinite Universe do I stand. The mortal spark burns deep within my being and I am flawed. The Divine spark burns deep within my being and I am flawless. Once I acknowledge the connectedness I share with the Source of All, I am complete and at one with all life in the Universe. I am a "Child of Starlight."

Feel the presence of the "Forces of Nature" surrounding your "*Nemeton,*" attracted to the "Circle of Light," that you have conjured. Acknowledge them by calling out:

I feel many varieties of energy imbued with Light and Life from the Otherworld coming to the edge of my Circle of Power. I hereby invite you in, all friendly spirits who aid in the positive magick of Nature. Witness and defend my ritual. Shield and protect this Sacred Nemeton, the Holy Mandala consecrated to the Light, the Children of Light, the Ancient and Shinning Ones. Being a Child of Starlight, I stand here to recognize and honor my ancestors and preserve the Elven Ways. May the Universal Spirit burn deep within my spirit.

Take the "pentacle" or "holed-stone" from the altar and go to the north. Trace your "Sign of Earth"* with the tool and see it green. As the portal opens, visualize a Sylvan Tree Elf emerge from the Otherworld (from the north) to join your ritual circle. It does not matter that you must at first envision or imagine these energetic events in your mind's eye. They are present even when we do not see them—just as much as there is electricity in the air and gravity accompanying condensed masses, we do not have to always "see" this unseen power to tap its potential. The energy is summoned in ritual by personally generating a like energy which is projected and will attract and exchange with other similar energies in kind. See the "Sign of Earth" blazing bright as you speak the Earth Key:

Moh-ar Dee-ah-el Heh-keh-teh-gah. Ahd-hoo-ee Glee-im Awe-guhs Foil-chah nah Speer-ohd-dee deh Cah-reeg en-duil-yah Awe-guhs Tah-lave See-uh ar aye-it sho. In the names of the Northern Quadrangle, I call thee spirits and powers of stone, leaf, land and the pentacle, to witness and defend this rite, shield and protect this "Magick Sphere." King and Queen of the Gnomes and Sylves, on this side of the Sacred Circle are you invited.

---

*   A personal symbol, glyph or "*Sign of Portal*" aligned with the element. Examples appear in the forthcoming section in this anthology regarding "Self-Dedication."

Go to the east and trace the "Sign of Air" with the wand, envisioning it yellow or purple. With the Air threshold veil lifted, envision an emergence of a "Sylphen Fey" coming to your circle from the (eastern) Otherworld as you intone the Air Key:

Oh-roh Ee-bah Ah-oh-zodpee. Ahd-hoo-ee Glee-im Awe-guhs Foil-chah nah Speer-ohd-dee deh Spay-er en-ghee-huh Awe-guhs Nay-all See-uh ar aye-it sho. In the names of the Eastern Quadrangle, I call thee spirits and powers of the sky, wind, air and wand. Shield and protect this "Magick Sphere." King and Queen of the Sylphs and Sprytes of the breeze and flowers, on this side of the Sacred Circle are you invited now.

Bring with you to the south your "sword," 'sickle' or 'blade,' and trace your "Sigil of Fire" in the air with the tool, seeing it red. As you open the portal of the south, you see a draconian figure emerge from the Otherworld, coming forth to join your magickal rite as you speak the Fire Key:

Oh-ee-peh Teh-ah-ah Peh-doh-keh. Ah-nahsh Glee-im Awe-gu-hs Foil-chah nah Speer-ohd-dee deh Gree-uhn Awe-guhs chin-nuh See-uh ar aye-it sho. In the names of the Southern Quadrangle, I call thee spirits and powers of the skystar, sun, flame and sword. Shield and protect this "Magick Sphere." King and Queen of the Fire-Drakes and Dragons, on this side of the Sacred Circle are you invited now.

Take the 'cup' to the western direction and use it to trace the "Water Sign' and see it blue. From the west you can imagine merfolk, or 'undine,' appear from the Otherworld mists, as you intone the Water Key:

Em-peh-heh Are-es-el Gah-ee-oh-leh. Ah-neer Glee-im Awe-gu-hs Foil-chah nah Speer-ohd-dee deh Gah-lahk En-oo-esh-ka Awe-guhs mwir-uh See-uh ar aye-it sho. In the names of the Western Quadrangle, I call thee spirits and powers of the moon, sea, water and grail. Shield and protect this "Magick Sphere." King and Queen of the Merfolk of the wave, on this side of the Sacred Circle are you invited now.

Leave each of your representations of the "Gifts of Faeire"—the "Elemental tools"—at their respective directions. After all these "keys" are activated, return to the altar (central workspace) and affirm:

Guh Renv-en en-na Too-huh deh Dahn-non Bahn-ahk-tree or-een. Coseent en Nuh-dee-huh doh are aye-it show. Etz-are-peh. Heh-coh-mah. Nah-en-tah. Bee-toh-em. In the names of Akasha, Nyu, Spirit of the Quintessenal Fifth Element, I call the Spirits of the Tuatha D'Anu, the

Danubian Sidhe, the Ancient and Shinning Ones. High Elves of the Otherworld, shield and protect this "Magick Sphere." Spirits of the Wood Elves, you too are invited to my Circle of Power.

Visualize the boundary of the magic sphere clearly, as it descends into the ground beneath you and into the sky above. See its auric shield as a bright "force field" of light and energy complete with your "Sigils of Elemental Portals" burning brightly in each cardinal direction. Each of the Elementals called to the circle stand guard near their respective seals. Meditate on what is happening and hold the images clearly in your mind. Finally intone:

Elemental Spirits of the Otherworld shield and protect this "Magick Sphere." Be a witness now and co-magician in the magick I summon here in this Sacred Space. Guardians of the Universe, Watchers and Portal Messengers, come now to witness and aid in the celebration of Light and Love enacted here in my ceremony. May the grace and blessing of the Source of All Being and Creation pervade in my spirit forever and always.

The "Circle of Power" or "Nemeton" is now ready for magickal work. Remember to "Extinguish the Powers of the Magick Sphere" before completing your ceremony and departing from your Sacred Space—as given in the next section.

extinguishing the circle of power

In every tradition that casts or summons a "Circle of Power," there is a similar concluding rite where all energies called *in* during the ritual are thanked and dismissed. Elemental energies used for crafting or casting the "Circle of Power" must be extinguished too. This is an important formality maintained by Elvish Wizards and Druids. Without a ceremonial manner of etiquette for opening a circle so closed, there is nothing to distinguish the Sacred Space or *Nemeton* from the ordinary surrounding space. The "Magick Sphere" exists as a psychological and spiritual thought-formed boundary to confine and focus the energy channeled by the Wizard. It has a second purpose—as a "Circle of Protection" for Wizards when they are channeling raw energy currents. And finally, it represents a fractal reality, as discussed previously.

To open a circle sealed by magick—or otherwise extinguish the powers of the circle so cast—move around the boundary of the circle counter-clockwise, thanking and dismissing the Elementals while retrieving the tools left there. If you have traced any sigils, lore suggests that you retrace them in reverse—"erasing" them and closing the portals that they access—even if they are "only" mental doorways for a novice—you usually don't want to leave these "open."

If you began (or oriented) your *Nemeton* to the north (Earth Element), then you will want to finish there—so begin in the west. If you started in the east, begin extinguishing in the north—always working backwards, counter-clockwise ("*tuathal*") when opening the circle at the end of a rite. Use the following formal incantations in the order most appropriate to your needs.

> WEST: *Slahn Ah-we-leh Speer-ohd-dee deh Gah-lahk En-oo-eesh-kah Awe-guhs Mwir-uh. Guh-rehv Mee-luh mah Ah-guhv. Depart in peace Western spirits of moon, sea, water and grail. May the energies of the Water Element return to your place of dwelling until you are again called.*

> SOUTH: *Slahn Ah-we-leh Speer-ohd-dee deh Ghree-uhn Awe-guhs Chin-Nuh. Guh rehv Mee-luh mah Ah-guhv. Depart in peace Southern spirits of skystar, flame, sun and blade. May the energies of the Fire Element return to your place of dwelling until you are again called.*

EAST: *Slahn Ah-we-leh Speer-ohd-dee deh Spay-ir En-ghee-huh Awe-guhs Nay-ahl. Guh rehv Mee-luh mah Ah-guhv. Depart in peace Eastern spirits of sky, wind, air and wand. May the energies of the Air Element return to your place of dwelling until you are again called.*

NORTH: *Slahn Ah-we-leh Speer-ohd-dee deh Cah-reeg En-duil-yuh Awe-guhs Taw-luhv. Guh rehv Mee-luh mah Ah-guhv. Depart in peace Northern spirits of leaf, land, stone and pentacle. May the energies of the Earth Element return to your place of dwelling until you are again called.*

When the final ritual tools are retrieved, bring them back to your central working space and address the Universe with:

Slahn Ah-we-luh En-too-huh deh Dahn-non Awe-guhs. Guh rehv Mee-luh mah Ah-guhv. Skee-uh deh Dree-uckt Show. Many thanks and blessings to the spirits who have gathered here. Depart in peace spirits of the Tuatha D'Anu, Wood Elves, Sidhe, and all Ancient and Shinning Ones who have blessed me with your mystical presence. Return to the Sidhe Hills and Faerie Dwellings until you are again called forth. May the grace of the rays of the Source of All Being and Creation go with all who have come to join in this magickal work. I depart in peace to my place of dwelling until I return here again in magick's hour. The Magick Sphere stands open now, but is never broken. Awen (Ah-oo-een).

With these last words, the energies of the circle itself are extinguished. You may raise your arms and see the bluish-white energy of the "magick sphere" burn brightly—and then as you quickly lower your arms, see these energies of the *Nemeton* ground and fade.

consecrating the symbols of power or "gifts of faeire"

This rite may be used for "charging" or "consecrating" ritual tools—particularly "Elemental tools" representing the *"Gifts of Faeire."* It may also be used to ceremonially charge amulets and talismans for other magical purposes. Essentially, all implements or "tools" of magic must be consecrated—dedicated and "charged" for "magickal" purposes—prior to incorporation into ritual and ceremony. Otherwise they are simply mundane objects. A "Magickal tool" is so considered because a Wizard is able to use it to connect to the energy that the tool represents—or is a catalyst for. Remember: *like forces attract like forces* in magic.

CONSECRATING THE SYMBOLS OF POWER

Conjure your "Circle of Power"—then say:

> *May peace and love fill my spirit so I may be a beacon of light and life projecting such energy outward in all directions of the Universe. May the Ancient and Shinning Ones hear my call. I ask the spirits of the Earth who are friendly to the Elven Ways to join me in consecrating this sacred icon to thy tradition. Come now and bless this [name(s) of talisman(s) to be consecrated], so that you will more easily recognize it when I present it to you in the future.*

You will need your item(s) available when you conduct the ritual. This simplified rite should be used only for "Elemental tools" or if not, an item that is used for more than a single-use "spell." For example, you might charge a runic pendant to attract love energy into your life, but Elven Wizardry is not used to gain the specific love of so-and-so, such as you might find in a targeted love-spell. True "Elvish Magick" is timeless and not restricted to a specific event or person (usually) and therefore the construction of general talismans that attract love would are more appropriate for this rite than a "love spell." Other examples may just as easily be applied here.

When the tool is "ready"—assuming it was just constructed—say:

> *Hail to the Sidhe, the High Ones, and to the Sylvanus, the Sylphs and Sylves and the Wood Elves themselves. Hail to the Lords and Ladies of the Land, Sky, and Sea. Greetings to all Creatures of Faerie—all ye welcomed here. Mark well what you witnessed this day/eve and remember.*

May the Eternal Source of Everpresent Light, look favorably on the magick I conceive.

In order for this consecration to be effective, you must charge the item with your intentions. This requires some proficiency in the ability of energy channeling. For those eyes falling upon this with no prior experience, you are bidden by these words read here now—to never misuse what is discovered in our grimoires of rites and secret spells. By *this oath* between us I will offer the clue needed to make this work...

In this practice of magic, you need to feel (and "see") your thought-form, goal or Elemental current clearly outside of yourself. Breathe this energy—or aetheric matter—in and feel it completely wash through your body as you absorb it through your every pore. Feel it run through your entire circulatory system. You are Assimilating this energy in total—so it had better be 'positive' or for your 'highest good'—and focus it on your arms and hands; project it from within and release (or push) it into the 'item'.

Take your "symbol of power" to the north with the "bowl of salt." Set the bowl on the "pentacle"—or Earth-stone (unless you are consecrating your Earth-tool for the first time, then the ground will work) and set the item in the bowl of salt and/or sprinkling some of the salt on it saying:

Look here and witness ye Spirits of the North. By sprinkling this [n.] with the Salt of the Earth do I consecrate it by the names and Seals of the Earth Element.

Take your "symbol of power" to the southeast, bringing your "incense burner" with, and if there is not already sufficient smoke, add more incense resin. For this rite you will want to select an essence to burn that correlates with the talisman or purpose of the rite. Pass it through the smoke and say:

Look here and witness ye Spirits of the East and South. I pass this [n.] through burning herbal resins that waft through the air. In doing so I now consecrate it by the ancient names and seals of the elements Air and Fire.

Continue your clockwise movement to the western direction, and use your "bowl of water"—or *'sacred vessel'*—to sprinkle some of the water onto the "symbol of power" saying:

Look here and witness ye Spirits of the West. I pass this [n.] through your realm by sprinkling it with your water of life and renewal. By the secret names of the Sea do I consecrate this symbol as witnessed by the Water Element.

If consecrating symbols representing "Gifts of Faeire" using this rite, it is customary to call on—and charge the tool—with energies appropriate to the original *Tuatha d'Anu* artifacts. ["Faeire" is an archaic spelling, applied here just as in the original handwritten manuscript.]

"THE GIFTS OF FAEIRE"

- Stone of Fal—North/Earth, Master Morfessas
- Spear of Lugh—East/Air, Master Esras
- Sword of Nuada—South/Fire, Master Uscias
- Cauldron of Dagda—West/Water, Master Semias

An 'item' is ritually consecrated prior to its use (or ritual application) as a sacred tool—but, there is no strict arcane dogma concerning how long tools will hold a charge—or how a blatant recharge is necessary, if at all. Items will also take on a charge 'naturally' over time with regular use as focal instruments. Gems and metal objects tend to hold a charge longest; followed by wood; then liquid.

the basic rites of faerie-calling

The "Children of Faerie" do not submit themselves to the will of Wizards like those spirits conjured and encountered from medieval grimoires—which are in actuality thought-formed ancestral and cosmic extensions of ourselves and our own consciousness as One with the ALL. "Children of Faerie" will certainly not so easily cater to Human whims. Thus, there is no ritual or ceremony that will ensure "conjuration" of the "Elven-Ffayrie" beings.

However, various methods are hidden in esoteric lore of Druidism and surviving remnants of those teachings of the Elven Wizards and Mystics once restricted to initiates of the "Ancient Mystery School." Therefore, what we may include here are "suggestions" to entice, gain favor or otherwise develop working relationships with nature-bound spirits. This is a prerequisite for any ceremonial or "at will" contact in Elven Wizard traditions. Of course, magical work of this nature will require access to the physical "Green World"—where you believe "nature spirits" reside. You need not even bother with this in a purely urban setting where you are almost guaranteed to find disappointment.

Once initial contact is made, initiating it in the future is increasingly easier—and more innate—with each success. When a relationship has commenced, be sure to ask the spirit(s) their names (and signs) and their preferred method of future contact. This is the only manner by which Fey-Touched Humans become privy to a true mystical apprenticeship with the Elven-Ffayrie far surpassing what has been considered "acceptable" by *them* for me to print in this tome.

I am permitted only inclusion lore that will be used by *them* to test *you* as a potential initiate. We should expect that they will certainly screen potential "Elf-Friends" and "Ffayrie-Allies." So as to safeguard our own existent Oaths, the *Elvenomicon* series is prepared as an objective mystical guide—relaying to potential initiates Nature's own "recruiting manual" for an awakening available to those truly enlightened folk that have not fully invalidated and forgotten who they are in a world of depersonalization and disenchantment.

If you are reading these words in the dark half of the year, you may still have time to prepare an initial rite of contact on a forthcoming Beltane or Midsummer. For this you will need a "Silver Wand"—an apple-wood wand with three silver bells hanging from white ribbon.

It should be consecrated prior to this rite. Use this wand to conjure your circle. Then, starting in the northeast, sprinkle "Primrose flower petals"—moving *deosil* around the boundary of your circle, As you say:

> *Under stone, under sea, under every blade of grass. In the winds, in the flames, in the circle that I cast. Elf and Ffayrie, come to me. Grant me favor and be blest.*

Ignite your incense coals in your sand-filled "cauldron" or "burner" at the south-west. Heap on some incense—an herb-and-twig mixture followed by sweet-smelling resins—and feel the smoke radiating from your "Magick Sphere" and into the Otherworld dimension, acting as a beacon to your call:

> *I have studied the way of Sidhe. I shall awaken every tree. I have called to share my home, with Undina, Sylpha, Elf and Gnome. I emerge from a world of mortal strife, here to partake in Faerie life.*

Prepare three small "shot glasses" in the northwest with "elderberry wine" or "milk and honey." Set out 'sweetbreads' or "cookies" alongside this. Then, take up your "bowl of salt"; sprinkle a circular boundary around the food offering as you speak:

> *Gifts of Faeire granted me, Elemental tools here on display. Now a gift I give to thee, to ignite a bond 'tween you and me. Overnight I'll leave this food, in hopes we'll meet here some day.*

Remains of the food may be removed the next day. Essences of the offering will already have been taken—or not. The physical food itself may or may not. "Nature spirits" also send their animal allies to feast on the physical foodstuff once they have accepted the sentiment of the gift.

Typically, Elvish Wizards will make regular food offerings to the Otherworld Fey—and a particular location at regular intervals. "Circles of Power" for the sole intention of calling the Elven-Ffayrie spirits may be consecrated or conjured differently. Elemental callings may even be modified to meet the needs of contacting members of the Sylvanus Folk—those maintain their own Elemental hierarchy.

The following are the suggestions listed in the original Elven-Faerie Grimoire:

SYLVANUS CORRESPONDENCES

EAST : Air Element—"Tree Elves"

SOUTH : Fire Element—"Sprytes"

WEST : Water Element—"Mushroom Fey"

NORTH : Earth Element—"Woodland Gnomes"

ELF-KING : "Lord Oberon" (Auberon)

FAERIE-QUEEN : "Lady Titania"

In your woodland travels or spiritual walks in the forests, valleys and mountain ranges throughout the Middle World, you may very well find something in Nature that your inner voice tells you is a gateway threshold to the Otherworld. At these places you can conjure a circle for the purposes of Faerie-calling but be advised: do not disturb the physical environment; do not make a lot of noise; and keep ritual incantations to a minimal and lighthearted—which is why many of those included in this book seem so whimsical. Keep them directed specifically toward "nature spirits." You might speak something like:

I am a spirit of peace. Let peace ring throughout the entire Universe. May my energy and vibration be that only of peace, love and harmony that I extend to the Creatures of Elphame. Know that I [your magickal name] come to you in admiration and respect. I seek contact and initiation to your Otherworld, in grace and goodness. I shall not disturb, trespass or break the solemn vows shared between us. I seek to be your companion and will adhere to the boundaries of that friendship. By the grace of the All-Source, please come forth and make thyself known.

Elven-Ffayrie lore suggests that animals as messengers of the Otherworld. Some are considered "more sacred" or more iconic to specific aspects of the tradition than others—but *all* woodland, marine and flying creatures are sacred as representing interconnection of All life as "One" in the Universe with ALL life—meaning that all life is one and equal at the Source of All Being. Animals maintain a role, almost as if ambassadors, negotiators or again, "messengers" between the "World of Men" and the "World of Nature"—or the physical visible world and the unseen Otherworld. As a general species the Humans have not treated their stewardship of Earth with due respect—nor is it it shown to our animal brethren as it should be. Working with animals in both the physical world and in the spirit realm (or astral) may even grant favorable attitudes toward you from the fey.

introduction to elven-faerie spells

Elven Wizards and Druids create their own unique 'prayers', which others might just as easily call "spells"—and still there are others that refer to it as "creative visualization therapy." Our minds, the *Self* and its interconnection to the All, may be described in various ways, names and traditions. We are most concerned with techniques that do yield results—regardless of various methodologies and semantics applied to the same use of "Cosmic Law" for thousands of years.

"Elven-Faerie Spells" may be created by an individual for any particular need or occasion. Remember: "magick" to Elves is a creative art—one that the Masters take great pride in. In order to "write your own magick," however, you should be acquainted and proficient with traditional rites and the rules of spellcraft.*

A "spell" is a small act or short magickal working performed in a "Circle of Power" in order to bring about a desired result or movement of energy toward a certain direction. This does not necessarily occur immediately; it may take days, weeks, months and even years (in some instances) to manifest—depending on the situation.

Most common uses of "Faerie Spellcraft" include protection, fertility and abundance, prosperity and wealth, and the banishment of negativity and/or warding away of unwanted energy. There are many other uses of magick—such as the ever popular "single use love spell," which is not dealt with in this tradition of magick. According to lore, the most popular days for magical work in the Elven tradition are "Elf Day" or "Tree Day" (*Tuesday*) and "Fey Day" (*Saturday*).

Every day is *magical*. Each of the planet-oriented days of the week represent attributes connected to a "ray" of the "Elven Star"—which allows us to glean the Sevenfold Schema of the original source tradition in the *Ancient Near East*. Note here: there are seven days—thus seven colors, seven notes of music and naturally seven (6+1) points on the "Elven Star" are all correlated within the paradigm of Elven Tradition.

SEVENFOLD SCHEMA (or ELVEN STAR)

MONDAY: Moonday; blue; "G" note; pearl stone; silver.

TUESDAY: Elf Day/Tree Day; red; "C"; ruby; iron.

---

* Additional details are given in later sections of this anthology volume.

WEDNESDAY: Woden's Day; orange; "D"; opal; mercury.

THURSDAY: Thor's Day; indigo; "A"; sapphire; tin.

FRIDAY: Freya's Day; green; "F"; emerald; copper.

SATURDAY: Fey Day; violet; "B"; onyx; lead.

SUNDAY: Sun Day; yellow; "E"; diamond; gold.

Herbs sometimes appear in lore as "Elf Amulets." Acorns aid in fertility rites—and those found by moonlight are symbols of prosperity and abundance. Acorns are essentially the fruit and seed of the oak tree and carry a history of traditional use for fertility, love, and protective spells and charms. They should, unless otherwise advised, always be gathered in daylight hours, preferably at noon. Keep your chosen intention for the amulet in the mind while collecting them.

In ceremonial magick, wands made from oak are often capped with a large acorn tip. Cones (pine, &tc.) may also be used for this—making excellent tools of growth magic.

In divination for "love," a couple may each drop an acorn in still water and watch to see how they respond to each other.

In a spell to encourage a friend to initiate a romantic interest, seven acorns are placed on a small square of white cloth and tied up with a red cord or ribbon to form an "amulet bag." After sleeping with it under their pillow for three consecutive nights, it is buried beneath a rose bush and then the person calls out for the other to come. The acorn is also a nut-food or it may be crushed into "oak flour."

Apple-seeds are natural items of love-drawing magic—though also poisonous in large quantities. The common apple tree is actually a hybrid effort—the result of years of crossbreeding to bring us the familiar fruit we know today. The original apple species—the crab apple (*malus hupehensis*)—produces much smaller fruits, resembling cherries. The *Rosaceae* family of apples is shared by over 3,000 different species, including the ash, bay/laurel, cherry, hawthorn, peach and plum trees. In Druid folklore, apple is also associated with *Queris* or *Quert Ogham* and is the traditional wood of love magick.

Most Celtic scholars associate apples with the Isle of Avalon, called "*Emain Ablach*," which some also interpret as "Isle of Glass." In fact "*Affalon*" may be a mutation of "Appleland"—perhaps an ancient orchard or grove. One famous magical tool in lore—referred to previously—the Celtic shaman's wand, called the *"craebh ciuil"* or "Silver Branch," was fashioned from apple-wood. The fruit is also sacred to Mystics because it bares the image of a pentagram when cut at its midsection, and is particularly significant to the harvest—the festivals of Lughnassadh and the autumn equinox. In ancient times, the harvest traditionally began with a toast of cider. At Yule, apple-wine *"wassail"* is used ceremonially for tree blessing. Apples are found in natural healing remedies for anemia and are good sources of Vitamins A and E, which may assist purifying from toxins and lowering blood pressure.

According to faerie lore, bay leaves ward away the enchantments, spells and glamour of others when placed under the tongue. Pinecones—when found by moonlight—are symbols of good fortune, health and well-being. Perhaps the most famous herbal 'Elf-Amulet' is the *"trefoil," "trifolium," "shamrock"* or *"clover"* that is so commonly identified as a symbol of luck—or to ward away warfare. All herbs require cutting or removal from the land, so it is customary to "ask the plant's permission" in order to officiate an understanding that a spiritual intelligence exists within all life. A common incantation of the "magical herbalist" is:

> *"With this strike may you grow stronger."*

"Magical herbalists" have also designated specific herbs that are held particularly sacred in Elven-Ffayrie Magickal Tradition. These include: dandelion root; chamomile; mistletoe; elder flow'r; hops; Irish moss; rosemary; rose-hips; raspberry leaf; mint; mullien; skullcap; and slippery elm bark. These may be used by themselves or in conjunction with each other for attracting the attention of "Otherworldly folk" in ritual as well as mixed with black tea and drank as an infusion. They calming herbs—and they may aid one in attuning to the energies of the "Green World" and "Faerielands."

To protect a home, an Elvish shaman might use sage and fern to clear out negative energy. Personal sigils of protection could be traced on the four outer walls to conjure a "magick shield." One might use the "Elf-Sign" (star) or a protective 'rune', 'Ogham' —even the "Dragon's Eye"—will generally suffice for banishing and warding against "typical" types of unfriendly (or malignant) energy. A traditional Gaelic-Welsh incantation for this purpose is:

> *Cosaint agus beanachtai yn n'Deith do talamh seo. Dibir na ole agus dona.*

Ask the aid of "helpful" Elementals. Decide and fix on a target or energy current (or ray) that you wish to block. Envision a representation of the unwanted energy or current and feel that it is the embodiment of what are you are warding away. See the auric energy projected from it/them as being blocked or shielded—as if encased in a bubble—which dissolves into nothingness as you say:

I command you, by the names and letters of the Most High, to depart in peace!

Keys to effective spellcraft are: clarity of intention; the ability to raise internal energy and merge it with assisting external ones; visualization of desired goals clearly; and the willpower to properly release energy so summoned from within and without. The keys—in this order—form the fundamental steps taken in all practices of "spellcraft." The following are some additional tips to aid your faerie spell-weaving:

—Incorporate only tools and items of a "like energy" to that which you wish to connect with. All others are distractions.

—Visualization skills make-or-break your mystical prowess of directing energy with the Mind, according to Cosmic Law.

—Only call forth or summon spirits and energies specific to your purpose; and only those that accelerate your cause.

—Ask the "Universe" (and/or "spirit guides") to assist carrying ("channeling") or directing release of energies via the appropriate channels.

—Do not dwell on a ritual working already performed, or on what the nature of the results will be, for at least three days afterward. This keeps any energy used for that ritual-spell "out there" "working for you" and not contained or restricted to the vicinity of your thoughts locally.

—Most importantly, it is essential that you believe in your abilities. Remember the ancient proverb that: *all intentional Self-determined acts are magical.*

the elven wizardry of healing and protection

Consecrate a "Circle of Power" in a place receiving blessing, protection and/or healing. Set out your ceremonial tools—or representations of the "Gifts of Faeire"—in their correlating directions. Enter the circle from the northeast by procession if there are multiple practitioners. Go to the center of your workspace unless you are working in a group that allows for using "Elemental Stations." Light a white candle and say:

"May there be peace within my being."

Each participant should do the same. You can then proceed to address each of the directions from the center (altar)—or if performed in a group, other participants may be stationed at each Elemental "quarter."

NORTH: *May peace ring out and extend across northern expansions.*

EAST: *May peace ring out in the east and extend across the furthest plains.*

SOUTH: *May peace ring out in the south and extend to the peaks of the tallest mountains.*

WEST: *May peace ring out in the west and extend to the depths of the deepest sea.*

Light more white candles—as well as a blue and a red one if this rite is for "healing." You may even state affirmations as you light them, before continuing with the rite.

NORTH: *May peace, love and harmony extend to every living being and space in the Universe, especially [name of what/who is to be blessed/protected/healed]. Great Bear of the North, I call now on your strength and the wisdom of the Earth Element. Offer your blessing towards me and extend your protective/healing power on [n].*

EAST: *May the purity of the Air Element enrich all work performed here. May the Winds aid me in purifying the energies of [n]. Hawk of the Eastern Dawn, I call now on your agility and the wisdom of the Sky Element. Offer your blessing toward me and extend your protective/healing power towards [n].*

SOUTH: *May the purifying flame purge and annihilate that which is unclean, especially in this place/for [n]. Great Stag of Southern Flame, I call on your virility and the wisdom of the Fire Element. Offer your blessing toward me and extend your protective/healing power towards [n].*

WEST: *May the blessing of the purifying and healing powers of the transforming waters be upon me in the work that I do towards [n]. Wise Salmon of the Western Sea, I call upon thy True Knowledge and the wisdom of the Water Element. Offer your blessing toward me and extend your protective/ healing power towards [n].*

Return to the center of your workspace and recite the "Elvish Wizard's Benediction"—or the "Gorsedd Prayer" of Druidism. You may use a version from some other ceremonial source or the more commonly known one, provided here:

Dyro, Dduw, dy naw erth, deall Ae yn heal gybod; Ae yng n gwybod, gwybod y cyfiawn; Ae yng ngwybod y cyfiawn; Eigarn Ac a garu, caru pobhanfod; Ac ym mhob hanfod caru Duw. Duw a phob dai oni.

Grant us O God, thy protection; and in protection, strength; and in strength understanding; and in understanding, perception; and in perception, the perception of righteousness; and in the perception of righteousness, the love of it; and in the love of it, the love of all life; and in the love of all life, the love of God and all goodness. May the Source of All Being and Creation extend currents/rays to protect/heal this place/person.

Bless the "target" with "saltwater" and "burning incense." A "smudge-stick" of sage, reed or fern might also be used. Bless the "bowl of water" and sprinkle it on the person and around the person, or in each room of the house and around the outside of the property. With the "salt-water," say at each point:

By the Elemental Powers of Earth and Water do I so cleanse and consecrate [n].

With the incense, at each point:

By the Elemental Powers of Flame and Wind do I so purify and bless [n].

Returning to the center of the circle, complete this portion of the rite by saying:

> *May there be peace [in this home/at this place/with this person]. May it/they absorb the protection/healing channeled to this space "now made sacred"* [or if at the Grove, *"most sacred"*].

If there is a faerie-shaman or Druid present, they may wish to seek the nature of an ailment of a person—or the energetic disturbance of an area—by communicating with Otherworld "shadows," "spirit guides" or other kind of energy work that allows for astral communication. Supplemental healing and protection spells may be performed here. Once the ceremonial goals are satisfied, thank the powers and extinguish the energies of the "Magick Sphere."

elven way: self-dedication rite

Regardless of whether or not you formally decide to join (or develop) a "coven," "circle" or "grove" of the Elven Tradition —whatever name you use to call such a close-knit magical group—you will first need to perform a personal "Self-Dedication" rite to the Elven Way.

Dedication rites are traditionally different from "initiations," because a dedication rite is performed in solitary—while alone in the woods or wilderness. This ceremony is not necessarily a "magickal spell" in the traditional sense—it is a personal "Rite of Passage" observed much like the "seasonal celebrations" of the "Wheel of the Year."

The Self-Dedication Ceremony is a form of psychological magic—it effectively changes an internal set or mode of thinking that determines our perspective in life. One such premise for a true Self-Dedication Ceremony: the Elven Wizard—or Elvish Wizard-*to-be*—has just discovered some strange arcane tome, such as the one you currently hold, and realizes —or awakens to a realization—that either they personally share the Elven-Faerie-Dragon legacy themselves, or for some "unknown" reason, they feel a peculiar inclination to these mysteries, innately drawn to the path via self-initiation.

Although this rite did not appear at the beginning of the original "Elven-Faerie Grimoire"—which the current author has made every effort to relay here in proper tribute—it would be logical that this is among the first, if not *the first*, ceremonial observation made by a practicing Seeker (since it may be performed without 'tools').

Focused concentration, meditation and self-dedication rites performed in Nature may aid in bridging a relationship with the natural, spiritual, or otherwise "metaphysical" side of Reality. All skill and ability is accumulated over time as a result of consistent growth of this relationship, which breaks down the artificial barriers of fragmented separation between the *Self* and the *Cosmos*—what is considered "Magical Authority" or "Power," but which is really derived from the ability to operate the *Self* in perfect clarity—or what we call "*Self-Honesty.*"

Conjure the "Magick Sphere"—or *Nemeton*—in a manner that you have practiced—even if you have only envisioned doing so in your mind, as you read this "grimoire," which is a form of magic in itself when energy is properly directed. This time, as you move about to trace the boundary of the circle, by hand (or wand), you will set out an "Elemental Candle" at each cardinal direction—a common practice in all forms of Elemental Magick and Wizardry. Choose one of an appropriate Elemental color for each direction. Wait until you address each Element during the Self-Dedication Rite to light the candles. Use incantations from the "Casting the Circle of Power" section of this grimoire only after performing a "self-dedication."

Once the area is deemed "Sacred Space," go to the center of the circle —you do not need an "altar" for this rite—and stand or kneel, facing north, saying:

> *In my mortal form I am known as [given name] but today/tonight I come to you in my Elven-Ffayrie form with the name [a chosen magical name]. I come to you now, Spirits of the Universe as an "Elf-Child" ["Fae-Child" (female); and "Elf-Friend" for mortal practitioners who are not certain they personally represent the Elven-Faerie legacy.]*

Take a "bowl of salt" and remove a pinch, placing it on your tongue. Feel the salt of the Earth entering your bloodstream and becoming a part of your entire body as you say:

> *I am a child of Earth. I am a child of the stars. I have studied on my own in preparation, but now I seek the Spirits of Nature to be my teacher, to instructor me in the true sciences of the Cosmos. Hidden in your folds lies the answers of Creation and Life. We are one. I am one with the entire Universe. I seek to share a relationship with thee.*

Stand and move to the north, light a "green candle," saying:

> *Spirits of the Enchanted Forest, of plants and rocks and trees, awaken and know me [magical name]. I come with peace within, seeking your aid in learning thy mysteries. I vow to ever uphold thy secrets, walking the path of wisdom and enlightenment. I present myself to this magic circle as a follower of the Elven Ways.*

Trace a seal or symbol of the Earth Element that you will use regularly in your rites to incite energetic activity of the Elements.

Examples shown here are based on the traditional Druidic interpretation of Elemental Magick. Envision the "Sign of Earth" as green in color, as you intone:

> *By this Sign shall we know each other.*

Go to the east; while lighting the "yellow candle," say:

> *Spirits of the Enchanted Breeze, of winds and sky and Air, awaken and know me [magical name]. I come with peace within, seeking your aid in learning thy mysteries. I vow to ever uphold thy secrets, walking the path of wisdom and enlightenment. I present myself to this magic circle as a follower of the Elven Ways.*

Trace your "Sigil of Air," envisioning it yellow, saying:

> *By this Sign shall we know each other.*

Move to the south and speak the following as you light the "red candle" there:

> *Spirits of the Enchanted Mountain, of sun and star and flame, awaken and know me [magical name]. I come with peace within, seeking your aid in learning thy mysteries. I vow to ever uphold thy secrets, walking the path of wisdom and enlightenment. I present myself to this magic circle as a follower of the Elven Ways.*

Trace your "Fire Sign" and see it red, saying:

> *By this Sign shall we know each other.*

Move to address the west, light the "blue candle" and say:

> *Spirits of the Enchanted Sea, of waves and lakes and rain, awaken and know me [magickal name]. I come with peace within, seeking your aid in learning thy mysteries. I vow to ever uphold thy secrets, walking the path of wisdom and enlightenment. I am a follower of the Elven Way*

Trace your "Seal of Water" in blue as you intone:

> *By this Sign shall we know each other.*

Return to the center and take some anointing oil—a type of your personal choosing. Spiritual traditions teach to "anoint" with oil from the feet to the head (upward)—and bless (wash) from head to foot (downward). Anoint your feet and say:

> *Blessed be the feet that bring me here this day/night and enable me to touch the ground, to walk the path of the Ancients, treading the 'Right Way' always, never deviating from the path of enlightenment and wisdom.*

Anoint your knees, saying:

Blessed be the knees that bend to give reverence to the Higher Power of the Universe, to the Source of All Being in the Cosmos that gives me the strength to move forth on the path of light and the ability to make or break my stride.

Anoint the palms of your hands and say:

Blessed be the hands that lift in praise of the Universe and all Life. They are my commanding hands I raise in power and I acknowledge their ability to direct my will, as they are extensions of my active mind.

Anoint the heart—left breast—saying:

Blessed be the flame that burns within my heart, that I may know the True Love of the Universe and in so doing, that I may recognize the Right Way by what I feel deeply burning in my very spirit.

Anoint the lips and say:

Blessed be the lips that speak the sacred words of incantation. May the words they speak only advance my evolution further and never idle or in vain. From my mouth, I utter the words of power and share in the breath of the All, yet remaining silent to non-believers.

Finally, speak the following as you anoint your forehead:

Blessed be the mind that seeks to understand its own nature and connection to the true Self, that allows me the ability to seek true knowledge and guidance from my true Self into this body, which is at one with my mind. Let my thoughts be pure and only of a nature that will contribute positively to my Ascension.

Elven Wizards and Mystics often consecrate a personal item, emblem or artifact—like a pendant or necklace—which is later worn as a symbol of dedication to the Elven Way. Hold up your talisman saying:

May the Spirits of Nature and the Universe beyond, see and bless this symbol of my dedication—recognizing it and me in our future exchanges.

Thank the energies called to the rite and extinguish the circle, completing the ceremony.

elven-faerie circle-initiation rite

"Sylvan Magick" is mainly related to trees and so groups of practitioners coming together to learn and practice the Elven Way will often call themselves a "grove" instead of a "coven." Magick may certainly be performed solitary, but 'circle magic' or 'group magick' generally requires a minimum of three people—one to represent each of the most basic Elemental Stations: Land, Sky and Sea. Traditional 'Elemental schema' run as high as nine different "*duile*" or Elemental aspects that participants may occupy as 'Stations' without dividing the system further. Larger groups may designate tree or "Ogham" names for a larger 'outer circle' of practitioners if necessary.

A "coven" or "grove" logically begins with members initiating each other. But this doesn't always make much sense at the initial inception of a group. In the past, the leader of a coven was so by her status; a leader of a grove or Arch Druid might be elected by a council. These High Priests and Priestesses are not "initiated" into their positions; they are "installed" into the group by other initiated members.

It is difficult in modern times to actually find a group using an authentic Elven-Faerie Tradition that is not diluted by the general pop-culture interpretations of Western Magickal Tradition. This is not surprising due to lack of true mainstream Elven-Faerie lore to draw such practices, especially those not restricted to a specific lineage or family tradition. With a rising underground popularity of the *Elvenomicon* series, this may change in the future.

This following rite was adopted in 1998 by the "*Elven Fellowship Circle of Magick.*" The area of initiation should be an outdoor *Nemeton*. Choose a place where the group can meet repeatedly and form a connection with this terrain over time. This place must allow for an absence of worldly distraction and the ability to practice rituals without the unnerving discovery from disruptive onlookers. Construct a *Nemeton* of stones, being sure the diameter is large enough for all participants. A group of three can often use a circle nine feet in diameter. Do not overlook the significance of the "Megalithic Yard" when constructing these henges. A single unit (1-MY) is equivalent to 2.72 feet, making appropriate ceremonial sites approximately 8.16 or 10.88 feet in diameter by this rule. Be creative.

A "Magician/Sponsor" leads a blindfolded "Initiate" to the northeast corner of the *Nemeton*, where the Leader—a group founder or other "ceremonial magician" hereafter referred to as the "Guardian of the Grove"—greets them. The "Guardian" stands in wait at the northeast threshold, holding a sword.

GUARDIAN OF THE GROVE: *Who is it there that you bring here to the very Gates of this sphere most sacred and secret?*

MAGICIAN/SPONSOR: *A child of Earth and Star seeking entrance—to be set on the path of our mysteries.*

GUARDIAN: *Do you then present this person to the Grove, vouching before us for their conduct and their dedication to our circle and the Elven Ways?*

SPONSOR: *I do. I sponsor this child of Earth and Star, and must take responsibility for them now . They remain in a state of darkness—blinded to the mysteries of our Nemeton.*

GUARDIAN: *Then, as Guardian of this Gateway, I open the Portal to our Sphere—but it is never broken. You may enter this time by the Unspeakable Password.*

The "Magician/Sponsor" guides the "Initiate" to the center of the circle, where they are set before the existing membership of the Grove.

GUARDIAN: *Answer, Initiate. Do you seek entrance into the mysteries of the "Elven Fellowship Circle of Magick"* [or another name for your personal group]?

INITIATE: *I do.*

GUARDIAN: *Answer, Initiate. Do you come here of your own free will, free from the pressures of peers or others and free of ulterior motives?*

INITIATE: *I do.*

GUARDIAN: *And finally, answer, again: Are you willing to swear an oath to the secrecy by the ancient covenant of the Mystic Wizards of the Earth now raised before you, and this Council, and the spirits we have called to our nemeton?*

INITIATE: *I do.*

GUARDIAN: *Kneel and submit yourself to this Elven Druid Council.*

The "Initiate" kneels and the "Guardian of the Grove" begins to encircle them in *deosil* rotation—drawing up the primal energies of the Earth planet.

> GUARDIAN: *You are now entering deep woods, the Enchanted World of the Elven-Faerie unsolicited. You step foot on the ground held most sacred to the Keepers of the Earth that maintain and celebrate the ancient Ways. Under penalty of death, no mortal shall step foot on our court unbidden, and thus you now render yourself to the mercy of the Court. You enter a place that is not a place in a time apart from time and still you are here. Fear has no place in our world—here in the Otherworld—and it is our will that you should perish from the spear-blades and arrowheads aimed at you by our Elven military as a sentence for such blasphemy. If you bring mortal fear in your heart to our world, you will undoubtedly summon your demise. How do you enter our world, Initiate?*

> INITIATE: *With perfect love and perfect trust.*

> GUARDIAN: *I ask the Sponsor: has this Initiate been properly prepared? Has s/he completed their Self-Dedication to the Elven Way? Is the Initiate recognized by the Elemental Portal Guardians of the Watchtowers?*

> SPONSOR: *They are prepared. They are dedicated. They are recognized by the Elemental Realms.*

> GUARDIAN: *We shall find out. May the Source of All Being and Creation grant us protection; and in protection, strength; and in strength, peace; and in peace, understanding; and in understanding, knowledge; and in knowledge, wisdom; and in wisdom, love; and in love, the love of all things; and in the love of all things, the love of the Universe.*

The "Sponsor" summons the "Initiate" up from their knees, guiding them on a cross-quarter Elemental journey before returning the center again. In ancient times, this would have been conducted in a cave or underground labyrinth. This text is read as the "Sponsor" guides them first to the south, as the "Guardian" reads from the center of the circle:

> *In the beginning was the infinite void of Nothing, a canvas with no form, a screen without picture. But then came Light, the Dragon, the Cosmic Law, that which gave all existence its form, waves of potentiality sprawling across the matrix-fabric of the Universe.*

The "Initiate" is brought to the east:

When the fires of life burned down to glowing embers, they breathed into existence the Air, the element of knowledge, and the Elven-Ffayrie spirits of the trees and breeze.

Across to the west:

More and more tangible did the formless Spirit of Light become, when the Waters emerged, ripples sent out to every corner of all encompassing sea. But the currents of energy chased one another and became even more solid.

And, around to the north:

The Formless Fire gave birth to Air; the gaseous Air gave way to water. The sea would yield finally to the land, to the Element of Earth, a powerfully strong and stable foundation to hold up the less tangible manifestations. This Earth is the planetary spirit of G'ea and She has had 'Keepers' and 'Guardians' at all times and places to maintain the balance of the Elemental World and thwart all that would cause disharmony on Earth.

Returning to the center:

As you have come to us in the darkness of ignorance, know that we are the 'Keepers of the Earth,' the 'Guardians of the Green World' and 'Scions of the Secret Knowledge' from the ancients. As you emerge, reborn into a realm of Light and enchantment, your existing name is no longer appropriate and is retired at the boundary of the Sacred Grove. We shall know you as [circle name for the Initiate]. Welcome Elf/Ffayrie Child, Lord/Lady [n].

The blindfold is removed. Existing members come forth and greet the Initiate, followed by a celebration in their honor.

eisteddfodd festival liturgy

The *Nemeton* may be conjured by means already suggested, an astral version thereof, a mixture of "Casting" and "Group Liturgies," or simply by using this rite alone. Some incantations used in solitary Ritual Magic are not necessary to observe seasonal *Alardana* celebrations or "rites of passage."

The liturgy presented here is named for a gathering of Welsh Druids and Bards, called an *"Eisteddfodd"*—which is a public festival event still held annually in Wales. This rite may be amended for any type of group energy work, gatherings and "circle magic" for any number of participants. The ceremonial observation is most effective within a circle of trees and/or stones. Once participants are prepared, procession to the northeast corner of the *Nemeton*, bringing all tools and necessary items with you.

—OPENING BENEDICTION—

ELF-KING: *May the Source of All Being and Creation grant us favor and protection; and in protection, strength; and in strength, peace; and in peace, understanding; and in understanding comes the True Knowledge of the 'Right Way'; and in the grace of this knowledge may we be granted the will to use it; and in that will, the wisdom to temper the use of knowledge; and in temperance comes mercy; and thru mercy, love; and in love we find the Source of All Being and Creation.*

FAERIE QUEEN: *The recursive spiral path passes through Annwn ('ahnoon') and returns to the love and favor of the Source. Blessed be the All.*

ALL: Blessed be the Universe.

—GRAND INVOCATION—

ELF-KING: *To bathe in the aethyr of new light and life that swirls about the galaxy. To cleanse away iniquity and mortality so we may join in the harmony of all living beings. Here we stand, beneath the Oaks, beneath the Stones, coming to the place we watched our ancestors go to commune with the Spirit of the Universe.*

FAERIE QUEEN: *The stars shine brightly upon this meeting of our people. The Divine Star shines brightly on us at the hour of our meeting.*

—ELEMENTAL BENEDICTION—

FAERIE QUEEN: *Let peace ring out through the four quadrants of the Universe. Within our being may we find peace at the center. In the Secret Grove we meet to share peace. Then, as we go about the lives we lead on the 'Surface World,' we radiate the currents of love and peace and attract the same.*

ELF-KING: *Here we stand strong, coming together in answer to the call of our inner vow as Guardians and Keepers of the Earth. Here we stand, side-by-side, heart-to-heart and* [the circle joins hands] *hand-in-hand.* [Release hands.]

NORTH: *Guardian of the North, realm and spirits of the Earth Element, 'nature spirits,' Gnomes, Kobold and Drwyds of Falias, hail and welcome to this Nemeton. Extend the currents of peace and stability.*

EAST: *Guardian of the East, realm and spirits of the Air Element, Ancient and Shinning Ones, Elves and Drwyds of Gorias, hail and welcome to this Nemeton. Extend the currents that enable enlightenment.*

SOUTH: *Guardian of the South, realm and spirits of Fire, Dragon Priests, fiery sprytes, pict-sidhe and Drwyds of Finias, hail and welcome to this Nemeton. Extend the necessary energy for strengthening the will.*

WEST: *Guardian of the West, realm and spirits of the Water Element, ancestral spirits, merfolk, Drwyds of the past and the Otherworld city of Murias, hail and welcome to this Nemeton. Extend the currents of personal well-being and those that enable the insight of wisdom.*

—BARDIC VERSE & STORY—

Traditionally, a gathering of Elven-Faerie, Wizards, Druids and Bards includes recitation of lore and legend to preserve their legacy. It is this very practice that earns the liturgy the name "Eisteddfodd." As an example, these deities and heroes are recognized during specific '*Fire Festivals*' in the modern Celtic Gwyddonic Druid Tradition:

Samhain—Morrigan and Dagda
Winter—Kerridwen and Kernunnos
Imbolc—Bridget and Belenus
Spring—Viviana and Merlyn
Beltane—Belisana and Tarvos
Summer—Rhiannon and Manannan
Lughnassadh—Rosemerta and Lugh
Autumn—Triana and Hellith

—FESTIVAL OBSERVATIONS—

Perform magical operations or ceremonial celebrations that the group has come together to accomplish. You will need to "Cast the Circle" if performing "ritual magic."

—DISMISSAL OF ELEMENTAL SPIRITS—

ELF-KING: *May the Source of All Being and Creation grant us favor and protection; and in protection, strength; and in strength, peace; and in peace, understanding; and in understanding comes the True Knowledge of the 'Right Way'; and in the grace of this knowledge may we be granted the will to use it; and in that will, the wisdom to temper the use of knowledge; and in temperance comes mercy; and thru mercy, love; and in love we find the Source of All Being and Creation.*

FAERIE QUEEN: *Let peace ring out through the four quadrants of the Universe. Within our being may we find peace at the center. In the Secret Grove we meet to share peace. Then, as we go about the lives we lead on the 'Surface World,' we radiate the currents of love and peace and attract the same.*

WEST: *Guardian of the West, spirit of the Wave and realm of Sea, we thank thee for thy attendance this day/eve as you witness and remember the ceremony we practice in memory of the rites of our ancestors. May you return again when hence we call. Hail and Farewell. Go in peace.*

SOUTH: *Guardian of the South, spirit of the Flame and realm of Fire, we thank thee for thy attendance this day/eve as you witness and remember the ceremony we practice in memory of the rites of our ancestors. May you return again when hence we call. Hail and Farewell. Go in peace.*

EAST: *Guardian of the East, spirit of the Wind and realm of Air, we thank thee for thy attendance this day/eve as you witness and remember the ceremony we practice in memory of the rites of our ancestors. May you return again when hence we call. Hail and Farewell. Go in peace.*

NORTH: *Guardian of the North, spirits of Stone and Wood and realm of Earth, we thank thee for thy attendance this day/eve as you witness and remember the ceremony we practice in memory of the rites of our ancestors. May you return again when hence we call. Hail and Farewell. Go in peace.*

—CLOSING BENEDICTION—

ELF-KING: *Before departing from this place, we release the field surrounding this sacred nemeton, grounding the energy of Earth, releasing to the Sky* the energies of Air, pushing down the currents of Fire deep into the 'Core of Gaea' and pouring the Waters back into the Sea. So mote it be.

FAERIE QUEEN: *As we have come in peace, so do we leave in peace. We are the 'Children of the Stars,' beings of light, life and love. In departing, we project and radiate peaceful energy and positive power throughout the Universe, dispersing the energies of light and truth gathered here this day/night. Blessed Be.*

ALL: *Blessed Be.*

THE ALARDANA

the alardana
festivals and seasonal rites

Many modern neopagan traditions observe some formal annual "calendar" or "Wheel of the Year." Most are inspired by actual "pagan" holidays and festivals based on an ancient observation of "natural cycles" or "seasons," especially those related to agriculture. Observance of cultural festivals is a tradition as old as civilization.

During the early 1900's, a modern standard of eight "*sabbats*" or "grove festivals" was developed by Gerald Gardner (for *Wicca*) and his friend Ross Nichols (for *Druidism*).* The model remains popularly used today, evenly spaced festival observations six-to-eight weeks apart. However, there is some redundancy inherent in the symbolism.

For example: the Celtic festival of *Beltane* or May's Eve also correlates with the summer solstice; both are landmarks for the season of growth and maturation. Beltane is a 'flower festival' marked by an observation of short-lived "may-blossoms" visible in Nature. This begins the 'agricultural summer'. The 'astronomical summer' is observed as the celestial or astrophysical event called the "summer solstice"—which marks a "turning point" in the solar year.

To observe an eightfold cyclic "Wheel of the Year," four "*Fire festivals*"—Beltane, Lughnassadh, Samhain, and Imbolc—are drawn from Celtic lore, supplementing two equinoxes and two solstices each year. This is metaphorically referred to as a 'wheel' that is constantly "turning" the seasons through an annual cycle. Each regional-culture carries its own distinct language-vocabulary or names to define the same kind of seasonal celebrations—such as the Druidic Tradition practiced by many Elven-Faerie folk, which call the solstices and equinoxes the "*Four Albans*"—or "Four Lights"—coinciding with a traditional Celtic "Wheel of the Year."

Origins for popular customs are often taken for granted in mainstream consciousness. For example, the Roman Catholic Church (and "Celtic Church") set their own religious holidays to coincide with dates and relative symbolism of former pre-Christian "pagan" holidays ("holy-days") and festivals. Not only did this aid in smoothing over a conversion of rural agricultural pagan folk—but the Christians were still actively developing their "religion," and incorporated

---
* More details may be found in "*The Witch's Handbook*" by Joshua Free; also included in "*Merlyn's Complete Book of Magick*" anthology.

many aspects that do not appear in the Hebrew-Kabbalistic tradition that Jesus actually practiced. Keep in mind—Jesus was a Jew, but he was also shown in scripture as a descendent of the throne of David, and thus a part of an arm of the Dragon Legacy once preserved by the Essene and Gnostic sects. John the Baptist was also an Essene, evident by his use of Essene baptismal rites, borrowed from the pagans, and only used at that time and place by that particular mystic sect. The Church later took ownership of this type of ceremony as well.

The following are standardized dates of the traditional pagan festivals along with the more commonly known observances corresponding to the same times and/or energies. These seasonal Fae-festivals are called *Alardana* (plural) or *Alardan* (singular).

SEASONAL ALARDANA FESTIVALS

April 30-May 1: *Beltane*, May's Eve, Calen Mai ("First of May"), Tana's Day, Walpurgisnacht and May Day.

June 21 (20-22): *Litha*, summer solstice, Alban Heruin, mid-summer and St. John's Day.

July 31-August 1: *Lughnassadh* ("Marriage of Lugh"), Cornucopia, Calen Awst ("First of August"), Lammas and Lammas Eve.

September 21 (20-23): *Mabon*, autumn equinox, Alban Elved, harvest-fest, Rosh Hashanah and Thanksgiving Day.

October 31-November 1: *Samhain* ("Summer's End"), Shadow-fest, Calen Gaeof, Feast of the Dead, All Saint's Day, All Soul's Day and Halloween.

December 21 (20-23): *Yule*, winter solstice, midwinter, Alban Arthuan, Jul, Saturnalia and Christmas.

January 31-February 1: *Imbolc*, Brighid's Day, Calen Geaef, Oimelc, St. Blaise's Day, Candlemas, Valen-tine's Day and Groundhog's Day.

March 21 (20-22): *Ostara*, Eostre, spring equinox, Alban Eiler, Akiti, Sheelah's Day, St. Patrick's Day and Easter.

SAMHAIN – ALARDAN FESTIVAL

Controversy still exists concerning the time of a proper 'New Year' observation—but Celtic traditions often begin their annual calendar on Samhain, November's Eve, or October 31. This time period marks an energetic threshold, much like Beltane, when the "veil" between this 'physical world' and the "ALL" is thinnest—but in this instance, the Gate is accessible from the *outside.*

Pagans traditionally observed a "Feast of Ancestors" during "Samhain" (pronounced *sow-en*) meaning "Summer's End" (or '*samhraidhreadh*' in Irish Gaelic) and today we know the remnants of these ancient customs as "Halloween." This includes events like "bobbing for apples," "mask-wearing" and "pumpkin-carving" (reminiscent of the ancient gourd-carved heads).

"Faerie lights" or painted glass orbs with candles inside are suspended from the trees around the *Nemeton*—emitting a cool ultraviolet or cobalt blue light.* Seasonal rites may be performed within a *Nemeton* using the "Eisteddfodd" or "Group Liturgy." They may also be practiced as a solitary, addressing each of the directions in turn.

NORTH: I call thee Northern Spirits of *Lasse, Cloch, Arbor* and *Elessar.* Join me powers of Leaf, Earth, Tree and Stone, in this celebration of my ancestors. I come to the Sacred Grove this *estevar* ["evening"] to be reunited and guided by their *asha* ["spirit"].

EAST: I call thee Eastern Spirits of *Gaeth, Gwai, Nel* and *Fin.* Join me, powers of Wand, Sky and Cloud, in this celebration of my ancestors. I come to the Sacred Grove this *estevar* ["evening"] to be reunited and guided by their *asha* ["spirit"].

SOUTH: I call thee Southern Spirits of *Re'Aitai, Anar, Arva* and *Teine.* Join me, powers of Skyfire, Sun, Flame and Fire, in this celebration of my ancestors. I come to the Sacred Grove this *estevar* ["evening"] to be reunited and guided by their *asha* ["spirit"].

WEST: I call thee Western Spirits of *Kh'dek, Muir, Kyela* and *Pehlora.* Join me, powers of Ice, Sea, Water and Love, in this celebration of my ancestors. I come to the Sacred Grove this *estevar* ["evening"] to be reunited and guided by their *asha* ["spirit"].

NORTH: *Glora Duath.* The Sun is overcome by darkness. On this *estevar*, a night outside all other nights, the invisible *evala* ["cloak"] between this world and our ancestor's realm in the Otherworld is thinnest— from their side.

EAST: I call upon the ancestral power of Elvenkind within me. Give me clear knowledge of *Kaloren* [the "Right Path"].

---

* Similar to a '*Pelen Tan*'; described in *"21 Lessons of Merlyn"* (Douglas Monroe).

SOUTH: I stand on a threshold between time to witness the death of one year reborn to another. As Keepers of the Earth, Guardians of the Elven *Cor Anar* ["Wheel of the Sun/Year"], I charge the *Duath* ["darkness"] to give way to *alb* ["light"] at Midwinter—the turning point of the Sacred Earth Year.

WEST: In the name of the covenant sworn by Ancient Elvish Wizards that first enticed and communed with spirits of the Otherworld with food offerings, I call out to my ancestors from *Arth Asha* ["spirit world"] to share in this feast with me. Take from this offering the essences you so require. You may then celebrate your feast. Be sure to leave a portion of it in the northern quadrant as an offering.

NORTH: Behold, I see before me, the Sidhe. They have graced my vision with their presence. They manifested to me, crossed over, transitioned from the Realm of the King. From ancestral mounds they have come this night to celebrate the *Samhain Alardon* ["Festival"] with me.

EAST: Here I stand at *Saeth Duir*, Guardian of the Threshold. I am a portal messenger. Before me the winds rise up to offer their hail and I thank thee spirits of the eastern direction for celebrating with me.

SOUTH: As the ancestral *asha* ["spirit"] depart, I wish peace and love for them on their return to the ancestral plane. I ask only that you leave me with your hereditary guidance that it may be a light to illuminate *Kaloren* ["the Right Way"].

WEST: From the ninth wave I emerge and from nine elements was I created. In nine states of being I channel my power and radiate peace multiplied times nine. By the power of nine may I hope to enjoy the fruits and bounty of another year.

NORTH: Here, I stand in the north on Earth as Guardian of the Threshold. I here seal the Otherworld portal. The ancestral energy and spirits of the dead have passed by this gateway and I bid them peace on their departure. New life comes from death and Nature once more unfolds her mysteries to her initiates. As Keeper of the Earth I shall await the New Light when we shall again meet this winter.

ALBAN ARTHUANN – ALARDAN FESTIVAL

Long before modern observations of Christmas, ancient cultures celebrated the rebirth of the Sun King at Midwinter on the evening of December 21st—the longest night of the year. In some cultures, the

Sun is lured or coaxed back to power with prayers and hymns. Pine trees; evergreen wreaths; symbolism of Oak, Holly and Mistletoe—all originate with pagan Druids. Circular wreaths symbolize the cycle of Life, represented by the annual 'Wheel of the Year'. We have retained customs of "Santa Claus"—that *"jolly ol' elf"*—where we encourage a visit by leaving a "fairy offering" of milk and sweetbreads (cookies).

Use red, green and white candles to illuminate your evening rites, all of which are traditional colors of Druidism and winter solstice. You might even affix the candles to a "Yule Log." The *"Alban Arthuann"* festival—meaning the "Light of Arthur" or "Light of the Bear"—is observed in the evening. After this night, the daytime grows longer and so the Sun is deemed "reborn."

NORTH: I call upon the Spirit of the Forest this eve. Come forth *Aldaron, Herne, Dagda, Kernunnos*—the Green Man and the Antlered One. You do I call upon, the strength of Earth, the elemental forest spirits, on this the darkest of nights.

EAST: *La'Aer, Gaeth, Suk'anar Estevar.* I call upon the power and energy of the Winds and spirits of the Air Element, on this darkest of nights, and a time of new beginnings.

SOUTH: From the south I bind energies of *Re'-Aitai*, Skyfire, *Leollyn*, Great *Anar*, Sun—whose power grows steadily.

WEST: *Muir. Muir. Suk'anar Estevar.* I call upon the power and energy of the tides, activity of splashing water, spirits of the wave and sea, on the darkest night of the year, as Midwinter turns and the Sun's course follows.

NORTH: The turning point is a new birth, one marked by the growing power of the Sun Father, *Leollyn*. As Keeper of the Earth I stand witness to new life coming from death. I stand guard to a gateway of the Cosmic Law that all things changes.

EAST: The *Cor Anar* ["Wheel of the Solar Year"] turns. I stand waiting encased in a season of hibernation. I am the Morning Star *"el tuile"* ["Spring"] and offer a season of new beginnings and new hope.

SOUTH: *Gaea. Vasta. Gaea. Vasta.* I awaken and arouse the Earth Mother to bare witness to the rebirth of the Sun King. Send forth your energies of creativity and inspiration. Lend us your fiery strength.

WEST: In the *Suk'anar* ["darkest"] *Estevar* ["night"] I call the energy of *Leollyn* ["Sun King"] who is born and reborn here at *Alban Arthuann* [the Winter Solstice] as the "Child" Sun King. From *Numen* ["the west"] I ask to receive the intelligence and wisdom to better use my abilities. Through self-knowledge, I increase my understanding of the Universe.

Light the solstice candles on the Yule Log in the north. If you use evergreen wreaths, light candles in these too.

NORTH: On this *Suk'anar* ["darkest"] *Estevar* ["night"] I call forth the Lord of the Forest by the names: *Aldaron, Ninastre* and *Saelr'ir*, to celebrate and observe the great mysteries of seasonal change and cosmic cycles.

EAST: The time draws near. The Sun King is to be reborn as a child. May all spirits and animals of Nature awaken and know his birth.

Wait in your circle until midnight, continuing your festivities until you wish to close by celebrating the Sun-birth itself. You can continue at midnight, have an all-night vigil until dawn, or you may return just before dawn the following morning.

EAST: *Vasta. Vasta.* Come forth and awaken, power and spirits of *Gaeth* ["wind"], energies of *La'Aer* ["the Air Element"]. Hear me; hear the call of the *Ekahal* ["Elven Wizard"] as I rouse you from hibernation. Rejoice! Rejoice! The Sun King is reborn!

SOUTH: *Vasta. Vasta.* Awaken ye powers and spirits of *Arva* ["flame"], energy of *Teine* ["the Fire Element"]. Hear me; hear the call of the *Ekahal* ["Elven Wizard"] as I rouse you from hibernation. Rejoice! Rejoice! The Sun King is reborn!

WEST: *Vasta. Vasta.* Awaken, powers and spirits of *Muir* ["the sea"], energy of *Ear Pehlora* ["the Water Element"]. Hear me; hear the call of the *Ekahal* ["Elvish Wizard"] as I rouse you from hibernation. Rejoice! Rejoice! The Sun King is reborn!

NORTH: *Vasta. Vasta.* Come forth and awaken, ye powers and spirits of *Aldaron* ["the forest"], energy of *Lasse* and *Gael* ["leaf and stone"]. Hear me; hear the call of the *Ekahal* ["Elvish Wizard"] as I rouse you from hibernation. Rejoice! Rejoice! The Sun King is reborn!

IMBOLC – ALARDAN FESTIVAL

Imbolc is a Celtic "Candle Festival"—observed with a candle light vigil from the evening of January 31st into the following dawn of February 1st. Even if a vigil is not observed, a candle may be left to burn all night for the protection of the home and family. Meditation on the candle flame has an ability to put you into a trance-hypnotic state. Fire gazing, in general, is known to produce similar calming states. Such activities allow the "inner mind" to be more receptive to visions and prophetic skills may be heightened. Such divination may be performed; most of the subtle energies of this time of year are received at night and during dreams. Imbolc is often dedicated to Brighid (in Celtic Traditions)—elsewhere to Venus and Diana. A 'grain-doll' is sometimes made in the image of such a goddess.

NORTH: I call thee Northern Spirits of *Lasse*, *Cloch*, *Arbor* and *Elessar*. Join me powers of Leaf, Earth, Tree and Stone, in this celebration: a turning of the *Cor Anar* ["Wheel of the Solar Year"] and the strengthening of *Glora Anar* ["the Sun"]. Bless now this *Tuile Alta* ["Springtime Light"] and lend your powers to this candle. [Blessing a candle to be used for the vigil.]

EAST: I call thee Eastern Spirits of *Gaeth*, *Gwai*, *Nel* and *Fin*. Come join me, powers of Wand, Sky, Cloud and Rain, in this celebration of the turning of the *Cor Anar* ["Wheel of the Solar Year"] and the strengthening of *Glora Anar* ["the Sun"]. Bless now this *Tuile Alta* ["Springtime Light"] and lend your powers to this candle.

SOUTH: I call thee Southern Spirits of *Re'Aitai*, *Anar*, *Arva* and *Teine*. Join me, you powers of Skyfire, Sun, Flame and Fire, in this celebration of the turning of the *Cor Anar* ["Wheel of the Solar Year"] and the strengthening of *Glora Anar* ["the Sun"]. Bless now this *Tuile Alta* ["Springtime Light"] and lend your powers to this candle.

WEST: I call thee Western Spirits of *Kh'dek*, *Muir*, *Kyela* and *Pehlora*. Join me powers of Ice, Sea, Love and Water, in this celebration of the turning of the *Cor Anar* ["Wheel of the Solar Year"] and the strengthening of *Glora Anar* ["the Sun"]. Bless now this *Tuile Alta* ["Springtime Light"] and lend your powers to this candle.

NORTH: May all of the Nature spirits and beings, woodland creatures and bipeds, find security, warmth and protection in the *Alta Nwyrve* ["light of the sacred fire"], which I extend as an expression of peace, radiating perfect love throughout the Cosmos.

EAST: From the Radiance within and the new *A'lahn* ["light"] that shines in the *Aiet* ["east"], may all the beings of *G'ea* ["the earth planet"] no longer be subjected to impenetrable *Duath* ["darkness"].

SOUTH: *Tuile F'yonn*, the "Light Season" is soon upon us. As some sprigs of *Tuile* ["the spring season"] and new hope od life appear, the Elven-Faerie Wizards come to commune with the "Elements of Nature," gathered here in this *Kirc* ["sacred circle"] in springtime anticipation.

WEST: *Gaea* breathes the breath of renewal, weaving a web of enchantment that spreads across the land. May the spirits of *Tuile F'yonn* ["the season of light"] bless this land with love and abundance. Energies of *Ear Pehlora* ["the Water Element"] send forth thy spring rains to nurture all life as it strives to grow and mature.

NORTH: Great Lord of the Forest ["*Aldaran*"], come forth and use your ancient magicks to bless the land, making it fertile and green. Bring renewal to all life—every living *Asha* [spirit/soul] of *Arda G'ea* [the earth-planet plane of existence] above and below the Surface World.

EAST: Voice that beckons in the winds of dawn, grant me guidance and inspiration.

SOUTH: Voice echoing strangely through the stillness of the noon's midday heat, speak quietly your secrets.

WEST: Vision that emerges to give form to the voice heard at sunset and in the moonrise, bless me with thy gifts.

Where the liturgy may be amended for use by any number of participants, you will retain the "I" (singular tense) as the following imagery is visualized or imagined.

EAST: I am the wind across the plains and sea. I am a hawk high above the cliffs. I am a raven on a Druid's shoulder.

SOUTH: I am the fire inspiring the minds of sentient spirits. I am the flame that burns in the passion of lovers. I am the beacon of light that permeates throughout the Universe.

WEST: I am a wave crest of the sea. I am the variegated sound coming from the rushing waters. I am a valley lake nestled between two plains.

NORTH: I am a hill of poetry. I am finest of flowers and trees. I am a stone standing watch since the beginning of creation.

Thank and dismiss the energies—wishing them peace as they depart—as with all ceremonies. Then return to your place of dwelling; taking your blessed candle with you. You may consecrate an area of prosperity and protection in the home with it—and if possible, allow it to burn down, extinguishing itself.

ALBAN EILER – ALARDAN FESTIVAL

The Spring Equinox goes by many names, including Ostara, Eostre, Ostera, Eastre and finally Easter. *Alban Eiler* is often observed on the dawn of March 21st. These kinds of festivals once ran three or more days in duration—observed perhaps from the 20th to the 23rd. In ancient Babylon, the New Year festival of Akiti and first month of Nissanu began on this day—observed by the whole urban population for ten entire days.

If ground and weather conditions allow, you might make this a seed-planting ceremony. You may even use pots if outdoors is not an appropriate choice. Both the spring and autumn equinox mark observable times of equality (or balance) between daytime and nighttime—or else, the Sun and Moon.

NORTH: I call upon the Spirit of the Forest at the dawn of the *Tuile F'yonn* ["Spring Season of Light"]. Come forth *Aldaron, Herne, Kernunnos*—you who come when I call on the strength and power of the Earth Element and forest energy. Merge your stream with this Grove, this Sacred *Nemeton*. Come and celebrate the Springtime Equinox.

EAST: *La'Aer, Gaeth, Tuile F'yonn*. I call upon the power of the winds and energies of the Air Element on the dawn of the Spring Season of Light, this time of new beginnings. Be here now to witness and remember my ceremony.

SOUTH: From the south, I bind the power of *re'-aitai*, the skyfire, and *Glora Anar*, the strength of the Sun that has returned. The air of the east blows to the south and it is warmed. Come now and celebrate *Alban Eiler* ["the spring equinox"].

WEST: *Muir. Ear Pehlora*. Energy and power of the waters and sea, I call thee here now to share in an ancient observation of the equinox, the festival of balance between day and night.

NORTH: As all beings yield to the new *A'Lahn Tuile* ["light of the spring season"], I plant new seed and call upon powers of the "Elements of Nature" to bless and encourage its growth.

As part of a seed-planting ceremony, you might choose an appropriate flower/herb for each direction, or use "pots." If necessary, you may even visualize the seed-planting process.

EAST: At the eastern ward I plant new seeds of psychological well-being.

SOUTH: At the southern ward I plant new seeds of spiritual well-being.

WEST: At the western ward I plant new seeds of emotional well-being.

NORTH: At the northern ward I plant new seeds of physical well-being.

EAST: Spiritual powers of *La'Aer* ["the Air Element"], caretakers of all flowers and trees—take and scatter my seeds among fertile soil. Bless and keep safe all new life that begins in *Tuile* ["the spring"].

SOUTH: *Sier Arva* ["sacred fire"], searing flame, spirits of the same, ensure that the Radiance of *E'Graine Glora Anar*, bright sphere of the Sun above, shines down to nourish these seeds with life-giving warmth and light.

WEST: Spirits of *Ear Pehlora* ["the Water Element"], the gentle rains and *Muir*, Element of Sea, come forth and bless this new life with your lustral waters, moisture and nourishing rains.

NORTH: I place the life of all new seed in the hands of *Gaea* and the invisible caretakers of the Green World of Nature. O Spirits of *Talamh* ["the Earth Element"] accept the seeds of new life into your folds.

EAST: Spirits of the *Duile* ["fey elements"], you have been called to this *Kirc* ["sacred circle"] *Nemeton* to observe, recognize and remember the ancient tradition observed.

SOUTH: Today, I call upon and receive the strength of the heavens, warming light from the Sun, to invoke the splendor of the Element of Fire...

WEST: Depth of the Sea and radiance of the Moon...

NORTH: Stability of Earth and firmness of stone...

EAST: Speed of lightning and swiftness of Wind.

NORTH: The cyclic phases of *Gaea* and the laws of the Green World of Nature are marked and observed with the rotation of the *Cor Anar*. The Great Wheel turns again.

BELTEINE – ALARDAN FESTIVAL

The *Belteine* or *Beltane* festival is named such after the "Fires of Bel" or "Belinos"—most likely a remnant of Bel Marduk or "Lord Marduk," the patron god of Babylon, known elsewhere in the mutation of "Baal." It was actual on the dawn of an ancient Belteine when the *Tuatha d'Anu* arrived in Ireland and set fire to their own ships. The most frequently cited tradition of May Day is, of course, the "May Pole"—erected as a symbol of the "World Tree" and then usually danced around while weaving ribbons.

By some calenders, Beltane was observed in mid-April, when 'May Blossoms' are first visible. "May Day" is, of course, May 1st, though the festival often begins the night before—on May's Eve—with construction of two large bonfires built side-by-side, which are consecrated to Bel, then set aflame. Ancient Celts marched cattle in procession between these two flames as they led them out to pasture for the year. Some evening observances may be held, however this following rite is typically observed at noon.

NORTH: I greet you *Alardon*, Spirit of the Grove, Spirit of the Green World. I call forth northern energies of *Lasse, Cloch, Talamh* and *Arbor*. Join me, powers of Leaf, Stone, Earth and Tree as we celebrate the mysteries of creation at the height of *F'yonn Thuile* [the "season of light"].

EAST: I greet you *Gwai,* Spirit of the Sky. I call thee forth from the east to celebrate the forthcoming *Laer Reudh* ["summer season"] marked by the Fires of Bel. Energies of *Gaeth, Fin* and *Nel*—spirits and powers of the Wind, Air and Cloud—grant me thy inspiration and guidance.

SOUTH: Spirits of *Laer Reudh Arva* ["the summertime flame"], now is the time to emerge, come forth and shine brightly. Power of the southern spirits, open your *Evala Duir* ["hidden door"] of mysteries. Join me in celebration of summer's anticipation.

WEST: I hail from the *Kirc*, this sacred *Nemeton*. Hear me, *Kh'dek, Muir* and *Ear Pehlora*. Spirits and powers of the last receding Ice, the warming Sea and the Element of Water, join me now, this *Beltaine Alardon* ["Beltane festival"].

All ritual candles should be lit from a central flame or bonfire consecrated to *"Bel."* In the event that candles are not appropriate, you may substitute lanterns or torches. Color themes for Beltane are red, yellow-gold and green.

NORTH: Lady of the Earth, Lord of the Greenwood, Spirits of the Grove, nature spirits and woodland creatures, come now to this *Nemeton* and share in the spiritual fire of *Bel*.

EAST: May this sacred time of *Belteine* rekindle the heart and inflame the spirit of all living things in creation.

SOUTH: As a Keeper of the Earth, Guardian of the Elemental Mysteries, I stand to observe a turning of the *Cor Anar* ["Solar Wheel of the Year"]. *Glora Llew Anar* ["spirit of the Sun"] I await the day of your solstice apex and keep watch as you grow in strength each day.

WEST: *F'yonn Thuile*, the Light of Spring is coming to a close, making way for *Laer Reudh* ["the summer season"]. Today begins *Twythron Thrimidge* ["the month of May"] sacred to the *Dwyr* ["great Oak Tree"].

NORTH: Elements of Nature, Forces of the Green World, heed my call this day. Open up your oaken door and reveal thy mysteries to me, a servant of the Earth Planet and follower of the Elven Ways. I seek the wisdom of creation and abilities to channel all energy currents of the cosmos. And to the same, I am a keeper and guardian for all my days.

At this juncture, you may consider a recitation of the "*Cad Goddeu*," or "Battle of the Trees." In any case, retain the "I" in these following statements as they are visualized.

NORTH: I am a *Cloch* ["stone"] hidden in the *Saeth* ["unseen folds"] of *Talamh* ["the Earth"] and in *Milana Abrahor Terrest* ["an ancient emerald forest"].

EAST: I am a yellow *Alta* ["ray of light"] of *Glora Anar* ["blessed Sun"].

SOUTH: I am a *Dwyr Arva* ["flaming door"] concealing the secret laws of creation.

WEST: I am a blue-crested wave under *Isil El'orel* ["the Moon"] concealing mysteries of the purple depths of *Muir* ["the sea"].

You may observe the tradition of the Maypole and feast. After the feast and any activities, the convocation concludes.

NORTH: *Laer Reudh* ["the summer season"] comes upon us quickly. It graces now by every bud, blossom and leaf.

EAST: On the dawn of the morrow, the Earth shall be set upon her "Golden Path" toward the season of maturity.

SOUTH: The great *Cor Anar* ["Solar Wheel of the Year"] continues to turn once more, now bringing us every nearer to the "Red Season," but ever turning.

WEST: And may peace radiate throughout the universe.

ALBAN HERUIN – ALARDAN FESTIVAL

The "Summer Solstice" marks a time of mystical significance throughout ancient Æurope. For as long as we can remember, Elves, Druids, Mystics and Wizards have performed Midsummer Rites. In Western Europe, these were frequently vigils held at sacred stone "*Kircs*," like Stonehenge on the Salisbury Plains in England. Thousands of "*Kirc*" remains are scattered throughout the mainlands. While the festival may begin the day before, this rite begins approximately ten minutes before the dawn of the solstice itself—usually June 22nd. It is the longest day of the year.

NORTH: I call upon the Spirit of the Forest in the twilight of the great Elven-Ffayrie Rade between the worlds, before the dawn of *Laer Reudh*, the "Red Season" of summer maturity. Come forth *Alardon, Herne, Kernunnos*, the Green Man—those entities that arrive when I call on the strength and energy of the Earth Element and the Enchanted Forest. Share your energies with this Sacred Grove.

EAST: The threshold is drawing near. The forthcoming power of *Glora Anar* ["the Sun King"] peaks to bless the lands of *G'ea* in celestial marriage. May the spirits of *La'Aer* come forth to share in this great observation of the season.

SOUTH: Hark! On the horizon awaits the Sun on the longest day of *Cor Anar. Arva, Teine*. I summon the spirits of flame and the power of high noon's heat to come forth on the occasion of this *Alban Heruin* ["summer solstice"].

WEST: The dawn of *Glora Anar* ["the Sun"] is upon us/me, only moments away. I call ye spirits and energies of *Muir* ["the sea"] and *Duile Ear Pehlora* ["Element of Water"] to come forth and share celebration of this Summer Solstice with me.

NORTH: *Glora-Anar*. Mighty Sun Father, share your power with me now in your time of greatness. I am a Keeper of the northern ward, and Guardian of the Earth while you sleep.

EAST: *Glora-Anar.* Mighty Sun Father, share your power with me now in your time of greatness. I am the Keeper of the eastern ward, guarding the direction of your birth.

SOUTH: *Glora-Anar.* Mighty Sun Father, share your power with me now in your time of greatness. I am a Keeper of the southern ward, Guardian of the mid-day peak during your travels through the sky.

WEST: *Glora-Anar.* Mighty Sun Father, share your power with me now in your time of greatness. I am the Keeper of the western ward, guarding the station of your daily retirement.

Moments before dawn, the leader says: *"Mighty Sun, be here now."* Then the rite continues after dawn has peaked.

EAST: As Guardian of the East, I hail that the Sun is upon us.

SOUTH: Hail to the Great Sun King Llewollyn rising in the sky.

WEST: Hail to the Great Sun King that warms the oceans and the sea.

NORTH: Hail to the Great Sun King, the supreme light bearer parading through Enchanted Forests.

EAST: I smell the fragrance of the summer flowers.

SOUTH: I am warmed by the spirit burning within all life.

WEST: I am blessed by the love in all life flowing throughout the Green World of Nature on Earth and in the Universe.

NORTH: May the love and energies called here for the *Alban Heruin Alardon* ["festival of Summer Solstice"] be radiated as perfect peace by all spirits present for this occasion.

LUGHNASSADH – ALARDAN FESTIVAL

The ancient Celtic festival of *Lughnassadh*—pronounced "loo-nass-ah"—is observed on August 1st (or on the eve of the same) and means literally: "The Wedding of Lugh"—a solar deity in the Celtic pantheon derived from the *Tuatha d'Anu*. This marriage of the "sun and sky" with the "land" marked the first harvest festival and start of the harvest cycle—which runs through the autumn season until the eve of *Samhain*.

The *Lughnassadh* festival is a time for blessing an forthcoming harvest and offering the first grains cut as a sacrifice back to the Earth and its spirits. For this ceremony, bring a sufficient supply of fresh bread and wine to the *Nemeton*. Traditional lore also suggests the custom of "*Lammas Towers*"—a competition to see who can build a larger bonfire that stands upright for the longest period of time. The rite is aligned to the sunset/dusk (autumn) threshold.

NORTH: I call thee Northern Spirits of *Lasse, Cloch, Arbor* and *Elessar*. Join me, powers of Leaf, Earth, Tree and Stone, in this observation of another turning of the *Cor Anar* ["Wheel of the Solar Year"]. Bless now this harvest time. Darkness appears distantly in the north as the Wheel continues to spin.

EAST: I call thee Eastern Spirits of *Gaeth, Gwai, Nel* and *Fin*. Come and join me, powers of Wand, Sky, Cloud and Rain, in this observation of another turning of the *Cor Anar* ["Wheel of the Solar Year"]. Bless now this harvest time as we must prepare for an inevitable winter.

SOUTH: I call thee Southern Spirits of *Re'Aitai, Anar, Arva* and *Teine*. Join me, powers of Skyfire, Sun, Flame and Fire, in this observation of another turning of the *Cor Anar* ["Wheel of the Solar Year"]. Bless now this harvest time, spirits of *Dan Harad* ["the southern direction"].

WEST: I call thee Western Spirits of *Kh'dek, Muir, Kyela* and *Pehlora*. Join me, powers of Ice, Sea, Water and Love, in this observation of another turning of the *Cor Anar* ["Wheel of the Solar Year"]. Bless and observe this harvest, and the wedding feast of Lugh here observed by the ["name of the Grove"].

NORTH: This *Calen* ["day"]/*Estevar* ["night"] I gather in the sacred *Nemeton* of the Grove to observe the Ancient Elven-Ffayrie festival of *Lughnassadh*. Here we mark the beginning of the harvest season. Here we celebrate the wedding feast of *Lugh*, hence all friendly spirits are invited.

KING OF THE ELVES: In order to eat, whether plant to us, or meat to other-kin, something must die. This is the law of Nature: that no energy shall be created or destroyed, only finite in number, changed and altered through processes. The energy may be exhausted if not renewed, so it must be maintained responsibly.

FAERIE QUEEN: When we eat of the sacred harvest, or the hunt, honor must be given to the sources of that energy that we take into ourselves. By this we honor the being that is the source of the food and its life, and the Source of All Being and Creation who is the source of the essence of life that is within the being and food, and life must be maintained responsibly.

Go to the central workspace and take up the bread, holding it outward and asking for benediction from the spirits present.

NORTH: Elemental powers of the ancient and sacred *Terrestai* ["the everlasting or eternal forest of the Universe"], spirits of Nature, Earth and Stone, you that arrives when I call on the power of *Tuath* ["the north"], spirits of the fields and harvest, spirit of the grain, I thank thee for your precious wheat, fruits and roots. All who share in the feast of this bread will also share in your eternal blessings of bounty and prosperity.

Return to the central workplace and replace the bread with the wine, taking it up and extending it outward as you ask the spirits for benediction.

WEST: *Duile Muir Ear Pehlora*, Elemental powers of Water and Sea, powers of of *Muin* ["the vine"], I thank thee spirits for your precious drink, as we might drain blood, so do we drain the wine from the grape in our harvest. Spirit of the wine, bless this drink and all who share it.

NORTH: All ye friendly spirits gathered at this Sacred Grove, this most holy *mandala* ["magic circle"], may you share in this feast in honor of the first harvest, the covenant of agricultural tradition, shared in offering for the wedding celebration of *Lugh* to the land.

Here you may celebrate the feast, sharing the "bread and wine." Remember to bring a portion of this feast in offering, placed at the northwest, saying: *"May the spirits of Nature accept this sacrifice, sowed and reaped using the knowledge granted by the covenant between the Earth Children and the Ancient and Shinning Ones."* Each participant may wish to offer a portion of their feast in a similar fashion before completing the rite.

NORTH: Nature is the greatest of all teachers. The Keepers of the Earth share these mysteries of creation as Guardians of the *Cor Anar* ["solar year"]. We come each turn in seasonal celebration eight times annually. Here in the sacred place of ancients I gather Elemental energies to weave a place worthy of such celebration.

EAST: Split wide the fruit of the seeds that have been sown and open the door to the ancient mysteries. As we share in the harvest, we share the wisdom of the cosmic law and the universal energy that makes all growth and life possible.

SOUTH: Source of All Being and Creation, kindle the formless and sacred *Nwyvre* ["divine fire"] of *gnosis*, inspiration and true knowledge in my head. Share in the eternal *Alta* ["light"] that is inextinguishable and an ageless source of true wisdom.

WEST: Great Spirit of the Western Winds that blow over the sea, energies and beings radiating from the sunset's beauty and evening twilight, come and share these blessings from the "elixir of wisdom" before departing this *Nemeton* in peace and perfect love.

NORTH: Deep within the secret folds of the forest lies the source of Elven knowledge—the Sylvan Library. Open your "Books of Light" and grant us true knowledge. Share with me your ineffable wisdom as I share with you the ancient covenant woven into this mystic elemental temple, consecrated here and now to observe *Lughnassadh*. Partake in our harvest and accept the sacrifice of ["name of the group or Grove"].

EAST: Change is ever upon us as the great seasons cycle. We must prepare for this each year, the changes. So, the harvest must be brought in to sustain life in a season of death. Spirits of *La'Aer* ["the Air Element"], *Giet Romen Gaeth*, powers of the Eastern Wind, come and share in the energy of this "Magick Sphere," bless and receive this combined sacrifice—a labor of love between the Earth and its children. Depart in peace to spread the winds of fortune on all harvests in the world.

SOUTH: Behold the passion of *Laer Reudh Anar*, the "Summer Sun" that dims as the *Duath* ["dark"] half of the year turns. Its lifeforce received in growing things which we receive in our nourishment. But change is always present in Nature, and we must observe and live in harmony with these changes, as the cycle of life, death and renewal turn once more. Mark well and remember this observation of the ancient covenant, departing in perfect peace and perfect love, and returning to this place again when we celebrate the turning of the Wheel.

ALBAN ELVED – ALARDAN FESTIVAL

An ancient name for this festival may be translated literally as *"Light of Elves."* This ceremony is traditionally practiced as a part of a "Thanksgiving Feast" in honor of the harvest, and as an observation of the "Autumn Equinox," the rite is part of a festival that peaks on September 21st.

As with *Alban Eiler* (the Spring Equinox), forces of light and dark—or day and night—are in balance with one another. With light giving way to darkness, the season of death is soon setting in. Harvest festivals are often observed at dusk. [This liturgy incorporates a "consecrated feast" and creation of a *"satchet"* ("pouch") containing "Mistletoe."]

NORTH: This *Kus'anar* ["evening/twilight"] I do call upon *Aldaron* ["spirit of the forest"], *Herne, Dagdha, Kernunnos,* and Green Man's spirit. You are summoned to gather here for this *Alban Elved* ["Autumn Equinox"] observance. I call to you that answer when I summon the solidity of Stone and powers of Earth. Come forth now and be present to celebrate these ancient mysteries.

EAST: This *Kus'anar* ["evening/twilight"] I do call upon *La'Aer* ["Element of Air"]. You are summoned to gather here for this *Alban Elved* ["Autumn Equinox"] observance. I call to you that answer when I summon the intensity of Wind and powers of Sky. Come forth and be present to celebrate these ancient mysteries.

SOUTH: This *Kus'anar* ["evening/twilight"] I do call upon the Southern Ward, radiant energies of *Re'Aitai*, Skyfire and the final rays of strength extended from *Glora Anar* ["the Great Sun King"] now fading. You are summoned to gather here to observe this *Alban Elved* ["Autumn Equinox"]. I call to you that answer when I summon up the strength of Flame and powers of Fire. Come forth and be present to celebrate these ancient mysteries.

WEST: This *Kus'anar* ["evening/twilight"] I do call upon *Muir, Ear Pehlora,* and the spirits of the place where the Sun sets. Hear the summons to gather here and observe this *Alban Elved* ["Autumn Equinox"] ceremony. I call to the spirits that answer when I summon forth the fluidity of Sea and powers of Wave and Water. Come forth. Be present to celebrate these ancient mysteries.

NORTH: At this time of year, those who live by the ways of nature—magical folk and woodland creatures—all make haste to ready their harvest before the frost. Now we take rest and offer thanksgiving to the spirits of the harvest and of Earth.

EAST: I come to acknowledge and observe the ancient ways; ancient ways that I maintain and uphold whenever I remember and keep the Elven Tradition. I adhere to the secret and sacred covenant between *G'ea* ["spirit of the Earth planet"] and the Keepers of the Earth, her mysteries and traditions.

SOUTH: I stand in recognition to observe the ever turning *Cor Anar* ["wheel of the Solar Year"] at the time of equinox, the bal-ance of light and dark. The harvest season is midway and all preparations must be made to survive the winter. The last scythe shall fall at *Samhain*. So, we come to extend our thanks for the food that will sustain all life through the dark months.

WEST: From *Gwaith* ["shadows"] of *D'yonn Reudh* ["the autumn season"] comes the cycle of *Hrive D'yonn* ["winter"] and death. *Gaea* ["the Earth Mother"] shall never perish so long as her faithful Elven-Ffayrie Guardians are there to serve and protect her. This is our responsibility.

NORTH: As the harvest is taken in, winter plans are made. I guard a season of inner exploration as the Earth ["*Gaea*"] and Sun ["*Glora Anar*"] hibernate in winter ["*Hrive D'yonn*"].

EAST: The secrets of the *Cor Anar* ["Wheel of the Sun"] are symbolic and well-hidden, but they offer to us the keys of self-realization. I will stand guard and wait for the season of new growth and beginnings as *Gaea* ["the Earth Mother"] and the Sun ["*Glora Anar*"] awaken in *Tuile F'yonn* ["spring season"].

SOUTH: The ancient power of the Elves, Faerie, Druids and Wizards shall never perish if the traditions do not cease to be observed. This is our responsibility. At this time of year, the Keepers of the Earth gather in the secret forest to reaffirm their Oath to Nature and remember the ancient covenant as it recedes in slumber. Let Earth rest easy in her season of hibernation, knowing that her Guardians are ever-present in stewardship while she sleeps. I stand guard a wait for the season of fullness and maturity as *Glora Anar* ["the Sun"] warms in *Laer Reudh* ["the summer"].

WEST: It is the equinox. At this time *Isil El'orel* ["the Moon"] sits in balance with *Glora Anar*. I stand guard and mark the ebb and flow of Autumn [*D'yonn Reudh*] and ask all the forces of nature to bless our food, our spirits and our path.

At this juncture, members prepare an amulet-bag containing the herb, mistletoe. It is consecrated in ceremony (using the consecration rites), then later hidden away for future use. At the northern quarter, each participant blesses their amulet-bag.

NORTH: May this sacred herb of the ancient—the Mistletoe—be consecrated for the future uses of *Sylvan Druidecht* ["Elven Forest Magick"]. May its contents activate all herbal remedies and potions that I prepare during the forthcoming year with goodness and love. May this amulet bag itself be charged as a symbol to guard away misfortune in my life and home.

Invite friendly spirits gathered at your *Nemeton* to join in the essence of the feast you have prepared, making certain to leave a formal offering in the north—inviting the energies or entities present to partake in the bounty before thanking and dismissing them.

The annual "cor anar"
de'ea canayen istari elandra

DYONN—"The Dark Season"

Narbeleth: Winterfilthe (October)
2nd – Alardenna: Festival of Spirit Guides
31st – Samhain: Night of Ancestors

Yestare: Newmoth (November)
1st – New Year's Day
11th – Lunatasidhe: Eve of Faerie

Rithon: Foreyule (December)
21st – Alban Arthuann: Winter Solstice
24th – Holly Day
25th – Oak Day

Narvinye: Afteryule (January)
18th – Danuhal: Festival of D'Anu

FYONN—"The Light Season"

Ninui: Solmath (February)
1st – Imbolc: Festival of Brighid
15th – Hal Pan: Festival of Pan

Sulime: Rethe (March)
21st – Alban Eiler: Spring Equinox

Virith: Astron (April)
7th – Yn Offeryn: Day of Sidhe Offerings
23rd – Hal Kernunnos: Green Man Festival

Lothron: Thrimidge (May)
1st – Beltane: The Fires of Bel

REUDH—"The Red Season"

Norui: Forlithe (June)
21st – Lithe/Alban Heruin: Summer Solstice
23rd – Elnassadh: Wedding Festival of Faerie King and Queen

Cerveth: Afterlithe (July)

Uruime: Wedmath (August)
1st – Lughnassadh: Wedding Feast of Lugh

Iavaneth: Holymath (September)
21st – Alban Elved: Autumn Equinox

The calendar is partitioned to correspond with 'months' that a modern reader is most familiar with. Lore suggests that when plotted on a fixed calendar, transition from one month to another occurs on the 21st; not the 30th etc. Some versions align with lunar phases, beginning a month with a "full" moon, a "new moon" or even the "sixth day of the moon."

The Elven-Faerie Spellbook

a brief introduction to the elven-faerie magical tradition

Elven-Faerie magic is quite different from other occult systems of "magick" that 'New Age' publications propagate. It is dependent on a unique relationship that is maintained between the practitioner and the Cosmos—and is not very concerned with deciphering cryptic formulas or other esoteric ceremonial specifics. As such, it has specific appeal to a certain segment of *Seekers* that find a unique affinity with the "Green World" of Nature, the environment, and of course, the wildlife—plant and animal—residing there.

Unlike other systems of magickal practice, where a magician might enact their craft as an 'outsider' enforcing demands on spirits or enticing them with strange glyphs, the Elven-Faerie Tradition takes the viewpoint that a practitioner shares an innate kinship with Nature, but also the "elemental" world—which encompasses all the spiritual intelligence that is *behind* and *directing* Nature.

In Celtic countries, there are remnants of a true Elven tradition inherent in what they call the *"Fairy-Faith"*—but the reality is that encounters with the spiritual intelligences of the natural world may be found in most all cultures in history, and not exclusively those of Western Europe. In some traditions they are referred to by names or titles that differ greatly from more typical faerie lore. As such, the factual existence of a universal application of Elven-Faerie tradition is still mostly concealed and misunderstood.

In non-Celtic traditions, earthbound nature "angels" are concerned with local affairs on this planet—and were only later treated as "elementals" by mystics and magicians. But at the beginning of present Human civilization, these matters were primarily handled by the 'priests' and 'priestesses' of holy and divine magic. These practitioners maintained a better Cosmic understanding than is generally relayed in common 'New Age' material today. As such, they understood their relationship with the Cosmos on a different level—and from a different perspective—than what is commonly maintained in today's standard-issue consciousness.

Where Humans are concerned, the Fey Folk do not exist without judgment. They favor those that maintain a physical existence in harmony with Nature; and they essentially shun those that are abusive and irreverent in their relationship with the natural world.

By definition, a personal relationship with 'Nature Spirits' is best established and developed *outdoors* in Nature. This contrasts greatly with the cold ritual chambers of ceremonial magicians in other traditions. The Fae are particularly fond of flower gardens and trees, forests and valleys, bodies of water and prairie wildernesses.

It is common for practitioners of the Elven-Faerie Magical Tradition to maintain a personal '*Fairy Garden*' in their yard. This becomes a sacred locale for Elven-Faerie magic—a place where the magician communes with Fairy-Folk and other nature spirits. The method of communication does not always have to be vocalized out loud, unless such feels comfortable and natural to the practitioner. Unlike other forms of 'magick' that often seem "unnatural," Elven magic is brought about by one's own innate nature.

Elemental encounters are more commonly experienced by those that make an active effort to remedy the environmental negligence inherent in the modern world. The type of person that exercises ecological responsibility in their everyday life is quite simply going to find this magic more effective than others. Quite simply, the Fairy Folk and other Elementals are not otherwise interested in assisting Humans—or maintaining a relationship with them—finding them to be a source of great unbalance on Earth.

The Elven Way often demonstrates an understanding of what is otherwise referred to as the "spirit of a place" or locale, meaning the inherent spiritual intelligence that is present, but unseen, in time and space. As a result, we find experiences described where "flower faeries" assist a 'gardener' or the "household brownies" (or gnomes) had assisted someone in 'selling their home'. In essence, these "personalities" are identified as the entities responsible for 'pulling the strings' behind-the-scenes of our reality; and they are only experienced by those that understand the symbiotic and harmonious relationship we maintain with the Cosmos.

The "Fairy-Faith" is called such, not only as a result of a *belief* in Elves and Fairies, but also because of the near-religious level of spiritual practice that synchronously ensues. An individual's "Fairy Garden" has the same associations as an 'altar'—and quite often it is complimented by an assortment of "statues" and "icons" representing Fae.

Perhaps one of the most common 'New Age' experiences with 'Nature Spirits' involves the subject of *healing*—whether physically or spiritually; whether concerning the individual themselves, or some other animal or plant-life in Nature. It is believed that since they live in closer proximity, affinity and harmony to *Life on Earth*, that they not only have a better understanding of it, but also a better working knowledge of how *Life* can operate or be maintained most optimally.

Fairy-Folk are notorious for their relationship with animals—something that is even observed by practitioners of the Faerie Tradition with their own "familiars" or pets. They are particularly protective of, and interactive with, pets and animals—including those kept primarily indoors.

The past several generations witnessed an increased 'psychical' sensitivity in children, and this is a trend that continues today. In truth, the young have always had a better chance at experiencing 'Nature Spirit' encounters just by '*accident*'. It is possible that this is simply because young people were not yet as clouded or distracted by worldly affairs—although this too is changing during the present information-tech age.

There are also many practitioners attracted to the Elven-Faerie traditions because they have an innate sense of kinship with Faerie beings —as if they are descendents of Fae or else that the 'Elementals' (as they are more commonly understood in occult lore) are, in fact, distant ancestors, or even reflections of lifetimes spent in another world, part of another Universe, resembling a *Faeryland*.

All of these are facets of the modern Elven-Faerie tradition as it is observed and practiced today—and as presented within this text in series with the other volumes that correlate with this instruction. May its suggestions and information prove beneficial to progressing your *Crossings into Faerie.*

MARDUKITE MASTER COURSE ACADEMY LECTURE #18[*]

"Danubian Druidism"

Although in the ancient Celestial, Mythological and Pantheistic systems that were derived specifically from the "planets," those traditions, such as in Mesopotamia, are observed as more of a "priestly" practice; with more religious connotations really attached to specific deities.[‡]

Now, when you look at either end of this—whether you move to the East or you move to the West—you see more of an emphasis on "elementalism," and "elemental" patterns. And a lot of that, in the Celtic tradition or in the Western tradition—a lot of associations with that are attached to the origins of Druidism; specifically 'Danubian'—or *"Danubian"* Druidism—those primarily connected to what you've seen as the *"Tuatha D'Anu"* in the '*Book of Elven-Faerie*' part of *Elvenomicon*. And *that* is a nomenclature that *I actually* developed. It's ironic to see it now being used elsewhere to connect "Ancient Druids" with the "Anunnaki"—but that was something I actually developed specifically in my works. And it was not very popular at first.

Unfortunately many still cling on to a very specific semantic paradigm viewpoint in regards to these studies—these mystical studies, which are supposed to be opening up one's considerations and freeing individuals to conceive and perceive of all these different things. Most semantics that we carry, even to the present day, in regards to ancient history, really pertains to the way it was documented by some classical writers—primarily the Greeks and Romans—as opposed to how we might understand it from the actual point-of-view of these individual cultures themselves.

Even our words "Druid" and "Celt" come from Greek writings pertaining to European encounters. The Greek writings eventually classify the entire Order and System of the "Druids" based on these encounters; and of which we continue to use today as our classical sources for understanding Druidism.

---

[*] Transcript of a lecture given by Joshua Free on September 23, 2020; revised from *"Druids, Elves & Dragons: Mardukite Master Course Academy Lectures (Volume II)"*—also contained in *"The Complete Mardukite Master Course."*

[‡] This transcript begins with the lecture already in progress, as did the original audio recording.

We find the same thing taking place with our traditional understanding of Mesopotamia. For example, Mesopotamia was never referred to as "Mesopotamia" by the ancient *Mesopotamians.* That's again, a Greek classification term for the region, meaning "Land between two rivers" in the *Greek* language; but not in any Sumerian language. Even the concept of "Sumerians" or "Land of Sumer"—the Sumerians, as we know and refer to them, never actually referred to *themselves as* "Sumerians." You see? This is something that's later done by others.

In "Sumerian" language there is no word for "Sumerian." In terms of the language or culture or the "land"—it's always referred to as, for example, the "language" is written *in* Sumerian as, "mother tongue." And then, the land: "mother land" and so forth. It's not classified the way that *others* later accounting for it, or referring to it, from the *outside*, are classifying it. It is *always* these *outside* perspectives that are primarily explored in the pursuit of conventional history.

This is why we deal with things as *"esoteric archaeology."* We don't deal in the "common everyday" version of history—of which has mainly been spoon-fed by those that are really in no better position to define or describe it as the next person. But it's become the common denominator of understanding; common knowledge; the information we assume that all "players" are basically aware of. This common knowledge is really some of the lowest-level information or "postulates" to base a Life and Reality on as you could get. To look any deeper that requires willingness to actually look or face up to these facets of society for what they actually are—and not just for the way they've been presented.

CHILDREN OF THE STARS

As our story goes: we begin with the *Tuatha d'Anu;* or "Children of the Stars" is what is really meant when you look at the semantics behind this. You can trace the vocabulary; you see references to these beings pop up as either the "White Folk" or "Shinning Ones" or "Light Beings" or "Star Beings." You see this appear throughout many different indigenous mythologies and in the lore behind a lot of different "mysticism" that relates to "ancestral deities" or any of the "Faerie"-type elementals—or any of this type of thing.

These "Children of the Stars," they *arrived* in Keltia—which is what we refer to as all of the "Druidic" or "Celtic" lands in the materials and in the Master Course—and they arrived on Beltane, which is

May's Eve. And so we see an emphasis here on a specific point: and this is the origins, of course, of the specifically Celtic observation of May's Eve.

There's other aspects to observing Beltane traditions today—such as those that follow "Great Bear" constellation circle around; and different ways to plot magical timing and calendars—but the significance of Beltane, or *La Baal Teine*, means the "*Fires of Bel*" in Celtic languages. The *Tuatha d'Anu* arrived and apparently, as the story goes, the local air was enshrouded in smoke for three days after they burned their "ships."

They burned their "ships"—whatever they arrived in—just burned them to cinders. This, of course, has begged the question to some: "is that like a *crash landing* of some kind?" or "did they just straight up burn the ships?—some kind of sea-faring ships..." But the references in lore, of course, just saying "ships," and then, of course, being "burned to cinders"—there's obviously no traces or evidence of them thereafter.

When the "Danubians" arrived in the Western Celtic lands, they arrived in Ireland according to ancient texts. And they discover that it is already actually inhabited by essentially a different Faerie race—descendents of "Nemed" or "Fir Bolg"—which means "Men of Bags"—but the Fir-Bolg, as it explains in the *Book of Invasions* (which is an Irish manuscript), they were forced to take shelter as a result of the smoke and fog and everything... They weren't really sure what had actually taken place when the Danubians arrived and basically treated the event as an invasion—a hostile invasion—as recorded in an Irish manuscript called the *Book of Invasions*.

And so you actually have this "war" ensue between these two "Faerie" races in ancient times; and it's probably not what we would consider "war" today, in terms of activity. But the fact remains that there was already a preexisting society existing in the "Celtic" lands when the Danubians moved through and, kind of, set themselves up as the "higher minds" or "authority" amidst them.

You then start to see a lot of associations—very specific—to "Elemental Magick." Those emerge specifically in relation to lore that's presented in, for example, the *Book of Invasions*. Each of the elements is ascribed these associations. For example, Earth is aligned to "North" and Air is given as "East" and we find many reasons why we can *qualify* this to be the case in later-derived traditions of ritual magick and in regards to Elementalism—but when we're dealing with Druidism specifically and ancient Druidic lore, it concerns the Danubian Druids being represented by *four* "Leaders," each coming from a different "Otherworld Kingdom" in their own rights prior to their emigration to the Celtic lands, and each of them carrying with them a particular "Magical Artifact."

THE "GIFTS" OF "FAEIRE"

And it just so happens the ancient Faerie lore corresponds... For example, the "Cauldron," which is associated with "Water" and associated with the "Western" direction—just so happens to be represented by a figure, the King of the Western Kingdom, which carried the Cauldron—and then a King of the Southern Kingdom, representing Fire, carried the Sword of Nuada. And Lugh, from the Kingdom of Air, carried the Spear, which is the equivalency of the Wand, in the East. And then the sacred Stone, the Stone of Fal—the Sacred Stone of Destiny—on which the Kings were later "crowned" in Ireland, came from a Northern Kingdom, represented by an Earth (elemental) Guardian.

These are referred to in lore as the "Gifts of Faerie." Then, you know, it's just a matter of simple transference to see how an Air Spear from the East becomes the Wand in ceremonial magic and so forth. In reenacting Irish Druidism, a modern practitioner might use these tools, as suggested in the works of Steve Blamires. So, in the north you're setting out a huge stone (for the Stone of Fal); and you consecrate a large Spear of Lugh and place that in the East and so forth.

So the idea to apply ancient iconic imagery and symbols this way—the concept of applying them to the elements, using them as ritual correspondences and so forth—this is an ancient concept. Of course, we know the ideals of "Magick" and "mysticism"—the "Power of the Self"—and all that, is not restricted to or allocated to any or one ritual tool, but we see these tools take a presence *in* the tradition as it's finally solidified, in terms of "Celtic Druidism" and "Elven Way" and "Faerie Tradition" as a way of reenacting—or of dramaticizing—these various ritualistic and ceremonial applications.

In the outline for *Irish Book of Invasions,* I have written here that it "ascribes the origins of Danubian Druidism; that it's linked to the La Tene culture" which is the culture—it's actually described by historians (by the way it designed its art and pottery styles and some of the ways in which the "spiral patterns" and, kind of, familiar "Celtic" designs can be traced back to the Ancient Near East, based on the use of it, by this "La Tene" culture.

That's what kind of clued me in—particularly the fact that one of the routes that had been taken was called the "Danube River" and I thought, that seems almost too simple, and as it turns out, yeah—it's for sure related to this tribal migration that took place.

The *Book of Invasions* also describes that there were multiple "racial" invasions of the Celtic lands in prehistoric times. And by "pre-historic," we mean prior to history being recorded first-hand in writing. This really can apply—it's not a specific date—it really applies to at any point in a culture where history is not yet being recorded by that culture.

Even after the invention of the mass-duplication of materials and so forth—the manuscripts that we refer to that are the basis of Druidism, like these Irish manuscripts here and so forth—they are making accounts as though they are very ancient knowledge. But even these materials are all mostly less than 500 years old as written materials. Prior to that, we don't really have much recorded because of the enforced over-Christianization and other dogmas that, ever since the Roman Empire, really suppressed the ability to communicate the true "Celtic" tradition.

Prior to that, all of the libraries and storehouses of information and so forth were destroyed by the Romans. I mean, the Romans spent 1000 years actively working to eradicate any traces of Druidic tradition. And then they ended up—their Empire ended up falling themselves. That's how that went down.

But, yeah, multiple racial invasions—the *Nemedians*, which were the "Sons of the Sun"; the *Fomorians*, the "People of the Sea"; the *Fir-Bolg*, which I translate here as "Men of the Dark Earth." And then finally, the "Children of Anu" or the "Children of the Stars." This marks emergence of Danubian Druidism, which is about where we begin to pick things up in terms of our understanding of Druidism: what Druidism represents; the Elements as I mentioned; the ritual tools and so forth. Granted, they have their own lore attached to how these classifications and elemental correspondences have come together; but it's no less effective when we compare it to the other "Elemental" paradigms; they are all working within the same Elemental tradition under various languages.

A concise synthesis of this "fundamental-elemental"—the ritual concepts that were all devised from it—the fundamentals can be derived directly from these *"Gifts of Faerie."*‡ So, we have the *Stone of Fal*, from the Northern city of Falias, coming to us from Morfessa, the High Wizard of the North. This was then set at *Tara*, the "Seat of the Kings" —literally "Dragonkings of Ireland"—and it would scream out whenever a true king had set foot on it.

And this is an integral part of the ancient "Dragon Legacy." The esteem of leadership and sovereignty and what it represented is specifically tied to this legacy—and there is a certain truth inherent in it. We see the same thing with, kind of, our everyday knowledge of "Excalibur"—the whole "Sword in the Stone" motif of Arthurian tradition—that it could only be released from the stone if the "True King" came along, and so forth.

And *that* is actually even related to, and derived from, the *"Sword of Nuada"* coming from the city of Finias, carried from the South by Uscias—according to this Mythology. And yeah, this is the archetypal "Magic Sword"—the Blade, *"Albion," "Caliburn," "Excalibur"* and such. Of course, it also had the "magical" ability to deal a direct fatal or critical blow with each strike. It was a symbol of the certainty and cutting will—the searing edge of power—directed by the operator.

Thereafter we allocate the Sword or Blade as a symbol of Fire and the South. And then the *Spear of Lugh* is another—also known as the "Spear of Destiny." I should mention that all of these tools are also referred to as the "objects-of-destiny"; so—The Stone of Destiny; The Spear of Destiny; The Sword of Destiny... the concept of Destiny seems to run pretty rampant here.

But the *Spear of Lugh*—according to the lore—emerged from the Eastern city of Gorias and it's carried by Esras. And it's the spear that essentially never missed its target—much as the *Sword (of Nuada)* could be wielded and it would be a critical hit every time—this spear always found its target. So it would, like with a *wand*, direct the flow or attention to the target. It became a symbol of the Element of Air and allocated to East and which again, we can represent with a *Wand*.

And then finally, the *Cauldron of Dagda*—it's also... well, in Celtic Mythology it reappears as "Kerridwen's Cauldron of Rebirth"—and that's directly related to Pheryllt lore. But the legends explain that it came

---

‡ Written/spelled as *"faeire"* in some versions of Elven-Faerie lore regarding these "gifts."

to Ireland by Master Semias, who came from the city of Murias (from) the West and aligned to water.

In one of the legends, the Cauldron acts like a "Horn of Plenty"—it just keeps filling itself with an endless supply of food. Another bit of lore suggests the artifact played a part in "healing rituals," where it could revive and cure the wounded—repair them; you know, you could stick your hand in and it would fix your hand. In later "Arthurian Traditions"—which emerged out of British Welsh Druidism during the Celtic period, or during the Christian period, rather—by that time, the Cauldron motif is connected—via Christianity—with the "Holy Grail" as a life-giving symbol, and the pursuit of the "Grail" as carrying the "Great Mystery" or the "Legacy."

In our present day understanding, there are other connections to the "Dragon Legacy," which is specifically connected to what you've actually found in some of the "alternative history" and "da Vinci Code"-type work—"*Holy Blood, Holy Grail*"—and so forth. You'll find that there's a "Grail Tradition" also, that emerges, in the Celtic lands, that's connected directly to Jesus, the Jesus bloodline, the Jesus legacy and so forth.

I've focused on the more basic themes for our exploration in Grade-I Route-D at the Academy, particularly for the "Celtic" tradition—then we move into Mesopotamian tradition in Grade-II. But once you explore, for example, "Druidry" and "Mesopotamia" and this particular stream as it evolved into the Western Magical Tradition, it really doesn't matter from there—if you examine, for example, other forms of Western traditions or African traditions or Eastern traditions or other semantics, you will see the common ground and correlations easily... And even the Egyptian and the Roman and the Greek philo... the mythologies and so forth—you will begin to see certain common parallels.

And these various cultural mythological figures: although each one is presented within their own cultural paradigm or point of view as, pretty much, the *epicenter* of all existence—or the known world—when you take a step back, you'll find that each one of these *epicenters* was actually correlating with all these *other* epicenters; and that they were actually all having, you know, very similar experiences with very similar "*beings*" and phenomenon that all contributed to very similar background stories and so forth.

But each was relayed just a little bit different and specific to the language, the culture, the values, the ideals, and the geographies of different places. A certain mountain would be a home of the God—and if you went 3000 miles in a direction, you'd find another mountain, which was the home of the Gods and was the birthplace of whatever and if you, you know; each one had established their own version of this. And this is—it's not until you really start to see mass migration of human populations that any of this started to be able to be brought together under the banner of a *new* "Mystery School."

Unfortunately, these human populations—as ignorant as they were as they migrated—really just carried with them *their own* values, their own tradition, held on to their own specific paradigms as their stable datum and then, you know, set out to use it to either interpret or invalidate whatever they came along with each step of the way.

But... now, at this point: we're here in the 21st century; and we've got a Master-level understanding that we can access from the Mardukite Academy of Systemology which to work with all this material; and we no longer have to be restricted to any one or another paradigm or semantic-set, when we set out to realize and discover what is actually *true*.

MARDUKITE MASTER COURSE ACADEMY LECTURE #19[*]

"the faerie tradition"

The "Elven Histories" and the History of the Druidry and the Elven Way—the Faerie Faith as it evolved; as it developed—is relayed very succinctly in the *Book of Elven-Faerie* portion of *Elvenomicon*, or in *Merlyn's Complete Book of Druidism*. It may be explored and relayed in a diversity of ways; it could be connected very easily to studies of the "Dragon Legacy" (as relayed in the *Draconomicon*); it also relates very clearly to Mesopotamia in Grade-II.

When you consider history and cultures and the "mystical" developments from ancient times and then how it later evolved as the religions and traditions carried through the Classical period—what you end up seeing; you see this with Mesopotamia and the Anunnaki; you see this with the presence of those same Celestial Deities when they are appearing in other cultures, whether it's the Greeks or the Egyptians; and you see this present even in populations of the "Elven" and "Faerie" and "Dragonfolk" directly, in terms of ancient history—and this all concerns the *Rise of Humans*. As you see a greater rise in the *Human* population, you see, basically, those that are preexisting in "power," kind of bowing out—and setting up other infrastructures and traditions.

Now, in the case of, for example, the Anunnaki in Mesopotamia—I mean this was kind an "archetype" or a "blueprint prototype" area of development. So, you see an institutional "class" step in, where you have Priests and ambassadors and a specific lineage of "Kings" that's all tied to the Anunnaki directly. There's considered a "bloodline" or a "legacy"—a specific "genealogy"—that is carried forth; and you see "Kingship"—you see this in the concept of the "Dragon King," you see this in ancient China, all throughout ancient Mesopotamia, in *Pharaonic* dynasties of Egypt; you see this in any classification or use of "Dragon" iconic imagery to represent "Kingship" and "sovereignty" all throughout Europe.

Of course, this all goes back to a specific programmed association between the "Dragon," "The Land," the ordering of cosmic systems

---

[*] Transcript of a lecture given by Joshua Free on September 23, 2020; revised from "*Druids, Elves & Dragons: Mardukite Master Course Academy Lectures (Volume II)*"— also contained in "*The Complete Mardukite Master Course*."

and sovereignty of "Kingship." And so this symbolism gets laid out and we find these specific "beings," which at first are essentially "gods" when you look at the very root of it; the farthest back—the Anunnaki, the Celestial deities—these are considered 'gods'.

And we don't mean "God" with a capital "G" as the 'Origin of All Things'—but their status; their status and their relationship with the Physical Universe. And the status of the ruling power and its representation with the "Divine Right to Rule" is always a mirror of this higher idea. So, it was put into place—it was implanted—in consciousness, that in the absence of these "gods," then we would have specific "Priest-Kings" and a specific lineage of mystics and so forth, you know—might be half-breeds or quarter-breeds or hybrids or however you want to look at that—they were considered a separate class of beings by comparison to the rest of the population.

Now, a lot of this gets related back to physical bloodlines. This of course, begs the question—and a lot of *hoopla* gets brought up about this on the internet—concerning RH-negative blood-types and all this stuff. But, really what is relayed here is just an example or demonstration of various genetic manipulation down through the ages. It led to establishing various 'shadow traditions' and 'underground traditions' allegedly carrying specific lineages of genetic memory that would otherwise be lost, watered-down or diluted through the common population...

And so, these are all important aspects, but when we look at it from a systemological paradigm, to consider, any of these aspects purely from the physical perspective is to be incredibly limiting about our understanding about the Human Condition. And herein lies the beautiful trapping of Grade-I, Route-D. To limit anything to any one or another "genetic vehicle" type, we know to be a falsehood. That only further contributes to fragmentation of a clear and true understanding.

We know that these vehicles, as the Human Condition, are actually capable of an incredible amount, regardless of any of their ancestry. We also know that genetic memory can be systematically resolved for an individual—as far as a separation of that identification with *Self* as a *Spirit*.

We know that *Alpha-Spirits*[†] come in and out of this Universe or Planet

---

[†] A term used in Systemology to indicate the *Self* or actual "I"—or the individual as a spiritual being that is independent of any material body for its existence.

all the time. We know that beings have experienced not only countless lifetimes in *this* Physical Universe, but other universes as well, are able to come in and assume points-of-view and command and control over physical action of a "body."

It's when a person is entrapped in that body and identifies *Self* with it that we start to get into trouble. It's only when consideration of "Self" is *for and as* the "body," we start to get into trouble. And so when we refer to these various "Races" and types—well, certainly in ancient times, significant differences existed between various populations and cultures; most of which operated fairly remotely to one another, up until 2500 years ago.

2500 years ago is around the time when the Greeks *first* encountered the Celtic people and Druids and began writing about them in history —about 500-600 B.C. And between then and now, there was *that same amount of* time taking place before that—if you consider the origins of Stonehenge and things of that nature—a couple thousand years *before any* Classical encounters, or the Greeks or Romans or anyone else that encountered prehistoric Celts to write about them for the history that *we* still use today.

And so, anything prior to that in the "Celtic" lands is essentially "prehistory," because it becomes open to archaeological and anthropological consideration and speculation. We can carbon-date various sites all we want, or try to. We make comparison between certain styles of art and pottery that is unearthed, but when it comes to the written records, we actually have to dig much farther and go back to the Ancient Near East and the cuneiform tablets to find records of the type of antiquity that we are often looking to go to—and those begin about *6000* years ago.

There aren't many literary records prior to encounters of the Classical world with the Celts to differentiate or determine a traditional or universally accepted academic history concerning Druids and other "Elven" and "Faerie" traditions; all of the Celtic traditions, all of the "Faerie Faiths"... All of that. And so forth most part—in terms of the "academic world"—most historians have left that area alone.

FAERIE TRADITION & THE NEW THOUGHT.

When we consider that the Spirit is eternal, and that these beings, which would have been intermediaries or descendents of, you know, the "Children of Anu," and descendents of "Priest-Kings" and "Dragon-lineages" and so forth, from very distant times. We would assume that they would, of course, have an increased capacity of ability.

The concepts that later get relayed—in terms of elementals; elemental beings; Elementalism—we know at one point, spiritual entities would have the ability to choose and discard bodies at will; or even be able to inhabit a wider range of existences. For example, you see increased appreciation for "Nature Mysteries" and natural traditions as "Danubian Druidism" goes from being a practice *by* the Elves themselves, the Faerie folk, the Dragon Kings and so forth—and later becomes traditions practiced by a class of Priests or Druids; those that are dispensing a "Human" version of the tradition to the common Celts.

In the beginning, contrary to popular definitions, Druidism is *not* a "religion" practiced by the common Celtic people. Druidism was originally the tradition practiced exclusively by the "highest minds." It was later systematized, codified and then used to establish or organize Celtic society. But, for example, when the "Pheryllt" are present in Wales or the Tuatha d'Anu are showing up in Ireland, we're talking probably 2000 B.C. or so. This is a different point in the evolution of common culture than what is understood today when you just see what it all eventually evolved to.

The idea that there's an Otherworld, Faerielands and alternate existences, is pretty common to virtually every ancient tradition; as is the idea that an individual decides to be the Spirit of a "Place"—to locate themselves as, for example, a Guardian Spirit of a particular "locale" or even the point-of-view or Beingness of a "Tree" thereafter. These are not ridiculous concepts. We see these elements intermixed between the lines of what is considered "Celtic Faerie Lore" or traditions of the "Faerie Faith" and "Elven Druidism" and so forth.

I mention this because when we deal with Elementals or talk about the Spirits that are inhabiting Nature and consider the amount of time that ancient Druids spent in "communion" with and "communicating" with natural surroundings, it might begin to make a little more sense. And clearly, when the Milesian Celts began showing up and the "Human" populations, races and cultures were starting to all push westward, these ancient beings had the ability to "transition" in to an Otherworldly "Faerie Country"—being driven from their Earthly homesteads.

I traced these prehistoric migrations, for example, based on the patterns of the La Tene culture, based on the way which these individuals set out from the Ancient Near East—whether it was Galatia, like modern-day Turkey or closer to Mesopotamia. But, this evolution showed that as the populations were growing around them, the Faerie were moving farther and farther west themselves; and they had reached the western point around the time of, at least, Stonehenge.

This is why you see a lot of issues with the classification of what is "Druid" versus these "Pre-Druidic"—the Danubians or "Pheryllt" — which we still consider "Druids" and such. And the big argument has always been "well, Stonehenge was there at a time before the Celts were there..." Well, I guess that would be true if you consider that the "Celts" were only encountered and labeled for the first time by the Classical writers in 600 B.C.

Communication and true understanding of history is quite obviously fragmented. There is little dispute about that. Understanding its truth is often a matter that reaches beyond what realizations can be earned from books. It's really a matter of *where* a person is placing their attention that determines what's going to be considered *real* or *acceptable* or within their *reach* of understanding. Because most of the time, their attention has really been diverted everywhere *but this*; and "history" has been treated as such a dry boring subject for a long time.

When individuals start to realize that pursuing any of these esoteric mysteries deeply also means encountering rigorous history lessons—reconsidering all of what has been learned about history; some people become incredibly overwhelmed by that and just sort of put all this "history stuff" aside because it seems like too much to go through.

ELVEN DRUIDISM & SYSTEMOLOGY.

A "Master"—with a Master-level understanding earned at Mardukite Academy—knows that we are treating the "Route of Druidism, Elven-Faerie Tradition and Dragon Legacy" as just the *First Veil*. We consider it part of the *Lunar Level* or *Gate*. We consider it part of the level which has a lot to do with the "magick" and "enchantments" and "glamours" of the various lights and elements and symbolism found in mysticism. To an individual just starting out on the *Pathway*, all of this stuff seems like an incredible new world; it's a "whole thing" when people finally open to that "all of this is there and exists" and "hey, it can be studied without being a devil worshiper—or some other connotation. It is an entire realm in and of itself; its own "continuity"; it's its own "level"—its own Grade or plateau—entrance into it, its own "*Gate.*"

This is really first steps for some people; and to consider that any of this has even taken place in this past on this planet, just thousands of years ago. It's a place to begin. And so this is why this all falls particularly within the domain of Grade-I for the Academy.

And then one particular benefit of Route-D, Druidism or the "Nature paths" is that—in terms of the *Pathway to Self-Honesty*—it does put one in greater contact or communication with the *Fifth Sphere of Existence*, which is "All Life on Earth" or "All Physical Life." This is one step beyond only treating "Human Life" or the point-of-view of the "Human Condition" at the *Fourth Sphere of Existence*. So, it allows someone to begin to operate—or *Be*—or consider point-of-views, or establish lines of communication, with that which is actually "exterior" to strictly a "Human" experience.

That's what is suggested by "shamanism" or "shape-shifting" traditions and such lore—what you see is basically the ability to establish a point-of-view; to establish the center of Beingness *outside* of a consideration of strictly just the "Human Body" or "Human Condition."

So, you have someone that can basically project and command a point-of-view beyond the physical body that they're tied to; the ability to go out and *Be* a "Tree"; to go out and *Be* the "Wolf"; go out and *Be* these other points-of-view, which are points of "Beingness" and points of "Knowingness." And we know that the highest echelon of "Knowing" is "Being"; and *being* something and *knowing* as a result of *that* point-of-view is essentially the highest point of Awareness or understanding that you could have on something.

This is something that we see in the "Nature traditions." Rather than putting an emphasis on just getting along better in the "physical world" and "what rituals can we do to get a better job in this material existence" and, you know, "how to entice the affections of the girl in the neighboring farm" or something like that; this becomes more about an individual 'mystic path' where a Seeker is reaching out and establishing lines of communication with the existence all around us.

And there is no danger behind this pursuit, so long as—like we referred to in previous lectures—that this doesn't become simply a matter of finding more of points agreement with the Physical Universe; or agreeing to facts that the physical and material existence is *all* there is. Fragmentation entraps an individual to this particular point-of-view.

The purpose should always be towards "Ascension." A simple survey of these types of traditions and a simple pass through or just read through with no higher-level comprehension of this stuff, really doesn't get an individual *there*; it doesn't get someone necessarily to these higher points of realization or the ability to understand the concept of *Beingness*, and point-of-views and Awareness—relating it to Nature, natural surroundings, other lifeforms. There's no guarantee that a *passive* or simply a *common* contemporary survey or participation with these "mysteries" is going to get an individual any further.

There we see boundaries—as I've explained—of Grade-I, or the *First Gate*, versus the *Second Gate*. And when we're talking about these "Gates" and "levels" of realization, we're still treating, systematically, the same existence; we're still treating our understanding of universes; we're treating Self; we're treating the concepts of what we can know and what we can do in the directing of energy.

The only difference being exactly what that entails: the parameters and what we're willing to encompass as that understanding— that kind of gets bigger and bigger and we move Awareness up through these 'Spheres' or "Gates" or "Levels"; these points of realization and existence. Because we're moving *up* and this is the point that we start to see this transition—even in the Mardukite Master Course; because pretty soon here, we are encroaching on our Grade-II work.

Grade-II work, for our purposes, *does* centralize on the points and geography in history that is the Ancient Near East—Mesopotamia and Babylon—but the principles, the truths behind all this, as I've tried to explain prior: that which makes any of things effective, and that which has given any of them the ring of truth, carries forth as we move forward—we're able to bring that with us. It isn't a matter of "Oh, well, we spent all this time doing this and that's *all* now nonsense." That really only becomes the case when a person gets *stuck* on a particular level. The actual passing through of this knowledge—the moving through of all the Master Course materials—can actually be done quite swiftly and with total comprehension, so long as a person doesn't get too exclusively immersed, or stuck or hung up on any one of the points.

You're, of course, entitled to your own opinions and to discover what works for you and what works best for the Seekers you instruct—but its important that we have this standard of delivery for the Academy; and that your personal experiences, inclinations and opinions do not affect that standard of delivery when you represent the Academy or this material. We try to eliminate as much of the "reactive programming" in our Pilots and Instructors before we just turn them loose on the world.

It's important that I have demonstrated that the Mardukite Master Course is a fixed set of material an individual can access; whatever edition a Seeker uses, the material still falls within the standards and curriculum outlined for this material. This way nobody is getting lost on it and it's really up to you Masters and Instructors—watching the cues of your Seekers that you're working with—to determine the direction and flow of this information; for *you* to have a complete understanding of it; for your to be able to *relay* it as best applied; and to be sure that your personal inclinations and experience aren't getting in the way of the clear transmission and communicated duplication of this material.

THE ELVEN-FAERIE SPELLBOOK

enchantment of the faerie realm

From the perspective of the physical realm or material world—or Earth—(or what is referred to as *Beta Existence* in Mardukite Systemology) there is an intermediary realm between *us* here and a truer, more infinite, "Spiritual" (or *Alpha*) Existence. The intermediary realm is often referred to in Elven Lore as the "Middle Kingdom" (and in Systemology as the "Magic Kingdom"—the residual of a former "Magic Universe"). In the traditional Semitic Kabbalah, it is represented as "*Yesod*" (or elsewhere in esoteric lore of the "Ladder of Lights" as the "Moon") or "Lunar" level of all potential existences—a Universe only thinly veiled from our own.

Intuitive and mystically inclined *Seekers* are frequently relaying experiences where they have gleaned a "sense" of this other realm; or occasionally have caught a "glimpse" of the 'elemental beings' and "Nature Spirits" that sit silently watching—peering out from between the folds of woodland foliage, the mists, or even riding the backs of animals.

There are vast differences in the portrayal of Faerie races throughout history and by various cultures. In one sense, they reflect the deities and heroes of ancient legend; in another, they seem almost 'angelic' or 'etheric'. A *Seeker* might easily compare the way in which we read of the humanoid "Tuatha d'Anu" of ancient Europe in contrast to the nature of the more 'Otherworldly' "Spirits" that do not necessarily inhabit typical human conditions of existence exclusively.

Even among 'New Age' practitioners, only a select few are drawn directly by inclination to immerse in Elven or Faerie traditions. In many cases, humans are not likely to take the ancient "fairy" and "Danubian" lore literally; they view the bulk of this subject as anthropomorphic misunderstandings about natural phenomenon, weather or biology. There is no 'deeper' (or 'higher', depending on your semantic preferences) understanding accessible to these individuals beyond the physical—or perhaps even what *they* consider the "Mind" (which, itself, has been almost completely misunderstood by mystics and scientists alike).

Reflecting the very qualities of 'Nature', the 'magic' of the Elven-Faerie Druid tradition is perhaps more 'subtle' than other esoteric occult practices. Memory of our direct experience with "Nature Spirits" from childhood often fades with time. The beliefs and practices maintained by the Fae themselves (and also the Elven Wizards that follow this tradition as metahumans in a mortal shell) are representative of Cosmic Order and the spiritual unity inherent in all Creation. It is not concerned with learning methods that coerce spirits or enforce some arcane pact by means of "blasting rods" or any such ridiculousness found in 'ceremonial magick'.

Those who are more 'sensitive' (or develop or 'sensitivity') are more easily able to increase their *Awareness* to perceive subtle effects from the spiritual intelligences that surround us on Earth and during our everyday lives. Such a 'belief' does not carry with it a necessity to believe that we are in any way victims or the effects of a myriad of obscure entities. Yet, all mystics and wizards are called such because they are aware of the interplay of existences that results in the visible manifestation we experience.

Interaction with entities occurs in a variety of ways, depending on a practitioner's sensitivity and also their own unique perceptual 'style'. Some individuals experience things more visibly; others, more audibly; or, even through tactile (touch-based) senses. Most practitioners of the Elven-Faerie tradition also intuit a nearly continuous presence of a particular 'Guardian' or 'Guide' from the Faerie realm. Various traditions obviously interpret the nature of this differently—but many of those drawn to these beliefs are likely to already have at least some sense of reality on '*Faerie Spirit Guides*'.

Unlike the manner of goal-implanting "To Survive" inherent in the Human Condition operating within an experience of *this* material existence, the Fae and 'Nature Spirits' operate from the Magic Kingdom existence that emphasizes a goal "To Enjoy." As a result, these beings are attracted to more light hearted and joyful environments and individuals. When 'Guides' notice a *Seeker* getting 'too serious' about the Human game, they may even intervene by playing small pranks; the most common being to 'hide objects', prompting you to be more aware.

There is also phenomenon associated with portals or 'thresholds'—not only those that are outdoors in 'Nature', but also those that are inherently a part of home-construction; such as doorways, windows, closets, hallways, and of course, mirrors. And this says nothing of those 'magical constructs' made by 'New Agers' intentionally to serve the purpose of such a 'portal'—or 'relay point' for communications between *this* existence and the 'Otherworld'. A sensitive individual may get a 'sense' of subtle energetic differences resonant with these 'thresholds'—even when they are not considered 'active'.

Encounters with the 'Faerie Realm' require a special etiquette that is not altogether common among Humans. There is a respect and courtesy involved that is reminiscent of aristocratic "courts" of legend and history. There is also a special etiquette involved in actually 'addressing' the Fae. It is not likely that a magical practitioner will learn the "true-name" (or "real name") of a specific 'entity' or 'nature spirit'. The name that *is* often given to you by these spiritual intelligences is only for the convenience of having something to call them—nothing more.

Common classifications for the Elven-Faerie 'types' or 'races' are included in traditional lore, but they serve the function of magical conveniences for 'Elemental Magick'—they are not strictly accurate of the Otherworld (Magic Universe). What they do reflect is an even more 'solidly condensed' reality that is relatively 'beneath' the Physical Universe that is identified with the experience of the Human Condition. They do not reflect the "Magic Kingdom" from which *this* Universe condensed from, so much as they are perfect infinite expressions of those 'elements' that we *do* find manifest in *this* Universe.

Fractioning of the "Elemental Realms" into four parts is illustrated in the contemporary standard of the *Hebrew* "Kabbalah" that is used in 'ceremonial magic' and 'esoteric orders' such as the Golden Dawn. In that cabalistic model, *this* Universe is represented as the "Kingdom" (or '*malkuth*') at the lowest (most condensed) order of manifestation. The remainder of the 'Tree of Life' is indicative of the progressive or cumulative descent of the '*Spirit*' (*Self*) and the Universe it considers itself to occupy. This is based on Anunnaki lore of the Ancient Near East.

The lowest '*sephiroth*' ('station' or 'sphere') of the traditional "Kabbalah" is often depicted as a circle with an "X" dividing it into four parts. Each of these parts or fragments is indicative of an 'Elemental Realm' that is a further condensation of elements in *this* Universe. Therefore, an Air Realm might be conceived of as infinite (or recursive) space or a 'plane' or "wind" extending in all directions; much like what we conceive for a Water Realm that would consist of *water* in place of "airy space"—but also perceived as extending 'infinitely' in all directions. Since the "Magic Universe" is more 'fluid' (meaning less condensed) than these descriptions, we must conclude that these are extensions of *this* Material/Physical Universe.

The lowest-most 'compartmented' Universe or Realm represented by this model *is* actually the very extension of *this* Universe that will represent the next level of degradation for the '*Spirit*' and its reality considerations; and we mean of course the Earth Realm of 'rock' and 'stone'. If one could imagine that a plane of infinitely recursive solidity could extend as a Universe, then one can see the future for *this* dwindling spiral of existence.

According to lore, spiritual intelligences of Nature are not tied to permanently physical bodies and forms. 'Nature Spirits' use "faerie glamour" to affect the visible appearance of their size and shape when they manifest more concretely in the Physical Universe. As such, there is little value in emphasizing the various ways that Humans have chosen to conveniently classify or categorize their various encounters with the Other; information that is often passed off as genuine magical lore, when in fact it is simply the local vocabulary of one or another culture, communicating about universal phenomenon.

The earliest recorded cultures often associated 'Nature Spirits' with other lore regarding 'angelic beings' and 'Divinity'. However, in the present text—and in regards to the ancient Eurasian Elven-Faerie Druidic tradition—we are referring specifically to those 'spiritual intelligences' inherent in the living systems found on the Earth planet. By the term 'Nature Spirit', we mean specifically those entities found in 'Nature'—or else the 'Green World'—and quite often we also mean those 'Elemental Beings' encountered frequently by ritual-magicians.

Inviting the nature spirits into your realm

Our existence and reality is multifaceted or manifold; it is composed of many interconnected parts or dynamic systems. The first and most critical step toward inviting these spiritual intelligence into your life and reality *is* the belief and acceptance—or rather, agreement—with that reality. Phenomenon is taking place all around us in the Universe all the time. Our perceptions are, of course, restricted to the degree of awareness or attention that is directed by an individual. We are not referring to 'made up' things in this book that are not there;

we are placing our attention—or shinning a light—on a facet of existence that is simply not often explored.

The second step toward inviting the 'Nature Spirits' into your life is to simultaneously make a place for them (metaphorically and physically) while proving your worth as a 'fairy ally' or 'elf friend'. It is often said that "every flower has its fairy; and every tree has its spirit." Humans carrying this knowingness in their lives are more likely to experience its reality; they are more likely to effectively invite 'Nature Spirits' into their own lives. Consider, for example, how many 'people' there are in the world—and yet if you don't know anything about someone, have any 'affinity' or 'communication' with them, then there is no relationship at all—and their "existence" seems rather inconsequential, no matter how "real" it may be.

When examining the various collections of lore passed down to us, it is quite clear that 'practical' applications generally surround the tending of herbs, flowers, animals and trees. Doing so forms a 'link' or strengthens a 'bond' that allows the interconnectivity of realities or *realms*. By sharing in the agreement of considerations concerning Elven-Faerie folk, we thereby open our lives to the potential of sharing such a *reality*.

One way in which a practitioner can bridge this *reality* is through intentional acts—or what some have referred to as *magic* in the past. The most common of these include herb and flower gardens, 'fairy-gardens' or other prepared 'natural' areas that are dedicated to the Fae and Faerie traditions.

A "Sunflower Portal" is easily constructed, economically grown and maintained to support a perpetual *bridge* between *realities*. This is more challenging in dense urban environments—but is preferably on one's own property, where it is readily accessible for use, observation, and of course, watering. As is often taught in 'magical lore', the preparation and maintenance of 'sacred space' is of particular interest to practitioners that seek to initiate 'magical activity' from *this* side of existence.

One might note that the Elven-Faerie folk are known for fashioning their 'dwellings' from the natural terrain—using their magic and patience to intertwine and entangle the growth of wood and plant-life to meet their own domestic needs when they manifest in the Physical Universe. Magicians and wizards believe that this is simply a reflection of their "Otherworld" 'dwelling-places'. In imitation of this activity, a practitioner will often find results by crafting their own version of the 'Enchanted World' that Elementals and Fae have a preexisting affinity for. The "Sunflower Portal" is a perfect example of this duplicative effort or 'magical act'.

The "Sunflower Portal" is one possible version of a 'planned fairy circle'—or rather, a 'planted' one. To accomplish this, a practitioner designates a particular area for sacred space. It is not required to be a large circle, since most of the Elven-Faerie tradition is practiced (or developed) in solitary. It should, however, be large enough to lie down in—so, at the minimum, using your own height as the diameter of the innermost clearing (circle). Sunflower seeds may be planted every few inches around the outer perimeter of the circle—making sure to leave a couple feet clear for an entrance.

According to traditional lore, 'fairy contact' occurs most often in places and times that are designated "thresholds" or "betweens." By this, we generally mean 'transitions' or 'shifts' from one distinct point to another. These generally reflect the personal or internal 'shifts' in "consciousness" that practitioners experience when they effectively pierce the "veil between worlds" that is all a matter of perception and Awareness—and not so much a matter of physical locales. The actual 'Spirit' or 'Self' has never been truly confined to the Physical Universe.

Thresholds or "between-points" appear all throughout esoteric lore. They are the 'magical' times and spaces assigned to various rites and spells across history and cultures. Clearly the ancients observed (or "sensed") heightened mystical—or otherwise "Otherworldly"—activity taking place during such times. It became evident that the energy —or at least a presence of Awareness—of such periodic states could be most effectively 'tapped' or 'perceived' in systematically aligned "places" specifically "tuned" to resonate or amplify such thresholds.

Although many books claim an expertise on the subject of "*natural magic*," much of the true enchantment experienced from Elven Magic and the Faerie Tradition results from personal exploration into these mysteries directly. The 'Secrets of Nature' are gleaned only by direct "initiation" into the folds of its mysteries—which are concealed only because we are no longer accustomed to 'look' beyond the surface world of 'Human Games' that we are indoctrinated into. The 'Key' to the 'mysteries' then, is not found in spells of incantation and fancy symbols, but in elevating *how* to 'look' and 'perceive'.

natural magic: the ancient craft of elven wizards

More than anything else, the esoteric arts of Elven-Faerie Tradition are classified as '*natural magic*'—meaning that they regard the 'aspects' and 'elements' of Nature, but also that these practices themselves come naturally to the Fae, even innately. Their type of "magick" differs greatly from what is found elsewhere in the 'New Age' concerning 'ceremonial arts' and 'grimoires'. It is born from a 'natural' understanding of 'Nature' and the 'Universe', and an understanding of the true relationship between "*Self*" and all existence in creation.

As increasing Human populations began to also observe practices of the 'nature spirits' the cultural charms and enchantments that they imitated came to be called 'folk magic'. It does not consist of ornate priestly rites involving a lot of specialized elaborate tools or obscure glyphs. They are the customs of the 'peasant folk' and practices inherited by 'gypsy witch' family lineages.

The types of 'magic' written down in other volumes of this series—such as '*Elven-Faerie Grimoire*' and '*Enchanted Forest*'—are intended to both preserve the styling of a specific tradition and provide a synchronous coherent focus when practiced in a group, or even individually among those 'sharing' in a tradition. But the words themselves—and the ritual gestures, *&tc.*—are not where the actual 'magic' is to be found. Such aspects are simply meant to systematically orient a practitioner's attention-energies in a specific way. Eventually, this ability to shift in 'Awareness' or 'consciousness' does not require the ritual 'triggers' and ceremonial 'stimuli' that a practitioner is first introduced to during their developmental period. And such a period may extend for the entire lifetime of some individuals.

'Thresholds' and 'Between-points' are one way a practitioner becomes accustomed to observing (or sensing) phenomenon. These include the solstices and equinoxes, phases of the moon, transitional times of night and day—and places where light meets shadow, water meets land, the forest rises up from the plains, and mountains meet sky.

The "simplicity" of *natural magic* reminds us of what 'true magic' *is*. Too often a practitioner becomes overly absorbed in correspondences and dramatic rites—they lose a clear vision on the actual 'magic'.

For as long as 'magic' has been a concept in this world, there has been a general understanding that it constitutes the act of applying *Will* via *Intention*. It is, by nature, "metaphysical" because it introduces something into this Physical Universe that would not otherwise be present. The 'origination' *or* 'Source' of *Intention* is not locally present anywhere in the Universe, because the actual *Self* or '*Spirit*' exists in a state beyond the confines of *this* Universe. Therefore, we are imbuing or 'impinging upon' *this* world when we induce change via the *Will* and *Intention* from *Spirit*. And it is generally only from this heightened or elevated perspective or awareness from *Spirit* that a practitioner is not only able to experience the enchantment present around them, but also be aware of their own participation in a magical life where an individual is in control of their own '*destiny*' and is able to exercise their own self-determinism in all ventures.

Druid magic, the Elven Way and other Faery Traditions all represent this higher understanding of 'magic' and the 'mysteries' of 'Nature'—even if not all of the practitioners that operate under such a 'title' or 'name' have actually achieved the elevated realizations that are embedded within this 'magical work', otherwise called the 'Great Work'.

At a practical—or 'modern'—level of reality, *natural magic* shines light on the remedy for the encompassing sickness that plagues the Human Condition and *our* world. It suggests just how 'out of touch' and 'out of communication' the Human population really is—having lost sight of the interconnectedness of all life and existence in this Universe.

If one chooses to find it, there *is* a 'high magick' inherent in the simple glamours and charms found in Elven-Faerie lore and wizardry. It is not always immediately obvious, except when one realizes that these simple acts are 'intentional acts'—and therefore, 'magical acts'. Efforts to unnecessarily complicate the field of spiritual mysticism and metaphysics often only occur in an absence of true knowingness and experience.

Enacting the arts of 'Elven Wizardry' is only a matter of opening up lines of communication and affinity with the reality of Nature—and living with the awareness of a 'Fairy-Realm' in your day-to-day beliefs and lifestyle. Doing so allows a practitioner to better shift their 'consciousness' (or 'focus' of one's 'attention' and personal energies) to a higher '*meta-state*' than what's conditioned in the "normative" perceptual level of the Human Condition.

Naturally, the Elven-Faerie tradition is not the *only* route by which this is achievable—but, it is the one presently of concern to this text. Even those esoteric traditions that do not appear to emphasize "Nature" and the "Green World" in their practices must still rely on systematic organization of the *Cosmos* in this Physical Universe for their methods and models to operate as a coherent paradigm of ideas and techniques. For example, you tend to still find many elemental and celestial (planetary) alignments in operations of 'ceremonial magick' or the 'high magickal arts'. There are obviously many parallels between our local Universe and the Otherworld or 'Magic Universe'.

natural magic: tuning into nature

The 'Mysteries of Nature' are no "mystery." Everything is 'hidden in plain sight' as they say—but, of course, one needs only adjust their vision to *see*. What we call "nature" is actually a 'manifestation' of *this* Universe—and as such, everything that we must know about *Life* and the *Universe* is everywhere around us. This includes the lessons that we might learn which yields greater *Self-knowledge*. For as the wise mystics have said: *Seek to understand yourself and you will understand the Universe.*

"Magic" is the application of "Will" as directed by personal "Intention"—aspects of *Self* (or *Spirit*) that originate from a higher plane or level of existence. Technically, it is this power of "Will" that we impress upon this *Universe* that causes any action or manifestation to occur. These operations take place systematically as a relay of communication (or 'energy') from *Self* that ultimately results in the 'emotional energy' and '*physical efforts*' manifest in this Universe.

The more elaborate rituals and formal rites appear in the companion text—"*Elven-Faerie Grimoire.*" They form the more traditional structure expected from a 'New Age' practice, complete with initiations, consecration of tools and seasonal observations. However, the 'fine tuning' of the "magic" is not inherently present in ceremonial texts themselves. This results only from practice and experiencing true realizations that advance an individual's progression on their spiritual journey. True 'faerie magick' is not dependent on stringent adherence to a ritual text. It is a clear communication of *Will.*

The '*natural magic*' described in this "spellbook" is based on the premise of 'living in the moment' and applying 'presence' and 'intention' to acts and activities—including the more "esoteric" displays. Whether it is the act of placing stones in a certain way or wearing a type of crystal; arrangement of a garden or gathering flowers and herbs; the burning of incense or taking a purification bath in times when emotional clarity is required—all of these things become 'magical acts' when an individual truly and clearly *Self-determines* that they *are* 'magical acts'.

In many ways, *natural magic* and '*folk magic*' are synonymous to one another. They both concern 'simple' charms and enchantments in contrast to more technical "kabbalistic" ceremonialism present in renaissance-era "grimoires" and similar variations inspired by them. As such, the more 'basic' or simple magical arts that survived among the "rural folk" traditions are often overlooked by the more elitist and philosophizing 'magicians'. An innate need exists among many Seekers to *find* a more complicated formula or decipher one more 'spirit name' or 'sigil'—and it often becomes the "gambler's fallacy" in which one more 'pull of the handle' *will be* the 'winning' final secret needed, &tc.

In *natural magic*, the elements and tools of effective practice are *given* by Nature—and with the power of *intention*, a stick becomes a 'wand', a stone becomes an 'altar', herbs and crystals and incense all resonate the desired frequencies or vibrations... Every thing comes together so long as the operator is fully *aware* and *present* and acting with *Self-determined* 'intention'. The most carefully crafted ritual text is powerless if it includes any aspects that are not understood.

The basic principles on which *natural magic* is based—and on which it is effective—may be embellished or elaborated on as a means of personalization. However, a practitioner should be careful not to make this the emphasis of their work. Various gestures, vocalized incantations and other regalia may be involved when it effectively assists an individual in achieving their 'focus' and 'contacting' a specific shift in 'consciousness'.

As a basic fact, an individual—when operating from '*spirit*'—does not require any additional tools in achieving a desired state. But where we are concerned with an experience of *this* Universe from the 'vantage point' of the Human Condition, some 'assistance' is often helpful for developing preliminary gains and greater certainty in one's *Self*.

'*Nature Spirits*' are the spiritual intelligence embedded in the very physical systems or natural manifestations that a 'magician' or 'wizard' seeks to enact a "change" in when they perform what we consider "magic." It is considered wise, even among magicians, to operate along the clearest path of least effort and resistance when transferring energy or communication of *Will* and *Intention* from our higher spiritual source down into the interactions we exchange and manifest on more tangible, visible, or physical levels. By working alongside the 'Nature Spirits' in a cohesive relationship, the wizard accomplishes their goals in alignment with various agreed-upon 'Laws' and 'Systems' of the *Cosmos,* rather than in opposition to them.

For example: the basic principle behind the "healing magick" found in a variety of texts (for the 'New Age') is the concept of '*transference*'. This means 'displacing' or 'moving' an (undesired) energy from a point where it is interfering to another point where it is not interfering (or else is diluted or transformed). This only effectively operates as a matter of *Self-determined Intention.* Any symbolic representation employed or verbal incantation uttered is only an 'assistant' to a magician achieving this desired focus with all of their *Awareness.* As a *spell*, an organic substance—like a 'fruit'—might be rubbed on a wound or afflicted area as a 'transference tool' (or catalyst), which is then buried in the earth. And if simultaneously vocalizing the intention is helpful, then do so.

The Sunflower Portal is *Self-determined* 'Sacred Space' where you might go to 'recharge' or 'get grounded' as the case may be. This isn't the only place you might lie down flat against the surface of the Earth, but you'll likely feel more comfortable in a familiar space. In this wise, you can imagine or visualize emotional turbulence "falling away" from you and sinking deep into the Earth. Or else, you might simply spend some time in 'meditation' "tuning in" to the rhythms of Nature—the heartbeat of planet Earth. It does not require a lot of ritual hype in order to achieve this centeredness.

herbcraft and earth power

The planet Earth provides all the tools that a magician requires to practice *natural magic.* In many traditions, the Earth is anthropomorphized as the feminine "Mother" to all living things that require this planet for its existence. In some traditions, the Earth is represented—and even named—as a 'Goddess'. In one way or another, *she* is a provider of the *leaf, stem* and *bud* that appear in the magical 'rites' and 'spells' of the Fae.

The practice of "herbalism" or "herbcraft" is an inherent part of *Faerie* 'charms' and 'spells'. In fact, flowers, leaves, plants, roots and sticks—as found in Nature, or reared in a personal garden—are the basic tools and ingredients of *natural magic*. Recommendations and ritual texts employ these ingredients based on "magical correspondences" found in ancient Elven-Faerie and Druidic traditions. These were later carried over to modern times by various cultural vocabularies and traditions throughout history.

The practice of *natural magic* requires care and reverence—and ultimately respect for the 'spiritual intelligences' inhabiting the natural world. This is particularly important when '*using*' any part of Nature —which is to say, '*removing*' any part of Nature for personal use, even "magical" uses. This factor is not stressed enough in magic texts and is an underlying factor in many experiences of "failed magic" and sudden bouts of "bad luck" or similar. While 'spirits' of the Green World of Nature may reflect life-giving beauty and whimsical bliss inherent in creation, there is also the darker side of the equation, where the Universe can also seem quite cold and unforgiving at times.

At one's own basic 'spiritual' state—the 'Alpha' state in Systemology —there is no requirement for creation in a Universe. It is only a matter of deciding—or *postulating*—the 'beingness' or '*is*-ness' quality of something for it to exist. Of course, in the Physical Universe—to play the 'game of *Life*' in *this* material existence—there is a certain set of 'ground-rules' or 'natural laws' that we must have 'spiritually' agreed to in order to experience the Human Condition.

One of these Cosmic Laws—at least as we have agreed to for *this* Physical Universe—regards the 'give-and-take' relationship inherent in a 'closed system' such as planet Earth (or even the greater existence of the entire Universe as a whole). Scientists understand this as a the 'conservation of energy', which is a nice thought for their own physical paradigms, but it is not altogether 'spiritually true'. For example, the actually intention and thought that the '*Spirit*' impinges upon a 'body' is not from within this Universe—it comes from *outside* (or *exterior to*) the closed system of material existence.

In our local system—here on planet Earth—we have agreed to a game whereby every thing has its 'costs'; that there are 'actions and reactions'; that 'polarity' exists; and, of course, all 'forces' are constantly enacting to 'equalize' existence toward a theoretical 'balance' point that never actually perfectly occurs—but it keeps all things in a state of 'motion', or at least the appearance of such. In recognition of *Cosmic Law,* an Elvish Wizard (or practitioner of the Faerie Tradition) must act as a steward, guardian and caretaker for the realm which they take from.

While most of the elements and ingredients for *natural magic* are, indeed, found in the natural environment, there is one exception: the tool used to '*cut*' or '*remove*' those ingredients from Nature. In most modern traditions of 'magical herbalists', this tool or blade is referred to as a '*boline*'—a white-handled knife used exclusively in cutting plant-life for "magical" purposes. Use of a 'sacred' or 'consecrated' tool simply adds to the 'presence' of *awareness* being provided to the 'physical effort' as a 'magical act'. A wizard '*lives deliberately*'. This is what a 'magician' is really practicing with the 'magical arts', though it is not often realized.

In Druidic-oriented Elven traditions, it is not uncommon for a '*boline*' to be a crescent-bladed hand-'*sickle*'. Many practitioners prefer to harvest herbs and plants (for dietary and magical purposes) from a personal garden—something that is very much connected to the Faerie tradition. It is by no coincidence that the earliest pagan cultures were primarily 'agricultural' and their very survival was materially dependent on an understanding and relationship with the land.

When handling living plant-life, particular care is taken so as to not needlessly tear or damage the plant—especially if only a part of it is removed so the main plant (or tree) can continue growing. On smaller plants, the *blade* strike should be made as a single sure upward motion. It is removed silently after first asking '*permission*' from the plant and uttering the intention: "*With this strike, may you grow stronger.*" The act is finalized with a statement of "*Thank you.*"

Flowers play a major role in many Faerie Traditions. Practitioners commonly wear fresh flowers in their hair. Wreath-crowns as headgear is very popular among pagans. The 'magic circle' may be observed in your 'Sunflower Portal'—but when a temporarily 'circle' is made, or when 'casting' a circle for a group, flowers may be scattered along the perimeter (or a 'garland' may be used). Many details regarding the 'magical use' of *trees* is found elsewhere within this series-anthology. An entire section—"*The Enchtanted Forest*"—is dedicated to such subjects, along with its companion '*Book of Ogham*'. Therefore, such information need not be repeated here.

the faerie magic of herbs and plants

'New Age' material—particularly that which is on the market regarding 'druidry', 'fairies' and 'herbalism'—must be especially careful in its relay of "folk remedies" and "plant lore." During the rise of the "New Thought" movement in the 20th century, several of its pioneers were forced to confront 'legal' ramifications for the "illegal" dispensing of 'medical cures' or 'spiritual healing'. Even to this day, literature and other products distributed in 'New Age' marketplaces are required to carry various disclaimers. Thus, even in the present tome, we are dealing with a collection of archaic "folk lore" that is not meant to steer critical life decisions by a practitioner without consulting other professional sources in addition to our own.

A practitioner of these arts *should* have a well rounded knowledge base in the matters they intend to practice; whether those matters are those pertaining specifically to the 'spirit', or those that are intended to affect well-being by treating the 'physical'.

'*Faerie Magic*'—as it pertains to plants and herbalism—concerns both the physical and 'spiritual' aspects or facets. We find use of particular herbs in connection to rituals of various intentions due to their 'spiritual' or energetic qualities. We also find the type of "folk lore" that regards the type of 'remedies' and 'potions' concocted by the original *alchemists* of ancient times—and distributed by the very first *apothecaries* or *physicians* that predate the modern pharmaceutical industry of our present-day society.

Within the *Faerie Tradition*, practices of magical herbalism—or *herbcraft*—appear most frequently when applying incense, anointing oils (or perfumes) to a ritual working or "*spell.*" Additionally, various "folklore" concerns "*charms*" (and suggestions) for carrying specific flowers, leaves and/or herb-filled sachet-pouches as '*amulets*' to ward away a particular type of misfortune. Some very basic herbal magic *formulae* include:

Lunar Meditations (Moon)—frankincense, jasmine, mugwort, sandalwood.
Love and Romance—apple, cinnamon, rose, patchouli, sandalwood.
Peace and Serenity—acacia, bay (laurel), chamomile, sandalwood.
Wealth and Business—allspice, cedar, cloves, dill seed, nutmeg, poppy seed.

Studying and Learning—cinnamon, mugwort, rosemary, vervain, yarrow.

Success and Charisma—benzoin, cinnamon, dragon's blood, fennel, ginger.

Protection and Safety—anise, basil, frankincense, parsley, rosemary, sage, sandalwood, thyme.

In examining just a few of the uses of herbal amulets in "folklore"—consider that during the 1960's, the 'lucky' four-leaved *Clover* (and larger Irish *Shamrock*) were frequently carried by those seeking to "ward away" military service (or in this case, avoid the "*Draft*"). Elsewhere we find lore of *Nettles* being carried to protect against evil and to overcome fear; a wreath of *Mistletoe* is made to ease the pain of childbirth; *Vervain* is carried to escape one's enemies; *Acorns* are worn to remain youthful and vigorous; fishermen carried *Hawthorn* sprigs to ensure success at sea; ...such a list goes on and on.

Herbal incense and 'magical aromatherapy' are common subjects in the 'New Age'. Not surprisingly, many of the more commonly used 'scents' and 'essences' are frequently available even in your local grocery store—although there are varying grades or qualities of incense to be found on the market. Some of the most common include:

Apple—love, happiness, relaxation.
Camphor—psychic power, clearing.
Cinnamon—protection, sexual vigor.
Eucalyptus—healing, purification.
Jasmine—love, sleep/relaxation.
Musk—courage, sexual prowess.
Myrrh—protection, purification.
Patchouli—peace of mind, confidence.
Rose—love, peace, harmony, unity.
Sandalwood—healing, protection.

Use of incense is a long-standing tradition in practically all ancient forms of '*religion*' and '*mysticism*'. It is pre-manufactured for today's market, though a part of the ancient craft included knowledge to make it.

Archaic books and 'grimoires' record some of the more popularly used incense mixture formulae of ancient times—some of them known best as "temple blends" originating in the Ancient Near East.

In the 'medieval magic' lore preserved in *"The Sacred Book of Magic of Abramelin the Mage,"* the balm of *Cedar* (or *Aloe*) is mixed with *gum* and *storax*. *"The Key of Solomon"* suggests a blend of many sweet smelling *gums—Aloe, Nutmeg,* and *Musk*. Another famous "temple blend" employs equal parts of *Frankincense, Myrrh* and *Sandalwood*—and, in fact, these three frequently appear in 'ceremonial magic'.

A practitioner of the Elven-Faerie Tradition is likely to know at least one method for making their own incense. The most basic formula is for small blocks or cones, which is made from a 'dough'. You can even work the 'dough' around a thin stick. The charcoal-free recipe-formula calls for: (6 parts) powdered *Cedar, Pine* or *Sandalwood*; (2 parts) powdered *Frankincense, Myrrh* or *Benzoin*; (1 part) ground *Orris Root*; (6 drops) of a fragrant oil; and (4 parts) of some other powdered incense —worked like a baker's 'dough' mixed with *tragacanth gum-glue.*

Amulet Bags—or '*sachets*'—are made exactly like 'pouches'; or else, the practitioner may fashion a similar-style 'bag' using a four-inch square swatch of cloth (of an appropriate *color*). Herbs and small items are placed in the center of the square, then its corners are brought together and tied like a pouch. Alternatively, you could weave a draw-string through holes around the outside of a cloth circle.

If following traditional *Elven-Faerie* lore: 3, 6, or 9 different 'herbs' or 'items' are added to a single *Amulet-bag* before it is *consecrated* and *charged* with the "intention" of a practitioner using a formal 'ritual' or 'spell'. To achieve the desired effect, it might then be carried, slept with (under a pillow) or given away—whichever is most appropriate. The following are just a few basic suggestions to include for some common applications:

Protection (*white*)—ash, basil, bay/laurel, dill, fennel, mistletoe, mugwort, periwinkle, rosemary, rowan, saint john's wort, trefoil, vervain.

Healing (*blue*)—cinnamon, eucalyptus, garlic, lavender, myrrh, rosemary, saffron, sage, sandalwood.

Love (*red*)—apple, coriander, dragon's blood, jasmine, lavender, mandrake root, marjoram, rose, rosemary, vervain, yarrow.

Wealth/Prosperity (*green*)—basil, benzoin, cinnamon, clove, dill seed, nutmeg, patchouli, pine, sage.

alchemical herbcraft

'Herbal Alchemy' is most certainly found at the heart of ancient proto-Druidic *Pheryllt* and *Elven-Faerie* traditions. It is the primary facet of 'magic' exposed by *Welsh* lore of "Ceridwen's Cauldron"—and it is clear that *Vervain*, *Mistletoe* and *Oak* are among the most sacred of herbs used by the *Druids*, and of course, Ceridwen's "*Elixir of Wisdom.*"

Concoctions, brews, tinctures, 'mead' and other libations are an inherent part of cultural traditions. Recipes for such 'draughts' may also be found in *Elven-Faerie Druid* lore. In fact, the oldest records we have of these ceremonial *draughts* in European tradition relates very specifically to the *Faerie Folk*—the *Sidhe* residing in the hills and mounds. Often the *Elves* would be seen, during the dark half of the year, collecting ingredients.

In one version, referred to as the "*Draught of Oblivion,*" a practitioner smashes up one gallon of *Elder Berries* into three gallons of good clear well or spring water. This is then boiled together for an hour. Then the substance is strained, and three pounds of dark clover honey is added. When it has cooled, but still warm, one ounce of brewer's yeast is stirred in; then it is covered and left to ferment for two weeks. It is skimmed from the top into dark bottles and corked until fermentation ceases. To perfect such an art, some supplemental "brewing" knowledge might be sought by a practitioner from other sources in addition to *this* book series.

Fragments of lore allude to various "*Elixirs of Sight*"—meaning a type of mystical 'Otherworld Sight' or 'Fairy Vision'—that which would allow a practitioner to be sensitive to (or literally. '*view*') "between worlds." In one *Welsh* version, we read of a Druid's ability to extend their lifespans beyond the normal allotted years—and of course, along with this is supposed to be an increased gift of *prophecy* or the "second sight" as it is often referred to in the European Celtic lands.

European *White Pine* is of the 'Ailim Ogham' energy current, though traditionally it is given in lore as the *Silver Fir*; but there is a hidden 'Ogham' called *pingwyddon*—or *Pine*. The *Pine* needles are gathered on the 'Sixth Night' of the New Moon. These are made into an elixir by infusing them in hot water; but using water drawn from the deepest wells, which have never seen the light of day. It is ingested once every three days.

* * * * * * *

Elsewhere in occult lore, we find alchemical preparation of a 'psychic condenser' (a 'focal accumulator' or 'catalyst') in the training provided by esteemed magician *Franz Bardon*—and notably introduced to American paganism by *Ed Fitch*. The instructions for the most basic of these is to:

> "Bring two-tenths of a pint of distilled water to a rapid boil. Add two tablespoons of dried chamomile flowers. Remove from the heat and allow to cool, then filter into a clean container. Keep refrigerated for later use."

Another formula is given for a 'Universal Condenser' along with the suggestion that our aforementioned 'elixirs of youth' and 'cauldrons of wisdom' from legend were, in fact, "well-prepared psychic condensers." The "universal condenser" formula is a list of components —much like what we find in other fragments of spells in legend: *Acacia* leaves, *Cinnamon* flowers, *Peppermint* leaves, *Tobacco* leaves, *Viola-odorata* leaves and *Willow* leaves, all brewed together.

These types of potions or "condensers" are later used as 'magical ingredients' or 'components' in themselves—such as in place of an 'anointing oil' to activate a magical item or artifact, or to be used inside of a 'poppet' or 'golem' intended to represent the 'body' of a "magically created" elementary being.

* * * * * * *

Elemental, chemical and spiritual 'alchemy' are all systematized classifications of knowledge relating to the separation, identification and incorporation of various 'parts' in Nature. These may be 'elemental', 'chemical', 'metallurgic'—or, in *herbcraft*, they are concerned with the various parts of plants. And one might have noticed that many of the herbal formulae given throughout this book—and other sources of magical lore—often indicate whether the *root* or *stem* or *flower* or *leaf* is used as the component.

Philosophically—or elementally—speaking, each part of a donor-plant is aligned to a particular 'energy' *in addition* to whatever 'energy current' the plant represents as a whole. For example, feminine 'producing' parts of a plant—those that are operate under the domain of *earth* and *moon*—are the parts that are actually *in* the ground-soil and assist to deliver *water* to the remainder of the plant. These include the roots, main stem (or wood) that grows beneath the outer skin (or bark).

Looking at the other pole—of masculine energy—we find those more visible parts of a plant that are exposed to the *sky* and *Sun*: the leaves, flower petals and outer skin (or bark). So each plant (or tree, &tc.) carries its own unique attributes or qualities, as a species; then too, we have these correspondences that are alchemically associated with each part. This all contributes to a greater understanding that a practitioner will carry with them while operating *natural magic.* Far more than incantations, it is "high quality certainty" that makes '*magic*' effective.

elven-faerie druid herbal miscellany

Anointing Oils—frankincense, jasmine, lavender, lily-of-the-valley, rosemary, vervain.

Banishing—cedar, clove, cypress, elm, fern, mugwort, rue, st. john's wort, vervain, yarrow.

Binding Spells—apple, cypress, dragon's blood, pine, rowan, wormwood.

Black Willow Bark—one of the hormonal-control herbs of male continence used to decrease sexual drive among male Druids, particularly during developmental training.

Catnip—chewed by ancient Celtic warriors to increase their fierceness in battle.

Divination—cinnamon, hazel, laurel (bay), marigold, mugwort, nutmeg, rowan, sandalwood.

Healing Spells—apple, cherry, cinnamon, clove, hazel, lavender, myrrh, peppermint, rowan, sandalwood.

Hops—also known as 'beer-flower'; one of the hormonal-control herbs of male continence used to decrease sexual drive among male Druids, particularly during training.

Juniper—an incense for sacred visions.

Love Spells—apple, birch, catnip, elder, heather, honeysuckle, jasmine, juniper, lavender, marigold, mistletoe, patchouli, vanilla, vervain, wormwood, yarrow.

Marigold—also called 'sun-bride'; like dandelions, may be rubbed on the eye lids to assist in achieving 'Faerie Sight'.

Mistletoe—also called 'all-heal'; a small pinch of this was added to all druidic herbal remedies and formulae.

Moonwash—made from a half-ounce jasmine flower, half-ounce eucalyptus bark, and a half-ounce mugwort herb, soaked in a dark jar of one-quart rubbing alcohol for one week before straining.

Mullein—also called the 'velvet plant' or 'graveyard dirt' in some formulae; used in various types of necromancy and dark magic.

Narcissus—one of the hormonal-control herbs of male continence used to decrease sexual drive among male Druids, particularly during developmental training.

Rue—an anti-magic herb used in defense against the magic of others; also used in general purification rites or exorcisms.

Sunwash—made from a half-ounce chamomile flower, half-ounce cinnamon bark and half-ounce oak leaves, soaked in a dark jar of one-quart rubbing alcohol for one week before straining.

Valerian—a powerful sedative used for restful sleep and lucid dreaming, often in combination with black-willow tree bark; it also appears in some love-spells.

Vervain—also known as the "enchanter's herb"; found in various magical offerings and rites for warding off attacks, spatial purification and acquisition of wealth.

White Pond Lily—One of the hormonal-control herbs of male continence used to decrease sexual drive among male Druids.

Yarrow—also called 'woundwort' or 'milfoil'; an herb of love and unity.

Women's Wisdom: Emmenagogic Herbs and Fertility*

An '*emmenagogue*' is a hormone-affecting substance—usually a plant or chemical synthesis of its properties—that affects feminine fertility. It is the basic component of modern-day pharmaceutical birth-con-

---

* Paraphrased from "*The Great Magickal Arcanum*" anthology by Joshua Free, first published in 2008. Included here for educational purposes only.

trol, but its origins extend quite far into history. The functional purpose of an 'emmenagogue' is to promote menstruation as a means of contraception—either in the earliest stages of a pregnancy, or as a regimen of normal use in order to prevent such. Apothecaries and rural witches possessed this knowledge during the "Dark Ages"—and they provided 'potions' to those 'customers' seeking to maintain control over their own sexuality.

The safest way of administering an *emmenagogue*, or maintaining a regular regimen, is in a "tea" and/or "tincture" form. Many of the herbs are also available as extracts. For example, *Pennyroyal* tea is safe enough to drink—but the "essential oil" form of the herb (on the market) is toxic if ingested. In fact, most "oil" forms are toxic and used only for 'anointing' or for their 'aroma'. A pinch of *Myrrh* is sometimes added to these formulae—but very little should be used, and again, never in 'oil' form. However, this is originally why *Pennyroyal* tea was popular among 'high-society ladies' in the past.

In ancient Roman times, the *Willow*—particularly the leaves of the *White Willow*—were used to help control fertility and regulate feminine hormones later in life. It is natural source of "*estriol*"—which has since been synthesized in 'labs' for similar purposes. The berries of the *Chaste Tree* are found in the same formulae—and are actually named so for their effect. Some 'Native American' recipes include *Blue Cohosh*. In some Wiccan traditions, *Mugwort* is also added.

To begin a regimen, the above ingredients may be brewed together as a "tea" and consumed daily (even multiple times per day) during the period of a menstrual cycle. This will not only assist in alleviating some symptoms of discomfort, but will also begin to allow the body to associate the properties of the herbs with the menstrual cycle. This cycle should also be kept track of on a calendar. The herbal tea regimen may then later be started in preparation for—or prior to—when the cycle is expected to start. It may also help to promote regularity of the cycles, and in some cases shorten the duration of the actual period itself. When fertility is no longer a concern, the same regimen may be used to alleviate some discomfort associated with menopause.

the faerie gem*

In addition to the *"Elf-Stones"* (as described elsewhere in this anthology), there are many legendary '*Amulets*'—gems and stones—that appear throughout magical lore. As relayed in the *Celtic Researches* of author Dudley Wright:

It is said that every Druid wore around his neck, encased in gold, what was known as the *anguinum*—or *"Druid's Egg."* Pliny, in his '*Natural History*', gives one account of it:

> "There is a kind of 'egg' held in high esteem by the Druids, unnoticed by the Greek writers. It is called the *serpents' egg*... Its virtue is highly extolled for gaining lawsuits and procuring access to kings; and it is worn with so great ostentation that I knew a Roman knight who was slain by the Emperor Claudius for no cause whatsoever except wearing one of these 'eggs' on his breast during the dependence of a lawsuit."

The Druids themselves were called *Nadredd*, or snakes (adders) by the Welsh Bards; and there is no doubt that this famous object of Druidic superstition was manufactured. The serpent was a sacred reptile to the Druids. They supposed its spiral coils to represent the eternal existence of the 'All'. This *snake stone* is traditionally associated with Midsummer's Eve.

In Scotland, the 'egg' was known as the Adder's Stone—and it was in great reputation for the foretelling of events and divination, the working of miracles, curing disease and the gaining of lawsuits.

It is suggested in several sources that 'glass beads' were "earned" by Druid apprentices as symbols of achievement when progressing through various levels of learning. They were often hung on a cord as a 'necklace' as symbols of cumulative mastery or true authority over the 'mysteries' of Nature.

* * * * * * *

Another interpretation of the "Faerie Gem" or *Glain Neidr* (*Gleiniau Nadredd*) is that it is manufactured from 'glass'—possibly even transparent enough to "see through"—and thereby '*view*' the Otherworld Faerieland. In any case, the "glass gem no larger than an apple" (re-

---

* Paraphrased from "*Draconomicon 2: The Pheryllt Researches*" by Joshua Free; also available in the anthology, "*Merlyn's Complete Book of Pheryllt*."

ferred to in some legends) is directly connected to the 'Motherhood of Avalon'—which is to say the 'Isle of Apples' or 'Isle of Glass' (now Glastonbury).

It has been further suggested by certain scholars, notably Lady Flavia Anderson in "*The Ancient Secret*," that the original "serpent's eggs" were spheres of clear crystal used to 'light' the Druidic Beltane and Midsummer "need-fires" via focused sunlight—"sacred fires" that could only be naturally 'lit' by the Sun, by friction, or by lightning.

Some Words of Light: Elven-Faerie Tradition Dictionary for Spells and Rituals[*]

ABRAHOR: (A) The woodland realm of the Forest; the Wood Elves.
ABROREN: (A) Elves of Abrahor, meaning literally of the Forest and woodlands.
AETHYR: Substance of the Astral World; a sub-atomic field, which light travels on.
AFTERLITHE: July
AFTERYULE: January
AICME: (G) A set of five Ogham letters. There are four in the original system.
AINE: (G) The Queen of Faerie
AIRE: (Q) Holy or divine.
AIRBE DRUAD: (G) A mystical force field, esp. an impassable barrier or hedge.
AISILING: (G) A mystic vision or dream.
AIYA: (Q) Holy One, not in reference to God.
AKASHA: Fifth Element; spiritual fire; union of all Elements; quintessence at the core of all existence.
ALARDAN: (M) A festival or gathering of Elven-Ffayrie.
ALB: A prefix or root often referring to Elves; literally "Light."
ALBAN ARTHUAN: (G) Yule or Winter Solstice.
ALBAN EILER: (G) The Spring Equinox
ALBAN ELVED: (G) The Autumn Equinox
ALBANIA: "Land of Elves"
ALBAN HERUIN: (G) The Summer Solstice

---

[*] Extracted from the original "*Book of Elven-Faerie*" as compiled from rituals and lore contained in "*Elven-Faerie Grimoire*" and other notebooks for the *Elvenomicon*.

ALBANY: "Land of Elves"
ALBION: "Land of Elves"
ALBREDA: (G) Wisdom of the Elves
ALDARON: (Q) Lord or spirit of the trees and forest.
ALDEA: (Q) Treeday, Trewsday or Tuesday.
ALFERIC: (SY) That which is Elvish Magick or Druidic Forest Magick.
ALFI: (G) Elf Power
ALFRED: (G) also *alfredo*; white or Elf-wise, meaning both "counsel" and a "council."
ALGER: (G) Spear
ALTA: (Q) A brightness, bright light or light.
ALURED: (G) Elven council or court.
ALVA: Lugh's sister-in-law in Celtic Mythology.
ALVAR: (G) An army of Elves.
AMA: (SH) Blood
ANAIL: (G) Breath
ANAR: (Q) Sun
ANDUNE: (Q) West
ANG: (SY) The element and metal of Iron.
ANGA: (Q) The element and metal of Iron.
ANNUN: (SY) West
AOIFE: (G) The Queen of Faerie
ARDA: (Q) A plane or region.
ARTH: (S) A plane or region.
ARVA: (A) Flames, esp. the energy current of the Fire Element.
ASHA: (SH) Spirit or soul.
AUBREY: (G) Elf King
AURE: (Q) Daylight or sunlight.
AVERY: (G) Elf King
BA'ISTEACH: (G) Rain, esp. the energy current of the Water Element.
BAK'YAH: (A) A magick word used for counter-spells.
BARDD GWEWLL: (G) Specific shade of azure sky blue; dye used for Bardic cloaks.
BEAN-SIDHE: (G) A mourning spirit appearing around the time of one's death.
BLEEDING: Part of *foison*; inside of foodstuff removed, outside looks the same.
BRICHT: (G) Spellcraft or magick requiring a vocal incantation or spoken component.
BROWNIES: Earth Elementals; the Elven-Ffayrie "chefs" of Faerieland.
BWCA: (G) also *bwbachod*, meaning Brownies (earth elemental faerie).

CAERLLEN: (G) Ffayrie-mounds; literally "Ghost Hills" or "Spirit Hills."
CALAN: (S) Daytime or sunlight.
CERMIE: (Q) July
CERTA: (Q) A glyph, character or rune; pl. *Certar.*
CERVETH: (SY) July
CHOR'N: (A) A dark or black auric energy, esp. putrescence.
CIR: (SY) Circle or ring, esp. a stone circle.
CLOCH: (G) Stone
COIMIMEADH: (G) A Co-walker or Elemental being who appears to be Human.
COIRC: (G) A sacred vessel, esp. the ceremonial cauldron.
COOMLEAN: (G) An Elvensteed or horse.
COOSHIE: (G) An Elven Hound or familiar.
COR: (SY) Circle or ring, esp. a stone circle.
COR ANAR: (Q) The Solar Wheel of the Year
COROLLAIRE: (Q) Ffayrie-hill or "*howe,*" literally "green-mound."
CRANNCHUR: (G) The divinatory art of casting sticks, esp. Ogham.
DAETENIN: (A) Dark or unseelie, esp. dragons or dragon-like elementals.
DAEVAUN: (A) Woodlands or forest.
DAN: (SH) South
DEEA CANAYEN: (F) Calendar
DELPHINE: (T) "Elven" [usually feminine]
DESH-IRIAL: (T) Sister [proper]
DESH-KETAI: (T) Father [proper]
DESH-MIEVE: (T) Mother [proper]
DESH-MIRIAI: (T) Guardian of the Home
DESH-NERAIN: (T) Brother [proper]
DESHTAI: (A) To be honorable in following one's destiny.
DES'TAI: (TU) To be honorable in following one's destiny.
DEVIR: (A) To divert from the right path or follow the wrong destiny.
DICETIA: (G) A charm or spell.
-DOR: (Q) Suffix indicating a world or plane.
DORAI: (TU) Loyalty and duty felt towards loved-ones.
DRAKYR: (A) Dragon
DRAVIDIANS: The Tuatha D'Anu and later Sidhe.
DRYS: (GR) An Oak Tree, spirit of the tree or wren (bird).
DUATH: (S) Darkness
DUILE: (G) The Faerie Elements or Spirit of the Elements.
EA: (Q) also I'ria, the Source of All Being and Creation.

EAR: (Q) Sea
EASA'AHAE: (L) Peace
EDAPHIC: (SY) Stewardship lifestyle, tending soil/Earth,
        esp. Elven/Sylvanus.
EKAHAL: (SH) Elf Wizard
EKAHUA: (SH) A female spiritual adviser or Ffayrie Enchantress.
EKAHUEI: (SH) A male spiritual adviser or Elf Wizard.
EL: (A) Prefix or root indicating Elf or star.
ELA: (SH) Stars
ELAITH: (A) The spirit of a being or Star-Essence.
ELAITH TOR: (A) "Tower of Spirit"; auric-chakra personal energetic
        life system.
ELAN: (A) An Elf, literally Child of the Stars.
ELANDRA: (A) Elven
ELAYNOR: (A) also *elynor* and *elinor*, literally Star Dragon.
ELEN: (TU) Elf-Star or Elf-Friend.
ELENARI: (TU) Elf-Friend or Saturday.
ELENYA: (Q) Saturn-day or Saturday.
ELESSAR: (Q) Elf Stone
ELF-DAY: Tuesday
ELF LEAF: Rosemary (or sometimes Elm)
ELFRIDA: (G) Elf Power
ELFSHOT: In reference to when a mortal is struck by an Elf Arrow.
ELGAR: (G) Noble Elf, High Elf, or Danubian Sidhe.
ELIA: (A) The spirit or soul of a being.
ELM: Tree of Elves
ELOR'EL: (A) Moon
ELOYA: (A) Star-Heart
ELPHAME: Elfland, literally Protected-by-Elves.
ELVEN HISTORIANS: see remembrancers.
ELVEN HOLOCAUST: The Dark Ages, a period from 751 AD-1736 AD.
ELVIN: (G) Elf-born or Elf-Friend.
ELVIRA: (G) Elf-Friend
ELWIN: (G) Elf-Friend
ENDOR: (Q) The Middle Earth world of Humans or Physical Plane.
ENNOR: (SY) Derived from endor, meaning world of Humans.
-ENYA: (Q) Suffix meaning day or light.
ERA: (T) The Earth, land or Middleworld.
ERLINA: (G) An Elf, Sylph or Ffayrie.
ERU: (Q) The Source of All Being and Creation.
ERUSEN: (Q) Children of the Stars or Tuatha D'Anu.

ESHE: (SH) Elf-Friend
ESTEVAR: (A) Tonight, this night, evening or nighttime.
EVALA: (SH) Cloak
FAERIELIGHT: A folklore name for the Jack-O'-Lantern.
FAERIE RING: A naturally occurring circle or ring of high grass or mushrooms.
FANA: (IT) Goddess of the Woodlands
FANA: (Q) An invisible veil, esp. veil between worlds and dimensions.
FAUNI: (IT) Female equivalent of *silvani*.
FAUNUS: (IT) God of the Woodlands
FAY: (FR) Ffayrie
FEAS: (SE) Love towards a material object, e.g. "I love books."
FELONIA: (A) Sacred
FELN: (SE) Love towards magick and the Elven Way.
FER-DAN: (G) Bardic Druid scouts, messengers and news collectors.
FER-LAOI: (G) Bardic Druid metaphysical poets and musicians.
FEW: (G) An Ogham runic character
FEWS: (G) Ogham runic characters, plural.
FFERYLLT: (G) *Pheryllt*.
FIDTH: (G) An Ogham runic character.
FIN: (SH) Air Element
FIRIMAR: (Q) Mortal humans
FOISON: (SY) A game where Otherworld beings steal Human food.
FOLLETTI: (IT) Female woodland spirits; Etruscan Kingdom (Northern Italy).
FORELITHE: June
FUTHARK: (SC) The Norse Elven Runic alphabet.
F'YONN: (SY) Rebirth season, spring, literally the "Light Season."
GAEL: (A) Stone or gem.
GAETH: (G) Wind, esp. the energy current of the Wind Element.
GALADHAD: (Q) Trees, plural.
GALDROSTAFFYR: (SC) Using Norse Runes in manners similar to Ogham Magick.
GE'A: (A) also Gaea and Gaia, Spirit of the Earth.
GEIRT COIMITHETH: (G) see just-halver.
GEIS: (G) A mystical restriction or prohibition, ban or taboo.
GILLACHT: (G) Puberty
GLAM DIAN: (G) The most severe Druidic curse: excommunication.
GLAMOUR: A mystical enchantment where the physical nature/reality is altered.
GLAMOURY: An Irish-Celtic revival of Elvish Otherworld Tradition.

GLORA: (SH) Sun
GNOMA: (GR) The genetic family of the Gnomes, Kobold and Dwarves.
GNOME: Guardians of the Earth, Keepers of the Soil, esp. rocks
    and gems.
GRAIN: (G) Sun
GREENWORLD: The physical world region synchronous with
    Elemental Realms.
GWAI: (AL) Sky
GWAITH: (Q) Shadow
HAL: (SH) Festival day
HARAD: (SY)
HERMETIC MAGICK: An underground Greco-Egyptian mystical
    tradition of origins in the Ancient Near East (Babylon).
HISSIE: (Q) Mist
HITH: (S) Mist
HOLED STONE: also Holey Stone; Druidic Birth Stone or tool of the
    Earth Element.
HRIVE: (Q) Winter
HWESTA: (Q) Breeze
HYARMEN: (Q) South
IMBAS: (G) Divine inspiration or gnosis; literally "Fire-in-the-Head."
I'RIA: (T) The Source of All Being and Creation
ISH'MAEN: (F) Unseelie Wizard [slur]
ISILYA: (Q) Moon-day or Monday.
ISTAR: (Q) Wizard; pl. *istari*.
JANDA'HAI: (D) Mortal Humans, literally "Round-Ears."
JUST-HALVER: also *Geirt Coimitheth*; a spirit feeding on essence of
    what one eats.
KALEANAE: (L) Watcher, esp. of the Universe or a plane/dimension.
KALOREN: (A) The bright path or right way.
KANITH: (A) Lunar energies
KEMEN: (Q) Earth Element
KEROTH: (TU) Brother
KH'DEK: (Q) Ice or glass, esp. when used as a magick tool or catalyst.
KIERAN: (TU) Sister
KIRK: (G) from Scottish *Circ*; meaning a sacred sanctuary, esp. a
    stone circle.
KOBOLD: also *kobolda gnoma*, the blacksmiths of the Elven-Ffayrie.
KUSANAR: (T) Twilight
KYELA: (SY) Love
LA'AER: (A) Air Element

LAER: (S) Summer
LAIRE: (Q) Summer
LANDS ABOVE: The physical world or world of Humans.
LANDS BENEATH: The Underworld or Otherworld of the Sidhe.
LASSE: (Q) Leaf; pl. *Lassi*.
LAVENDER: Elf Herb
LEOLLYN: (G) The Sun Father, esp. Llew/Lugh of Celtic Mythology.
LES: (G) An herbal medicine bag or "juju pouch" carried by Shamans.
LIA FAIL: (G) Stone of Fate brought to Tara in Ireland from the Otherworld.
LINCHETTO: (IT) Night Elves, a lineage from the Etruscan Kingdom.
LIVEWOOD: *Wizardwood*.
LOR: (A) To shine or shine bright, esp. in relation to knowledge.
LOTESSE: (Q) May
LOTHRON: (S) May
LUMBULE: (Q) Darkness
LUVA: (W) Elvish bow
MACDACHT: (G) Prepubescent childhood
METONIC CYCLE: Great Year, an observable astronomical period of 19 Earth years.
MIDDLE EARTH: The physical world of Humans.
MILANA: (T) Forest
MIR: (SY) Jewel
MYHIDR: (AL) A lover who is a Life-Mate but not necessarily a Soul-Mate.
NAIDENACHT: (G) Infancy
NAN: (SY) Valley
NARBELETH: (SY) October
NARIE: (Q) June
NARQUELIE: (Q) October
NARWA: (SY) To "remember," as like an "awakening."
NARWAIN: (S) January
NARVINYE: (Q) January
NEL: (G) Cloud
NIA: (A) Master
NIEVE: (T) A lover who is not a Life-Mate.
NINASTRE: (T) Master of the Woods, esp. Kernunnos or Dagda.
NINUI: (S) February
NISHTAI: (A) Not to walk or follow one's destiny.
NISSA: (SC) A Sylph or Sylve, esp. female.
NOLDO: (Q) High Elf or Danubian Sidhe.

NOLE: (Q) Lore, folklore or knowledge.
NORUI: (S) June
O'FORFAMAR: (SY) Leadership
ONLAY: (G) A charm or spell fixed on a home or specific area.
OR'MN: (A) The Surface World, Middle Earth or world of Humans.
ORNE: (Q) Tree
ORTH: (G) A charm or spell.
OSTARA: (G) also Ostre, Ostera and Easter, *Alban Eiler*, Spring Equinox.
PARMA: (Q) Book
PEHLORA: (A) Water
PERIZADA: (G) Ffayrie-born or Fey-touched.
PHERYLLT: (G) A race of pre-Druidic Dragon priest-kings in Keltia.
PIXIE: (G) often defined as female winged sprytes; actually Scottish Pict-Sidhe.
RAELL: (A) Refuse or trash, esp. energy/habits one wishes to be rid of.
QUENDI: (G) The first-born Elves of Aeurope.
QUENYA: (G) The original language of the *Quendi*; depeicted as "(Q)."
RADE: Times of mass transition of the Seelie Court.
RE'AITAI: (G) Star, esp. the energy current of the SkyFire Element.
RECOGNITION: Innate ability for sensitive Elven-Ffayrie to recognize other ones.
REMEMBRANCERS: Elvish historians and loremasters.
RETHE: (G) March
ROCH: (A) Elven-steed or horse.
ROMEN: (Q) East
SAETH: (SY) Cloak, esp. of invisibility.
SAELR'IR: (A) Spirit of the Forest
SALAMANDER: also *draco salambe*; Elemental Fire-Drakes or fire-elementals.
SALAMBE: (GR) The genetic family of Salamanders and Fire-Drakes.
SALAN: (G) Salt, esp. the energy current of the Earth Element.
SATURDAY: Fey-Day
SEAN-SGEAL: (G) A folktale or faery-tale.
SEELIE COURT: The Blessed Court, esp. Elven-Ffayrie of the Sidhe.
SELEK'TAR: (F) A spiritual advisor, usually female.
SENACHIES: (G) Bards specializing in Ogham, esp. historical scribes/musicians.
SENDACHT: (G) Old age
SHADOWLAND: also Summerland, realm of the ancestral spirits of the past (or else a resonant "memory" of such spirits).
SHAMROCK: also *Trefoil* and *Trifolium*; the four-leaved clover.

SHEA: (G) Fey-touched and/or genius/brilliant.
SHELTIETH: (T) Unseelie, unblessed or dark in polarity.
SHOL: (SY) Elven Breath, like the Dragon's Breath, esp. healing energy.
SIANA: (SY) Yes
SIDHE: (G) pronounced "*shee*"; the High Elves of the Seelie Court, esp. Danubians.
SIDTH-BHRUACH: Silverwand or Ffayriewand, esp. made from the Apple Tree.
SIER: (A) Fire Element
SILPHE: (GR) The genetic family of Sylphs and Sylves, esp. the Sylvanus Folk.
SILVANI: (IT) also Sylvani, a masculine spirit of the woods, esp. an Elf.
SIMULACRA: An imitation or substitute, esp. Human shells an Elf spirit resides in.
SLATAN DRUIEACHD: (G) A Druid's staff.
SLAUGHMAITH: (G) The Good People, esp. the Sidth or Sidhe.
SOLMATH: (G) February
STEMLINE: The straight or middle line used to align Ogham notches.
STONE OF SCONE: Lia Fail or Stone of Destiny.
SYLVA: A treatise on trees or Elvish Forest Magick and wood use.
SYNDARIN: also Sinddarin, a Sylvan Language of Wood Elves, used by Tolkein.
SULIME: (Q) March
TAGHAIRM: (G) Necromancy; summoning (talking to) the dead.
TAURE: (SY) also taur, Forest.
TERRESTAI: Everlasting Forest, perhaps a reference to the Universe.
TIR-NAN-OG: (G) A mystic island of perpetual youth; a reference to the Otherworld.
THUILE: (SY) Spring
TOR: (A) Tower, lookout tree or tree hideout.
TORLO: (A) Intense strength, brilliance or brilliant light.
TORLORNOS: (A) World Tree or Tree of Life.
TOROTH: (A) Strength of the Oak Tree or immovable Oak.
TRANSIGNATION: An Elemental projects their Alpha spirit into a mortal body (viewpoint).
TRANSITION: The movement between world and dimensions.
TREE OF LIFE: also Yggdrasil, the metaphoric World Tree.
TREFOIL: also Trifolium, the Shamrock or four-leaved clover.
TROSAD: (G) A ceremonial or ritualistic court for Wizards.
TUAITHBEL: (G) Counterclockwise

TUATHAL: (G) Counterclockwise
TUILE: (Q) Spring
TUESDAY: Elf-Day
UBAID: An ancient Mesopotamian proto-Sumerian "Anunnaki" dynastic civilization.
UIAL: (SY) Spring
UNDOME: (Q) Twilight
UNDOMIEL: (Q) Elven-star, esp. a seven-rayed star.
UNICORN: A Creature of Faerie; an icon of innocence, love and beauty.
URIME: (Q) August
URUI: (S) August
VARDA: Queen of Stars; also Anu and Eru, literally "Star Mother."
VASTA: (SY) Awaken
VIRESSE: (Q) April
VIRITH: (S) April
WEDMATH: August
WINTERFILTHE: October
WIZARDWOOD: also *livewood*; wood removed from the tree by an Elf Wizard.
YEATA: (S) Fire Element
YGGDRASIL: (SC) The World Tree, usually the Ash Tree.
Y TYLWYTH TEG: (G) Name of race residing in Celtic *Caerllen* or Ffayrie-mounds.
ZEISATU: (SY) Consciousness or thought-forms.
ZHA: (T) The future or what is to come next.
ZORVAIN: (SY) Mystically charged, esp. with an intention.

[KEY TO ORIGINS: The source of a word is indicated by the letter or letters immediately following each bold entree. They are (A) Abroren; (AL) Alloryne; (D) Drae'sturi; (F) Firefen; (FR) French; (G) Gaelic-Welsh/Celtic; (GR) Greek; (IT) Italian; (L) Lis'tarii; (M) Miaren; (Q) Quenya; (S) Syndarin; (SC) Scandinavian/Norse; (SE) Silver Elves; (SH) Shiri; (SY) Sylvanus Folk; (T) Tyr Tylwyth Teg; and (TU) Tulari.]

The Enchanted Forest

the magick of the enchanted forest

Green is the universal color of Life and Nature—a color most sacred in Elven-Faerie Tradition, from which the *"Green World"* is named: the "place of enchantment" where "Forest Magick" permeates the air. True "Elven Magick" is performed in the "Green World" and pertains to its elements more strongly than any other magical system. The place of operation for this "Green Magic" is *in* Nature itself—no dank chambers or elaborate ceremonial vaults will do.

The *"Green World"* is described in lore as that space in the physical world that resonates an affinity with all natural energies of the Elemental Kingdoms—and therefore raw forces of Cosmic energy may be tapped, unhindered by the intrusion and tampering of humans. Practice of "Forest Magick," by definition, is primarily concerned with the Earth and Air Elements. It is in these forms and manifestations that an Elven Wizard, Mystic or Druid is able to use to capture the essence of "Earth Magic" as related to trees.

In Elven-Faerie Druidry, a *"silva"* (or '*sylva*') is a magical treatise or discourse cataloging the nature and function of the forests—with psychological, spiritual and emotion properties coinciding with physical lore. Most current forms of "tree magic" linked to the Druid *"Ogham"* (also spelled *"Ogam"*) are derived from the *"Book of Ballymote"*—also known as the *"Sylva d'Ogam."* That information is collected in a separate section within this series-anthology titled: *"The Book of Ogham."*

The present section examines the "Greenwood Grimoire" of the original *Elvenomicon* series. It is based on—and includes—a manual titled '*Sylva Druieachd*' which means "Treatise of Forest Wizards" or "Treatise on Elven Forest Magick" within the same tradition that provided the present author with materials for the *"Elven-Faerie Grimoire."* For those with a deep inclination toward "Tree Magic," this book will serve as an incredibly faithful guide to the Enchanted Forest.

It is important, from the start, to address an idea put forth by anthropologists called "tree worship." Ancient Druids, Elves, Mystics and Wizards *did not* "worship" trees any more than a person might worship some other sacred symbol used to represent the "Divine" in a religion.

Elves *revere* trees as an icon of the ALL, the Source-of-all-Being and the Cosmic Law that guides and defines all existence. By understanding the trees and the way in which they grow, Elves also understood the expansiveness of fractal existence of Reality long before and far clearer than Fibonacci and other modern mathematicians.

All life, matter and energy across space and time is a progression of Cosmic Law that moves or grows in the same manner, code or program as trees. This is an important key to the system of Elven Magick. It is often thought that trees are simply inanimate and unintelligent beings, and yet this could not be more untrue. Although they may not share the same degree of "movement freedom" as many other creatures in the wild, their "Earth memory" is far older, clearer and more accessible than what is encoded in shorter-lived beings.

Trees also have an ability to be charged (absorb energy) from their natural surroundings, and like other lifeforms, prefer to live in "groups" and "communities." They also like to communicate with one another.

"Awakened" trees—those interacting with active Elven magick—will more easily communicate with one another, and if there is a shortage of trees to talk to, they will produce them, through *"layrs."* The branches or roots will actually re-root to form a new tree, while still connected to the mother. The more we interact with them and learn, the more we realize that trees are actually quite sentient beings. They have the ability to communicate with us when their spirit is "Awakened" or "remembered" intentionally with Elven high magick.

Traditional lore describes the "spirit of a tree" as a *"Dryad"*—borrowing the Greek term used to define a female Druidess, or 'Lady of the Woods'. The *Dryad* "spirit" is an intelligence or spiritual growth program inhabiting and driving the living system manifestation that we call *"tree."* The same patterns of tree-like consciousness are seen in neural formations of the brain called *"dendrytes"*—the word *"Dryte"* is a masculine equivalent to *"Dryad."*

The "spirits" within the trees—which have many names in the Elven Tradition—are a part of any wood taken from it for magical purposes, just as a fractal or genetic print retains the entire code within each part. In fact, nearly all tools used in Elven Forest Magick are crafted from trees. It is the manner in which the wood is taken and how it is used that distinguishes the Elven Way from the ways of Humans. This begins with a high reverence for the Green World and all life in Nature, including asking permission from the spirits of a tree before taking any part of its lifeforce. We see a similar practice among both archaic shamans and modern herbalists. By "permission seeking," a practitioner further develops a communicable relationship with the Green World—and this is reinforced in consciousness with each "communion."

With exception of the title for this "grimoire," the term 'wood' is hereafter applied to parts of a tree no longer attached to a living tree —either from intentional removal, or some other natural means. There are essentially three types of "wood" indexed by loremasters of Elven-Faerie Druid Tradition:

> Deadwood / Dredgewood
> Wickwood / Wetwood*
> Livewood / Wizardwood

Wood that you find littered all throughout the forest floor is *deadwood*. For whatever reason, it has been broken away from the trees— and it naturally does—mixing with fallen leaves and decaying foliage to form soil after its decomposition. It is good for kindling fire, but be sure not to completely clear it away from the forest floor, as it is a necessary part of the ecosystem. Deadwood may be used for amulets, talismans and various magical crafts, but is not traditionally preferred for permanent ritual tools. A wizard may enjoy the discovery of a perfect wood specimen for a wand or staff already broken away from a tree. There are no absolute rules that discourage this; only many suggestions regarding cutting live trees.

Wickwood is *any* wood taken from the living forest that is not properly removed by a magical practitioner. This means any wood harvested as lumber or broken by carelessness without following Elven-Faerie codes of permission. When wood is taken in this manner, the spirits of the tree actually retract from it, making it quite unsuitable for magical work, particularly of the Elven-Druid variety. Humans have a tendency to remove plants and trees with hostility and ignorance. Such energy is also present in wood harvested by that same sentiment.

Wizardwood is that wood taken from a living tree by an Elven Wizard, Druid or Herbalist following Elven-Faerie codes. This includes permission and thanks for its sacrifice. The article removed will respectfully preserve the spiritual essence of the living spirit of the tree—as a res-

---

*   Called "*greenwood*" in former versions; too often confused with original title of grimoire.

ult the wood is blessed by "Nature spirits" and is positively charged with perfect love, peace and cosmic unity. If you feel inclined to leave an offering to these "Nature spirits" in exchange for their sacrifice, then by all means do so. *Always follow your intuition when walking the path through the enchanted forest!*

elven high magick

Many techniques of Elven High Magick are categorized as "energy work," "light work," or "astral work" using New Age vocabulary. An ability to use currents of natural or cosmic energy in "magick" is dependent on the true understanding and realization of a "higher omni-dimensional web-matrix" or "field" in which all energy exists and acts beyond the surface images and forms we believe we are interacting with. It is really this underlying energy that is exchanging and moving, and only bands of light within a specific spectrum give rise to visible manifestations in the "world we see."

It is essential that an Elven Wizard is fluent in their knowledge and use of the "subtle" underlying currents of universal cosmic energy found throughout all Nature and within and as all Life. These frequencies or vibrations—often interpreted as "auric energy"—emanate from all systems: people; animals; trees; rocks; minerals ...*everything*. Certain individuals may even increase their sensitivity to regularly perceive these energetic interactions at the most basic underlying degrees of awareness. A kaleidoscope of energetic currents or "rays" are abundantly processing around you—and through you. Energies transmitted through all environments, actions and thoughts are in constant interaction with each another, even when we are not "aware" or do not see a visible change.

Try this exercise:—Go outside on a clear day when the sky is light blue and lay down in the grass, perhaps on a hill. Allow your attention to drift as you quiet your mind. Focus on clouds, if any, or the blueness of the sky. Bring your awareness away from the things of a "mortal" world and life.

Raise your arm and hold your hand about a foot in front of your face so that your vision of the blue sky is backing it. Place your index finger and thumb together as if you are pinching something and rub the slowly in a circular swirling motion. Bring them apart about an inch and soften your gaze to look between them. *What do you see? What is that?*

Energy streams and strings are indeed all around us. They project from all living things and may be altered with emotion and intention. Even physical placement of non-living objects—as made famous in recent revivals of *"feng shui"*—has the the ability to affect the motion of energy currents around us, and in turn, our own vibrational states in their presence.

"Dowsing-With-Your-Feet" is a technique Elven/Sylvan (Forest) Wizards use to assist sensitivity development. They learn to free (clear) their minds and allow inner intuition to guide their "actions" (movement) when selecting a particular tree, rock, stick, &tc, which we might relay as having a particular aspect "speak to us," or that a particular tree &tc has "chosen" us. The relationship between a Wizard and the Green World is unique for each instance—and nearly impossible to "grade" as many have attempted in their formation of certain 'Orders' and 'Lodges'—which is why "Inner Teachings" are always revealed by Nature *herself*.

The core material in the *Elvenomicon* series is meant to provide an intrepid Seeker the keys necessary to unlock the "Great Mysteries" by sheer dedication and sincere desire. Potential "Forest Wizards" will have to enter the Green World for an extended period of time to work with these energies directly—yet, once we shared communion with these forces, the "Astral Grove" always exists within us to work from.

According to Elven Tradition, *all* trees have healing qualities. Almost any species of tree is capable of channeling pain and negative energies down into the magma core of the Earth for transformation. It may seem odd to send such energies down to the Earth to be incinerated, but they are more destructive when left unchecked on the surface.

Wizards must cure their own pain to properly ease the pain of anyone else—including the Earth itself. Equally so, it is actually in our best interests to help in relieving the suffering of the surface world—ourselves and our environment—so that it does not restrict the future global process of Ascension that we are all participating in.

In some ways, everything is connected together in the Universe—meaning all of *us*—and what one or two people may feel in one place, is not at all restricted to affecting only them alone. Every course we take sets out causal ripples or tides of manifestation across seas of infinity—and we must take the responsibility for every single one of them if we are to assume any "control" over their "power."

You might practice "Dowsing-With-Your- Feet" for intuitively selecting a "Healing Tree" to perform the following exercise. Ask the tree's permission to heal your pain—emotional, physical, &tc.—then soften your gaze and attempt to perceive a visible auric glow emanating from the tree, similar to the bands you may have seen between your fingers in a previous exercise. Sit up straight with your back to the tree—using its trunk to support your spine, keeping sure you are in a comfortable position. Feel and see your "auric body" merge with that of the tree.

Focus on your connection to the tree until you no longer easily distinguish boundaries between your body and the tree. Bring your pains to the surface and send them down the trunk into the ground with each breath.

Feel and see that you and the tree are pushing it deep down into the fiery core below for incineration and recycling. You may wish to visualize any remaining energetic cords or ties to the energy as equally dissolved. Always thank the Nature-spirits when you have completed energy work in the "Green World." It is also customary to "tend to"—or "groom," in the Animal Kingdom—the fellow life in Nature that we are stewards of or share kinship with, furthering our ecological responsibility.

Whenever activating your consciousness within and as an "astral form"—just as you would in order to partake in 'astral travel'—you enter your "Light Body" or a "Body of Light." If you do this in wakened states without the intention of Astral Projection, you may be able to use this shift in consciousness as a catalyst for better recognizing 'subtle energies', 'streams' and 'strings' that seem otherwise invisible to the uninitiated. This "astral preparation" technique is the same method used for other 'energy work', 'light work' and Tree Magick.

Entering the "Light Body" is an application of Visualization and Will to direct intention—just as in all other 'energy play' and 'light work'. Such methods differ greatly from the vocal dramas and ceremonial forms of ritual magic popular in other systems, including "Elementalism." Energy currents of the forest are strong, but are slow in their build-up of "eventual power."

"Forest Magick" does not carry the same 'flare of immediate accessibility' that many practitioners search for—such as we see in the more active Elements of Nature and its corresponding "spirit world." In the forests, progressive learning and communication efforts tend to be slower—matching speeds of frequency in the Green World. To participate in "woodland magic," a Sylvan Wizard slows their vibrations to the "heartbeat of the forest" and envision their own "light-shield" as the same brilliant emerald green.

Try this:—Sit comfortably with your back erect or lie down. I do not suggest sitting cross-legged, with any parts of the body crossing, or without back support, when first attempting. Begin by focusing all your awareness as a light in your feet, initially drawing this energy up from the ground, and concentrate all your focus and awareness on this area until it is completely filled with light. Slowly bring this light awareness throughout your entire body, moving it from your toes, feet, ankles, legs and knees upward into your thighs, pelvic region, solar plexus, stomach, chest and shoulders, then finally into your arms, neck, head and reaching its destination in forming a halo-crown about the top of your head. By this method, the Wizard becomes a "Pillar of Light." Feel this light extending from your body and strengthening your auric shield. [The "Western magical tradition" even observes a similar version of this rite, called the "Middle Pillar."]

Accessing the "Astral World" begins first with the ability to project one's consciousness into their "Light Body." Secondly, the Wizard consciously detaches their "Light Body" from its fixed awareness to the physical simulacrum that it localizes as a "home" or "genetic vehicle" (for the physical degree of material existence within the Human range of normative sensory perception). In Forest Magick, the Wizard does not detach into the astral, but maintains this heightened sense of awareness as a magical prerequisite to performing any light-work or energy-work—in Nature or otherwise. The Shaman that visits the "Otherworld" to perform their "magic" does this too. Rather than performing a ritual or ceremony within the physical *Nemeton*, the magic is conducted directly on the "Astral Plane" within the "Astral Grove" or some other locale.

"Astral Travel" taps an imaginative part of our consciousness that is most active in children before civic systemology takes a greater hold on neural activity. But we are all "Children of Light" and "Children of the Stars"—and it is that "star-light" for which the "*astral*" is named. By raising our consciousness and awareness to connect with that ancient source of our *Self*, we are reaching closest to the light to become the free spirits again that we once knew as children, to partake in the amazing spiritual bliss that results from communion with the ALL. To visit your "Astral Grove" it is critical that you first become proficient in entering your "Light Body."

Once you're able to enter the "Light Body," practice of "Astral Travel" may be achieved by envisioning a catalyst for teleportation—meaning a 'threshold,' 'gateway' or 'portal,' to launch your astral form through. The Water element is a powerful "portal" element—representing the most fluid-like, yet physical, essence that bridges between "worlds." Females will find a sense of familiarity using dark pools and mirrors as a doorway. The "Earth portal" or stone megalithic "Trilithon" gateway is another stereotypical "portal" icon, popularly used in Druidism. Other Personal symbols or glyphs may be used to direct awareness as you pass into "Faerie."

Whatever method you choose, you project your conscious awareness into your Light Body and then project that body through an envisioned portal or representation of a door. This helps trigger the subconscious into releasing Awareness (or the mind) into the "Astral Field" and appropriates our attention awareness in the process. Simply envision the portal firmly, seeing it standing before you in your mind's eye. Some practitioners have also found success by visualizing a "Flaming Door." Spend time practicing and refining your skills in assuming this state. Note all of its details of the visualization until it seems as real as any other experience. Using Will, you may direct your astral form through the portal, and maintain a belief that you occupy *this* physical body in the "Astral."

Once you have successfully launched yourself through the imagined portal, anything might occur. You may emerge in darkness—the Underworld Initiation—in which you will be forced to move your mind through a complex labyrinth, often a result of blocks or barriers of the uninitiated mind. You may find yourself in a "astral stellar void"—where all kinds and natures of energy and light moves this way and that, existing as "waves of possibility" and never really taking on a concrete form in one shape or another, known as the "White Place." Or, perhaps you will cross to the Abyss and find the shell of the void—before the First Cause—where all is the Infinity of Nothingness.

If you fix in your mind the intention to reach the "Astral Grove" upon entering this state of consciousness, then you may arrive in a 'greenwood forest setting'.

The "Astral Grove" is within the "*Infinite Enchanted Forest*," and if you do not directly arrive there from your portal, you must "will" yourself there. Your "Astral Grove" is composed of infinite streams of light and energy, formed and constructed by your intentions. Nothing on the astral plane has form except as a finite perspective of an individual observer experiences it and interacts with it. Thus, there is a lot of room for games, magical practice and other experience in the Otherworld, especially if your access to a physical grove is limited.

enchanted trees, forests and groves

"Elemental Magick" is explored within the '*Elven-Faerie Grimoire*' volume of this series. It is usually practiced within a ritually consecrated 'circle'. "Forest Magick" of Elven-Ffayrie Druidic tradition also uses a circle: a natural clearing for rites, one that is in the midst of a "grove" of trees. This "grove" is treated as the *Nemeton* for an Elven Wizard.

"Groves" were once intentionally planted and tended by Elvish Drwyds or Druids. A ring of specific species of tree and plantlife was maintained as an observatory-temple. The concept of a "tree calendar" most likely emerged from such practices, where wise Wizards were capable of literally "reading the signs of Nature" and interpreting natural conditions from the appearance of these trees—including the time of season.

Many have assumed that Ogham lore is primarily a means of "fortune-telling" or mundane divination, yet these natural observations could also predict weather, animal behaviors and other natural effects of the environment. Certain times of year, or other natural conditions, were reflected by the different species of the grove in specific ways—and this lore was carefully observed and cryptically recorded.

Elven Forest Magick lore describes no requirements concerning the boundary of a "ritual circle" or its marking. Large stones are not always appropriate, and they may even disrupt natural energies of groves and clearings that may already visibly appear as distinct "circles." Practice of Forest Magick is less formal, and more intentionally deliberate, than "ritual magic"—even when performed in a woodland setting. A practitioner might carry a small pouch of smaller gems/stones used to temporarily designate points of the circle or as a focal aid.

Circle stations are not often clearly indicated in the rites of Forest Magick as they are in Elementalism and traditional ritual magic—unless they are intended for groups. This is because magical work performed by Forest Wizards is primarily internal and often practiced alone. An urban citizen may find difficulties in planting and tending a physical grove. The ability to do this not only distinguishes the type of "magick" involved, but also the type of individual that is able to advance through the Elven Forest Magick system. The natural area guarded is revisited frequently for both mystical operations and meditative exercises which contribute a "charge" or quality of "Enchantment" to the terrain. The following groupings of tree species repeatedly appear in Elven-Faerie and Celtic-Druid lore:—

· The Elven-Ffayrie Triad Trees are *Oak, Ash and Thorn*.
· The Seven Chieftain Trees of the Cad Goddeu are *Apple, Ash, Hazel, Holly, Oak, Pine and Yew*.
· The Seven Noble Trees of the Grove are *Apple, Alder, Birch, Hazel, Holly, Oak and Willow*.
· The Nine Sacred Woods of Needfire include *Ash, Apple, Cedar, Hazel, Holly, Mistletoe, Oak, Pine and Poplar*.
· The Traditional Tree Calendar Grove consists of *Birch, Rowan, Alder, Willow, Ash, Hawthorn, Oak, Holly, Hazel, Apple (or Vine), Ivy, Reed (or Pine) and Elder*.

The following rites may be used individually or in succession (as the application requires).

THE BLESSING OF THE SAPLINGS

Before planting a grove or breaking ground, take all of the trees you intend to plant to the location. All members of the "fellowship" may also be present. Any participants involved should perform all tree-work from the "Body of Light." The leader (or land steward) stands in the center and says:

Here I [we] have [are] gathered in this place of light. Here I [we] find a place to weave a Sacred Space that I wish to honor with the planting and stewardship of a Sacred Grove of trees. May this Holy Nemeton be a place of peace and power.

Conjure the circle, using stakes to mark its boundary—marking where trees are to be planted. Use the most appropriate liturgy. Nature-spirits of the forest will not be as concerned about your "ritual formalities" as they will be with your planting.

> NORTH: *I [we] come forth to this sacred place and call the spirits of the land to join us here. At this Nemeton do I [we] ask permissions to raise and tend a Sacred Grove of trees, following the tradition of my ancestors.*
>
> EAST: *Here at this sacred place do I [we] acknowledge my [our] vow[s] as Keeper[s] of the Earth. Here I [we] pledge to be Guardian of the Grove, a consecrated Nemeton ever sacred. Here may the sylphs, sylves and Nature-spirits of the woodlands, come and bless, making holy and enchanted.*
>
> SOUTH: *May these future trees of this Grove, these saplings presented here, be blessed by the good Creatures of Faerie, the Four Elements and the Sun above. May the light, love and strength of the cosmos nourish these trees and offer all life sanctuary when visiting here in peace and love.*
>
> WEST—holding hands over buckets of water: *May the spirits and powers residing in the Elements of Water, Sea and Rain come forth and bless these vessels of water. I use them to now share you blessing with these saplings, that they may receive your grace. I ask that you be generous in nurturing this Sacred Grove with your gentle life-giving rains.*

Burn incense, carrying it thrice around the circle boundary, clockwise. Feel the energy in the area equalizing to the land changes about to occur. Conjure a clear image of the completed project and project it as you inform the spirits of Nature—and the trees to be planted—of your intentions. Say:

> *By the grace and permission of the Forces of Nature and the Spirits of the Universe; in accordance with the covenant sworn between my ancestors and the Ancient and Shinning Ones; I now break ground in perfect peace, perfect love and compassion and understanding. I open this circle now to perform the work, but the circle is never broken.*

CONSECRATION RITE FOR A NEWLY PLANTED GROVE

After planting the grove trees, bring some remaining soil to the center of the grove circle and say:

> *May all good Spirits of the Earth and Land bless this soil, the land where it is used and the life in nourishes. Bless those who use it as an expression of perfect love to nurture this newly planted life.*

Bring this consecrated soil to each of the trees, sprinkling it over the topsoil around each one. Depending on species and climate, wood chips may be used if more appropriate. Feel the love and compassion for Nature and life flowing through you as you complete the planting stage for each of the trees. Return to the center to consecrate more water, saying:

> *May the Spirits of Water and Sea bless this water, the land where it is used and the life it nourishes. Bless those who use it in their expression of perfect love to nurture this newly planted life.*

Take the water around to each (as previously with soil). Then clean and clear the area before performing a *"Dedication."*

THE RITE FOR PLANTING A SINGLE GUARDIAN TREE

This rite may be used to plant a specific "Guardian Tree" or it may be used for each tree planted in the "grove." Go to the space and ask the spirits of the land for permission before you break ground. Follow the basic steps outlined in previous rites—performing all work from a "Light Body." As you dig and plant the single tree, say:

> *I plant this tree in perfect peace, love, compassion and understanding. May it be to others and myself a symbol of the same.*

When are ready to complete the work with topsoil and/or woodchips, consecrate the materials, saying:

> *May this earth feed and nourish this sacred life, a symbol of perfect peace, love and compassion and understanding.*

Complete the planting, then consecrate vessels of water, saying:

> *May this consecrated water bless and nourish the life of this sacred tree. May all good Elemental Spirits of Sea and Water ensure the rains to ever maintain it.*

Water the tree liberally with your consecrated water and then connect with the auric/light field of the tree—something that becomes easier as your proficiency in Tree Magick grows—saying:

> *By the Elements of Nature were you sown. By perfect peace and love are you grown. I am a Keeper of the Earth and have overseen your birth. I am a Guardian [Scion] of Elven Ways and your steward for all my days.*

Close the rite (if planting a single tree)—or continue with each tree of the grove before performing a *"Grove Dedication."*

GROVE DEDICATION & STEWARDSHIP

A grove is consecrated and dedicated prior to its use as a *Nemeton*. The rite may also be used repeatedly over time. You may even use this rite to dedicate existing groves growing in the wild.

> NORTH: *May the Sacred Grove awaken to the mysteries of the Everlasting Forest. May it grant Elven Wizards, and those who come in peace, the same strength and protection the Sacred Grove offered the Ancients. May the sacred ground on which it stands, be purified and blessed.*
>
> EAST: *Here now before the Sacred Grove and the Nature-spirits awakened and drawn to my work, do I vow stewardship to the Sacred Grove and the mysteries of the Everlasting Forest. I am a Guardian of the Earth Mother, keeper and protector of her ancient ways.*
>
> SOUTH: *I summon forth the energy and power of the Sky and Sun. Come forth spirit that grants light and life to all creatures on the Earth. Send forth thy Rays of Radiance and instill strength and well-being throughout the Sacred Grove.*
>
> WEST: *May the spirits of the Water and Rain Elements look upon and bless this Holy Nemeton, consecrated and dedicated to the mysteries of the Universe. Nurture and give life while protecting from deluge and fierce storms.*

You may wish to supplement this rite with individual "Tree Awakenings" and various other rites to more intensely "awaken" and "enchant" the land. With repeated use, this Grove portion of the forest will eventually stand apart, noticeable to folk with even the slightest sensitivity, and may even appear more "alive." Such is the nature of true *Elvish Druid Forest Magick!*

rays of light and energy play

According to traditional Bardic and Druid lore, "Three Rays" compose all energetic manifestations, passing through the "Three Spheres"— or great divisions—of Existence. The smallest inner circle is *"Abred,"* which is the physical world, a plane of condensed energy, including the "Green World of Nature." The next sphere is "*Gwynedd*," the Otherworld—or Astral—which exists as a "higher" spatial dimension that envelopes the physical world. Finally, there is "*Ceugent*," which is to say "*Nirvana*," or the "Kingdom of Heaven," where resides the Source-of-All-Being-and-Creation and, in some traditions, those spirits that have achieved "Supreme Ascension"—those who have successfully climbed the "Ladder of Lights" back to the Source.

True Elven Magick—energy work and light-work—requires calling on and using Divine Radiance, which manifests as colored 'Rays' of the Forces of Nature. These auric streams of energy and consciousness are summoned by will, intention and emotion collectively. Once a Wizard has projected awareness into the Light Body, the color of the auric "Light Shield" may be altered to meet a desired energy vibration. Call the energy down as a beam of light from the stars and then allow yourself to assimilate its essence.

The properties of the "Three Rays of Awen" are of Divine or spiritual "silver," "crystalline" and "gold." These are further divided—fragmented or condensed—into the *seven* bands of light. The primary Rays are called upon in Elvish High Magick. Modern practitioners find that identifying the *Rays* by color is a most convenient and accurate way of differentiating their relative degrees on a continuous "spectrum."

The color—and thereby, nature—of one's own "Light Shield" is transformed by the work to match and attract the desired energetic currents. Remember, as you experiment with the *Rays* and light-work, that these various colored degrees are all derived from three primary rays, which in turn are the manifestations of a singularity of *All-ness*. Using visualization and Will, you may call down the radiance of the "*Rays*" and allow yourself to absorb it through all of your pores and then radiate it from your aura and each breath. Classifications of the *Rays* are as follows:

THE SILVER (LEFT) RAY

Sound/Letter: I ("*ee*")
Polarity: Female, dark, passive, lunar.
Quartile Element: Water (some Earth)
Elvish Element: The Sea
Physical Manifestation: Mineral Kingdom
Threshold Time: Dusk, sunset, autumn.

Elessar (Elf-Stone): Silver (hematite)
Light Bands (Rays): Indigo, violet and blue.

The Silver Properties of the Light Rays

VIOLET (Saturn): Astral vision, darkness, Otherworld work, wisdom, wards.
  Domain: Element of Vapor/Cloud
INDIGO (Jupiter): Beauty, enchantment, emotions, love, music, play.
  Domain: Element of Rain
BLUE (Luna): Compassion, dreams, healing, peace and understanding.
  Domain: Element of Sea

THE GOLD (RIGHT) RAY

Sound/Letter: O ("*oh*")
Polarity: Masculine, light, active, solar.
Quartile Element: Fire and Air
Elvish Element: The Sky
Phys. Manifestation: Animal & Human Kingdoms
Threshold Time: Dawn, sunrise, spring/summer.
Elessar (Elf-Stone): Gold (tiger's eye)
Light Bands (Rays): Yellow, orange and red.

The Golden Properties of the Light Rays

YELLOW (the Sun): Knowledge, intellect, confidence, and inspiration.
  Domain: Element of Skyfire
ORANGE (Mercury): Communication, courage, being aware, wishes.
  Domain: Element of Star
RED (Mars): Transformation, healing, strength, willpower, and leadership.
  Domain: Element of Flame

THE CRYSTALLINE (MIDDLE) RAY

Sound/Letter: A ("*ah*")
Polarity: Neutral, crystalline, reflective
Quartile Element: Earth ('Quintessence.')
Elvish Element: The Land
Physical Manifestation: Plant & Tree Kingdom
Threshold Time: Twilight, midnight, winter.
Elessar (Elf-Stone): Black (obsidian) or Green
Light Band (Ray): Green

The Crystalline Properties of the Light Ray

GREEN (Venus): Life-force, balance, healing, growth, true love.
   Domain: Element of Earth

The traditional "Elven-Faerie Star" is a seven-pointed septogram. Elemental symbolism differs from the "pentagram"—which obviously represents Earth, Air, Fire, Water and *Akasha*. Elvish Wizards see elements as manifestations of Seven Rays of Creation, powers descended from the Source-of-All-Being that make up the myriad of lights that we call manifestation. The Seven Rays also correlate to the traditional "seven energetic centers" of the body—called "calen" and "astyr" or "chakras" in various traditions—all related back to the primary Three Rays and the holistic singularity.

> ### VIOLET RAY—INTERCONNECTEDNESS
> Spiritual Element: Fire-of-Spirit (*Nwyvre-of-Akasha*)
> Light-Centre: The Crown or Flower of Life (*7th Chakra*)
> Gemstone: Amethyst specifically.

A core belief and teaching of Elven Druid Tradition concerns unity of life. Everything shares energetic ties to everything else—and everything is connected together at the "highest" spatial or spiritual plane of existence. Sylvan light-work—such as that which allows a seed to grow faster and stronger—is dependent on a premise that "thoughtforms" and emotion have abilities to charge or affect the energy around us. This energy may be focused as a colored *Ray*—filtered with intention and emotion, as if placing a piece of colored film over a white light projection. The energy of the "Violet Ray" is the highest frequency—and shortest wave-length—of all the vibrations treated in this system. As such it should be only used for the highest caliber of mystical work, Ascension work and Transcendental magic—matters involving activation of the "true Self," inner development, "star-walking" and reconnecting with the ALL.

> ### THE PURPLE RAY—THE SEA
> Spiritual Element: Water-of-Spirit and Water-of-Earth
> Light-Centre: Heart or Merkaba (*4th Chakra*)
> Gemstones: Quartz, quicksilver, silver, sapphire, and turquoise.

The Sea is powerful. It is the perfect "liquid" manifestation of the "inter-connectedness" envisioned at the first point. The tides of the Cosmic Sea are the waves of potentiality—they represent the Will and Ability of Cosmic Law in motion. The Sea and Water Elements possess a long-standing association with the Moon and "emotional condition" of our make-up—which bridges the "Mind" with the "physical body," a vast network of energetic communication and exchange. The ebb and flow of these waves of energy manifest as both gentle tides and fierce rushing currents. This "Purple Ray" is called upon to aid in centering and purifying our emotions and, in effect, the proper use of Will and intention. It is the second 'highest' "magick" on the 'Ladder of Lights', by which one can reach a *Self-Honest* experience of life from the Violet rung.

> ### THE BLUE RAY—THE MOON
> Spiritual Element: Earth-of-Water and Water-of-Air
> Light-Centre: Sex Organs (womb) and Spleen (*2nd Chakra*)
> Gemstones: Hematite, Pearl, Topaz and Lapis Lazuli.

Indeed, the Sun is a necessary condition for life derived from light, but the Moon *influences* the beings of light. The ancients believed that the Moon was a luminary body, but of course, we know now that it actually reflects the Sun's light—much like the reflective surface of the Sea. Tidal cycles of water are influenced by a magnetic pull on the earth from the Moon. There are thirteen lunar cycles in a 365-day solar year—and just as many menstrual cycles for a woman. The Moon may affect cyclic psychological, hormonal and behavioral biorhythms on Earth. Different people generally maintain "higher" or "lower" energy levels cycling with different times of day, week, month and year. These patterns are unique to each individual and may be discovered only though self-reflection and self-analysis. The "Blue Ray" is called for perfect peace and protection—such as for casting a Circle of Power. Disruption of the Blue Ray (*2nd Chakra*) causes depression and anxiety—the polar opposites of the peace and security spectrum—and so use of this *Ray* may aid in restoring a personal balance as needed.

> ### THE GREEN RAY—THE WOODLANDS
> Spiritual Element: Earth-of-Earth and Earth-of-Air
> Light-Centre: Ground (feet) or base of spine (*1st Chakra*)
> Gemstones: Amazonite, Aventurine, Emerald, Moss Agate.

An inclination toward the "Green World," and its currents, is the epitome of "Elven Magick." Woodlands and forests are for the Elven-Ffayrie what water is to fish. The "Green Ray" life-force energy is used in all "tree communication rites" and "growth magick." A subversion of the "Green Ray" in its pale (greenish-yellow) form may produce jealousy, envy and discord. When used properly, a Wizard will change their "Light Shield" to match color hues of the forest they are communing with. Trees are the most sacred icon of the "Green Ray"—growing their branches out like the dendritic snowflake, the "Sign of Awen" or the "Elf-rune." Additionally, the "Green Ray" may be used in rites/meditation for personal grounding (centering) and to assist healing.

THE YELLOW RAY—THE SUN
Spiritual Element: Earth-of-Fire, Starfyre and Air-of-Fire
Light-Centre: Mind (Third Eye) or Brow (*6th Chakra*)
Gemstones: Citrine Diamond, Gold, Tiger's Eye and Topaz.

As the Moon is the celestial sphere most sacred to the "Silver Ray," so the Sun brilliantly illuminates the "Golden Ray." All Three Rays of Illumination were once thought to originate with the Sun—which like all other Stars, must originate in the "White Place," a plane of *Infinite Light*. White Light is indicative of the Middle or "Crystalline Ray," and the use of a prism reveals that all Seven Rays are actually contained within one. Crystals may be charged with any *Ray*-color (frequency) or intention through Will and Emotion.

The "Yellow Ray" is called forth in connection to the intellect, mental faculties and the accumulation of wisdom—by whatever class (and color) that may fall under. It is interesting that the "Blue Ray" and "Yellow Ray" on either side of the "Green Ray" also share some of the reflective properties of the Green Ray—and as we know in our experiences with artistic colors: mixing yellow and blue results in green. The Elven-Faerie Star paradigm is quite fluid in this way, demonstrating interconnectivity, *not* separation.

THE ORANGE RAY—THE WINDS
Spiritual Element: Air-of-Air, Air-of-Earth and Fire-of-Air
Light-Centre: Throat (Respiratory) or Breath (*5th Chakra*)
Gemstones: Amber, Carnelian, Jacinth and Opal.

Winds are particularly sacred to the Sylph-Ffayrie types. It is the power of the Air Element, with warm currents driven by the Sun, that blows seeds containing the spark of life ensuring the continuation of Nature. Powers of the breeze or wind element are often overlooked because they are represented by the most intangible and unseen symbols—but reflect some of the strongest manifestations of energy in motion. When the wind is "at your back," in may help carry you further. If blowing in the proper direction, in may aid in delivering clear communication at a distance. Otherwise, the "Orange Ray" is only used to relay information that you *really* want to stand out and draw attention to. Next to red, it carries the longest-wavelength, and demands attention, which is why so many in positions of leadership radiate orange in their "Light Shield."

THE RED RAY—THE MAGICK

Spiritual Element: Fire-of-Fire and Spirit-of-Fire
Light-Centre: Solar Plexus (stomach) (*3rd Chakra*)
Gemstones: Red Jasper, Red Agate, Ruby and Rose Quartz.

Practical Magick—such as the "Elementalism" introduced earlier in this *Elvenomicon* (in the "*Elven-Faerie Grimoire*")—is often a *seeker's* first step on the path to clearing and defragmenting the programs of the "Mind-system" and the Reality experience of the Human condition.

Ritual-magic and similar forms of ceremonial practice may aid the novice in understanding and developing their own abilities—but we must make sure that we do not falsely attribute power to these "rituals" themselves, and that we do not fall into the trap of over-identifying with the ritualism or dependent on such "external" forms as our only means of thinking and acting "magically." All truly intentional actions—or movements of energy intended from the true Will—performed deliberately are considered "magical," and only when a true conscious understanding of these principles and dynamics becomes automatic second-nature to us, do we begin to say that we are practicing or operating "magick."

Much more than rituals and spells, degrees of initiation or fancy dress, the purpose of the magical pursuits is to engage on a specific process or pathway—a progressive journey toward active participation as *Self* in *Self-Honesty* with Cosmic Law of the ALL—and these are not affirmations of someone who lives life only in response or as a victim, no indeed, we are actively creating with the "Red Ray" and it manipulates the emotional states of passion, consummate love and anger—currents with the longest wave and most immediate tangible results.

communing with nature

Prior to working with the entire spectrum, an initiate might begin their journey into "Light Work" or "Energy Work" with the "Three Rays of Radiance." The following "Triad Rite" assists with this. Once a basic familiarity with the system is reached, Rites of the Rays may be performed anywhere—in a physical setting or purely while working on the 'astral' or 'mental' plane—and always from the perspective of *Self* within an activated "Light Body."

THREE RAYS OF RADIANCE
"THE TRIAD RITE"

• Face the northern direction.
• Call down the Radiance of the "Silver Ray."
• See and feel the "Silver Ray" descend upon you, and to the left of you, as you intone the sound "I" ("ee").
• Raise your arms as you inhale the tone; bringing them down to your sides as you exhale and intone the sound—using your arms to draw or pull down the "air" (*Ray*).
• Do this with the Middle or "Crystalline Ray."
• See and feel the "Crystalline Ray" descending upon you, and through you, with the sound "A" ("*ah*").
• Repeat the process, calling the "Golden Ray" down upon you, and to the right of you, with the intonation "O" ("*oh*").
• With practice, the rite may conclude by drawing down all "Three Rays" combining the three processes: "I-A-O."
• Try experimenting with other sequences; such as "A-O-I."

Elven lore includes many references to an "Astral Grove" and "astral plane"—suggesting this environment as most suitable for meditation and ritual work. But this is only available to those with proficiency in accessing such state of consciousness. To assist in this development, there is an effective exercise—called "A Day at the Pool"—that 'New Age' teachers offer their students to practice directing (projecting) mental energy in an 'astral', 'mental' or otherwise imagined universe.

Try this:—Enter the Body of Light and begin first at your Astral Grove, asking for the grace of the Cosmic Source to protect your Beingness as you work. Now travel through the *"Everlasting Astral Forest"* until you find a still pool or lake—making certain you are experiencing all of the sensory details of your surroundings as you move through this fluid-like degree of existence: the colors; smells; the feeling of the ground beneath your feet...

Then begin to practice your intentional interaction with the environment—drawing in energy (inhale through your astral form) to make deliberate movements and actions with the Astral Body. For, example, extend the energy with an exhale as you bend down to pick up a rock from the waters edge. Hold it a while, feeling it completely in your hands, making certain the imagery is concrete as you build your Will and to focus. Continue to perform simple actions, tossing the rock from one hand to the other, inhaling energy and exhaling action. Then use your will (and exhale) as you cast the stone across the still waters of the pond—releasing and projecting energy. Pause a moment to witness the results. Did you see ripples across the pond as consequence of the energy you directed? [This type of exercise may be repeated as desired for cumulative experience.]

To summon the Radiance of peace and protection about yourself—or to a specific locale—conjure a "ball" of compressed blue-white energy rays between your hands. Feel its radiance warming and cooling your hands simultaneously. It may help if you perform a "Triad Rite" first and call on the "Blue Ray" directly as you construct the "ball." Use the "Three Rays" to give the ball substance, then incorporate the "Blue Ray" to provide its "shield" or energetic filter.

If this does not work for you at first, try rubbing your hands back and forth together repeatedly while initially drawing down the Radiance, and then bring them apart several inches and focus your energy and attention on the space between your hands. When the ball is adequately visualized and experienced, feel the *"Radix"* or *"Rad"* of the ball emanating out, affecting the surrounding environment with its radiation, driving all out-of-phase frequencies and negative conditions away. Then direct the "positive" Radiance of the ball toward a target, or absorb it internally. This practice is otherwise known as a *"Blessing."*

We have mentioned Light Shields of living systems (beings) in passing —but these same "auric covers" exist for all things. They are the "energetic frequency signature" of that "thing"—fragmented from the Unmanifest as a "thing" in exclusion to "other things"—a filtering determinant of the energy projected and received by that existence and in relation to other existences.

Colored bands associated with living beings are consequences of energetic activity moving through the body on all degrees/levels of existence. These colors may typically distinguish what energy type is most actively projecting into the field. Each color carries frequencies associated with basic attributes that may be either "under-stimulated" or "over-active"—with the ability to generate "positive" constructive frequencies in our daily life and work, or "negative" wave-interference patterns. The choice is ours.

Understand that we are not here speaking in absolutes—"good" and "evil"—but, what we *have* discovered is that there are modes of operation (thought and activity) that contribute either *toward* or *away from* progression on our "Path of Ascension." These also tend to solidify or manifest in our daily lives and directly relate to spiritual evolution, emotional well-being and yes, even our physical health—all of which is interconnected; nothing treated is in exclusion.

There is nothing wrong with treating physical ailment symptoms with physical medicine as a tool that might enable the "Mind" and "Spirit" to focus on its own degrees of health. But when we focus on the physical ailments and remedies in exclusion, the underlying "problems" continue to resurface.

Esoteric lore from the "Ancient Mystery School" also alludes to the existence of the colors and Rays in descriptions of the degrees/levels of existence that make up the total identity of *Self* as it came to be more locatable in time-space (with the successive condensation of universes). It states that: at the innermost core of your being there is a "violet egg" or oval-like elliptical sphere containing the essence of your True Spirit. All of the rest—all the other bands and layers—are further and further shells that resonate increasingly condensed degrees of existence. This includes our "biochemical" genetic vehicle that the Spirit calls "home" for its earthly condition of experience.

Elven-Faerie lore describes a "violet egg" as "amethyst" (or violet quartz)—and that it is a "fragmented shard" of a now "Dark Crystal," something that seems to resonate with a certain brand of modern-day fantasy. The "amethyst crystal" of our True Spirit is protected in an encasement of spiritual skin—a pink shell that radiates the true love and absolute purity of the ALL. This violet-pink hued spiritual existence is the truest part of our spiritual identity, which came from and may return to the Source—the destination of Ascension called "*Ceugent*" in Welsh literature.

This true spiritual state is the connection link back to the Source—a column that is aligned directly with the "Middle Ray" or "Crystalline Ray" (from which both the "Silver Ray" and "Golden Ray" divert) that activates our personal energetic propulsion system (that some call *chakras*) as an "Identity"—the light centers that are anchored to us and within us that align to variously perceived degrees/levels that project our more material existence—and our ability to simultaneously exist—at all degrees/levels of the ALL at once. Without such a function, we would have no consciousness, no ability to relate to our created environment, and no memory to retain either across time and space—and all past spiritual lifetimes.

When the white crystalline energy of the Light Body has stabilized (equalized) or is "clear," it is then able to manifest all colors of the spectrum perfectly. These Rays use the body's *Chakra-system*—or "*Calen*" system—as an energetic "step-down transformer" connected to "Divine" Radiance of the Cosmos. According to lore: the fourth level of your "etheric body" consists of both a silver and a gold shell that wraps around the crystalline one, sealing primary auric energy in as part of the spiritual identity (independent of any body). The fifth level is the 'Light Body' itself—"outer aura" or "Light Shield." It is the part that people may see when they say they "see auras." Energetic and emotional states influence the type, nature and strength of the auric "Light Shield"—and *vice versa*, because all energetic activity is also an exchange (or communication).

It is possible to neutralize negative or destructive aspects of an emotion (color) by changing the "Light Shield"—and therefore conscious attention—to an opposing color. For example—a person might counter the "red" they see when angry with "blue" peaceful hues. When we meditate on the nature of this multiplicity of oneness that we perceive as levels of the "spiritual self," we may strengthen our abilities to consciously interact with these energies as a part of a daily holistic practice.

The same systems of consciousness and energetic interaction we apply to ourselves is also present in other forms of life—including animals and trees. Therefore, it is important that an initiate is first aware of how this energetic systems operates on *themselves* before attempting to interact, commune, or otherwise exchange energies directly with Nature or other living systems—and specifically the *trees* that the remainder of this "grimoire" is focused on.

Tree Magick is a uniquely personal form of mystic practice used by Elven-Faerie Wizards—and later Druids—to awaken the individual consciousness of trees on Earth, one by one. These awakened trees form groups or "chains," composing a complex network of communication—and energetic exchange—with the other awakened or "Enchanted" trees. Through "high magical" processes of "Communion with Nature," an Elven-Faerie Wizard or Druid is capable of learning otherwise untold spiritual lessons from Nature and awakened tree-spirits, because they are all linked to the planetary pool of "Earth Memory," just as each of us is influenced by encoded genetic memory within the design of these mortal body-shells that may even be billions of years old.

An advanced use of these abilities might include activating a ring of awakened trees to guard (monitor) an area around your home. Linking with the Forces of Nature, a sensitive adept may notice when the surrounding area has a "visitor" or is disturbed—like the strings of a spider's web. Other more abstract practices could include accessing data from the Elven Libraries—what some refer to as "Akashic Records."

The Forest Magickal Tradition is so vast and colorful that entire lifetimes could be dedicated to its ways and unlimited applications. To "Commune with Nature," any skills developed from previous exercises in Visualization and Willpower will be tested. The following are prerequisite steps of the traditional "Commune with Nature" spell-rite before performing any other specific acts.

- Go to the sacred woods where you practice your art of energy-play and light-weaving. This will most likely be the *Nemeton* ('magic circle' or 'grove') or place where you most often spend time developing your magical arts.
- Spend some time meditating on the "Elven-Faerie Tradition" or Druidry.
- Project your awareness into your "Light Body."
- Adjust or tune your "Light Body" to match the green energy vibrations of the woodlands.
- Use muscular inclination ("Dowsing-With-Your-Feet") to guide

you to a specific tree (assuming it is one that is not a part of the 'grove' or have not already selected). [At first you may want to work with only a few tree types—but eventually you may be able to awaken the entire forest.]
• When working with individual trees, approach slowly and from the north (when possible) and with a quieted "mind." Do not bring a head full of cluttered worldly matters to your Elven Green World energy-work.
• Sit close—within an arm's reach—and focus on both your "Light Shield" and the "auric radiation" of the *tree*.
• Spread your palms wide on the surface of the trunk.
• Match your frequency and vibration (color) with the tree and then merge the two energy fields.
• Retain contact with your left hand, completing the circuit with your right hand by using some catalyst for the energy—such as sticks, stones or the ground, depending on your other intended practices.

Now that the preliminaries are performed, what follows will depend on what type of 'Green Magick' you have intended. Not all Nature-communion sessions are for literal "communication." Basic communion is the first step regardless.

Visualize—and maintain an awareness—of a clear circuit of energy. The pillared trunk of the tree represents the "Tower of the Green Ray," the Middle Ray of pure crystalline reflection. Take this energy into your circulatory and nervous system through your left (or receptive) hand spread on the trunk. Make it a part of you, then send it forth to the ground (after cycling it through your catalyst or tool)—just as you would an electric circuit! The root structure of the tree takes this energy in, circulates it through its own internal nervous system—passing through trunk, branch and sprig—before it is passed back to you.

When both aspects ('terminals') are sending and receiving simultaneously, there is no energy "drain." When life-force energies are cycled, they are filtered as a result of the process, which may be beneficial when it is clear *Self-Honest* filtering—much like removing corrosion from a wire-connection or electrical contact. Such exchanges also take place during sexual encounters: energy is projected and permanently changes by the "energetic signature" of a partner, and then returns. When we engage in such activities without understanding energy properly, there is a risk of damaging or depleting auric energy from our "*chakra-system*" and/or "Light Bodies."

Once you commune, you can communicate:—Close your eyes and see a whitish etheric "cloud" between you and the tree, slightly above your head. Both of you share this 'field' and have the ability to project into it. Understand: trees are not verbal "talkers." They prefer—and are mostly restricted—to communicate in the timeless language of symbols and imagery; hence, in this case, a "picture *is* worth a thousand words."

So long as true communion exists between you and Nature, the verbal use of communication—for example, in rites and rituals—are mainly for your benefit, and to assist focus on actual communicable energy transmissions. Members of the animal and plant kingdom are more likely to hear and respond to tone and "emotional charge" (or your Light Body resonance) than the words themselves. Use the "cloud" previously described as a "thought-bubble" to facilitate communication. Then wait and be patient to see what happens. Tree communication is often slow work—even for an adept.

The Elven Forest Magick system is loosely aligned to the later Druidic classification of *Ogham* trees—a "systemology" derived from the former. There are three different traditional sets of "*Ogham Tools*" that are often all haphazardly referred to as "*Ogham Sticks*." Elven tradition gives each of the versions its own title and each are kept separately in their own magical pouch—called a "Crane Bag" in the *Ogham-ic* tradition and system.

OGHAM STICKS—Twenty sticks/twigs of the same type/species, cut to the same size and polished. An alternate version uses wood-chips as "runic wood-stones." Each stick or chip will have one of the Ogham glyphs burned (preferably), cut or painted thereon. "Ogham Sticks" are used for high-divination and "cryptomancy."

OGHAM WANDS—Ranging from eight to sixteen inches long, each wand is constructed from the correlating tree for each Ogham sign if possible—or tree of similar energy. The "handle" of the wand should be shaved flat on one side so there is a surface to burn or paint an Ogham sign. The other end should be sanded or filed to a stake-like point so it may be pushed several inches into the ground. During communion or communication, the Wizard holds the handle of the wand to complete the energetic circuit. "Ogham Wands" are primarily used for communication and spiritual communion with Nature.

OGHAM RODS—Twenty-one pieces of dowel or thin wood that are cut to equal lengths and used specifically for divination. Some scholars suggest this ancient tool set inspired the game "pick-up-sticks"—which is what an objective observer might see when the set of rods is cast, interpreted and retrieved. "Ogham rods" are held in one hand about a foot or so away from the ground, and then dropped. Using runic and Ogham signs as reference, the Wizard may interpret any omens found or "read."

When used in conjunction with tree communication and communion with Nature, even simple acts of "divination" may become powerful workings of "Elven High Forest Magick." The "*Elf Stones*" are another perfect example of this.

ELF-STONES—(*Elessar*)—are among the most sacred tools of "Sylvan Magick." They may be used for any purpose: divination, tree communication and various energy-work. Elven lore suggests many different versions—including all-blue and all-green sets—but always sets of three stones.

"Triscale Oracle Stones" (*Elf-Stones*) are the most commonly described in traditional Celtic lore—three equal-sized stones, each tapping into the energetic heart of one of the "Three Rays of Radiance" or Elven "*Awen.*"

> "Golden Ray" — Tiger's Eye
> "Silver Ray" — Hematite
> "Crystalline Ray" — Obsidian*

"Elf Stones" are a perfect catalyst for divination and tree communication, acting as a an energy-testor, similar to the function of a "pendulum" or "dowsing rods." A standard "Triscale Set" may be used to indicate 'positive' or 'negative' responses (answers) based on where the gold and silver stone fall in relation to the black/green crystalline indicator stone.

To use the Elf-Stones in relation to "Tree Magick," you might try the following:—Link up to a tree energy from your Light Body and ask it if it is in need of a Guardian and Caretaker or if it wishes to begin a mystical and spiritual relationship with you. Drop the stones at the base of the tree and see how they fall. If the gold one is closest to the

---

* Some sets substitute aventurine or bloodstone for the obsidian.

indicator, the answer is "yes." The answer is "no" if the silver stone is closer.

Practices related to 'Ogham Tools' and 'ElfStones' are all great for developing skills of "Elven High Forest Magick," but they are dependent on sensitivity and awareness of a practitioner for effectiveness. More information on these is found in our *"Book of Ogham"*—another title in this series. Such tools (and techniques) formerly described may also assist in "Awakening the Forest." In fact, one of the final rites offered in the original "Greenwood Forest Grimoire" is a direct suggestion to accomplish just that:

ELVEN-DRUID HIGH FOREST MAGICK
"THE TREE AWAKENING"

- Enter your "Light Body."
- Call down the "Radiance of the Three Rays."
- Make physical contact with the tree.
- Perform the "Tree Communion" spell.
- Speak the "Elven-Gaelic name" for the tree species three times, followed by the "English name," and finally the names "Aldaron," "Daghda" and the "Guardian-name" (associated with the type/species).
- Knock three times and break contact.
- The tree is *awakened!*

---

the "great tree" rite

The 'Great Tree Rite' first carried an exclusively lunar-orientation—used for Full Moon observances and complimenting the solar orientation of the traditional "Grove Festivals" marking the annual 'Wheel'. It may, of course, be also added to solar rituals used during these seasonal observances—such as those found in *"The Elven-Faerie Grimoire."*

This ritual text follows the same "elemental alignment" as other rites in the *Elvenomicon* series; and similarly, while originally written for group applications, may be modified for use by solitary practitioners. As a "rite" it is generally added to other magical and ritual work. It honors the 'Sacred Tree' of the Grove—one that is generally included in the 'Magic Circle' itself.

THE GREAT TREE RITE

LEADER: *We are here to give witness to the unity and strength of the magic circle, this mandala of love most holy. We, the Druids, the Children of Light, are at one with thee, Oh Sacred Tree. You, who stands as an eternal symbol of the Circle of Light and Life. You, who represent our eternal link with the ever-present Source. We honor and imitate you as the perfect living specimen of the Source of All Being and Creation. We watch you as you progress through the sacred Earth Year.*

NORTH: *The beginnings, middles, and ends of the sacred Earth Year.*

EAST: *The balanced forces and equinox equalities of the sacred Earth Year.*

SOUTH: *Tonight (today) we coven together, humans and tree, acknowledging the Sacred Grove.*

WEST: *We celebrate the strength, love, and unity of the Sacred Grove, and in that celebration we honor the central icon of its existence: The Great Tree.*

EAST: *From the Eastern Winds we are granted a season of growth, as the sun emerges in the spring.*

SOUTH: *From the Southern Flame we are granted a season of fullness, as the sun warms the summer.*

WEST: *From the Western Waves we are granted a season of transformation with the shifting tides of autumn.*

NORTH: *From the Firmness of Northern Ground we are granted a season of stability, self-reflection, and stillness, as the Earth hibernates and is renewed through winter.*

LEADER: *The calendrical month ___, the Oghamic month of the ___ tree in the ancient Druid's calender.* [Traces an appropriate Ogham sign in the air. Then continues.] *May the blessing of ___, and the corresponding energies of ___ be projected forth into our auric light.*

[continues on next pages]

> **GREAT TREE RITE—BASIC OGHAMIC KEYS**
>
> January: Alder Tree, *Fearn*, F, protection and power.
> February: Willow Tree, *Saille*, S, healing and enchantment.
> March: Ash Tree, *Nuin*, N, protection and peace.
> April: Hawthorn Tree, *Huatha*, H, love and purity.
> May: Oak Tree, *Duir*, D, strength and leadership.
> June: Holly, *Tinne*, T, purification and balance.
> July: Hazel Tree, *Coll*, C, intuition and creativity.
> August: Vine, *Muin*, M, meditation and prophecy.
> September: Ivy, *Gort*, G, protection and growth.
> October: Reed, *Ngetal*, Ng, intense energy and direct action.
> 13th Month:* Elder Tree, *Ruis*, R, completion and reflection.
>   Alternatively: Yew.
> November: Birth Tree, *Beith*, B, fertility and new growth.
> December: Rowan Tree, *Luis*, L, strength and insight.
> Winter Solstice: Silver Fir, *Ailim*, A, objectivity and longevity.
> Spring Equinox: Furze/Gorse, *Ohn*, O, fertility and inspiration.
> Summer Solstice: Heather, *Ur*, U, healing and support.
> Autumn Equinox: Aspen, *Eadha*, E, ascension and immortality.

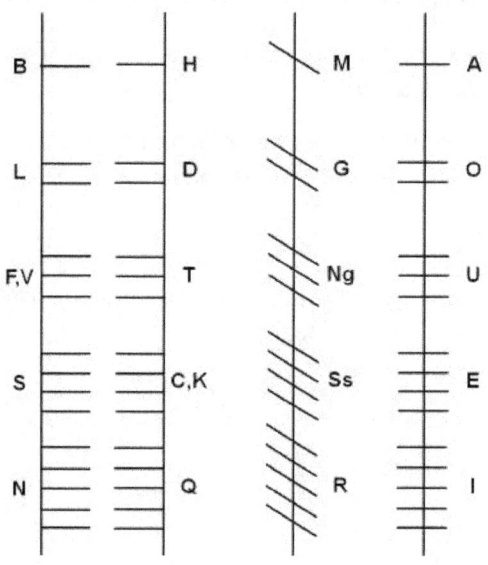

---

*   *13th Month*—ambiguously referring to either a "*Blue Moon*," or *Samhain*, or the three days leading up to a '*New Year*' observation.

EAST: *May the Sacred Grove and the Great Tree grant us the strength of the ancient Druids.*

SOUTH: *We hereby swear (reaffirm) our Guardianship of Gaea, the Sacred Grove, the Great Tree, and all life in Creation.*

WEST: *May the gentle rains bless all of Creation, nurturing and giving life, forever and always.*

LEADER: *The entangled roots of the Great Tree shall live deep within our being, offering nourishment and stability to all of its faithful guardians.*

NORTH: *And in between the roots and branches, we stand as the Guardians, the Keepers of the Earth, we who live in imitation of Oak Trees.*

EAST: *Our branches reach into the same sky proving that ascension is the purpose and goal of all life.*

SOUTH: *Great Universal Spirit, beings inhabiting this Sacred Tree, we stand here as your worthy guardians, and Keepers of the Earth and her mysteries.*

WEST: *May we grow to become our full potential from the seedlings we now are. May seeds plant in the world, bloom and flourish, spreading the true beauty and love of the Source of All, shared by all those receptive.*

LEADER: *[Traces appropriate Ogham sign on the tree; knocks three times lightly on the trunk, intoning names of the tree (often the English, Elvish-Celtic and Guardian names) with each knock. Then continues.] Oh Great Tree, you are hereby awakened by the Druids of the ancient and ineffable knowledge.*

NORTH: *May the ground that covers the roots, forever and always be blessed with all that is good and holy. May all of creation grow as the trees in the forest, each beautiful in their own uniqueness, yet still sharing the same Earth in which too spread roots and call home.*

LEADER: *We are united in our strengths, our faith, our love, and our trust. Ours in the bond that must endure all other bonds. The Truth Against the World.*

ALL: *The Truth Against The World.*

LEADER: *Through True Knowledge, Power.*

ALL: *Through True Knowledge, Power.*

LEADER: *So mote it be.*

by wand, ward and staff

The Druid Wand and Wizard Staff—called *"slatan drui'echt"* (literally: magic rod, wand or staff)—are iconic symbols of magic; and when made of wood, they represent a wizard's relationship with the woodlands and trees. Each is believed to contain the very essence of the *dryad* spirit that inhabits the tree—thus a regimen of reverently extracting a sacred wood specimen only after magically awakening a tree, asking its permission and doing as little damage as possible in the process. A cutting ceremony should also be performed, which includes casting a circle around the donor-tree and wizard.

Additional lore on the magical properties of each individual wood-type or tree (and suggestions of use as *wands* or *wards*) is found in the next section ('Sylvan Druieachd'). For the moment, we will simply distinguish the types of tools, themselves, which are referred to throughout the *Elvenomicon*.

WAND—a thin branch (half to three-quarters of an inch thick or so—although thickness often varies along its length) used as a focusing tool for directing 'streams' or 'currents' of energy—via attention—in 'ritual magic'. In Elven-Faerie tradition a *wand* is representative of the Air element and the action that is transmitted via thought.

WARD—a wand-like branch (usually four to sixteen inches long and decoratively crafted) used (or hung) as a 'talisman'—or protective magical artifact—to *ward* away certain energies. *Wards* are derived from Celtic lore, where an Elvish Wizard or Druid performs "magic" (called '*druieachd*' or '*druidecht*') by cutting or carving symbols on a branch and reciting a "spell." Some traditions refer to the *ward* as a '*rod*'. A longer (*staff*) version is often called a '*stave*'—from which we get the expression to "stave off" something. Interestingly, a '*stave*' is a name for a 'rung' on a ladder, and also a 'stanza' from Bardic poetry.

STAFF—a thick long branch, resembling a 'walking stick'—with medium-length ones often called '*rods*'. A staff acts like a vertical wand that maintains an axis connecting land and sky—or else the polarity of the seen and unseen, the material and the spiritual, or else *Beta-Existence* contrasting with the truer *Alpha* reality (if we are to include systemological terms). In the Elven-Faerie tradition, the *staff* or *rod* is typically representative of the Fire element—a symbol of the force and authority (presumably of Will) that is exercised by the wizard.

Now that we have established what is traditional, it should be noted that these 'rules' are not "dogma." As an example: lore suggests specific rules for sizing a wand—such as using the length of your elbow to palm, or elbow to fingertip, &tc. The truth is that a wand will either feel comfortable and natural when held by an individual, or it won't. And while traditionalists support extracting wand and staff wood from living trees, this is not an absolute rule either. Many fine tools have been crafted from branches of fallen trees and even store-bought wood.

Each wand and staff you construct is individually named during its dedication rite or consecration ceremony. Elsewhere in occult lore, the *Key of Solomon* instructs that the ceremonial staff should be constructed of 'elderwood', or 'cane' or 'rosewood'; and the wand from 'hazel' or a nut-tree—but made from *"virgin-wood."*

This term 'virgin-wood' is ambiguous and once meant: from a tree of one year's growth only that had not yet budded (or fruited). Anyone that has actually seen such a tree would probably not find it suitable for staff wood. It is more likely that the phrase indicates a tree that has not been previously cut on for any other purpose—but that is only a theory.

Much like a *'caduceus'* indicative of Hermes, the wand and staff is "sacred" (or 'aligned') to the planet Mercury. Therefore, the traditional time to cut or construct one is the "day and hour of Mercury"—which is to say Wednesday at dawn. Some of the common staff-wand types in Celtic lore include:

>   *Darkwand/Darkstaff* = Blackthorne
>   *Goldwand/Goldstaff* = Oak
>   *Silverwand/Silverstaff* = Apple
>   *Whitewand/Whitestaff* = Hawthorne
>   *Witchwand* = Willow or Rowen
>   *Wizardwand/Worldstaff* = Ash or Rowen

There is one other archaic tool from Celtic lore worthy of mention here: the "Druid's Rod" is little used among modern revivals, but this ancient tool was often created and carried by an *Ovydd* for their solitary rites during a probation period spent studying and meditating in the woodlands, among the company of trees. Technically, it is two rods connected by a cord, resembling a larger version of the familiar *nunchuk* weapon.

The two rods are attached with a cord so that when the tool is outstretched, there is a rod at each end with the cord between. By fixing one portion in the ground and using the other to trace the boundaries of a nemeton (or ritual circle), the Druid's Rod acts like a drawing compass. The tool could also be arranged to form a sun-dial. As such, it represents a mastery of cosmic knowledge, particularly regarding 'space-time'.

The "Druid's Rod" employs another important facet of little-known Druidic lore, called the 'Megalithic Yard' (abbreviated "MY"). A 'Megalithic Yard' is equivalent to 2.72 feet (which some modern practitioners simply round off to 3-feet). The complete "Druid's Rod" is composed of three measured parts, each 2.72 (or 3) feet long, making the total length approximately 9 feet, or 8.16 if using the strict 'Megalithic Yard'.

THE SYLVAN DRUIEACHD

alder tree

Elvish-Celtic Name: Fearn, Gwernen
Ogham Letter: "F"

Oghamic lore attributes the Alder Tree to the Fire element; yet, additional investigations into its mysteries reveal that it also carries an affinity for water—because Alder wood holds up quite well against it and is capable of actually living in water. For this reason, fortified villages floating on logs in Scotland and many "water-towns" (such as Venice) are built on piles and stilts of Alder wood. Since the Water element and magic of enchantment and glamour are closely related, Alder *wards* away (protects against) such enchantment from others. Due to its unique aquatic growth ability, it represents a bridge or link between the material world and the Otherworld—and, of course, it used to build "bridges" in general.

One clear indicator to the ancients that this is a sacred Faerie-tree is that when it is first cut, it appears as though it were bleeding. Such omens forced wizards to consider that this wood should not be often cut, and so there is a mystical taboo or "*geas*" concerning its use—though it is still often used. It allegedly makes good charcoal and the bark yields a blood-red dye. Fresh shoots produce a more cinnamon-hued dye.

The Fire element and red attributes apply to its use in battle. According to the "*Cad Goddeu*"—"Battle of the Trees"—Alders are at the head of the battle—"first in the foray"—right there on the front line. Warriors often sought Alder wood for their shields.

The blood-like sap is equally reminiscent of wounds in battle—such as those endured by Bran-the-Blessed. Alder energy drives the warrior spirit, allowing one to stand fast in battle or conflict, or when confronted with an overabundance of external pressures. Just as the head of Bran arrived in the midst of battle to reveal important prophecies, so must an Elven Wizard or Druid be open to hearing their own inner voice at all times.

Alder '*wards*' are highly effective. Of course, to obtain Wizardwood, you must touch the tree with a blade, which is taboo except by the most adept of Elven Wizards. Ask the *dryad* spirit of the tree to enter the *ward* and aid safeguarding against the will, magic and enchant-

---

* *Ogham* correspondences that originally appeared in this section are now incorporated with the material in the next section, titled: "*Book of Ogham*," for this anthology edition.

ment from others toward you, your family—or for the owner of the ward.

Alder is sometimes used for medicinal purposes. The inner bark may be boiled in vinegar and used to anoint the skin to remedy various skin conditions, it tightens gums when used as a mouthwash (or soothes a toothache) and has even been used to help kill head lice and assist with scalp recovery afterward. [As with any "folk medicine" discussed within these pages, the present author suggests the reader/seeker embark on extensive investigation into all homeopathic and holistic medicine—including discussion with a health care professional—before self-treating with any natural suggestions.]

apple tree

Elvish-Celtic Names: Quert, Queris, Afal
Ogham Letter: "Q"

Many Celtic scholars interpret the name of the ancient *Isle of Affalon* (or "Avalon") as the "Isle of Apples"—also known as the "Isle of Glass" and today, Glastonbury. The Apple Tree and Avalon both share a peculiar connection to the Elven-Ffayrie Otherworld. An examination of ancient lore and references to Avalon suggest it was called "Appleland"—and most likely home to a large orchard or elaborate arrangement of Apple groves. It is said to aid in perceiving other 'worlds'.

An Order—or secret society—of priestesses and Druidesses maintained a mystical tradition in Avalon sacred to the Silver Ray and using Apple Wand in their ceremonies. The *Craebh Ciuil* wand or "Silver Bough" is used for healing, beauty, peace and harmony, in addition to Otherworld Magick. The "Apple Branch" is also a central tool to several magick rites that summon or call the *Fey*. Lore suggests that it is a forked branch, unpainted, with three silver bells hanging on white, silver and/or blue ribbon.

Another reason Apple is sacred is that when the fruit is cut in half, you can see the image of the pentagram—the five-rayed star. *Quert* is sacred to the harvest, festivals of Lughnassadh and the Autumn Equinox. The tree flowers white blossoms near Beltane. A toast of cider is always conducted in the honor of the Apple Tree Spirits at the beginning of the harvest to bless and consecrate the harvest season. The tradition of wassailing occurs during the winter season. All dietary use of Apple hybrids (now common) first emerged from the original

Crab Apple tree—for which the Celtic Ogham letter is named. The also fruit appears in folk remedies for soothing asthma or for chronic pneumonia sufferers—possibly inspiring the old saying that: "...*an apple a day keeps the doctor away.*"

ash tree

Elvish-Celtic Names: Nuin, Nwyn, Nion, Unnen
Ogham Letter: "N"

There are three main wands of the Sylvan Faerie Druid Tradition—excluding the Silver (Apple) Branch formerly mentioned— and they are: Oak, Ash and Thorn. While *Drwyds* are best known for their Oak wands, the legendary Spear of Lugh was fashioned from Ash wood. The first Elven wands were possibly of the *Nuin* current, in imitation of this spear, and often carved into a spiral, like a Unicorn's horn—always representative of the Air Element. Ogham tools constructed from Ash wood are used for inspiration, enlightenment and most obviously, knowledge.

Ash is the most likely candidate for a "Tree of Knowledge" or "World Tree" (*Yggdrasil*) often referred to in Nordic-Elven lore—or even the Semitic Kabbalah, which is based on Mesopotamian lore of the *date-palm* as the "World Tree" or "Tree of Life." In all of its forms, the "World Tree" is a holistic microcosmic-macrocosmic representation or Cosmic model—its branches representing different degree/levels of existence (or dimensions) yet still a part of the singular Tree. Elves sometimes refer to the "Middle World"—or "physical plane" experienced by the Human condition—as "Mid-Branch."

As one of the few truly crystalline tree currents, Ash trees possess the ability to be one sex and then switch based on reproductive needs. According to folk remedy lore, Ash bark may assist in reducing fevers; and the leaves may be used to remove bio-toxins as a laxative, or externally to treat snakebites. When leaves are unavailable (or out of season), the bark is often used with similar results and the sap is sometimes added to teas and infusions to aid relieving kidney stones and bladder infections.

aspen tree

Elvish-Celtic Names: Eadha, Aethin, K'emmir, Poplysen Gwyn
Ogham Letter: "E"

The Aspen Tree is aligned to the use of intuition and the uncovering or revelation of secret or esoteric knowledge. Long have Wizards sought Aspens as "Oracle Trees." From a meditative state—the Body of Light—they watch as winds blowing through the leaves produce a sound and flickering sight that is conducive to skrying and receiving visions and prophecies. Slightly more robust, Poplar and Cottonwood Trees carry the same energy current. Cottonwood, particularly, is more highly aligned to masculine/solar polarities, also known as the "Giant Aspen."

The *Eadha* current represents mysterious lessons that are necessary to overcome in order for spiritual completion on the Earth Plane—and finally the "Grand Ascension." Aspen Trees have many associations with death, as both Jesus and Judas of the Judeo-Christian tradition hung from them. Aspen wands and *ward*-talismans represent overcoming death and bad habits. They are also used in "karmic balancing" rites and for revenge. The measuring rod used to fit coffins for people was once made of Aspen wood. But Aspen is not the final Ogham Tree in the twenty-fold system—it is nineteenth—reminding us that the physical death transition state is *not* the end.

Elves, Wizards and Druids all maintain a "Transmigration of Souls" doctrine that indicates that the "spiritual egg" at the center or core of our True Self is not physically tangible at the normal human degree of perception and is not destroyed when the physical body or vehicle perishes. It instead extends its own light to maintain a spiritual existence or vehicle fit for higher degrees/ frequencies of manifestation. If more lessons must be learned, the Light Body or spiritual self will travel to another catalyst or vehicle to access this knowledge—we sometimes call *reincarnation*—which continues until a True Ascension takes place, and the being or spirit is so full of light that physical incarnations are no longer necessary, except in cases where a self-actualized Ascended Master returns by will to assist teaching others. The Aspen Tree does not have many medicinal uses, save one famous one: Nature's Aspirin. The bark is powdered and administered—perhaps in capsules or tea—to relieve fevers and mild tension or pain.

beech tree

> Elvish-Celtic Names: Phagos, Sultan, Atarya Dwyrion, Ffawydden
> Elvish-Ogham Letter: "Ph"

Beech Trees are a secret Ogham character incorporated into a later system—possibly by reconstructionists themselves. It is an important tree, appearing in the first line of the "Cad Goddeu," yet it does not appear in any traditional twenty-fold Ogham system. The Beech and Oak trees are the subject of the first quatrain of the "Cad Goddeu" prose—and they share a connection, representing ultimate "Godparents of the Forest" (*Atarya Dwyrion*). Elvish lore often depicts the *Phagos* current as a more "feminine" counterpart of the "masculine" Oak.

Phagos is a sacred tree to both Elves and Dragons. According to lore, Beech is more closely aligned to humanoid energies than other trees —and its "Dryad" spirit is often more receptive to communication than many other species. In spite of this, the Beech Tree is often slighted out of "New Age" texts regarding "trees in magic" that are based exclusively on a modern 'Celtic Tree Oracle' popularized by Liz and Colin Murray. But there are other, and more antiquated, resources regarding Ogham lore—much of which is found within the *Elvenomicon* section titled: "*The Book of Ogham.*" Communication is significant integral of the *Phagos* current. Beech wood was once the preferred material for writing tablets and even hardcover books. Resonating with the "preservation of knowledge," the *Phagos* current may also serve useful when working with ancestral spirits. The Beech Tree produces an edible nut called a *"mast,"* which is also traditionally used to make cooking oil.

birch tree

> Elvish-Celtic Names: Beith, Beithe, Beth, Belwen, Bedwen
> Ogham Letter: "B"

The Birch Tree marks the New Year on most interpretations of the Celtic Tree Calender and as such is sacred to *Samhain*. Its purifying energies are called to drive out old spirits and static energies of the old year. Such is also the primary ritual function of a "magical broom." Traditional folk magic rituals often began with sweeping out of the area to neutralizing the energy of a magical workspace or *Nemeton*. The "flying" aspect of the witchcraft tradition more likely emerged from the use of mushrooms that grew in the Birch shade and provoked "spirit flight" when ingested. Such methods of "astral travel" would lead seekers into the Otherworld via hallucinogens.*

Beith is an energy of new beginnings, and the tree is notorious for producing new trees from fallen twigs. As the first tree of the Ogham system, it is commonly the first forest lesson encountered by an initiate. Only as a result of effective abilities to awaken, communicate and utilize currents of the Birch Tree, would a first degree student of "Elementalism" be permitted to enter the second degree of "Forest Magick."

The New Year marks the annual transition into the "Dark Half of the Year"—from *Samhain* to *Beltane*. And although not observed even close *Samhain*, the Birch Tree is most closely aligned to energies of Spring Equinox (*Alban Eiler*) forcing many scholars to question the validity of the accepted "Tree Calender" used by reconstructionists.

The Birch Tree is the "Lady of the Woods"—often replacing the Beech as the Silver Pillar (next to the Ash/Yew and Oak) in the Forest Magickal Tradition. Medicinally, the oil from the bark may be used to make a skin lotion, which may assist a variety of skin conditions. The buds of the Birch flowers are used to help stomach pains and ulcers. Chewing on twigs will helps keep teeth clean, and a tincture of the leaves and/or bark aids relieving mouth soars. Teas and tinctures have a purifying quality causing frequent urination when ingested. The oil in the bark may be used to repel insects. [Apparently, modern scientists discovered that a chemical in Birch known as *"methyl,"* makes this all possible.]

blackthorne tree

Elvish-Celtic Names: Straif, Straife
Ogham Letters: "St" "Ss" and "Z"

Blackthorne—also called "Wishing-thorne" or the "Faerie Tree"—actively reflects the "darker side" of Nature, and the thorns may be carried (or used in ritual) as a symbol of this part of the "Ffayrie Tradition." When allowed to grow wild, it forms an impenetrable bramble—yet it is important to clarify that when allowed to grow, Blackthorne is a tree, not a bush.

---

* For legal reasons we don't actually include details regarding this.

In the physical "Green World," a hedge of thorns may help to hide a grove or other "secret portals" to the Otherworld. If we apply the same symbolism to divination, the hedge may represent barriers and distractions which promote confusion and anger.

Dark Power is not restricted to "Dark Elves" and actually has nothing to do with the *Unseelie Court*. Darkness and shadows simply hide those parts of the world—and ourselves—that we do not readily see or accept, like the "Shadow Self." When we see observe the manner in which we handle frustration and anger, we are often left to deal with aspects we do not like and may seek to change. You can't change the fact that sometimes you get thwarted on your path and will come across barriers and challenges. You can change your programmed fight-or-flight response-reactions and your ability to cope, or manage the "Game of Life."

A "*Shillelagh*" or "Blasting Rod" is made from a Blackthorne branch with Ogham signs of power burned along its surface. Lore suggests that a repetitive sequence of personal names and words of power would be inscribed thereon. In spite of its many titles, this is not a tool of malevolence. On the contrary, it was used to protect against such malignant energy in an active manner—perhaps as the original "ward-wand"—so as not to leave one defenseless against "Dark Arts." Strength, wisdom and self-actualization occur when you can face and control your own dark nature without being controlled by it. It cannot be healthily suppressed as "evil," because in doing so you are rejecting a part of yourself that will only surface later, unbidden and uncontrolled, and usually with unhealthy and/or destructive consequences.

Blackthorne tea—concocted from powdered bark—induces a calming effect, as is a common aspect of many Ffayrie trees when ingested, which may help to slow one's vibration to "Green World" frequencies. Blackthorne produces a purple berry called a "*sloe*," which is a necessary ingredient for "sloe-gin" alcohol. Ink and dye are also made from the sloe berry. It is most sacred to *Samhain*, and second to *Beltane*.

cedar tree

Elvish-Celtic Name: Chakris
Elvish-Ogham Letter: "Ch"

Cedar is not a traditional Ogham tree. Along with the Beech, it was incorporated into the system more recently. The wood carries a long-standing tradition in the Ancient Near East for "binding" spiritual energies, and is traditionally used in construction of many sacred buildings such as Solomon's Temple.

Some "New Age" Ogham revival systems classify the *Chakris* rune as the "the Grove" ("*Koad*"), most likely named after the Ceder Tree's ability to purify the area of the Grove (*Nemeton*). The runic glyph and energy current, however, is more appropriately attributed to the Cedar as an individual tree. In Elven Forest Magick, Cedar wood (and essence) is a purification incense, used in a similar manner as "sage." The smoke may be assist consecrating the Circle of Power, especially if ritual intentions include spirit summoning, ancestral work, or any form of Mesopotamian Neopaganism. It is called the "Tree of Light," sacred to the *Imbolc* and, as an evergreen, to the winter season (*Alban Arthuan*) and "Yule."

cherry tree

Elvish-Celtic Name: Oadha
Elvish Letters: "Da" "Dh" and "Th"

Cherry is a popular wood for art and woodcraft because of its distinct coloration and ease of workability. The wood is naturally charged to amplify Will, alchemy or transformation magick. The current can be used for intentions that further an existing war, or to end and prevent them. Cherries are symbolic of sexual passion—the power and intensity of the orgasm, and is sacred to *Beltane* and Midsummer (or *Alban Heruin*). *Oadha* is not an official Ogham Tree and yet, it seems incomplete not to consider it in our catalogue.

elder tree

Elvish-Celtic Names: Ruis, Ysgawen
Ogham Letter: "R"
* NOT TO BE CUT FOR WOOD!
* LEAVES MAY BE POISONOUS!

Some superstitious folklore mistakenly attributes Elder as an "unlucky tree," but Elven-Faerie lore simply says that it is unlucky to cut one down, bring inside or even grow indoors. Those who cut them might fall to misfortune and death—and thus you have been warned now of this Forest Code. Elder Knowledge is "Crone Knowledge," demanding protection and preservation—just as the elders of a spiritual society and their folk memory require the same. For *Oghamancers*, the *Ruis* current is one of the most difficult to awaken for "Tree Communication."

Elder is not a particularly large tree, reaching only 30 feet in height at maturity—but it is powerful and resilient. Its wood is strong, withstanding many harsh conditions. Elder bark—found as deadwood—may be used to develop a very dark dye and the leaves yield a rich "forest green" hue often used for riding/traveling cloaks. When mixed with alum and salt, the wood produces a deep violet dye. The Elder Tree is very sacred in Elven-Ffayrie traditions, even apart from its Oghamic associations. According to lore, its sap may be used as to make a "Faerie-Sight" ointment—a headdress or diadem fashioned from Elder deadwood twigs may grant the same ability to its wearer.

As previously stated, Elder is the "Crone of the Forest," the "Venerable Mother." She is so sacred to the forest people that her wood is protected in Celtic society by a "*geis*," a taboo against removing livewood—even by Wizards. Those who use the wood for furniture and miscellany may be haunted by the spirits of the wood, and fall upon misfortune. [DeLorean cleared an ancient Elder and Thorn Faerie-forest to make room for a new car manufacturing plant in Ireland, and the company practically disappeared.]

"Dark-natured" trees, called "unlucky" by some, actually tend to be the best species/types for ridding a space of negative energy or clearing away illness. Folklore suggests a tincture of "Elder Flow'r" will purify the bloodstream. Leaves may be infused into a solution that for externally dressing bruises and swellings—or as a pesticide. Elderberries are rich in Vitamin C and are used to make a delicious wine. They may also be boiled down to make a shampoo that will have a darkening effect on the hair.

the fir-pine-elm current

Elvish-Celtic Names: Ailim, Ailm, Elma, Ffynidwydden,
Pinwydden

Ogham Letter: "A"

Fir/Pine/Elm trees represent pure primal Earth elemental and planetary energetic currents and an interconnectivity with all life in the Green World of Nature—which is the epitome of the "Green Ray."

The Elm is especially distinguished as the "Tree of Elves," and carries the same *geas* (taboo) against its use as the Elder Tree. The tree is frequently affected by "Dutch-Elm Disease" (giving appearance of dead branches in the canopy)—which is really caused by beetle infestation. Overcoming this barrier of disease reflects the true enduring strength inherent in this current—and certainly the Elm shares many spiritual attributes with the Fir/Pine (*Ailm*) earth-forest energy, with affinity for "invisibility magick," agriculture and protective rites.

Fir and Pine Trees are tall and slender in comparison to the Elm. They are also evergreens—whereas the Elm is deciduous. The tallness of the Fir, Pine and Redwood varieties demonstrate their "objectivity" and "high view"—their ability to see clearly and judge fairly. They are also quite communicative. They are able to grow new trees from old sprouts thought to be dead, making the Fir-Pine an iconic symbol of endurance, eternal life, and of course, regeneration—which is why it is popularly featured in winter.

We can use modern science to divide this current into hundreds of sub-species, but all of them represent the "Middle Pillar" and carry the energy of the "Green Ray" in its clearest form. Ease of communicating with this current and its frequent appearance in Sylvan Magick makes it a prime candidate for early novice "tree work" before approaching other primer trees in the forest catalogue, such as Birch and Beech. The *Ailim* current is useful for growth and fertility rites—for both the "Green World" and personal needs, as well as rituals and ceremonies pertaining to marriage and relationships. Pine is also a natural source of charcoal, tar and turpentine.

furze and gorse

Elvish-Celtic Names: Ohn, Piswydden
Ogham Letter: "O"

To call this Ogham a "tree" is bit of a stretch, but this hedge plant does grow a woody "bark" and it appears in the "*Cad Goddeu*" prose, describing a "Battle of the Trees." Some scholars believe the "Battle of the Trees" was a metaphysical skirmish to determine rank and stature of the species composing the later Druidic Ogham Tradition. This low prickly shrub—not typically taller than a Human—is often present for purification rites and/or burned as incense.

To work with this current directly in your locale, you may need to find a suitable substitute tree that shares its energy—such as a *Linden* or *Lime* tree—especially if you intend to construct an *Ohn*-wand. The Gorse-Furze Ogham is also closely related to "Broom" and "*Ohun*," the Linden Tree or Basswood—but Americans without access to a Gorse bush are probably not going to find a species of Linden Tree naturally growing nearby either. "*Ohun*" is sacred to stars and astronomy, but also to magical rites or enchantments regarding love, beauty, glamour and personal attraction. Its metaphysical/"*ray*" color is orange—as opposed to yellow for Gorse—but it retains a strong alignment with the element of Fire.

hawthorn tree

Elvish-Celtic Names: Huatha, Huath, Draenen Wen
Ogham Letter: "H"

Hawthorn is a "Faerie tree" with a special "*geis*" (taboo) against wood removal—except during a ten-day period preceding *Beltane* when wizardwood may be properly obtained in keeping with tradition. *Huatha* staves, wards and wands all have powerful protective properties, particularly against enchantment, spells or magic from others. This wood is also used to make the famous "Whitewand," just as Blackthorne wood is used to make the "Darkstaff." As with any cutting, a ceremonial rite should accompany wizardwood removal as a sign of respect toward the spirits residing within that otherwise may bring misfortune.

Often cut back to form a "haw" or hedge, the hawthorn may enjoy a long time—even by tree standards—and reach dozens of feet in height. It makes a frequent appearance in fantasy or "fairy tales" as a magical barrier or wall around enchanted places or castles. Some Elven lore refers to it as the "Wishing Tree." Hawthorn berries, raw or in tea, may act as a blood thinner with calming properties to assist relieving heart issues. If the oak-resembling leaves are added to the tea, it may help a sore throat—and is sometimes added to grain alcohol for the same result.

hazel tree

Elvish-Celtic Names: Coll, Koll, Collen
Ogham Letters: "C" and "K"

The Hazel Tree provides an energetic current of great insight. Its nuts fall into lakes, which feed the "Salmon of Wisdom." The stream of Hazel-Salmon energy is the current or path of "inner knowledge," what is often sought from oracles and in divination: "perfect cosmic knowledge of all things." Hazel rods may be used to form an entire set of divination sticks—when tied together or carried in a "Crane bag" or pouch, actually represent a powerful ancient protective amulet. Forked branches are sometimes used to make "dowsing rods"—tools of energy-testing, for finding water, or tracking "ley lines."

Elven lore suggests that the energetic current of the "Hazelnut Tree" represents the "Tree of Sacred Knowledge"—a catalyst for learning the true nature of the *Self* and the Universe, and should not be confused with Eden's "Tree of Knowledge," which is metaphoric—or ancient near eastern allegory—and related to genetics.

The nuts of the Hazel tree are edible, and may be powdered to infuse a drink to induce "spirit vision," as well aid relieving colds and sore throat symptoms. The Water element is strong in Hazel energy, especially when found growing around water. Its energy is most similar to that of the Willow Tree and *Saille* Ogham current.

heather and mistletoe

Elvish-Celtic Names: Ur (Heather), Uchelwydd (Mistletoe)
Ogham Letters: "U" and "W"

There are two types of *Ur*-Heather: red and white. The Red type attracts passion and is a symbol of sexual energy and lust. White Heather wards against passion and sex and symbolizes purity and chastity. While Red Heather is sacred to, and picked, at Midsummer (or *Alban Huruin*), White Heather is aligned to Spring Equinox (or *Alban Eiler*). Heather is not a tree, but is listed as one of the Ogham energetic currents, and is therefore listed here.

In some versions of the system, this Ogham sign and energetic current is represented by "Mistletoe," which Elven and Drwyd lore both suggest is among the most sacred of all herbs. Naturally, both Heather and the Mistletoe current share similar attributes.

Mistletoe lore is mainly the product of Celtic Druid Tradition. It was considered most powerful when found growing on Oak Trees—a rare but very real event (in spite of what modern skeptics have to say on it). Mistletoe is aligned with the Air Element because it passes itself along tree top canopies. It is a 'parasitic plant' that attaches to a host tree and does not root in the ground itself. When cut with the Druid's Sickle, a white linen sheet would be placed below to catch it, being sure that its sacred essence never touched the ground. This herb was then consecrated and later added to all Druidic medicines—lending Mistletoe the folklore name "All Heal."

holly tree

Elvish-Celtic Names: Tinne, Celynen
Ogham Letter: "T"

Many modern Christmas customs are derived from ancient Elven-Faerie Druidism ('*Drwyddon*')—the ancient national religion of Celtic people once dominating the British Isles, Ireland, and previously, the European mainland. Holly is actually an evergreen *bush*, but it may have served as the first traditional "Yuletide Tree." Of course, all evergreens share some affinity with winter. Holly berries also hang like red ball-ornaments, inspiring iconic color themes for its seasonal festivals. The three primary Druidic herbs significant to Yule actually represent three 'Oghams' directly—Holly, Ivy and Mistletoe.

Lore suggests to grow a Holly Tree in your grove or garden to attract positive currents and ward against negative energy. Holly-wood burns well when still green (freshly cut) but it is taboo and against the Faerie Code to do so. Burning any pre-dried wood, particularly a species held so sacred to Elven-Ffayrie, is blasphemous. Holly wands may summon lightning, suggesting fire alignment as is the relationship with war and allegorical conflict of ongoing struggle for annual supremacy between the Oak King, ruler of the "light half of the year" and the Holly King who is keeper of the "dark half of the year."

The *Tinne* current shares many of the same energetic attributes as the Oak Tree—and with good reason. The only major frequency difference (aside from obvious size) is that Holly is an evergreen and Oak is not. At Midsummer (*Alban Heruin*) the Oak King loses the battle over the Sun's control to the Holly King, who yields it back to the Oak King on *Holly Day*, or approximately Yule. This is metaphorical, of course, and the lore is used to describe or explain the properties and polarity of natural forces that ebb and flow at varying times of year. [Holly leaves may also be used to brew detoxifying teas.]

the ivy

Elvish-Celtic Names: Gort, Uruin, Eiddew
Ogham Letter: "G"

In the helix-style growth pattern of the Ivy, ancient Elves and Druids observed and recorded the "Golden Spiral"—else, the energetic serpent-entwining of DNA structures and life patterns. While not generally classified as a tree, Ivy possesses an ability to develop bark and grow strong when allowed to. *Gort* unifies the spiral with the wand—as a spiral (carved or metal) is sometimes wrapped around the length of a wand—or for a true herbalist, this might be the Ivy itself. Spirals represent active creation, so incorporating it with any magical tool (or object) provides an additional "active" quality. It is sacred to the Autumn Equinox (or *Alban Elved*).

maple tree

Elvish-Celtic Name: Shorin
Ogham Letter: "Sh"

The Maple Tree is not a traditional Ogham character. In fact, it is not mentioned anywhere in "Celtic" Ogham lore. Maple is included here because North American and Canadian practitioners *do* share access to this energetic current, and it is a powerful one—quite common to encounter in these geographic locales.

The Celtic Tree Ogham was refined by Ancient Druids of Ireland, a location where the *Shorin* current has little lore is ascribed to it. Its leaf structure is iconic—even gracing the Canadian national flag—visibly displaying the 'Sign of Elves' and 'Rays'. The leaves transition through all hues of green-to-red in Autumn, near "Equinox" (or *Alban Elved*). Maples may be used for magic to connect with similar energies —tree types or species that are not accessible to where the practitioner resides. Wands are appropriate for sex magick—in its purest sense: awakening inspiration or creativity and then manifesting it.

oak tree

Elvish-Celtic Names: Duir, Dwyr, Dar, Derwen
Ogham Letter: "D"

Oak-acorns are fiery seeds of life—perhaps one of the most famous elf-amulets found in Nature and used to attract fertility, love and protection. Oak Groves—collectives of trees—have a tendency to grow because, as is said, the "acorn never falls far from the tree." Elven and Druid lore suggests that eating the acorns—or using oak flour—may aid in understanding "Divine" (Cosmic) and ineffable truth via inspiration (or *'gnosis'*), as similar to the *Hazelnut*. The Oak is a very "busy" tree with vast long-standing traditions of mystic lore—and, if we adhere to such lore: it may very well be the most sacred tree on Earth.

Deep within the Greenwood forest stands a tall and gnarled Oak Tree branching out wide and drawing you nearer and nearer to the mysteries of the secret grove—the repository for all knowledge in Nature. There lies the "great door" leading to the inner mysteries of true initiation. True magick is what brings us "Absolute Truth" and contributes to our evolution on the "Path of Ascension."

Oak is often used to represent highest degrees or levels of study in Elvish Schools of Druidism, emphasizing a path to self-realization and absolute awareness. It embodies the final most notable lesson for Oghamancers in their advancement to the "*Drywydd*" degree and is listed seventh in the Ogham alphabet, perhaps demonstrating a hidden awareness and appreciation of the original and complete "sevenfold" system.

There is an old saying about how Oak is a long-lived tree: "300 years to grow, 300 years to mature, 300 years to die." In that time they will commonly acquire what are known as "galls." These spherical growths are sometimes the result of insect hives occupying beneath the trunk surface until their larvae are mature.

The "Grandfather of the Forest," guards the Oak door of May at *Beltane* and clearly aligned to the Fire Element. In fact, the *Duir* tree current carries such an affinity with fire that it has a tendency to manifest the element as lightning—which seems to strike Oaks more than any other species observed, almost as if they are "calling it down." Obviously the species defends its attributes of "strength and endurance" by withstanding such energy, resulting often in a more gnarled, tangled and "interesting" looking tree. The fiery energetic affinity between Duir and lightning makes a Golden Oakwand (a companion to the Silver Applewand) highly prized for powerful Nature-oriented magic.

Oak wood is a common material for ceremonial blade handles (corresponding with its fire alignment)—and another tree that closely shares the *Duir* energy current, though perhaps more passively, is the Hickory Tree or "*axara*." Its energetic attributes are similar to Oak, but applying to more worldly, mundane or tangible aspects—such as the acquisition of material gain, good fortune and abundance. In fact, oak-hickory forests are among the most common in North America east of the Mississippi River.

reed and broom

Elvish-Celtic Names: Ngetal, Corsen, Erun
Ogham Letter: "Ng"

Broom is a specific kind of tall wetland grass known as reed. It literally grows out of the water—and may even form an outer bark layer—making it the "Water Tree" of Elven Forest Tradition, though other systems often reserve this title for the Willow tree. But, while Reed is derived from the water, it is aligned with the Air element with a long-standing affinity for communication, writing and knowledge that originates in the *Ancient Near East*, specifically *Babylon*—where use of the "Reed stylus" was perfected for refined cuneiform script.

Reed represents a connection between the perceived "inner" and "outer" worlds and the harmonic balance of those energies. The Ngetal Ogham current is a subtle energy, slowly working its magic and enchantment from a point of stillness, with small ripples. Although aligned to air, the natural affinity between Reed/Broom and water makes it an appropriate addition to any rites aligned to an "aquatic" nature, or the consecration of water-elemental tools. The Broom type is actually named for its use in broom manufacture. In a previous lesson-chapter we discussed how brooms were used to sweep out and clear ritual space. Ironically, the Broom—both in its plant form or as an object—is sacred to *Samhain*.

rowen tree

Elvish-Celtic Names: Luis, Ceridinen
Ogham Letter: "L"

The Rowen (also spelled 'Rowan') Tree produces berries, which, much like fruit from the Apple Tree, contains a five-pointed pentagram, traditionally symbolic of Nature's Elemental forces. These edible berries are rich in Vitamin A and C.

Talismans of Rowen wood offer protection while traveling and from the enchantments of others. For this reason, it is commonly used for walking sticks or staves and its protective properties make it beneficial to plant a Rowen Tree at the entrance of your home, property and/or Sacred Grove. *Luis* is called the "Quickening Tree" because of its active magickal power—combining active Air Elemental qualities with the feminine current. This Air of Moon correspondence makes its wizardwood a prime choice for a traditional "witches wand."

The flowers and berries often bear a pentagram and along with the leaves, once dried, may be used as incense. Don't forget to add a pinch of Mistletoe. Burning this may call forth energies of the ancestral realm and Otherworld—as well as the "Nature Spirits."

The Rowen is represented by the Unicorn, the epitome of all that is beautiful and enchanting, also representing a link between worlds. The Unicorn current tempers that of the Dragon. These energies should always be used in balance of one another. It is easy to fall into the trap of over-analyzing and over-thinking and essentially all of the untempered qualities of the unbalanced "Dragonmind." It is most sacred to the annual beginning of winter (*Samhain*).

the vine

Elvish-Celtic Names: Muin, Gwynwydden
Ogham Letter: "M"

The Vine, though not necessarily a tree, is ranked among the Ogham currents because it may develop a hardened outer bark. Its sacred annual threshold time is the harvest, specifically the Autumn Equinox (or *Alban Elved*). It has been used to make grape-wine for thousands of years. A tradition of wine used to "reveal truths" is derived from its ability to gain information gathered via loss of inhibitions. *Muin* represents hidden, just-below-the-surface realizations—sometimes only brought to the surface when uninhibited—that cannot be healthily suppressed if we are to break through to the next steps of our progression. With an ability to scale walls, the Vine truly knows no boundaries.

willow tree

Elvish-Celtic Names: Saille, Awn, Helyg, Helygen
Ogham Letter: "S"

Willow Trees possess a high affinity for water: it drinks a lot of it, soaking up as much as possible to develop a fast growing trunk structure. A combination of water and the moon "*Rays*" contribute energetic qualities of intuition, emotion, beauty and enchantment. Willow represents the epitome of the lunar-water current resonating with the "Moon Goddess" or "Triple Moon Goddess," aligned to feminine rhythms and cycles, and not only regarding monthly rhythms, but the greater life-cycle phases of "maiden-mother-crone."

The Willow is metaphorically the "Grandmother of the Forest"—the one you can tell anything to because she has already been there herself. A Willow-wand may be used for lunar rites and/or water-oriented magick relating to feminine needs, as well as dreams and the old priestess tradition of "drawing down the moon." Its wood is also favored for fashioning 'dowsing rods'.

Saille is a healing Ogham, mostly on an emotional level. By linking/communing personally with Willows, you may open channels necessary to sort, retain and release past emotional pains and carried energy. Willow bark is also known for its healing properties, yielding the *salicylic acid* used in both aspirin and skin-acne treatments.

yew tree

Elvish-Celtic Names: Ioho, Ywen
Ogham Letters: "I" "J" and "Y"
* BERRIES MAY BE POISONOUS!

An evergreen marking the end of our magical forest journey, the Yew Tree reminds us that it cannot be a true ending—because nothing ends. By riding this energetic current toward Ascension, we are reborn and transformed into a new life. After completing the "Initiation of the Forest," the Initiate or "Oghamancer" may rightfully call themselves a "Sylvan Wizard" with the ability to awaken the woods and be known to all "Nature-spirits" as a forest-friend or "elf-friend."

Yew also stands at the finale of the Ogham alphabet. *Ioho* is the Oghamic sign of completion, in a manner much deeper than that represented by the *Ruis*-Elder Tree current. It is not so much an "ending," as much as it represents the gateway to the Otherworld—or that is to say the absolute promise that there is continuation of spiritual life after material death. *Ioho*-Yew shares an energetic frequency with a select few other Ogham Trees in the tendency to (re)generate new trees from its *"layrs."*

The Book of Ogham

the oghamic system: a brief history

*"Ogma, a man well skilled in speech and in poetry, invented the Ogham.
The cause of its invention, as proof of his ingenuity,
and that this speech should belong to the learned exclusively.
The father of Ogham is Ogma.
The mother of Ogham is the hand or knife of Ogma."*

—'Lebor Ogaim'

Ogham or 'Ogam' (properly pronounced as '*ow-am*' '*oh-wam*' '*oh-am*' '*ohm*' according to various sources) is a style of script—and, of course, 'sigils', 'glyphs' or 'runes' in New Age applications. It represents information once unique to upper classes of Celtic society—particularly the *Druids*, who in fact decreed it forbidden for the uninitiated to be given practical knowledge of the alphabet.

The surviving literary records of scholarly and mystical interest today are notably Irish (Gaelic) manuscripts and various esoteric British (usually Welsh) sources—all of which have been considered during preparation of this present handbook.

Ancient Celtic and Druid Ogham inscriptions do still survive today on hundreds of 'standing stones' and 'markers' in Ireland and the British Isles. Many more likely exist but are badly damaged. Notches or hash-marks (called '*fleasc*' or '*fleasg*') distinguishing each letter or *"few"* ('*fidh*'—or *"fews"*/ '*fedha*' plural) are written along a straight-edge—or the *"stemline"* ('*droim*'). Of course, when cut onto stone, the outer edges are most vulnerable to wear.

> *"Stemline"* (the straight-line) / *"droim"*
> *"Notch"* (hash-marks) / *"fleasc"*
> *"Few"* (an individual letter) / *"fidh"*
> *"Fews"* (letters, plural) / *"fedha"*

Ancient wooden Ogham artifacts rarely survived the ages. The best examples date only to the 1700's and relate to an entirely separate Celtic alphabet—the Bardic *coelbren*—used almost exclusively in the Welsh-Druid tradition and based on researches of Iolo Morganwg in Wales. But the secret alphabet of Ogham was not always intended for obvious permanence or detection. For example, wooden posts or temporary signs could be raised near remote settlements or villages that might alert a traveling Druid to secret grove meetings and perhaps inform of their location. To the uninitiated, such ambiguous notches would not seem significant.

Not surprisingly, origins of the Ogham are frequently attributed to Ireland—where a host of manuscripts and majority of surviving 'sites' remain. As with many of the other archetypes and stereotypes of "Celtic" culture, Ireland served as the last great stronghold for Celtic and Druidic tradition—meaning the most recently in our history.

Prior to this, the Celtic and Druidic influence dominated most of ancient Europe up until the 'Classical period' (the age of Romans and Greeks) when Celtic-Druid presence was forced westward—primarily due to ancient 'Romanticization' and later, the eventual 'Christianization' of Europe. Thus, as it is an alphabet, not a dialect, most surviving Ogham inscriptions represent the Irish language in Ireland.

The secret alphabet notably emerged into use during a time when hidden messages might need to be exchanged among Druids amidst interaction with a literate classical world of Greeks and Romans. It is difficult to determine the origins definitively, even archaeologically, because Ogham script was never intended for widespread open visibility or any common use among the Celts. But there is a surge of more visible usage in the Celtic world c. 100 BC.

According to the Irish texts, Ogham script originated (or was refined) c. 600-500 BC. by the scribe-poet-god of the Celtic pantheon: Oghma—named Ogma, Ogmios or Ogmas in other Celtic/Druidic traditions. In addition to gifting Druidism with knowledge of the Ogham script, he became something of a 'patron deity' in the Bardic tradition.

Oghma is listed as one of the "Tuatha de Danaan" (or "Tuatha d'Anu" in the original *Elvenomicon* series), or else the Danubian Druids that arrived in Ireland when it was formerly occupied by the "Fir Bolg" and "Formorian" races. As such, he is related to Dagda and Lugh (also famous Celtic deities). Although dating on any findings are often disputed, chalk slabs once excavated by Alexander Keiller in southern England (Windmill Hill, Avebury, Wiltshire) suggest that ancient prehistoric Oghamic use may have existed there as early as 2160 B.C. concurrent with a dawning 'Age of Aries' and the development of Mardukite Babylon.

The era of the historical Oghma is the same time, archaeologically speaking, that the 'La Tene' type of Celts are believed to have emerged prominently in Ireland—after migrated westward across Europe. This era is marked not only by increasing contact between Celts and the classical world, but also an internal Celtic integration of proto-Druidic, proto-Celtic and La Tene cultures.

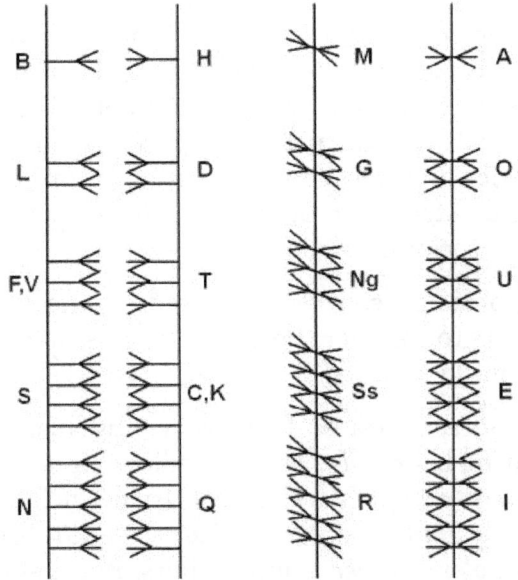

Ogham scale variation from Book of Ballymote.

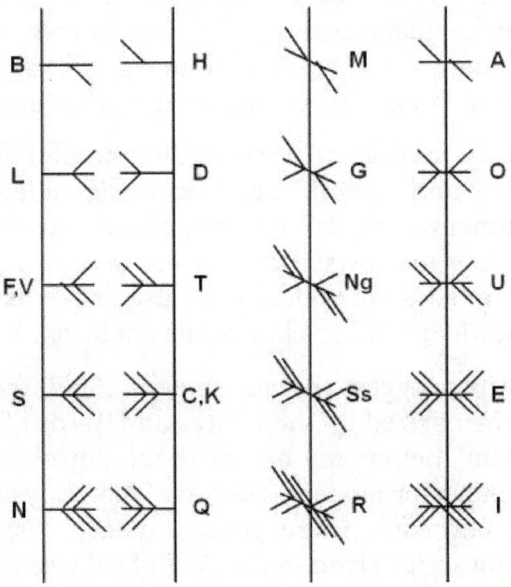

Ogham scale variation from Book of Ballymote.

THE OGHAM TREE ALPHABET

An Oghamic (or proto-Oghamic) tradition appears to be related to at least some methods employed to preserve Druid lore in ancient times. While historians are inclined to suggest that Celtic society was wholly illiterate, there is strong evidence to support the existence of ancient Druid 'tree libraries' in remote forests. Leaves, representing information, were hung on strings or 'stemlines', much like the 'written' or 'inscribed' Ogham script later represents.

The Romans reportedly destroyed hundreds of these forest libraries during their efforts to conquer the Celtic people—an effort that lasted for half of a millennium.

Modern Ogham lore is drawn from surviving manuscripts of antiquity, some dating back as far as the Medieval times, in the heart of the Dark Ages; most of which are, in fact, Irish—including *Book of Ballymote* and *Lebor Ogaim* (*The Book of Ogham*, also known as the *Ogham Tract*) and *The Scholar's Primer* among others. But it should be understood that these are archaic works *about* the Ogham; we have no surviving manuscripts actually written *in* Ogham.

The alphabet is structured into four groups of five *fews*; each group is called an *aicme*. Much like Nordic runes, it can actually be utilized to write in most any language. It is read left-to-right when the *stemline* is horizontal (meaning the right side of an upright *few* faces down), or it is read upward when inscribed vertically—an orientation point.

Although primarily used as a 'secret code' and alphabet among the elite, the scholarly and 'Druidic' applications included 'coded' references to all manners of birds, animals, stones, deities, places, and above all else for our interests: the names of *trees*. In fact, the Oghamic tradition concealed a mnemonic code used to assist recall of vast systematized knowledge lessons in Druidic tradition.

Archaic manuscripts suggest that as many as 150 different "Oghams" may have been memorized by the Ovates and Bards of the Druid College—"Tree Ogham" being only one of them, but obviously one that became most popular for modern 'New Age' metaphysical and/or magical (magickal) purposes. There are also nearly 100 variations (or "scales") of Ogham script given in the *Book of Ballymote* alone. Two are shown here.

Throughout the world of magic and mysticism, across aeons of folklore and mythology, trees have stood as the universal or cosmic symbol of the connection between all 'worlds' or "Universes"—referred to in esoteric lore as the "World Tree" or axis link between *this* physical-material Universe or level of perception (referred to as s"*beta-existence*" in Mardukite Systemology) and the true all-encompassing "Other" existence.

The theme appears in other esoteric models as the "Tree of Life"—such as in the "Kabbalah" of the Ancient Near East, &tc. Apart from the "Dragon," the "Tree" is the most commonly reoccurring ancient cosmological model of all Universes and Creation.

It is not surprising then that we should find evidence of both the 'Dragon' and the 'Tree' as definitive icons of Druidic Tradition. In the Celtic cosmology, the physical universe is likened to a "dragon" and the "tree" represents the conduit that connects *this* "Mid-Branch" (or "Middle-Earth") existence with *upper* and *lower* existences. Ancient Mesopotamians maintained similar lore in their mythological symbolism of existence. But, let us turn our attention more concisely to the Ogham itself...

[The following transcript is a special bonus for this edition that would not have been available for inclusion a few years ago.]

MARDUKITE MASTER COURSE ACADEMY LECTURE #22*

"the oghamic tradition"

One of the features of *Merlyn's Complete Book of Druidism*—as a Master Course edition for present purposes that wasn't available when we released previous editions of the past, like, as an anthology (*The Druid Compleat*)—but this edition has the my "*Pheryllt Researche*" notebooks and portions of the *Pheryllt Researches* were then spliced with excerpts that went along with those themes, when I released "*Book of Pheryllt*"‡ to accompany "*Deepteachings of Merlyn*" and Douglas Monroe's complete "*Merlyn Trilogy.*"

So, what I did in this edition is, I maintained the material that is in *Elvenomicon* presently still today as it's been for the last fifteen years, and then added as an appendix to the entire book, the "*Pheryllt Researches.*" And so, if you are going to deal with Master-level 'Ogham Tech' or forest magick and a "Druid School," this is all pretty critical stuff to incorporate.

I expect in the next couple years—I've been asked to expand on my work on the "Elven-Faerie Tradition" and "Druidism" and many other elements of Grade-I. Rowen Gardner contributed some 'Forewords' to, I believe, the *Druid's Handbook* and the *Draconomicon* in the past. I've done some work with them in the past. So, I decided to go ahead and probably work with them on expanding Grade-I material—for those that are using it, again, as an entry-point; and for those who are still coming into our tradition.†

So... *expect that* to be coming up here; but what I do want to do is present—a lot of the material is already present within the Master Course, it's just not set up that way. So, again, if you look through the material and the "Instructor's Manual" and look at the material of the *Pheryllt Researches* in addition to *Elvenomicon* and the *Draconomicon*, *Druid's Handbook*, you'll see that this time around already, the "Route-

---

* Transcript of a lecture given by Joshua Free on September 24, 2020; extracted from "*Druids, Elves & Dragons: Mardukite Master Course Academy Lectures (Volume II)*"—also contained in "*The Complete Mardukite Master Course.*"

‡ Now available in a collector's edition hardcover from JFI Publishing as "*Draconomicon Vol. 2: The Pheryllt Researches*" and within the new 2023 deluxe anthology, "*Merlyn's Complete Book of Pheryllt.*"

† Alluding to a second *Elvenomicon* trilogy, which is included in this present anthology.

of Druidism and Dragon Legacy" exceeds anything we were presenting as "*The Druid Compleat*" in the past.

At a Grade-I understanding, you will find a lot of material as you go into the "*Greenwood Grimoire*" of the *Elvenomicon*—or even another of our publications, the *Vampyre's Handbook*—you're going to see more of an emphasis on work with "Rays of Light," which is really just getting someone into a practice of handling "flows."

Handling "energy flows" directly is actually a very high level element of "Alpha" work—of Wizard work. It's practiced at Grade-I levels; but seldom mastered. Because when we're dealing with "Rays of Light," when we're dealing with the "flows," the channels between individuals, the "conduits," a lot of this... and the way it's explained in the *Vampyre's Handbook*, it's all handling, basically, raw energy directly.

Now, we've found as an alternative to this, that handling "mental imagery"—or even the concepts of which these various "flows" and "energies" and response-mechanisms are attached—is actually a lot more effective; a lot easier. There's nothing wrong with handling the "energies" directly. It's just that at a Grade-I level, when an individual is usually just now getting used to the concept that these even exist, it's usually considered higher-level work within even that grade, to start handling "Rays" and such directly.

The other element being: astral light—the concept of an "astral body." We know now at kind of a higher systemological level that these 'astral bodies' are kind of "blanketing" this existence that we have here; they're basically bodies that have actually almost—not deteriorated—but they no longer have the same "power" and "function" and "solidity" to occupy as a point-of-view as, for example, what we're kind of stuck in *here.*

And that's why we're trying to liberate an individual *out of* the Human Condition while we're doing Systemology work. These "astral bodies" do perhaps occupy a "mental plane"—"mental universes"—once operating very much as a "beta-existence" within themselves, but for whatever reasons enough barriers, blockages, withholding—in terms of wanting to reach, and withdrawing *from*—and other elements forced more and more condensed point-of-views of what we experience today as *reality.*

"Astral work"—"mental work"—*can* be employed; it's just that we have found at higher levels of practice that there are simply more effective ways (than what is demonstrated in conventional mysticism). I mention this because the concept of the "Astral Grove" is introduced within my writings—within the last fifteen years—mostly ever since I kinda came to the realization that there was a way to get back to this other "Magical Universe" that we've all descended from. One of the ways in which I thought practice of that could be involved, was getting back to the point where *Self* was able to experience... well...

There's a reason why those that are attached—or find an attraction to —have any affinity with "Druidic Paths," the "Elven Paths," the "Faerie Paths," things that involve "Nature," "Shamanism," animals and so forth; there's a reason why there's an inclination: because this restimulates a memory—probably several lifetimes worth of memory —involving this other Universe, this other existence, which one did engage in a very fluid communication and perfect understanding with what was treated *there* as the "natural world."

There is a "mirror image" of it on *our* planet, although not nearly as vibrant until you're actually able to peel away some of these "levels" of (fragmentation) that kind of dim our sight of this world. But there's a connection there because it does "remind" us exactly of that; and that when we looked at, for example in yesterday's lectures, some of the traditions and Faerie traditions and Otherworld beliefs concerning this existence and whatever existence that these once physical and inhabiting "elves" and so forth—"Faerie Races"—that inhabited this physical existence and we able to be identified as such, were then moving *back* to the "Magical Universe" and taking up residence there.

Now, what we've later discovered was that this Universe became kind of a lower-level consideration or "prison" or "penalty existence" of a lower-level Game than what was taking place in the "Magical Universe." At that level of existence, we had the original archetypes of what you see with "Wizardry" and "mysticism" and "magic" and the natural "elements" and related icons and themes that draw someone into this tradition.

As one of the "Masters" or the "Instructors" involved with the Mardukite Academy, you would then be able to recognize these elements and work with them later on in "processing"—if you get into "Piloting" or other elements and the higher "Wizard levels." Because these are direct links. These are what's going to get individuals out of the confines of the Human Condition.

Many that are taking up these paths already have some kind of inkling that there *is* something more and that they're not strictly "Human" as *Self*. I mean, these are all things that many carry with them today. Just because they're not involved with *us*, doesn't mean they aren't aware of these things. But...*selective directed attention!* That's what we've emphasized in Systemology; and most individuals that aren't carrying a *full* realization of what's taking place, it's overshadowed by all the other aspects of the material world.

In terms of "Elven Tradition," "Celtic Faerie Tradition," "tree magic," "forest magick"—there are ceremonies for the "Consecration of a Newly Planted Tree," a "Rite for Planting a Single Guardian Tree" and "Dedications of a Grove" or "Stewardship of an Area" are all within what was originally called the *Greenwood Forest Grimoire* in the *Elvenomicon.*

One of the reasons I had at one point encouraged more "Astral Grove" work was because the "Elven Fellowship Circle of Magick" was meeting in Denver. Most of the work I did on the *Elvenomicon*, up until 2004, was while living in Denver. Although there were a lot of parks and, of course, access to the mountains and Nature, I was writing, primarily at the time, for what is considered "urban" readership; and so the concept of using an "Astral Grove" or using "imaginative creative visualization" to operate "magick" was simply as an alternative to, you know, access to "natural terrain" or natural areas to operate.

So, if an individual wasn't able to physically actually go to a park or go to an area or have a "grove" to work from or maintain stewardship of or guardianship of, then using the "Astral Grove"—using visualization techniques—was an alternative. And this is something I still do impress as a very effective form of "magick" that virtually any of the results that can be achieved from actually working out a ritual area, drawing out a physical space, using physical tools, physical implements an all that—can actually be practiced *within* the "mental realm" because that's actually all you're trying to achieve anyways.

The *Self* is using the "body" and the fact it's kind of been restricted to this point-of-view of a "body" at still this point of Grade-I, that is has to basically get the body—what we like to do in "objective processing" in Systemology—we're command of the body involved, and more command and control of the Mind-System that's doing that, by doing these outward "objective universe" practices.

If the same states can be achieved in the Mind without that—if an individual is able to achieve that—then all of this can actually be done at that level directly; in simply the operation of the Mind-System. Of course, this doesn't replace what we're trying to impress with the "Natural Paths" and "Ogham Tech" and actually going out into Nature and engaging into these lessons directly. But again, this is one of the elements that's not necessarily relayed in the "ritual magick" texts or in what's considered "mainstream New Age mysticism"—that all of these are meant to be tools, meant to assist the individual Seeker, into achieving this greater control over the Mind-Body connection or control over the Mind-System or actually Actualizing Self as a Spiritual Being as the Alpha-Spirit.

That's what we're dealing with all the way up the *Pathway*. But like we've said before: sometimes a passive—or just a simple read-through—or basic demonstration into what we consider a Grade-I understanding of the "New Age" or "Magick and Mysticism" is not a guarantee that an individual is going to surpass that and reach to new levels of realization; especially if they're tied exclusively to a "magickal correspondence in the physical universe" type of understanding.

OGHAM TECH.

But in terms of these assistant tools—within Ogham Tech, we have Ogham Sticks: they're twenty sticks or twigs, same size, cut the same size, polished; I mentioned before you could use "wood chips" if you wanna make more "rune stone" styles. But these are specifically for divination and cryptomancy—and so each of them, you would have twenty, and each of them would have one of the standard Ogham *"fews"* or characters; either carved into, or if possible, burned onto.

And then Ogham Wands are a completely different set of tools. These can range from six to eighteen inches. And if possible, what you want to do is construct them from the correlating trees. Thus, you have a "hazel wand" that's taken from the "hazel tree" and so forth.

If you look into the *Elvenomicon*—in the back, where we deal a lot with the tree lore—you'll see that there's a lot of correspondences and other ways of connecting attributes of tree energies so that you can find substitute trees that could represent the same kind of energy pattern. And so each one of them, what you want to do is you have a long rod and then this kind of section up at the top that you have as like a handle, you kinda cut away this to shave it flat so that it kinda goes down into the middle and this kinda gives you this surface to either burn or paint one of the Ogham "fews" on.

Traditionally these are used specifically for "tree communication" and communing with Nature. So these wands we kinda sharpen the other point a bit, you know, cut it down to a point. And this is then put into the ground and so the individual, when their communing with a specific energy or their working on a specific "Path of Encounter" or what have you, they have this Wand into the ground and then they're holding the handle part here where the Ogham script is printed.

That's what these particular ones are for—and since their each used individually and their not "cast" as any kind of divination, you don't need to be too concerned with, you know, making them all the same size or anything of that nature. Each is an individual tool.

And then there's the Ogham Rods. Twenty-one pieces of the same size, like, dowels. You just cut dowels down into twenty-one little sticks that are all the same size, and you don't do anything to them. They're basically just "cast" out as, kind of like, the game of *"pick up sticks"*—they're just "cast" out and you "read" any... however they've fallen, you "read" any of the Ogham symbols or script patterns in there that you might then look up to interpret as some sort of "omen."

Traditionally they've referred to the "magic pouch" that an "Oghamancer" or a "forest wizard" would use, as the "Crane Bag"—because the crane is the animal of knowledge. When it would fly in the air—its legs and the way it would stand and different patterns it would make—they would interpret those as Ogham symbols as well. So they had these *bags* that are called "Crane Bags." And each of your sets—your Ogham Sticks and Rods— they could each have their own Crane Bag.

The Wands, you can kind of arrange those. I've—when I've done this in the past, I had my own little wooden chest that I made; and I just kept all the various lengths of wood in there that way. So those are several tools that you can use; and you can correlate—you know, throughout this material, there's all kinds of Ogham correspondences and correlations... ways of practicing divination and interpreting Earth mysteries; these are basically the tools you might use for that.

I should point out: although I don't really recommend the printed card medium for this, the original presentation, or the reintroduction actually of this lore, the idea of a "Celtic Tree Oracle" for the New Age, really is attributed Liz and Colin Murray, which in 1988 released the "*Celtic Tree Oracle*" with St. Martin's Press. It's this beautiful green hardcover book and these cards. This has been basically the inspiration for much of the modern neopagan and "New Age" Celtic Tree lore connected to the Ogham in the past few decades. This inspired interest in the Ogham, when prior to that, it was more of an academic or scholarly interest regarding Ogham inscriptions found on stones all throughout Celtic Britain and Ireland. There's actually even evidence that they existed in the mainland of Europe, and even the Americas.

And so this interest in using the "Celtic" Ogham to represent a system of "Celtic Tree Magic" sprung up from that. When mixed with thousands of years of tree lore it has since evolved into what's become an entire complete system and field of "magick." And there's many examples of... each tree listed in the back of the *Elvenomicon* or *Merlyn's Complete Book of Druidism*. *Pheryllt Researches* also include many correspondences and applications and just a wealth of material.*

TREE-ORACLE ELF-STONES.

One of the key tools also that I've kind of always popularized—I mean, I started this with the original *Sorcerer's Handbook*; it was given in the "Merlyn Stone" materials, and also I've expanded it for the *Elvenomicon*. This concept of "Elfstones"—they weren't necessarily referred to as "Elfstones" in ancient Celtic lore. What I did was... —I was fascinated with the "*Shannara*" series of Terry Brooks; and perhaps as one of his better known, it became the subject of the "Season One" presentation of it a few years back when they did actually make a televised version of it. Fans had been hoping for a motion picture of his book "*Elfstones of Shannara*" for decades—and it was finally picked up essentially as a miniseries.

In the original concept of the Elfstones, there are three stones which had significance as a powerful tool; this set of stones. In that particular version, they were three blue stones. And I have this set that are three blue stones and what I use them for is "clarity of vision." They were considered "seeing stones" in one version of the stories by Terry Brooks, and so that's one way that I've used them. I've also used three green stones as a way of basically getting in touch with the

---

* Much of this is synthesized and expanded on in the present section, *The Book of Ogham*.

"Green World" while working with the natural elements or "Middle Ray"—the "crystalline ray"—you know, things of that nature.

Traditional Elfstones that appear (in Celtic lore) are known as "sky stones" or "triscale stones." They've been popularized in some books of Celtic wisdom derived from mythologies; they've been found in—for example, the Pheryllt system in *21 Lessons of Merlyn*.

So, the traditional set is: a golden stone, a silver stone, and what would be a crystalline stone or a black stone. And these each represent: the "Golden Ray," the "Silver Ray" and "Crystal Ray" of the "Druid's Cabala"; and the "Ray" system of the "Rays of Light" as they pertain to, not only the "Elven" system, but any of the "Light-Center" systems or "Chakra" systems—any "Seven-Plus-One" systems that involve Lights, which we deal with all throughout the various grades.

And so these are actually a really good tool for getting in touch with basic divination and tree communication. They have kind of a "pendulum"—like a "yes-or-no" quality to them; and so when they're used, the crystalline stone or black stone is used as an indicator. The silver is used to indicate "no" and the gold indicates "yes." And when you throw them—or "cast" them—at the base of the Oracle Tree, whatever stone is closest to the indicator stone is your answer.

The traditional "set" consists of the Tiger's Eye for the golden stone, the Hematite for the silver stone and Obsidian for the black stone. And this, again, you can keep in a small pouch and keep separate; or if you want to make several steps the way I've... you know, a standard set that I've had since the 90's: the hematite, obsidian and tiger's eye. I also have (this) blue set and a green set and each I use for different purposes.

But these basic, just, focal tools—these basic implements... Again, it's not to put a lot of emphasis on the power that they themselves have, but over the significance that is attributed to it by using them—by using them as a focus or to concentrate on a particular "Ray" or particular state or particular aspect. And so for *that* purpose, they can be very useful; very useful tools for increasing sensitivity.

THE OGHAM LADDER OF LEARNING.

So, before closing this out, I *do* want to give a brief rundown of the actual Ogham trees—and the most applicable way to do this, for the purpose of our Master Course, is to look at it from the perspective of

"The 21 Paths of Encounter." You can look at the Ogham for their individual aspects—what they represent. Each Ogham represents a color, it represents a bird, it represents a particular magical lesson—it does also represent a tree. You can easily use all of these aspects in "ritual magic." You can also use all them for divinatory or oracular purposes.

But I thought, for the purposes of the Master Course, I would run through this "Druid's Cabala of the Forest" with you—and how it's presented in climbing the "Great Tree of Life" in the Oghamic tradition. The concept of "Ascending the Druid's Ladder" is interpreted from the Pheryllt tradition.

This is not in the "Master Course Instructor's Manual," but it is in our Master Edition textbook of *"Merlyn's Complete Book of Druidism"*—in the *Pheryllt Researches* section. And what this lore does is: this runs through the basic Ogham trees and the Ogham symbolism in the order in which it's given traditionally. And it's usually—they're in groups of five.

We start with the *Birch Tree*, which represents new beginnings, first realizations, self-sacrifice, change to a higher level, devotion to the Great Work, awakening on the path.

And then we move onto the *Rowan Tree*, the first action, the first move of a game, magical work begun, self-control, movement in the direction of your chosen path.

Then we go to the third path, *Alder*, which represents heated resistance, strength to face what's avoided, conquering adversaries, the material world opposes your choice but your aspirations are completely protected.

The fourth path is *Willow*: new journeys and inspiration, Otherworld contact, confidence necessary, enchantment. Your path now appears as a dream on a moonlit night.

The fifth path: *Ash*; personal resolve, resolute decision, changing outlooks, the inner and outer world meet as one, and the inertia to break the threshold. And by threshold, we mean approaching the veil—the first veil of threshold—which is the "death of the old."

So, we've ascended up the path to the sixth Ogham now, *Hawthorn*—where new blossoms awaken. This represents the first success or manifestation being purified, protection given as you accept the bitter and the sweet of the chosen Path. And the bitter and the sweet is interesting, because in the upper level, when we're talking about flows and concepts in upper-level processing, we're actually talking about the "beauty" and the "ugliness," the light and the dark, the compelling versus the repulsion and all of that. This is something that actually as you break through the "Death of the Old," this is actually what we're trying to *flatten* out; *flatten* out any reactivity to.

The seventh path, the *Oak*: higher powers experienced and called to you, the strong door to the inner mysteries. Oak is spoken "*duir*" in Celtic languages. This is where we get the word "*Door*"—and then, of course, the "*Oaken Door*" is a strong common use for the wood, traditionally. Personal reflection opens up to new possibilities; we're talking about opening up "doors" to inner mysteries.

Which leads us to the eighth path, *Holly*. This represents an encounter, the Guardian of the Gates—which of course, we're approaching this Door; this Gateway—self-worth is tested, balance of opposition, challenge is presented, things may not always be what they seem so dispel all illusion.

And then we work into *Hazel*. Hazel is the ninth path: the fruit of knowledge. As we know, hazelnut—this kinda goes with other traditions from Druidry—the hazelnut falls into the lake, which is then eaten by the salmon, and then the bear eats the salmon. And these all become animals and trees and symbols of "knowledge"—of ancient knowledge and paths of knowledge and ancient primordial wisdom. So, from the hazel, the fruit of knowledge is given, wisdom is accessible, your encounter yields straightforward harvest of secret intuitions.

The tenth path: *Apple*—the tree of beauty. So, we have this new enchantment that comes with breaking through this first veil—the enchantment—such as like the *lunar level* with these new realizations and awakening these prior purposes and feeling the enchantment of Otherworld contact. This brings us to the second veil or threshold, which is that "Matter Gives Way to Mystery." And so we're confronting "Mystery"—*flattening the* Mystery—eliminating "Mystery" now.

And the eleventh path is the *Vine*, which is a meeting of companions, fellowship is born and hidden knowledge is revealed between them, strength to face destinies, your path is entangled with... fate, prophecy of others.

The twelfth path: *Ivy*. And Ivy, of course, is the "spiral"—the "spiral" of the Path—when you look at the growth patterns of Ivy; overcoming restrictions—Ivy, of course, breaking through barriers to be able to continue its growth, gaining confidence, inner strength and continuing to face the world; confront.

And the thirteenth path is *Blackthorn*: facing material existence, the clutches of the world, transition and change along the path, death, loss, cleansing, clearing; when choices are taken away, the perfect path remains. And there you see another staple of the *Pathway to Self-Honesty*.

The fourteenth path: *Reed*. Experience in the world; learning from experience, understanding Earth systems, material struggle, survival, knowing selective conform; knowing when to bend.

The *Elder*: self-annihilation; purging the Self of all artificial, the darkness before dawn; the "Dark Night of the Soul" so to speak; facing hard truths, accepting the lessons given and seeing clear light ahead.

Which brings us to the last set—the Third Veil—which is "Visions of Victory." And here we're coming down the "Home Path" here. It begins with the *Fir* or *Pine tree* of high views, long sight, the depth of relationships; experience gives rise to new visions and new realizations; seeing past the illusions—and even getting past our own experiences —the distant clear path that is visible.

The seventeenth path, *Furze*: the sweet smell of victory; awareness of the seeds born of difficulty; struggle passes away; and there's time to rest as you collect yourself. Here's where you're basically reaching that *point* where you're—it's either going to be a divide and conquer or conquest versus succumb.

And so at this point, you also have the eighteenth path: *Heather*. Pause and reflection; healing of the spirit; examination of actions—we're talking about hostile acts and withholds, withholding from others and withholding from ourselves; we're talking about the responsibility, taking responsibility and Self-determination; we're talking about basically making one's Self "whole" so that one can aspire to the remainder of the journey.

Which, in the nineteenth path, *Aspen*: you have the rainbow kaleidoscope of spiritual achievement appearing before you; protection given on the "Rainbow Path"—you see many references here to the "horizons of many colors" and a "Rainbow Path." It's also—this is applicable to the Tower of Babel, and the "Tower" of the Tarot; and so we're talking directly here of a "Ladder of Lights"—Ascension—the 'Ascent' up the "Ladder of Lights" beyond what has been... Breaking the gravity of the material existence.

The twentieth path, *Yew*, is: completion, final realizations, Ascension, rising above the impermanent, the product of the journey—the end in the beginning; beginning in the end.

Finally, twenty-first path, *Mistletoe*, represents the "formless," the "not," the "unknowable." We're talking about the Infinite. So we have the twenty-first element representing "Infinity of Nothingness," which we know is, the true background beyond the ALL.

THE OGHAM DIRECTORY

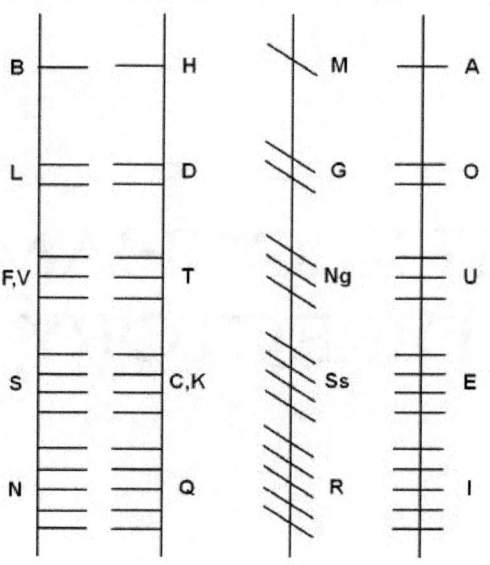

OGHAM FEWS DESCRIPTION KEY

"Standard Names (Celtic and English)."
"Esoteric Text Quote"
[Background Information]

ESOTERIC CORRESPONDENCE.

Alternate Names : Variations of spelling demonstrated by various Celtic languages (*Irish, Welsh, &tc*).

Alphabet Letter : Standard character.

Ogma's Tree : An associated tree of "Ogma Sun-Face" recorded in the Irish *"Lebor Ogaim"* ('*The Ogham Tract*').

Alternate Trees : Other species with similar energetic/spiritual properties.

Bardic Value : Numeric designation based on traditional Ogham sequential arrangement; also any reductions using *classical numerology*; the "Bardic Value" significance was popularized by Colin (and Liz) Murray's Ogham research for "*The Celtic Tree Oracle.*"

Forest Rank (British) : Using the hierarchy of the forest listed in the *Ogham Forest Tract* of British Druids—*chieftain, peasant, shrub* or *b ramble*.

Forest Rank (Irish) : As above for Irish Druids.

Quadratic Element : Corresponding 'classical element'—*earth, air, fire* or *water*.

Druid Guardian : Name given from the '*Boibel-Loth*' Ogham; used similarly in practice as 'patron saints'.

Celtic Deities : Avatars/heroes of the Celtic Mythos that identify with similar energetic/spiritual qualities.

Druidic Deities : Figures of Celtic Religion given on a mnemonic list (from at least the 1st Century B.C.) that is related to the Ogham alphabet.

Solar Month : A standard calendar month as adopted from Elven-Faerie Druidry (given in the *Elvenomicon*); there is *no* universal esoteric standard for a 'Celtic Tree Calendar'.

Lunar Month : A month of the pagan/lunar 'Wheel of the Year' or one of the 'Sabbats' (Grove Festivals); often based on the work of Robert

Graves; lunar months are traditionally named for their Full Moons starting with one closest to the 'Winter Solstice' (or Samhain as 'New Year')—however, there is *no* consistent Ogham calendar among sources. Some start the new month with a New Moon.

Color Ogham : As recorded in the Irish "*Lebor Ogaim*" (*Ogham Tract*).

Bird Ogham : As recorded in the Irish "*Lebor Ogaim*" (*Ogham Tract*).

Sacred Animal : As given in various *Ogham Tracts* and 'New Age' sources, &tc.

Sacred Gems : Corresponding 'gemstones' with a similar energetic/ spiritual quality, as adopted from Elven-Faerie Druidry lore and other 'New Age' sources.

Ogham Forest Tract : Additional practical, oracular and/or energetic/ spiritual expressions associated; keywords collected from *Tracts*, the *Scholar's Primer* and other records; an associated "art" or "craft" is also given.

DIVINATION SYMBOLISM.

Description : A written description of the graphic/glyph or '*few*' character.

Word Ogham (Morann mac Main) : Given in *Auraicept na n'Eces* (*Scholars Primer*); alternate name, Morainn mac Moin.

Word Ogham (Mac Ind Oic) : As recorded in *Auraicept na n'Eces* (*Scholars Primer*); alternately, 'Ogham of Aonghus'.

Tarot Equivalent : For divinatory purposes—a traditional Tarot Key (card) from the standard Major Arcana that represents this Ogham *few*.

Ogham Lochlannach : Corresponding (Norse) Runic Key interpreted similarly as given in *Ogham Tracts* of Ballymote.

Personality : When used to indicate specific persons, known or unknown, this Key may be consulted (as similar to use of "court" cards in Tarot); an 'inverted' trait is also included.

Oracular Meaning : A list of representative factors, states or aspects traditionally interpreted for each Ogham Key—derived from Celtic-Druid and/or Elven-Faerie lore; concepts/attributes may also be attracted by "ritual" or "meditation"; or for use as symbolism for talismans, &tc.

1. *beith* — birch tree

"The birch tree reminds us that new dimensions are opening for us. As they do, balance is necessary for greatest success in entering them."

—Ted Andrews
'Nature-Speak'

In the starting position of Ogham script, the birch tree signifies initiation and inception of a new journey or endeavor. A youthful vitality is infused in these new undertakings that is not reliant on experience. In fact, the birch is indicative of a need to release a hold on the past, clearing out old energies and taking up a path of spiritual Self-cleansing—or else the pathway of personal 'defragmentation'.

ESOTERIC CORRESPONDENCE.

Alternate Names : beithe, beth, belwen, beath

Alphabet Letter : "B"

Ogma's Tree : "birch in the forest"

Alternate Trees : beech (*phagos*), river-birch

Bardic Value : 1 (unity and purity); also the singularity or source, union of all forces/energies in rawest form

  Alternative (R.Graves) : 5

Forest Rank (British) : Chieftain

Forest Rank (Irish) : Peasant

Quadratic Element : Air

Druid Guardian : Boibel ('Babel')

Celtic Deities : Bel, Mabon; also Amergin (creativity), Blodeuwedd (learning lessons), Credne (creativity), Deae Matres (children), Evnissyen (responsibility), Finvarra (competition), Grannos (purification), O'Carolan (creativity)

Druidic Deities : Bran (the 'Raven', protection, power), Belinos (sun god of fire, healing, inspiration) Barinthus (the 'Ferryman', teaching, mystery)

Solar Month : November 1 ("New Year"); the day after *Samhain*, start of the first month

Lunar Month : December 24 – January 20/21; begins closest to Winter Solstice; Moon of Inception; Moon of Beginnings (uses 'Yule' as the 'New Year' or start of the first month); some esoteric discrepancy on whether a 'New' or 'Full' moon starts a 'lunar month'

Color Ogham : *ban*, white

Bird Ogham : *besan*, pheasant

Sacred Animal : cow (goddess, nurturing)

Sacred Gems : flourite, red-sard, imperial topaz

Ogham Forest Tract : wands, broomsticks, protection (wards) for children, healing, greatness, eagerness

Arts of Civilization : *bethumnacht*, livelihood

DIVINATION SYMBOLISM.

Description : one notch to the right of the stemline (or downward facing if a horizontal stemline)

Word Ogham (Morann mac Main) : "*Feocus foltchain*—faded trunk and fair hair"

Word Ogham (Mac Ind Oic) : "*Glaisiuni cnis*—most silvery of skin"

Tarot Equivalent : The Star—future accomplishments, high hopes and ideals, need for clarity and spiritual aid

Ogham Lochlannach : *jera*—fertility, harvest, peace; also 'year' or 'good year', alteration, transformation, turning, revolution of circumstance, fulfillment of plans; but also inversion, sudden setbacks, reversals; a major change; (also *berkana* rune or 'birch tree', beginnings, birth, &tc,)

Personality : happy
  Inversion : immature

Oracular Meaning : new beginnings (a new start at a higher level), renewal (revitalized energy), cleansing, purification, fertility, new birth (or rebirth), vitality, new dedication to the Pathway (the 'Great Work'), the 'Lady of the Woods'

2. luis — rowan tree

"Seek ever the way of the soul, whereby or by what order, having served the body to the same order to which it did flow that it may rise up again, joining action to sacred speech."

—Oracle of the Mystic Rowan
(Monroe Version)

The rowan tree indicates the first challenges faced after setting upon the Pathway—but the Seeker is well prepared to face (or confront) these directly, and is well-protected via new insights recognized. Some of the challenges come from 'within' when an individual is not properly 'grounded' in their realizations. But the foreknowledge is available to overcome or even avoid the possible pitfalls.

ESOTERIC CORRESPONDENCE.

Alternate Names : lois, ceridinen

Alphabet Letter : "L"

Ogma's Tree : "elm in the forests"

Alternate Trees : elm, mountain ash, red cedar, rosewood, the 'quickbeam' tree

Bardic Value : 2 (duality and polarity; as above, so below); also the 'Great Division', heaven and earth, land and sea, the seen and unseen, &tc.

Alternative (R.Graves) : 14

Forest Rank (British) : Chieftain

Forest Rank (Irish) : Peasant

Quadratic Element : Air

Druid Guardian : Loth

Celtic Deities : Epona, Macha, Math; also Airmud (healing), Baile (communication), Beli (divination), Beltene (spirit contact), Borvo (healing), Caradoc (divination), Coll (astral), Crom Cruaich (spirits), Dhonn (past-lives), Grainne (astral), Gwendydd (divination) Gwyn ap Nudd (spirits), Oghma (communication), Rosmerta (communication), Taliesin (understanding time)

Druidic Deities : Llew (god of all crafts and trades), Llyr (sea, rain, waters), Laighinos (teacher of battle skills)

Solar Month : December

Lunar Month : January 21/22 – February 18; Moon of Vision; Astral Travel Moon

Color Ogham : *liath*, gray, also red

Bird Ogham : *lachu*, duck

Sacred Animal : bear (the god, masculinity), unicorn (the goddess, femininity)

Sacred Gems : smokey quartz, diamond, yellow chrysolite, ruby

Ogham Forest Tract : personal empowerment, protection against enchantment, against control by others, astral or otherworld (spirit world) work (vision), patience, thoughtfulness, 'magical' work; planted outside the front door to ward off negativity

Arts of Civilization : *lumnacht*, pilotage

DIVINATION SYMBOLISM.

Description : two notches to the right of the stemline (or downward facing if a horizontal stemline)

Word Ogham (Morann mac Main) : "*Li sula*—delight of eye; the flame"

Word Ogham (Mac Ind Oic) : "*Cara ceathra*—friend of cattle; quickening-tree"

Tarot Equivalent : The High Priest—open-mindedness (or stubbornness, if reversed), recognition of truth, solidifying foundations

Ogham Lochlannach : *perth*—assertiveness, karma, initiation; also 'pear tree'; abundance, luxury, display, lavishness; also debauchery, decadence, excess, gluttony; physical pleasure

Personality : spiritual
Inversion : fanatical

Oracular Meaning : awareness and insight (inner understanding), self-control, empowerment, protection and nurturing (motherhood and fatherhood), evanescence, 'the tree of quickening'

3. *fearn* — alder tree

"Alder energy drives the warrior spirit, allowing one to stand fast in battle or conflict, or when confronted with an over-abundance of external pressures. Just as the head of Bran arrived in the midst of battle to reveal important prophecies, so must a wizard be open to the inner voice."

—Joshua Free
'The Enchanted Forest'

Having overcome challenges of starting up the path, a Seeker must maintain personal integrity in order to maintain their footholds upon it. This requires keeping aware of what's hidden beneath the surface all around us at all times. Rather than be 'on guard', we can simply increase our active awareness. In light of this, the Seeker may move ahead with utmost confidence and without the need to tread lightly and without succumbing to the basic upsets of material life.

ESOTERIC CORRESPONDENCE.

Alternate Names : fern

Alphabet Letter : "F"

Ogma's Tree : "alder in the forest"

Alternate Trees : maple

Bardic Value : 3 (triad, trinity, triangle); or 5 in some B-L-N systems (quintessence, Akasha)

  Alternative (R.Graves) : 8

Forest Rank (British) : Chieftain

Forest Rank (Irish) : Peasant

Quadratic Element : Fire

Druid Guardian : Forann

Celtic Deities : Bran ('The Blessed'), Macha; also Ambisagrus (weather), Arthur (self-sacrifice), Druantia (the eco-system), Figol (patience), Fionn (overcoming), Leucetios (weather), Nomenoe (service to others), Owen Lawgoch (self-sacrifice), Pryderi (duty), Saba (ecology), Scathach (teaching), Stine Bheag (weather)

Druidic Deities : Fionn (architecture, strategy), Ffagus (the 'Beech god', forgotten knowledge, lore), Formorix (invention, sea/air travel)

Solar Month : January

Lunar Month : March 19 – April 15; Moon of Utility, Moon of Efficacy, Moon of Self-Guidance; or February 18 – March 17 (on some tree calendars)

Color Ogham : *flann*, red, also crimson

Bird Ogham : *faelinn*, gull

Sacred Animal : fox (slyness, wit, cunning), ram (achievement through personal sacrifice), raven (protection)

Sacred Gems : beryl, serpentine, fire-garnet, obsidian

Ogham Forest Tract : charcoal, dye, housing foundations, protection/defense, foundation of wisdom/knowledge

Arts of Civilization : *filideacht*, bardic poetry

DIVINATION SYMBOLISM.

Description : three notches to the right of the stemline (or downward facing if a horizontal stemline)

Word Ogham (Morann mac Main) : "Airinach Fian—shield of the warriors"

Word Ogham (Mac Ind Oic) : "Comet lachta—guarding of milk, for of alder are made the vessels containing milk"

Tarot Equivalent : Strength—disillusionment, need for organization, use of personal strength

Ogham Lochlannach : uruz—strength, manifestation, sacrifice; also 'aurochs'; masculinity, freedom, energy, action, courage; also lust, rashness, violence; sexual desire

Personality : ambitious
Inversion : impulsive

Oracular Meaning : foundation, protection, guidance, resistance to water (or enchantment), shielding (overcoming difficulties, confronting), 'the tree of resistance' (inner strength)

4. saille — willow tree

*"The noble willow, burn not, a tree sacred to poems;
within his bloom bees are a-sucking, and all love the little cage."*

—Iubhdan

The feminine grace of the willow tree has captivated artists and poets since ancient times. It speaks to us of the subtler aspects of life: the nighttime dreamscapes and otherworldly faerie realms. It speaks to us of intuition, and of the tendency inherent in the human condition to ignore the 'inner voice' that is actually our own, but which is often washed out by the hidden influences, imprinting and emotional encoding of living in a fragmented world. By learning to hear and listen to ourselves, free of what we have taken on and carried with us as a burden of experience, the self-confidence and determination necessary to move forward can be assured.

ESOTERIC CORRESPONDENCE.

Alternate Names : sail, awn, helyg, helygen, suil

Alphabet Letter : "S"

Ogma's Tree : "willow in the forest"

Alternate Trees : n/a

Bardic Value : 4 (the cosmic cube, solid); foundation of solid manifestation, the four directions

  Alternative (R.Graves) : 16

Forest Rank (British) : Chieftain

Forest Rank (Irish) : Peasant

Quadratic Element : Water

Druid Guardian : Saliath

Celtic Deities : Silver Huntress, Arianrhod, Diana ("of the Forest"), Epona; also Boann (fertility), Cerridwen (shapeshifting), Dana (elves/faerie), Fand (elves/faerie), Maeve (femininity), Nantosuelta (fertility), Nessa (femininity), Rhiannon (fertility), Sheila-na-gig (femininity), Taillte (fertility)

Druidic Deities : Samhann (god of death, guardian of the Otherworld gate), Sucellus (fighting, assassination), Silvanus (herb-lore, plants, healing)

Solar Month : February

Lunar Month : April 16 – May 12; the Witch's Moon, Moon of Balance; March 18 – April 14 (on some tree calenders)

Color Ogham : *sodath*, fine-coloured; also fiery-coloured

Bird Ogham : *seg*, hawk (loftiness, nobility)

Sacred Animal : hare (intuition), cat (detach- ment) and owl (wisdom)

Sacred Gems : opal, pearl, sugulite, uvulite, peridot

Ogham Forest Tract : lunar magick, dream work, femininity, fertility, healing, baskets/wicker-work, Otherworld contact, an aid to divination

Arts of Civilization : *sairsi*, handicraft

DIVINATION SYMBOLISM.

Description : four notches to the right of the stemline (or downward facing if a horizontal stemline)

Word Ogham (Morann mac Main) : "*Li n-aimbi*—hue of the lifeless; of one dead"

Word Ogham (Mac Ind Oic) : "*Luth bech*—the activity of bees"

Tarot Equivalent : The Moon—dreams, hidden influences (hidden forces), intuition needed, self-reliance required, forthcoming subtle changes

Ogham Lochlannach : *laguz*—lake life, flow, fertility; also 'water'; river, ocean, dreams, fantasies, mysteries, the underworld; also madness, despair, obsession, suicide; the unconscious

Personality : wise
Inversion : bitter

Oracular Meaning : beauty, enchantment, rhythm, cycles, harmony, inspiration, an indication that emotional healing is necessary (confidence), intuition, flexibility

5. *nuin* — ash tree

"You ash, cruel tree... turn not aside
A foot's-breadth ye, straight at the heart fly free.
Nuin Neiagadin—spear shaft be!"

—Song of the Forest Trees
(Monroe Version)

Ash represents the "combination" of factors involved—the systems that make up the System. In many ancient European traditions, the ash tree is the 'World Tree' or 'cosmic axis' that connects all 'worlds' or 'universes'. It is the link between the 'inner' and 'outer'—and demonstrates that they are one and the same; that what is going on 'out there' is not independent of what is going on 'in here'. The ash bridges the aspects of 'beingness' and 'doingness'.

ESOTERIC CORRESPONDENCE.

Alternate Names : nin, nwyn, nion

Alphabet Letter : "N"

Ogma's Tree : "maw of a spear, or nettles in the woods"

Alternate Trees : redbud, ponderosa pine

Bardic Value : 5 (control of the soul), or 3 (in some B-L-N systems)
   Alternative (R.Graves) : 13

Forest Rank (British) : Chieftain

Forest Rank (Irish) : Chieftain

Quadratic Element : Air

Druid Guardian : Nebgadon/Nebuchadnezzar

Celtic Deities : Lugh, Ogma, Woden/Odin, Gwydion; also Biddy Mamionn (healing), Habetrot (healing)

Druidic Deities : Nudd (the 'cloud-maker', weather, storms, seasons), Nuada (wealth, water, power, dominion), Nwyvre (stars and planets)

Solar Month : March

Lunar Month : February 19 – March 18; Moon of Waters; April 15 – May 12 (on some tree calenders)

Color Ogham : *necht*, clear; also clear-green

Bird Ogham : *nescu*, snipe

Sacred Animal : adder or serpent (healing, transformation, life-force)

Sacred Gems : sapphire, sea-green beryl, peridot, smithsonite

Ogham Forest Tract : maypoles, spears (also pool cues, paddles/oars) wands, sea/water magick, empowerment, healing, increase of personal ability

Arts of Civilization : *notaireacht*, notary

DIVINATION SYMBOLISM.

Description : five notches to the right of the stemline (or downward facing if a horizontal stemline)

Word Ogham (Morann mac Main) : "*Cosdad sida*—checking of peace; the maw of the weaver's beam"

Word Ogham (Mac Ind Oic) : "*Bag ban*—fight of women, to wit, a weaver's beam"

Tarot Equivalent : The World (Universe)—end of a cycle, freedom, perfection, satisfaction, success, triumph

Ogham Lochlannach : *algiz*—life, protection, meta-human; also 'aesir' or 'one of the gods'; goodness, health, truth, harmony, wisdom, insight; vanity

Personality : charming
Inversion : egocentric

Oracular Meaning : triumph, protection, overcoming mental strife and boredom, change of outlook (viewpoint), 'World Tree' (connection between 'inner' and 'outer' worlds), awakening, 'the tree of personal strength', harmony (peace), rebirth

6. huathe — hawthorn tree

*"The power of 'H' is that it increases the power of other letters in a grammatical context. This applies equally on a spiritual level.
Once the magical or spiritual work is finished, you must expect a period of disruption, which should not be too severe or upsetting."*

—Steve Blamires
'Celtic Tree Mysteries'

Hawthorn begins the second *aicme* of five *fews* and represents the first challenges faced after this breakthrough on the pathway. Navigating safely through thorns requires patience, but is not impossible. Often these barriers are only erected to thwart those who have come this far on the journey from going further. But the passageway is much narrower than before—and as such, it requires that Seeker 'lighten their load' in order to proceed. The way ahead is only restricting when we have not adequately cleared away the debris.

ESOTERIC CORRESPONDENCE.

Alternate Names : huath, huatha

Alphabet Letter : "H"

Ogma's Tree : "test tree, or whitethorn"

Alternate Trees : whitethorn, sycamore, laurel, cottonwood

Bardic Value : 6 (time)

Forest Rank (British) : Peasant

Forest Rank (Irish) : Peasant

Quadratic Element : Fire

Druid Guardian : Huiria

Celtic Deities : Olwen, Hurle, Rhiannon; also Aine (summertime), Arianrhod (bindings), Lugh (fire)

Druidic Deities : Hagfgan (gems and stones), Hesus (prophecy, springs, caves), Heremonix (wells and underground rivers)

Solar Month : April

Lunar Month : May 13 – June 9/10; Moon of Restraint, Moon of Hindrance, the Summer Moon

Color Ogham : *huath*, terrible; also purple

Bird Ogham : hadaig/aadaig, night raven

Sacred Animal : goat (material life), dragon (power, vitality, energy)

Sacred Gems : amethyst, tanzanite, lapis lazuli, carnelian

Ogham Forest Tract : hawthorn wood is not usually taken; wands and wards are cut between April 21 and May 1 for love and magick marriage rites; grown as a living being for general 'magical' protection and success

Arts of Civilization : h-airchetul, trisyllabic poetry (triads ?)

DIVINATION SYMBOLISM.

Description : one notch to the left of the stemline (or upward facing if a horizontal stemline)

Word Ogham (Morann mac Main) : "Conal cuan—a pack of wolves"

Word Ogham (Mac Ind Oic) : "Banadh gnuisi—blanching of face in fear or terror"

Tarot Equivalent : Judgment—nearing completion, forthcoming renewal, looking ahead, guidance needed

Ogham Lochlannach : hagalz—hail, disruption, framework; also 'precipitation'; pain, loss, suffering, hardship, sickness, natural disaster; also testing, temptation; the 'Wrath of Nature'

Personality : passionate
Inversion : ruthless

Oracular Meaning : purity, restraint (being held back for a time), chastity (similar to the white-'heather' Ogham); also love and marriage proper (marital pleasure), prosperity, challenges (harshness, misfortune), healing of the heart (love)

7. duir — oak tree

*"When the beech prospers through spells and litanies, the oak-tops entangle,
there is hope for the trees.
With foot-beat of the swift oak, the heavens and earth rung;
stout 'guardian of the door', his name in every tongue."*

—Robert Graves
'Battle of the Trees'

Having passed through the thorn barrier, oak trees represent the enduring strength that is achieved. Oak signifies the layers of knowingness or realization—of which "Druids" named themselves after. Even thin layers combined will generate solidity. Universally, oak trees stand as the 'doorways' or 'gateways' of time and space—and thus a continuum to the past and future that is accessible to a Seeker. In these cases, the oak represents the "doors of perception."

ESOTERIC CORRESPONDENCE.

Alternate Names : dur, dwyr, derwen, dar, doir

Alphabet Letter : "D"

Ogma's Tree : "oak in the forest"

Alternate Trees : hickory, western cedar, sequoia; also related to 'holly' ogham

Bardic Value : 7 (lunar or faerie, dreams or enchantments); also, perfected knowledge of the local universe (seven days, seven ancient planets)

Alternative (R.Graves) : 12

Forest Rank (British) : Peasant

Forest Rank (Irish) : Chieftain

Quadratic Element : Fire

Druid Guardian : Daivaith (Dagda)

Celtic Deities : Belinos; also Abelard (loyalty), Awawen (friendship/loyalty), Artio (fertility), Cernunnos (the forest), Connla (wisdom, loyalty), Dagda (masculinity), Laeg (loyalty), Llewellyn (elves/faerie), Merlin (magic), Rohand (duty/loyalty)

Druidic Deities : Dagda (the 'Good God', 'All-Father', god of Druidism), Dian Cecht (healing), Dis Pater ('oldest grandfather of the races')

Solar Month : May

Lunar Month : June 10/11 – July 7; Moon of Strength, Moon of Security

Color Ogham : *dub*, black; also dark-brown

Bird Ogham : *droeii*, wren (the "druid's bird")

Sacred Animal : white mare (the earth/land), lion/tiger (sovereignty), salamander, adder-serpent

Sacred Gems : yellow topaz, amber, gold, white carnelian, moonstone

Ogham Forest Tract : doors (protection for homes), fertility; '*galls*' used for the '*naddred*' talisman (Adder's Egg or Druid's Gem), Druidic spirituality

Arts of Civilization : *druidheacht*, wizardry

DIVINATION SYMBOLISM.

Description : two notches to the left of the stemline (or upward facing if a horizontal stemline)

Word Ogham (Morann mac Main) : "*Ardavi dossaibh*—highest of bushes"

Word Ogham (Mac Ind Oic) : "*Gres sair*—carpenter's work"

Tarot Equivalent : Emperor—exterior authority, inner balance, responsibility, use of experience

Ogham Lochlannach : *thurisa*—gateway, door, defense; also 'Thor' or 'thunder'; also evil, malice, hatred, torment, lies; but also catharsis, cleansing, purging; a malevolent individual

Personality : fatherly
Inversion : dominating

Oracular Meaning : protection, strength, a 'doorway' (to personal growth), sovereignty, guidance, endurance, higher powers at work, security, truth, the 'King of the Woods'

8. tinne — holly tree

*"The holly, dark and green, made a resolute stand;
armed with many spear-points wounding the hand."*

—Robert Graves
'The Battle of the Trees'

Once a Seeker has broken through initial barriers and solidified their position, it is a time for *action*. But it also requires that one is clear about their endeavors before pursuing them. In some ways, holly represents the balance of forces through *action*—the inertia and resonance that ensues—and manifests visibly as movement through 'actions' and corresponding 'reactive' courses of motion. Like the oak, holly represents endurance, but of activity—and as an evergreen, signifies actively holding up against harshness and tests of strength.

ESOTERIC CORRESPONDENCE.

Alternate Names : celynen

Alphabet Letter : "T"

Ogma's Tree : "holly, or elderberry in the forest"

Alternate Trees : black walnut, holly-oak

Bardic Value : 8 (purification, the annual cycle or 'wheel-of-the-year'); also the 'magnificence of the sun'

  Alternative (R.Graves) : 11

Forest Rank (British) : Peasant

Forest Rank (Irish) : Chieftain

Quadratic Element : Fire

Druid Guardian : Teilmon

Celtic Deities : The Holly King (Holly-Man), Cu Chulain (strength); also Cernunnos (fertility); Dahud (sexuality), Fergus (sexuality), Flidais (animals), Guildeluec (choices), Macha (wisdom)

Druidic Deities : Taranis (the 'Thunderer'), Tigernonos (hills, mountains and valleys), Toutorix (war, power)

Solar Month : June

Lunar Month : July 8 – August 4; Moon of Encirclement, Moon of Polarity

Bird Ogham : *truith*, starling

Color Ogham : *tenien*, dark gray

Sacred Animal : warhorse (protection), warhound (loyalty)

Sacred Gems : ruby, rose quartz, blue topaz

Ogham Forest Tract : spear-making (combat and protection), chariot wheels, charcoal; grown to bring good fortune and ward off evil

Arts of Civilization : *tornoracht*, turning (?)

DIVINATION SYMBOLISM.

Description : three notches to the left of the stemline (or upward facing if a horizontal stemline)

Word Ogham (Morann mac Main) : "*Trian*—'another thing', the meaning of that today"

Word Ogham (Mac Ind Oic) : "*Smir guaili*—fires of coal"

Tarot Equivalent : The Chariot—application of energy, movement, travel, self-discipline, triumph, success

Ogham Lochlannach : *ehwaz*—movement, soul travel; also 'horse'; transportation, speed, a vehicle; also haste, blind rushing in; rapid progress

Personality : determined
Inversion : insensitive

Oracular Meaning : movement, vigorous action, vitality, energy, holiness (sacredness), 'lifeforce', natural cycles, a path between extremes (balance), the 'survivor tree'

9. *coll* — **hazel tree**

*"Why is the crane in the next place?
Not hard. This is the month of wisdom, and the wisdom of Mannan Mac Lir,
namely the Beth-Luis-Nion [Ogham], was wrapped in Crane-skin.
And brown are the nuts of the Hazel, the tree of wisdom."*

—Robert Graves
'The White Goddess'

The hazel tree symbolizes not only an acquisition of arcane knowledge and ancient wisdom but also its comprehension and communication. Synthesis and communicability of data is necessary for its effective use for any application—otherwise it simply remains in a pool of potential. The hazel tree and its nut represent pursuit of that potential and practical integration for a continuing existence. Hazel may also signify that divine guidance is at hand or attainable.

ESOTERIC CORRESPONDENCE.

Alternate Names : koll, calltuinn

Alphabet Letter : "C" and "K"

Ogma's Tree : "hazel"

Alternate Trees : nut-hazel, beech, pecan, white-oak

Bardic Value : 9 (the completion of wisdom and knowledge)

Forest Rank (British) : Peasant

Forest Rank (Irish) : Chieftain

Quadratic Element : Water

Druid Guardian : Kay (Cai)

Celtic Deities : Llyr, Branwen; also Bebhionn (spirits), Ban Naomha (wisdom), Cailleach (wisdom), Pwyll (justice)

Druidic Deities : Cernunnos (the 'Horned-One', animals, deep forests), Cromm Cruaich (darkness, death), Camulos (Mars, war, blood, conquest)

Solar Month : July

Lunar Month : August 5 – September 1; the Moon of the Wise, the Crone Moon

Color Ogham : *cron*, brown

Bird Ogham : *corr*, crane (hidden knowledge, patience, longevity)

Sacred Animal : *bradan*, salmon (wisdom, inspiration)

Sacred Gems : lapis lazuli, sapphire, opal, banded red agate, magnetite

Ogham Forest Tract : wands, baskets, thatch-work, divination sticks; nuts used for love spells and potions to aid inducing 'spirit vision', inspiration

Arts of Civilization : *cruitireacht*, harping

DIVINATION SYMBOLISM.

Description : four notches to the left of the stemline (or upward facing if a horizontal stemline)

Word Ogham (Morann mac Main) : "*Cainiu fedaib*—fairest of trees, owing to its beauty in the woods"

Word Ogham (Mac Ind Oic) : "*Cara bloisc*—friend of cracking"

Tarot Equivalent : The High Priestess—inspiration, intuition, spiritual connectedness, uncovering hidden influences

Ogham Lochlannach : *othila*—property and prosperity; also 'heritage' (estate); house, land of birth (mother land); what one is 'bound' to

Personality : generous
Inversion : deceptive

Oracular Meaning : divination (oracles), creativity (inspiration), intuition, spirit vision or inner vision, true sight (skrying), wisdom, knowledge, productivity (nut-bearing), insight (perceptions), the "poet's tree"

10. quert — apple tree

*"Sweet apple tree growing by the river, who will thrive on its wondrous fruit?
When my reason was intact,
I used to lie at its foot with a fair wanton maiden of slender form."*

—Myrddin the Bard
'Black Book of Carmarthen'

On the pursuit toward wholeness, apples signify the 'fruits-gained'. Fulfillment of wholeness at the level of material existence is often identified with companionate love as a means of correcting the symmetry of our own personal fragmentation. So while we are able to reach states of happiness and recognize the beauty in the world, we are also susceptible to misappropriating the sensory sensual fulfillment of this world as a substitute for the inner calling to reconnect our awareness and consciousness with the spiritual-Self that is eternal and superior to all human experience.

ESOTERIC CORRESPONDENCE.

Alternate Names : queris

Alphabet Letter : "Q"

Ogma's Tree : "quickening tree, or aspen"

Alternate Trees : crab-apple, orange

Bardic Value : 10 (the 'Divine Completion'); *red.* 1; or often unnumbered (as in the tree calendar count, &tc.)

Forest Rank (British) : Peasant

Forest Rank (Irish) : Chieftain

Quadratic Element : Water

Druid Guardian : Qualep

Celtic Deities : Kerridwen (or Cerridwen), Mannan mac Lyr

Druidic Deities : Affalon

Solar Month : n/a

Lunar Month : sometimes August 5 – September 1; sometimes not included in the calendar; also September 2 – September 29 (on some tree calenders)

Color Ogham : *quiar*, mouse-coloured; also green

Bird Ogham : *querc*, hen (femininity)

Sacred Animal : unicorn (beauty, purity, enchantment)

Sacred Gems : rose quartz, amethyst

Ogham Forest Tract : food (fruit), drink (cider), the 'apple-wand' or 'silver-branch', healing, link to the Otherworld

Arts of Civilization : *quislenacht*, fluting

DIVINATION SYMBOLISM.

Description : five notches to the left of the stemline (or upward facing if a horizontal stemline)

Word Ogham (Morann mac Main) : "*Clithar mbaiscaill*—shelter of a hind, i.e., 'a fold'; to wit, *boscell*, lunatic; that is *bas-ceall*, death sense, the sense that comes when one goes to their death"

Word Ogham (Mac Ind Oic) : "*Brigh an duine*—force of a man"

Tarot Equivalent : The Empress—fertility, growth, joy, prosperity, satisfaction

Ogham Lochlannach : *berkana*—birth, life, growth; also 'birch tree'; fertility, healing; also desire, passion, carelessness; a love affair or new birth

Personality : motherly
Inversion : weak-willed

Oracular Meaning : love, beauty, unity of mind and spirit between lovers, eternal life (perpetual youth), abundance, fertility, healing, personal wholeness (development or completion of spiritual work), sometimes indicates 'choices'

11. *muin* — vine

"Muin represents hidden, just below-the-surface realizations, sometimes only brought to the surface when disinhibited—that which cannot be healthily suppressed if we are to break through to the next steps of our progression. With an ability to even scale walls, the Vine truly knows no boundaries."

—Joshua Free
'The Enchanted Forest'

The vine leads off the third *aicme* with a moment of inwardness and introspection. This does not mean introversion or inactivity, and quite the contrary, the vine represents realizing and removing personal inhibitions that cause one to withhold energies and thereby withdraw outward participation in creation of reality. Naturally, the vine also warns against the dangers of drunken excess and extremes in this same regard.

ESOTERIC CORRESPONDENCE.

Alternate Names : min, gwynwydden

Alphabet Letter : M

Ogma's Tree : "vine, or mead"

Alternate Trees : mulberry, grape, blackberry (also the elm, a tree used in Britain to support the vines)

Bardic Value : 10 (prophecy) or 11 if previous 'apple' is numbered, &tc.; red. 1 or 2 (though some numerological schools don't reduce elevens, if this is counted 11)

  Alternative (R.Graves) : 6

Forest Rank (British) : Shrub

Forest Rank (Irish) : Shrub (?)

Quadratic Element : Water

Druid Guardian : Muriath

Celtic Deities : Brigantia; also Brid (protection), Caer (dreams), Epona (dreams)

Druidic Deities : Mabon (the 'divine youth', music, poetry, beauty), Math (magic, shapeshifting), Myrddin (magic)

Solar Month : August

Lunar Month : September 2 – September 29; Moon of Celebration; September 30 – October 27 (on some tree calenders)

Color Ogham : *mbracht*, variegated

Bird Ogham : *mintan*, titmouse (survival)

Sacred Animal : scorpion, lizard, serpent

Sacred Gems : aquamarine, amethyst, yellow serpentine, jasper

Ogham Forest Tract : grape-wine, intoxication, meditation, revealing truths, harvest (manifestation)

Arts of Civilization : *milaideacht*, soldiering

DIVINATION SYMBOLISM.

Description : one long notch diagonally intersecting across the stemline

Word Ogham (Morann mac Main) : "*Tresim fedma*—strongest of effort, i.e., the back of a man or ox"

Word Ogham (Mac Ind Oic) : "*Arusc n-airlig*—condition of slaughter, to wit, a man's back"

Tarot Equivalent : The Lovers—changes, determination, possible indication of relationship (romantic love)

Ogham Lochlannach : *gebo*—partnership, sexuality, lovers; also 'gift'; award, inheritance; but also sacrifice

Personality : sympathetic
Inversion : dependent

Oracular Meaning : inner-development, self-realization (introspection, inwardness), hidden knowledge (prophecy), comprehension, manifestation (harvest)

12. gort — ivy

"Around the ivy path, the Autumn turns the trees aflame with color.
Taliesin, wise man fleeing from the wrath of Cauldron Mother."

—The Roebuck in the Thicket
(Robert Graves)

Ivy represents inner growth and development such as is depicted in its spiral-like pattern. It also signifies abilities to overcome obstacles, even scaling walls. Its ability to scale walls is dependent on there being a wall present to assist. This reminds us not to be afraid to lean on good solid support when it can be found. It must be quality support, however, because as one progresses along the pathway of Ascension there are those that will be envious or jealous, and this is sometimes demonstrated in 'false help'—even when it occurs subconsciously and not blatant malicious attacks.

ESOTERIC CORRESPONDENCE.

Alternate Names : uruin, eiddew

Alphabet Letter : "G"

Ogma's Tree : "cornfield, or fir in the forest"

Alternate Trees : elm, blackberry (although also associated with 'vine' Ogham)

Bardic Value : 11 (maternity) or 12 (if using the alternative count); *red.* 2 or 3; though some numerologic schools don't reduce elevens)

  Alternative (R.Graves) : 10

Forest Rank (British) : Shrub

Forest Rank (Irish) : Shrub

Quadratic Element : Earth

Druid Guardian : Gahth

Celtic Deities : Swan Maidens, Cuchulain, Cernunnos/Kernunnos, Orion, Ogmios; also Brian Boru (leadership), Bres (compassion), Melusine (compassion), Niamh (leadership), Veleda (leadership)

Druidic Deities : Govannon ('divine smith', metalcraft), Gwyn ap Nudd (god of 'the Wild Hunt'), Grannos (corn, harvest)

Solar Month : September

Lunar Month : September 30 – October 27; Moon of Buoyancy, Moon of Resilience; October 28 – November 24 (on some tree calenders)

Color Ogham : *gorm*, blue; also sky-blue

Bird Ogham : *ge'is*, swan or "mute swan" (love, partnership, community)

Sacred Animal : boar (leadership, focus, the 'warrior')

Sacred Gems : chryso(beryl), green jasper, clear green jasper

Ogham Forest Tract : exorcisms/banishings, encouragement (support), determination

Arts of Civilization : *gaibneacht*, smithwork

DIVINATION SYMBOLISM.

Description : two long notches diagonally intersecting across the stemline

Word Ogham (Morann mac Main) : "*Milisiu feraib*—sweeter than grass; the cornfield"

Word Ogham (Mac Ind Oic) : "*Med nercc*—ivy"

Tarot Equivalent : Justice—the consideration of all factors (equality and fairness), possible outside factors

Ogham Lochlannach : *teiwaz*—gods judgment, warrior justice; also 'Tiwaz' (deity); victory, battle, winning disputes

Personality : ambitious
Inversion : lazy

Oracular Meaning : cooperation, community (support), healing, 'inner-spiral' (journey), restrictions (warnings), development (new skills, &tc.), taking time to consider all aspects

13. ngetal — **reed**

"You reed, swift to pursue... Skillful and slender, straight never-bending. Ngetal Ngoimar—fly ever-true!"
—Song of the Forest Trees
(Monroe Version)

Ancient Mesopotamians employed the reed to fashion their stylus-pens and manage literary communication. This is relevant to the Ogham because the "ng" *few* seems to have only been adopted to preserve writing in languages other than Celtic. Whether reed or broom, this Ogham represents a communication of knowledge—which also means application of knowledge or 'doingness'. Personal confidence in one's own Self-determination is dependent on maintaining elevated states of knowingness. It is only when in doubt—or enshrouded in mystery—that a person hesitates, falters, or otherwise lingers in a realm of maybe.

ESOTERIC CORRESPONDENCE.

Alternate Names : getal, corsen, erun

Alphabet Letter : "Ng"

Ogma's Tree : "broom"

Alternates : cattail, horsetail, broom, fern

Bardic Value : 12 (divine or royal purposes), or 13 if using alternative count; *red.* 3 or 4 (depending on which count and if reduced)

Forest Rank (British) : Shrub

Forest Rank (Irish) : Shrub (?)

Quadratic Element : Air

Druid Guardian : Noimahr

Celtic Deities : Olbaal, Gwydion, Morgana, Morrighan; also Bran (divination), Coventina (divination), Don (family)

Druidic Deities : Arianrhod

Solar Month : October

Lunar Month : October 28 – October 30 (the three days before *Samhain*); the Moon of the Home, Hearth Moon, Winter Moon, the Moon which Manifests Truth; also November 25 – December 23 (on some tree calenders)

Color Ogham : *nglas*, grass-green

Bird Ogham : *ngeigh*, goose (parental-style vigilance, reproduction)

Sacred Animal : stag (independence, pride),   dog, rat, owl

Sacred Gems : aquamarine

Ogham Forest Tract : writing pens, brooms, pipes, fertility/love magick

Arts of Civilization : *ngibae*, modeling

DIVINATION SYMBOLISM.

Description : three long notches diagonally intersecting across the stemline

Word Ogham (Morann mac Main) : "*Luth legha*—a physician's strength"

Word Ogham (Mac Ind Oic) : "*Eitiud midach*—a physician's robe"

Tarot Equivalent : Wheel of Fortune—the ups and downs of life, chance, cycles, opportunity, randomness (the randomness of life / the 'life game')

Ogham Lochlannach : *raido*—right action and movement; also 'ride' or 'journey'; travel, relocation, evolution, transportation; but also disruption, dislocation

Personality : adaptable
Inversion : indecisive

Oracular Meaning : effort (direct action), application (of effort or intention), further work needed for completion, clearing away the old to make way for what is necessary to finish, harmony

14. *straif* — **blackthorn tree**

"The surly blackthorn is a wanderer, and a wood that the artificer burns not; throughout his body, though it be scanty, birds in their flocks warble."

—Iubhdan

Blackthorn is often slighted out as a negative Ogham due to its association with *control*. And most individuals have had poor experiences with 'enforced control' and unwanted outside influence. The blackthorn represents another significant energetic barrier on the Pathway, whereby a Seeker must shed the conditioned and imprinted influences and enforced command from outside sources. Often times these commands are imprinted into circuits that an individual keeps on following long after the fact. While there is some benefit to social education (and observational learning) when one is seeking to fit into a society, the manner in which we become entrapped to a human condition and victims to this world is taking things a step too far.

ESOTERIC CORRESPONDENCE.

Alternate Names : straife, strife

Alphabet Letter : "ST"/"Z" and "STR"

Ogma's Tree : "willow-brake in the forest"

Alternate Trees : plum ('*emrys*')

Bardic Value : 14 when using alternate count; *red.* 5; or often unnumbered

Forest Rank (British) : Shrub

Forest Rank (Irish) : Shrub

Quadratic Element : Earth

Druid Guardian : Stru

Celtic Deities : Taliesin

Druidic Deities : Scathach, Skadi

Solar Month : n/a

Lunar Month : October 31 (*Samhain festival*); more often not included on the calendar

Color Ogham : *sorcha*, bright; also 'bright purple'

Bird Ogham : *stniolach*, thrush

Sacred Animal : wolf (the mysterious), toad (hidden power), black cat (sensitivity, intuition)

Sacred Gems : obsidian

Ogham Forest Tract : the 'Thunder and Lightning' Staff, the 'Dark Staff' a.k.a. *Shillelagh*, cudgel weapons, warding against evil and illness, channeling 'magical' power

Arts of Civilization : *streghuindeacht*, deer-stalking

DIVINATION SYMBOLISM.

Description : four long notches diagonally intersecting across the stemline

Word Ogham (Morann mac Main) : "*Tresiiu ruamna*—strongest of red, sloe red for dyeing things"

Word Ogham (Mac Ind Oic) : "*Morad run*—increasing of secrets, to wit, sloe"

Tarot Equivalent : Temperance—balance, seek harmony and security, a possible indication to slow down and 'temper' emotions

Ogham Lochlannach : *daguz*—prosperity, breakthrough; also 'daylight'; a day or cycle, period, span of time; also full circuit (full circle); completion

Personality : honest
 Inversion : deceptive

Oracular Meaning : cleansing, control, operating by force, confusion, restraint (constraint), resentment, coercion, threats, aggression, sudden change, renewal, strife, protection, stillness, severity, fate

15. *ruis* — elder tree

"Stoop not down afar, for a precipice lies below the earth: fearful depths drawing down through the ladder which has seven steps.
Beneath which stands the throne of necessity."

—The Oracle of the Elder Tree
(Monroe Version)

The elder tree stands at the end of the third *aicme* representing the completion of a cycle, transitions and/or initiation into a final phase of work. Before reaching forward to the next level, a Seeker must release themselves from the 'ties that bind' in order for their chance at the ultimate 'redemption'. This involves the forgiveness of others in addition to one's self. Some method of personal 'reconciliation' or pastoral confession may be found in virtually all spiritual traditions—and for good reason. Only when an individual is able and prepared to face (or confront) their past head on will they be truly free from its hold.

ESOTERIC CORRESPONDENCE.

Alternate Names : ysgawen

Alphabet Letter : "R"

Ogma's Tree : "elder"

Alternate Trees : bourtree, hickory, myrtle, persimmon

Bardic Value : 13 (rebirth and transmigration), or 15 in the alternate count; *red.* 4 or 6

Forest Rank (British) : Shrub

Forest Rank (Irish) : Shrub

Quadratic Element : Earth

Druid Guardian : Ruben

Celtic Deities : Boann, Niknevin; also Balor (protection), Diancecht (healing), Gwyddion (wisdom), Meg (healing)

Druidic Deities : Ronanorix (death, old age), Rhonabwy (dreams, prophecy), Ruadanos (travel, crossroads)

Solar Month : "the '13th' month" ('*Samhain*')

Lunar Month : November; Moon of Completeness; not included on some tree calenders

Color Ogham : *ruadh*, red ("blood red")

Bird Ogham : *rocnat*, small rook

Sacred Animal : badger (prudence, planning), black sow (abundance, nourishment)

Sacred Gems : bloodstone, red jasper, dark green malachite

Ogham Forest Tract : exorcism, banishing, regeneration magick, elderberry wine, faerie-sight oinment, healing, sacrifice, inspiration

Arts of Civilization : *ronaireacht*, dispensing

DIVINATION SYMBOLISM.

Description : five long notches diagonally intersecting across the stemline

Word Ogham (Morann mac Main) : "*Timieui rucce*—intensest of blushes, that is elderberry, to wit, the reddening or shame that grows in a man's face"

Word Ogham (Mac Ind Oic) : "*Ruanma dreach*—redness of face, to wit, blushing"

Tarot Equivalent : The Hanged Man—the need for foresight, changing direction (or indecision), transition (mid-life crisis), self-sacrifice

Ogham Lochlannach : *isa*—concentration and standstill; also 'ice'; treachery, illusion, deceit, betrayal, ambush, plots; also allure, seduction, entrapment; a cunning beautiful woman

Personality : intelligent
Inversion : unfortunate

Oracular Meaning : self-reflection (self-examination), change, end of a cycle (completion, evolution), crossroads (toward a next level)

16. *ailim* — **silver-fir tree**

"You fir, uncouth and savage... Untamed wood, you smash and ravage.
Ailim Achab—Be deadly in your mirth."

—Battle of the Forest Trees
(Monroe Version)

Having overcome our emotional encoding and feelings of guilt and betrayal, a new leg of the journey opens up to us as the fourth *aicme*. It is epitomized by the 'objectivity' maintained when one is freed up of artificial personality programming and filters that hinder the crystal clarity that is possible when viewing from Self and without fragmentation. Clearheadedness is imbued in the aura of firs and pines, which is probably why so many are instinctively drawn to these forests when the need to "center" or be "grounded" arises.

ESOTERIC CORRESPONDENCE.

Alternate Names : ailm, elma, ffynidwydden, pinwydden

Alphabet Letter : "A"

Ogma's Tree : "Scots-pine"

Alternate Trees : pine, elm, redwood, fir

Bardic Value : 16 ; *red.* 7; or often unnumbered

Forest Rank (British) : Bramble

Forest Rank (Irish) : Chieftain

Quadratic Element : Earth

Druid Guardian : Achab

Celtic Deities : Horned-Man (the Green-Man), Merlyn (Myrddin), Abban, Sezh, Arianrhod, Am-Mesh (Gaea), Cernunnos/Kernunnos

Druidic Deities : Amaethon (agriculture), Arawn ('otherworld king', hunting, hounds, the hunt/pursuit), Albiorix (poetry, orchards, streams)

Solar Month : n/a

Lunar Month : Winter Solstice (Yule festival)

Color Ogham : *alad*, piebald, speckled; also pale blue

Bird Ogham : *aidhircleog*, lapwing

Sacred Animal : cow or "red cow", stag or deer (independence, self-reliance)

Sacred Gems : agate (moss agate), clear quartz, tourmaline

Ogham Forest Tract : forest magick of all kinds, earth memory, teaching, sacred fires, the elves (elvenkind, otherkin faerie)

Arts of Civilization : *airigeacht*, sovereignty

DIVINATION SYMBOLISM.

Description : one long notch perpendicular across the stemline

Word Ogham (Morann mac Main) : "*Ardam iachtadh*—loudest of groanings, that is, groaning of disease, or wondering, that is, marveling at whatever circumstance"

Word Ogham (Mac Ind Oic) : "*Tosach fregra*—beginning of an answer; the first expression of every human being after their birth"

Tarot Equivalent : The Devil (Horned-One)—arrogance, bondage, egotism, pride, materialism, need for self-control

Ogham Lochlannach : *nauthiz*—constraint, persistence, deliverance; also need; necessity, want, poverty, emotional hunger; also resistance, survival; defiance of circumstances

Personality : outgoing
Inversion : introverted

Oracular Meaning : ancient knowledge, primal power, high views (objectivity, far sight, perspective, broad range of experience, new realizations), penetration, strength, 'the tree of leadership' (reign, vigor)

17. ohn — furze

"The nature of divine growth is neither stern nor savage, but alluring and calm. It causes not fear in those subjected to it, but attracts all things by persuasion and sympathy."
—Oracle of the Sweet Furze
(Monroe Version)

The furze or gorse Ogham represents the synthesis of information into *wisdom*. This means the illumination or true enlightenment that is sought or promised in all spiritual paths, but of which the Seeker seldom reaches their desired destination. At this point of the journey along the Ogham pathway—or up the ladder of learning—the destination is in sight and assured so long as the individual uses what they know to the best of their advantage.

ESOTERIC CORRESPONDENCE.

Alternate Names : onn, oir, piswydden

Alphabet Letter : "O"

Ogma's Tree : "furze, or ash"

Alternate Trees : gorse, spindle ('*gwyrthed*'), linden, basswood, silver-spruce, lime

Bardic Value : 17 ; *red.* 8; or often unnumbered

Forest Rank (British) : Bramble

Forest Rank (Irish) : Bramble

Quadratic Element : Fire

Druid Guardian : Oise

Celtic Deities : Lugh, Llew, Adraste

Druidic Deities : Ogma (eloquence, literature, writing/scripts), Ossian ('beautiful youth', swordplay), Owein ap Urien (leadership, war, reincarnation)

Solar Month : n/a

Lunar Month : Spring Equinox (March 21)

Color Ogham : *odhar*, dun; also yellow and gold

Bird Ogham : *odoroscrach*, scrat

Sacred Animal : rabbits (rebirth), bees (organization, community)

Sacred Gems : peridot, green quartz, jade, emerald

Ogham Forest Tract : honey and food for animals, fertility, eroticism, purification

Arts of Civilization : *ogmoracht*, harvesting

DIVINATION SYMBOLISM.

Description : two long notches perpendicular across the stemline

Word Ogham (Morann mac Main) : "*Conguaui- aid echraidc*—helper of horses, to wit, the *ennaid* of the chariot, i.e., the wheels of a chariot"

Word Ogham (Mac Ind Oic) : "*Fethim saire*—smoothest of work, i.e., stone"

Tarot Equivalent : The Sun—happiness, joy, brilliance, brightness, blessings, fulfillment, honesty

Ogham Lochlannach : *sowelu*—wholeness, victory; also 'sun'; power, flaming-sword, cleansing fire; also justice, destruction; 'Wrath of God'

Personality : prosperous
 Inversion : vane

Oracular Meaning : wisdom, spiritual fulfillment, optimism, projection (like rays) and protection, sometimes indicates discovery of new information, synthesis of information

18. ur — **heather**

"There are two types of heather—red and white. Red-heather attracts passion and is a symbol of sexual energy and lust, whereas White-heather wards against passion and sex and symbolizes purity and chastity."

—Joshua Free
'The Enchanted Forest'

The types of heather—red and white—represent the ultimate dilemma of continuation in material existence: reproduction versus personal immortality. During the course of one's life, the focus is generally on one or the other. In terms of material evolution: when environmental factors are favorable, life will usually choose reproduction; but when they are particularly turbulent, the emphasis is generally on one's own survival, growth and progression along a pathway that traverses lifetimes beyond just *this* one. In the end, we are left with ourselves, whether or not we produce offspring along the way— which means that ultimately, the quest must be to secure our own immortality.

ESOTERIC CORRESPONDENCE.

Alternate Names : uir, uchelwydd (mistletoe) [although 'mistletoe' is treated as a "blank" Ogham stick for divination]

Alphabet Letter : "U"

Ogma's Tree : "thorn"

Alternate Trees : silver-poplar, 'mistletoe'

Bardic Value : 18 ; *red.* 9; or often unnumbered

Forest Rank (British) : Bramble

Forest Rank (Irish) : Bramble

Quadratic Element : Air

Druid Guardian : Uriath

Celtic Deities : Grainne, Bloddwedd, Freya

Druidic Deities : Uath mac Imoman (the 'son of terror', ancient magic), Urias (ancient wisdom, supreme knowledge), Uaithne Umai (pipes, harps, music)

Solar Month : n/a

Lunar Month : Summer Solstice ; or the day after Winter Solstice (for mistletoe)

Color Ogham : *usgdha*, resinous; also purple

Bird Ogham : *uiseog*, lark

Sacred Animal : bee, lion

Sacred Gems : amethyst, peridot, amertine

Ogham Forest Tract : healing, attracting rain, perfume (heather), the 'goddess'

Arts of Civilization : *umaideacht*, brasswork

DIVINATION SYMBOLISM.

Description : three long notches perpendicu- lar across the stemline

Word Ogham (Morann mac Main) : "*Uaraib adbaib*—in cold dwellings, to wit, fresh; for from *uir*, the mould of the earth is *uaraib adbaib*"

Word Ogham (Mac Ind Oic) : "*Silad clann*—growing of plants, that is from *uir*, the soil of the earth"

Tarot Equivalent : The Fool (Heather current)—decisions, crossroads, taking measure before acting, new starts; or The Hermit (Mistletoe current)—experimentation, guidance, true wisdom, withdrawal (reclusive)

Ogham Lochlannach : *mannaz*—the self (on a path); also 'man' or 'humans'; skill, ability, craft, intelligence; also cunning, slyness, craftiness, calculating (the 'Magician')

Personality : carefree
Inversion : superficial

Oracular Meaning : clarity, understanding the 'inner self' (heather), healing (mistletoe, the 'all-heal'), personal development (success, gain)

19. eadha — **poplar (aspen)**

"The danger that you must guard against, even at this level of attainment, is falling into the trap of self-importance. Realize that you are still capable of falling from grace, of making mistakes, of upsetting the delicate balance of things, when you do what you want rather than what you will."

—Steve Blamires
'Celtic Tree Mysteries'

Nearing the end of our journey on this cycle, the aspen tree stands to give us the final test of our convictions—but it also represents the strength to overcome all final obstacles and barriers to our ultimate success. Its presence urges the Seeker to 'push ahead' to the end, which is surely in sight at this juncture. Fears of success—whatever those last pieces are that keeps us from accomplishment—are met and faced or confronted dauntlessly. There is no fear of 'losing' anything because Self will remain.

ESOTERIC CORRESPONDENCE.

Alternate Names : edad, ebad, eubh, aethin, k'emmir, beith-bhog

Alphabet Letter : "E"

Ogma's Tree : "yew"/"aspen"

Alternate Trees : aspen, white poplar, cottonwood

Bardic Value : 19 (or 21 as mistletoe); *red.* 10 or 1 (or *red.* 3 as mistletoe); or often unnumbered

Forest Rank (British) : Bramble

Forest Rank (Irish) : Shrub

Quadratic Element : Water

Druid Guardian : Essu

Celtic Deities : Brighid, Rhiannon, Keyne, Llyr

Druidic Deities : Eochaid Ollathar (the 'great horse father', animals), Esus (god of woodcutters and weaponry), Ethniu (language, speech)

Solar Month : n/a

Lunar Month : Autumn Equinox

Color Ogham : *erc*, red; also silver

Bird Ogham : *ela*, swan (love)

Sacred Animal : white mare (the goddess); also the serpent-snake (in some traditions)

Sacred Gems : gray topaz, opal, sapphire, citrine quartz

Ogham Forest Tract : shapeshifting, shields, divination, 'rites of passage', crossing over (transition, change)

Arts of Civilization : *enaireacht*, fowling

DIVINATION SYMBOLISM.

Description : four long notches perpendicular across the stemline

Word Ogham (Morann mac Main) : "*Ergnaid fid*—distinguished wood; a name for the trembling tree"

Word Ogham (Mac Ind Oic) : "*Comainm carat*—synonym for *friend*"

Tarot Equivalent : The (Falling) Tower—false hopes, sudden changes, breakdown, limitations of clinging to the old

Ogham Lochlannach : *fehu*—physical power, possessions and prosperity; also 'wealth' or 'cattle'; ownership; also slavery, bondage; a valuable object

Personality : caring
  Inversion : insecure

Oracular Meaning : overcoming barriers and problems, facing fears, overcoming death (transition, change), working through emotional distress, overcoming doubts (misunderstanding), overcoming final obstacles toward completion

20. ioho — yew tree

*"Although all things are comprehended by the Mind—
yet the Dweller exists beyond the Mind.
The first mind is reason. The second is intuition.
Within the third dwells the pattern, who is neither intellect nor inclination,
more excellent than all speech and notion."*

—The Oracle of the Silent Yew
(Monroe Version)

An 'end-cycle' has been achieved. Death of the old has made way for the new. The Seeker has shed skin and rebirth into a new cycle awaits. Yew represents the essence of the unadulterated Self, fully defragmented, or at the very least emerging onto a higher plane of realization and experience with the next cycle of the pathway—the next ladder—that awaits us. A sense of accomplishment is well-deserved, but the the gateway to a complete Ascension is still forthcoming.

ESOTERIC CORRESPONDENCE.

Alternate Names : idad, ida, ibur, ywen, iodha, idho, iubhar, uhr

Alphabet Letter : "I"/"J" and "Y"

Ogma's Tree : "Service-tree"

Alternate Trees : dogwood, cypress, hemlock

Bardic Value : 20; *red.* 2; or often unnumbered

Forest Rank (British) : Bramble

Forest Rank (Irish) : Chieftain

Quadratic Element : Earth

Druid Guardian : Iachim

Celtic Deities : Arawn, Arianrhod, Dagda Mor, Samhann

Druidic Deities : Ith (towers and buildings), Ialonus (cultivated fields), Iorix (astronomy, meteors and space)

Solar Month : n/a

Lunar Month : Day before Winter Solstice

Color Ogham : *irfind*, very white, also dark green

Bird Ogham : *illait*, eaglet (courage, renewal)

Sacred Animal : spider (the gateway)

Sacred Gems : emerald, diamond, star-ruby

Ogham Forest Tract : poison, poisoned weapons, archery-bows

Arts of Civilization : *iascaireacht*, fishing

DIVINATION SYMBOLISM.

Description : five long notches perpendicular across the stemline

Word Ogham (Morann mac Main) : "*Siniu fedaib*—oldest of woods; and *ibur*, a name for the service-tree"

Word Ogham (Mac Ind Oic) : "*Crinem feda*—most withered of wood, or sword, to wit, a service-tree"

Tarot Equivalent : Death—abrupt changes, letting go, transitions, unfortunate realizations; does not typically indicate 'physical body' death

Ogham Lochlannach : Eihwaz—life, death, the rebirth cycle; also 'Ingwaz' (deity)

Personality : enduring
Inversion : sanguine

Oracular Meaning : completion, changes, renewal, transformation, forthcoming rebirth, the next step, the life and death cycle, infinity, immortality of the spirit

THE OGHAM ORACLE

Divination in the Druidic Tradition

> *"[Druid] systems of divination are rather different to many modern methods of 'fortunetelling'. They used divination techniques to learn the hidden secrets about things, so they could be just as interested in divining someone's secret past as in determining the future. They understood that by knowing someone's secret past, the future can be predicted with a great deal of precision..."*
> —Richard Webster
> 'Omens, Oghams & Oracles'

READING THE LAND.

During the early developmental period of the Mardukite Research Organization, the present author traveled over 20,000 miles on the American Greyhound bus lines in just a few short years—most of them exceptionally long trips crisscrossing the United States—even coast-to-coast. Rather than driving, this chance to ride passively as a passenger, journeying across the surface of the land, allowed for observation and interactions at new levels of realization.

Although the concept is alluded to in many manuals of 'earth mysticism', the experience afforded opportunities for "reading" the resonant energy of various regions and landscapes. It was curious to note that although state-lines are indeed purely "political" boundaries, there are observable differences when crossing either side of these thresholds. The land and those that dwell on it are indeed *one*, and they clearly have an influential effect on one another. All is connected together.

Although the manner of understanding the specific projected energies of life is difficult to instruct in a book, the interconnected lore of the Oghamic tradition does reflect this. An individual that is high in awareness can easily "tune in" to sense these "subtle energies. But, a person does not really have to be all that 'sensitive' to perceive that the 'feeling' of an oak forest is quite different than an aspen forest—or notice the distinguished presence (or 'aura') of a lone elm tree surrounded by a circle-grove of pines. A systematic understanding of these qualities allows a Druid (or similar practitioner) the ability to "read" the land, in a sense.

ORACLES & DIVINATION.

Divination is a personal individualized application of metaphysical systems or magical traditions—and the Ogham is certainly among the most individually personal and intuitive means of 'reading' the omens of life. Still, all methods of divination depend on the operator's (seer, medium, magician, Druid, diviner) relationship with the system itself (its meaning, symbolism) and the actual implements (tools, stones, sticks).

Although we find no shortage of lore, tales and stories within Celtic, Druid and Elven-Faerie systems—all of which reach into the ancient pools of knowledge—we are often at a loss for precise methods of divination and interpretation that are held completely and one-hundred percent 'authentic' to original source-cultures thousands of years ago.

There are no absolute standards or rules toward handling oracles and divination in the Druidic tradition as it is observed today. We have only suggestions. And magical practices must be personalized to a certain extent in order to be effective anyways.

THE CRANE BAG.

The divinatory "tools" employed for an oracle are generally treated as "sacred" items. They are usually kept hidden away from the eyes of the 'profane' or 'uninitiated' and are often quite personal possessions. The traditional Oghamancer's 'shamanic pouch' or 'medicine bag' serves this purpose for the Ogham sticks. Drawing *fews* from a pouch or bag also replaces the need to "shuffle" or randomize a card-based system. This bag may be shaken up and its contents could even be emptied out all at once if desired.

In one Druidic tradition, invention of the Ogham was inspired by observing flights of cranes, which "form the characters of the letters as they fly." The phrase *crane knowledge* came to denote the hidden knowledge that Oghamic tradition conceals—and that divination is thought to reveal.

A bag or pouch is traditionally used to hold and store a set of *Ogham sticks*. During an oracle reading, *fews* may be drawn individually from the bag—or the bag may be used to drop the entire set onto a 'spread'. But even a single *few* may be drawn for some quick overall insight.

PRAYERS & SILVER-BELLS.

Divination is connected to the "Other"—or else piercing the veils of mystery and not-knowing that enshroud knowledge that is considered "Divine" relative to material existence and the human condition. In Celtic cosmology, the "Other" is often treated literally as the "Otherworld," which includes the *'Realm of Faerie'*. Druids (and other similar practitioners) have maintained a long-standing connection to the "Otherworld."

One particular connection to the "Other" is represented by the *Ogham* tree most sacred to the Avalonian Druidesses—the Apple. Its wood is used to fashion a traditional tool called the "Silver Branch"—also known as *'craebh ciuil'* or "Poet's Branch" in the Bardic lore and Oghamic systems. This "wand" serves as a catalyst to bridge the transmission of energy and information between the "Other" and the medium or operator.

To construct the tool, attach silver bells to a single branch of apple wood, twelve to sixteen inches long. It may even be a forked branch or with smaller offshoots to provide nodes for attaching three bells with blue and white ribbon. According to traditional lore, the hanging bells are meant to represent apples themselves. Before any type of divination is performed, the bells would be rung three times in order to purify the 'air' and ensure an accurate reading. A prayer or invocation might also be spoken—such as:

Hail to thee, Ogma Sun-Face;
Watchful Eye of the Great God;
Seeing Eye of the God of Glory;
Witnessing Eye of the King of the Living.

Pour down and bestow your blessing;
Pour down and bestow your skill;
Pour down and bestow your power;
Unmask the God of Life for this divination.

Oghamancy and the Art of Casting Ogham Fews

"In the 'Tochmarc Etain', the omen sticks are called 'eochra ecsi', or 'keys of knowledge'. The 'Senchus Mor' describes a type of judgment, used to find a murderer or thief, which is called 'crannchur', or 'casting the woods'. J. A. MacCulloch says that some early Irish saints used a kind of divination called 'fidlanna', which used pieces of wood..."

—D.J. Conway
'By Oak, Ash & Thorn'

Twenty (or twenty-one, including a blank) *Ogham fews* serve as the variable elements of the Oghamic oracle system employed in modern 'New Age' practices. Use of *Ogham fews* for any divinatory purpose is subject to the interpretation of an Oghamancer (magician, Druid, practitioner, &tc.) that is familiar with those energies represented by the 'Green World' of the Forest Trees. As a result, the system is generally referred to as the 'Celtic Oracle of the Forest Trees' or else the 'Celtic Tree Oracle'.

SPREAD-CLOTHS & CASTING-CLOTHS.

A special surface area is used for divination that may or may not surround an 'altar'—depending on the tradition—but should be at least temporarily designated as oracular space with some kind of 'cloth' material, especially if working indoors. Sometimes the ground may be used outdoors, but it is still distinguished with some type pattern or "spread" to indicate its application to the oracle.

The 'cloth' could also be printed with the 'spread' symbolism, if desired. In either case, it is *on* this 'spread' which one *casts* the Ogham *fews* from the 'Crane Bag'. Alternatively, one could trace an area out with chalk or charcoal, if we're staying true to natural applications.

A "spread" is any oracular pattern used to 'read' or interpret the meaning of more than one facet randomly selected from a divination system; or more than one Ogham *"few."* The "spread" involves applying a preassigned meaning to specific placements or positions within the pattern.

Any divination system, such as the Ogham, tarot, runes and so forth, require a combination of two factors, or a meeting point of two axis: the fixed environment, and the variable elements. The "spread" provides a fixed environment or "setting" on which the "variables" (the Ogham *fews*) are "cast" or "set" out upon. The type or manner of "spread" used is indicative of the 'standard' by which the cosmos are seen from the point of view of the Observer or Diviner. A particular "spread" (or "layout"), or point-of-view, is selected based on the type of information an individual seeks to gain.

FORFEDHA—THE FIFTHS SPREAD.

An additional *aicme* of five Oghams appear in the *Book of Ballymote*—called the *Forfedha* or "*Fifths.*" They are traditionally not used as *Ogham sticks*, but are instead the symbols on which *Ogham fews* are cast as a "spread." Variations of interpretation occur throughout 'New Age' traditions. The version provided here closely matches a system instructed to the present author during the 1990s. It has been since updated. As was stated in the *Pheryllt Researches:*[*]

> "As an Ogham oracle spread, the *Forfedha* are the fixed zones—a background matrix—on which the *fews* are variable elements. A combination of these two are what suggest the total 'reading'."

Some theorize that the *Forfedha* "Fifths" or 'Elemental/Directional' division used in the model represents the divisions of Ireland, and simultaneously, the Otherworld Kingdoms of Faerie (or presumably, the "Tuatha d'Anu"). For Ogham divination systems, the "Fifths" represent a microcosm of creation, a *spread* mirroring the cosmos. Continuing from the *Pheryllt Researches*:

> "*Forfedha* might be drawn on the ground before a sacred 'Oracle Tree', or imprinted on a 'board' or 'spread-cloth'. Design of this 'spread' should include a portion for each of the Four Directions, therefore the Four Elements, plus a 'center' area, which represents the 'fifth' position."

In contrast to the traditional *fèdha* or *fews*, there is marginal consistency between the various New Age interpretations of *forfedha*. Our *forfedha* model displayed here is based on a version of the Ogham 'scales' depicted in the *Book of Ballymote*. Four divisions are clearly visible, as is the "X" in the center. The image reproduced here features the remaining Ogham script as an ornamental addition, which is not required in your own graphic representation of the Fifths-Spread.

---

[*] Available as "*Draconomicon (Vol. 2): Pheryllt Researhes*" and reprinted in "*Merlyn's Complete Book of Pheryllt.*"

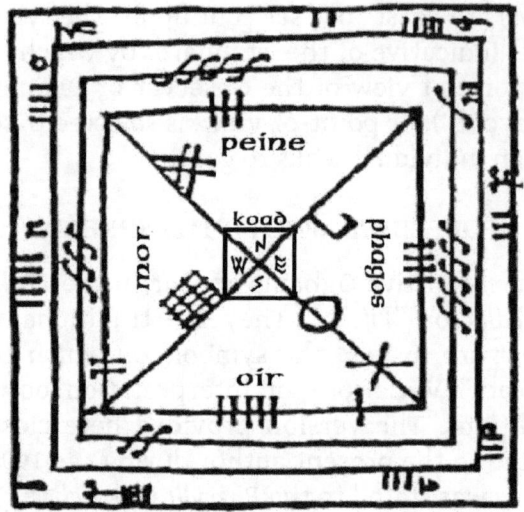

Interpretation of the *forfedha* given below is unique to this work—whereas other sources often designate different names and classifications, making any comparative research for this part quite difficult. Therefore, for this example, the present author relied on personal notebooks maintained in the 1990s for the *Elven-Druid* and *Pheryllt* systems.

pine — peine %
Alignment: north / earth
Alphabetical: "Pe" "Ui"
Aspect: the physical / foundations
Associations: manifestation and prosperity

beech — phagos @
Alignment: east / air
Alphabetical: "Ph" "Io"
Aspect: the psychological / communication
Associations: learning and knowledge;
ancient wisdom; guidance from the past

spindle — oir ◇
Alignment: south / fire
Alphabetical: "Oi" "Th"
Aspect: the spiritual / focus of attention
Associations: harmony; growth; delight;
happiness from achieving goals

the sea — ᛘᚑᚏ
Alignment: west / water
Alphabetical: "Xi" "Ae"
Aspect: the emotional / influences
Association: challenges and turbulence;
imprinting; also journeys and travel

the grove — ᚕᚑᚐᚇ x
Alignment: center (middle) / spirit
Alphabetical: "Ch" "Ea"
Aspect: the Self / etheric link between all
Association: where all things are connected;
Alpha-Spirit and Spiritual Timeline
(True Knowledge across all 'lifetimes')

Creative interpretations are discerned by combining the general 'aura' gleaned from the Ogham *few*—as previously catalogued—with the situation or environment represented by its position in the spread. For example, depending on the question posed: Birch ('*beith*') might represent 'new beginnings and vitality'. If we consider what introducing 'new vitality' to 'challenges and conflict' (in the '*mor*' position) essentially is, it would be like "fanning flames"—yet, this same 'vitality' in 'learning' (the '*phagos*' position) could indicate "over-eagerness."

There are no definitive 'rules' for "casting" the *fews*. You might choose to select a stick individually from a 'crane bag' and place it in each position around the 'spread'. One might also gather the sticks in their hand and drop them onto the 'spread' surface from above—our simply pour them all out from a 'crane bag' and interpret how they land across the 'spread'. It might be that any or all of these is appropriate, but that a diviner's intuition will guide their performance of divinatory actions by necessity.

If a diviner is pulling individual *fews* from a 'crane bag' to place onto the 'spread', there should be a sequential order for laying the *fews* down into positions. Traditionally, the energy-flow incited by such actions should follow a 'spiral-like' pattern—either toward or away from the center. For example, from *koad*, to *peine*, *phagos*, *oir* and *mor*. Or some diviner's might prefer another pattern.

As a divination system, Ogham requires a high level of intuition by practitioners, not to mention studying a language and style unfamili-

A CELTIC TREE ORACLE QUICK-START.

Although there is no substitute for intuitively understanding and applying the lore of the Green World to Ogham—as described throughout this present volume—the following 'New Age' interpretation from many decades ago may assist a beginner in 'jump-starting' their practical applications of the "Celtic Tree Oracle." This 'quick-start' list is only one possible way of interpreting the *Forfedha-Fifths-Spread* and is not a definitive standard that a reader 'must' adhere to. It simply suffices to at least get a Seeker moving in a practical direction.

1. BIRCH / *beith*
   in KOAD : new starts and beginnings
   in PEINE : fortune and riches
   in PHAGOS : youthful eagerness
   in OIR : turbulence and disturbance
   in MOR : new fanned fury (aggression)

2. ROWAN / *luis*
   in KOAD : protective (dominance)
   in PEINE : abundance and affluence
   in PHAGOS : new insight or discovery
   in OIR : productivity and advancement
   in MOR : overcoming adversity

3. ALDER / *fearn*
   in KOAD : fundamentals (basics)
   in PEINE : underlying challenges
   in PHAGOS : apathy or disinterest
   in OIR : overcoming doubts
   in MOR : acute vigilance

4. WILLOW / *saille*
   in KOAD : intuition or insight
   in PEINE : brooding or excess
   in PHAGOS : wit and cunning
   in OIR : passivity and femininity
   in MOR : securing the advantage

5. ASH / *nuin*
   in KOAD : world tree (seeking Infinity)

in PEINE : loss (starting over)
in PHAGOS : renewed interest
in OIR : new influences or interests
in MOR : mass gathering (abundance)

6. HAWTHORN / *huathe*
   in KOAD : weaknesses (integrity)
   in PEINE : shortage or poverty
   in PHAGOS : ignorance or stubbornness
   in OIR : disharmony or misfortune
   in MOR : defeat or sudden change

7. OAK / *duir*
   in KOAD : realizations and beliefs
   in PEINE : security and restfulness
   in PHAGOS : recognition and retention
   in OIR : discontentment (change needed)
   in MOR : destruction or overcoming

8. HOLLY / *tinne*
   in KOAD : steadfastness or sternness
   in PEINE : planning ahead (for harvest)
   in PHAGOS : discernment (decisions)
   in OIR : rejection and choices (action)
   in MOR : revenge and retribution

9. HAZEL / *coll*
   in KOAD : creativity and intuition
   in PEINE : created goods and arts
   in PHAGOS : teaching and instruction
   in OIR : accomplishment (satisfaction)
   in MOR : legal matters and judgment

10. APPLE / *quert*
    in KOAD : perfection (beauty)
    in PEINE : wholeness (duality)
    in PHAGOS : occult knowledge
    in OIR : rewards (harmony in life)
    in MOR : mistrust and betrayal

11. VINE / *muin*
    in KOAD : reserved (abstained)
    in PEINE : class or prestige
    in PHAGOS : moderation of intake

in OIR : shrewdness and subtlety
   in MOR : boastful pride (excess)

12. IVY / *gort*
   in KOAD : development (new skills)
   in PEINE : restriction of growth
   in PHAGOS : educational grades
   in OIR : attainment and persistence
   in MOR : ruin and stagnation

13. REED / *ngetal*
   in KOAD : direct action (will)
   in PEINE : etiquette and records
   in PHAGOS : symmetry (cohesion)
   in OIR : harmony (tranquility)
   in MOR : stillness and inaction

14. BLACKTHORN / *straif*
   in KOAD : stewardship (guarding)
   in PEINE : favors and debts owed
   in PHAGOS : tests (of the true Self)
   in OIR : violent (passionate)
   in MOR : capture and imprisonment

15. ELDER / *ruis*
   in KOAD : maturity and age
   in PEINE : sharing and generosity
   in PHAGOS : progress and advancement
   in OIR : new information (rethinking)
   in MOR : survivalism (quest for Infinity)

16. FIR / *ailim*
   in KOAD : objectivity ('high views')
   in PEINE : individuality and singularity
   in PHAGOS : accomplishment
   in OIR : discovery (magnification)
   in MOR : strategy (perspective/POV)

17. FURZE / *ohn*
   in KOAD : collected wisdom
   in PEINE : collected wealth
   in PHAGOS : collected knowledge
   in OIR : collected authority
   in MOR : collected experience

18. HEATHER / *ur*
  in KOAD : new inspiration (sources)
  in PEINE : greed and obsession
  in PHAGOS : zealousness (tenacious)
  in OIR : disturbance (fragmentation)
  in MOR : raging tides (before the calm)

19. ASPEN / *eadha*
  in KOAD : overcoming (success)
  in PEINE : effort (to complete actions)
  in PHAGOS : structure and discipline
  in OIR : overcoming all effort-force
  in MOR : force applied (to cause action)

20. YEW / *ioho*
  in KOAD : rebirth (eternity or Infinity)
  in PEINE : grief (losses along the way)
  in PHAGOS : disillusionment (clarity)
  in OIR : discordance or disharmony
  in MOR : fear (of unknown/next steps)

INTRODUCING THE ORIGINAL
MARDUKITE MASTER COURSE
ACADEMY GRADES I, II & III

The single most purpose of our *Mardukite Master Course* is to ensure professional qualifications for "mastering" an understanding the materials in the same way that an artist "masters" their craft. The complete *Mardukite Master Course* spans three *Grades* of knowledge. It is given to those *Seekers* that properly work through the different *Grades*, and may only then be rightfully considered *Masters* of this knowledge. Extents of such "mastery" should prove readily obvious (objectively), lending to increased qualities of *Self-Actualization*, personal leadership, a continuing pursuit in Systemology, and the certainty to instruct *Mardukite Groups*.

Current works available by Joshua Free—written and published between 1995 and 2019—all pertain to a singular stream of complete instruction that is now divided into three *Grades*, or knowledge *tiers*. The *Mardukite Master Course* is intended to grant a clear unification of all material presented across the three *Grades* under the *Mardukite Academy* banner. "Mardukite Systemology" is the name given to *Grade-III*. The two are interconnected (*Grade-III* and the *Master Course*); hence the complete *Mardukite Master Course* is usually delivered to *Seekers* at the completion of *Grade-III*. There are "higher" *Grades* within the domain of "Mardukite Systemology," but the *Mardukite Master Course* successfully covers all specifically "Mardukite Master" *Grades*: I, II and III.

It is important to clarify what we mean by *Grades* and distinguish the materials that pertain to each. In most instances, instruction for these *Grades*—as delivered in the materials (books) over the past 25 years—was all self-administered; meaning it has been explored independent of properly structured groups or trained instructors. In the past, *Seekers* selected a volume at random, "had at it" on their own for a while, then walked away with whatever level of understanding might be attained, even if severely fragmented. Most are unaware that the works—no matter what the theme—are all tied together. They are divided as follows:

    GRADE-I   Western Magical Tradition ("Magick")
    GRADE-II   Ancient Mystery School of Mesopotamia
    GRADE-III   Futurist/NexGen Mardukite Systemology

It can be said that the *Grades* are all a part of a single continuum—one which is explored in a "reverse engineering" style in order to provide the greatest certainty for effective workable future applications that will advance the spiritual evolution of the *Human Condition*, particularly the *Self* that is participating in and experiencing a co-creation of the Physical Universe and a continued existence of its conditions. As a single continuum, the *Grades* do actually overlap on many points—and often times these "bridges" between levels of understanding are what we are highlighting profusely for our *Mardukite Master Course*. This preferred approach—treating the universal knowledge and its records as a single wholeness rather than an emphasis on individual parts—developed after many years of experiment and discovery.

Direction of the *Mardukite Master Course* loosely follows a chronological pathway charted by Joshua Free from 1995 through 2019—meaning: from the release of the first "Merlyn Stone" *Grade-I* discourses on "magick" and "Druidism" until the recent completion of *Grade-III* as "Mardukite Systemology." Between these *Grades*, a *Seeker* discovers abundant source material known as the "Mardukite Core" comprising *Grade-II*. These *Grades* also loosely follow a premise for organization set out in the 1990's for *Grade-I* Alumni of "Merlyn Stone's School of Magick"* that is referred to elsewhere as "The Sacred Order of the Crystal Dawn." The outline for this premise in 1999 proposed structuring of "A New Illuminati" using the work published by Joshua Free over the next two decades.

There are no strictly enforced "title-badges" and/or "initiations" defining *Grades* when applied to individual *Mardukite Groups* (outside religious organizational function of *Mardukite Zuism* specifically) for "study" or "instructive" purposes. A *Master* may choose to adopt a particular regimen for their *Seekers* as applicable to each *Grade* and in alignment with themes and goals of a group. Starting with the original *Grade-I* "Merlyn Stone" volume by Joshua Free—THE SORCERER'S HANDBOOK—reissued for its 21st Anniversary as a collector's edition hardcover, sufficient material is now available in each "core" toward defining group structure as it pertains to the greater *"whole"* at each *Grade*.

Parameters assigned to formal progressive *Grades* are approximately equivalent to the *first three* "degrees" of the original "Crystal Dawn" program; which is the extent an individual "Chapter" or "Lodge" is allowed to administer (apart from authority of a "Grand Lodge"). For two decades, this clause permitted a *Master* of the *Third Degree* to launch a "Chapter" or "Group" as an official extension of the organization; so long as that *Seeker* had completed the *Master Course*. However, no such

---

* Also operating in Denver from 1998-2000 as *"The Elven Fellowship Circle of Magick."*

Grade-III materials were sufficiently supplied for such a "core" (until 2019) in which to make this possible. But, now, we have a *Grade-III*.

The basic pattern of development across the *Grades* follows progressive and cumulative ascent up the "Ladder of Lights" or "Gateways to Infinity" first described by the Ancient Mystery School of Mesopotamia as a sevenfold "Babylonian Stargate" system. The chronology of the *Grades* begins with the most apparent and recent influences of the contemporary "New Age"; meaning the modern communication and conception of "magick" and metaphysics—otherwise known as the Western Magical Tradition, which maintained its popularity for the past several thousand years in Europe. This is the essence of *Grade-I*, which is essentially the "Lunar Gate."

A *Seeker* exploring origins behind magickal correspondences, practices, ceremonies and ritualism of various European developments—including everything from ancient Celtic Druids to more modern esoteric Hermetic Orders—will at one juncture or another intersect with the even older Ancient Mystery School present in Mesopotamia—systematized in "Mardukite Babylon" at the inception of the *Age of Aries* (c. 2160 B.C.)—an extension of the former loosely organized Sumerian civilization, now collectively making up *Grade-II* and the key to open the "*Nabu Gate.*"

When a *Seeker* considers this logical progression: we begin with what is most readily familiar and accessible at *Grade-I*, loading the shot in the sling, and then pulling back to the extent that we may be certain, by examining the oldest literary records in *Grade-II*; the very basis for which our *Grade-I* material is actually based, albeit forgotten to the sands of time coupled with thousands of years of programming and encoding separating the two. History and tradition begins with "writing," and so we cannot be certain of anything further than what we have actual accounts of; yet still we find that these *Arcane Tablets* provide an understanding that is milestones beyond what is demonstrated in contemporary society today.

There are many ways of which we can demonstrate how the knowledge between these two *Grades* is bridged and overlaps in application and study; but the *Grades* are distinguished as they are for good reason—and we are not to muddy the waters of a *Seeker's* thinking by incorporating unnecessary complications to instruction. A line has been drawn, if only even from necessity, between the *Grades* by using the *Mardukite Chamberlains Grade-II* material as a benchmark for our evaluation of other materials.

Essentially—all volumes by Joshua Free pertaining exclusively to ancient Mesopotamia are considered *Grade-II*; all volumes pertaining to general mysticism, magick, esoterica, Druidism, &tc are considered *Grade-I*. This is not to say that "higher realizations" are inaccessible from lower *Grade* materials, nor is there a guarantee that "higher realizations" are gleaned directly from reading higher *Grade* materials. A *Seeker* working through the entirety of the first two *Grades* may reach all necessary "ledges" of "knowing" on their own merit, independent of outside instruction. But given that only one-way communication relay takes place from this book-learning, there is no guarantee that an individual will correctly gauge the distance between "ledges" of "knowing" on their ascent up as they leap about unaided.

An early premise of "higher" *Grades* comprised the ORIGINAL THESIS for a new flavor of "New Thought" provided exclusively to *Grade-II* Mardukite Alumni in 2011 as "NexGen Systemology." The official "Core" of *Grade-III* was not released to the public by Joshua Free until late 2019 as "Mardukite Systemology." It is from the vantage point of *Grade-III*, and a mastery of that same tier of knowledge, that we actually treat all of which the *Mardukite Master Course* represents. Although a *Seeker* could certainly remain at one or another *Grade*, an individual must demonstrate total understanding of all three *Grades* to be officially considered a *Master*.

Earliest contributions toward this *Course* from the 1990's are considered *Grade-I*, pertaining to practical magick, general metaphysics, the Western Magical Tradition and its archetypal scions, the *Druids*. The original *Grade-I* volumes pertaining to magick and metaphysics are THE SORCERER'S HANDBOOK and ARCANUM by Joshua Free. In addition to THE DRUID'S HANDBOOK, there are two volumes that, combined, complete the *Druid Cycle* and effectively "bridge" to the *Grade-II* elements that incorporate Mesopotamia: DRACONOMICON and the ELVENOMICON[*] anthology.

A *Seeker* working through the original *Grade-I* "Handbooks" may also choose to take an alternate "bridge" between the ritualism and ceremonialism of *Grade-I* with *Grade-II*, as described in THE VAMPYRE'S HANDBOOK by Joshua Free.[‡] The original 2015 release of these materials for *Moroii ad Vitam Paramus* served as a contemporary "holding point" for Alumni after the completion of *Grade-II* work, prior to the proper establishment of Systemology. Meanwhile, a "Core" for *Grade-III* developed behind-the-scenes until late 2019. For our purposes, this now means that

---

[*] *"Elvenomicon"* formerly published as *"Book of Elven-Faerie"* (from 2004 to 2018).

[‡] *"The Vampyre's Handbook"* formerly released as *"Vampyre Magick"* by Joshua Free; an anthology edition combining *"Book of V: The Vampyre's Bible"* and *"Cybernomicon."* A revised and expanded 10th Anniversary deluxe edition is anticipated for a 2025 release.

there are several "entry" points for a *Seeker* to experience glamour and enchantment of the *Grade-I "Lunar Gate"* on the way to *higher* avenues of *Self-Actualization*—which is the ultimate goal behind the *Master* level.

In 2008, existing ARCANUM and ELVENOMICON materials contributed to the establishment of *Mardukite Ministries*, an underground umbrella organization that took control of the former "Merlyn Stone" legacy of Joshua Free as a "ledge" for developing *Grade-II*. By 2009, the *Mardukite Chamberlains* emerged—a global network contributing to progressive generation and dissemination of a "Mardukite Core" of materials, providing the inception of the modern "Mardukite" (and "Mardukite Zuism") paradigms. This living spiritual philosophy dispensed at *Grade-II* is drawn heavily from the ancient cuneiform tablet records of Mesopotamia/Babylon.

Mardukite Chamberlains participated in developing the bulk of material for *Grade-II* from 2009 through 2011. These materials were simultaneously presented in two guises—the *same* materials, but dispensed in two different formats: one emphasizing the *Anunnaki Legacy* as a demonstration of more "academic" and "intellectual" pursuits into ancient history and its esoteric traditions; the other, emphasizing the title of the NECRONOMICON due to the high correlation and association of "New Age" data regarding the ancient "Mardukite Babylonian" tradition. When treated in its entirety as the *Complete Anunnaki Legacy* from within the Mardukite paradigm, presentation of the two "formats" is essentially identical. *Grade-II* should not, however, be confused with *any* other outside treatment of the *"Necronomicon"* subject.

Starting in 2009, the original source book of *Grade-II* developed into an anthology composed from individual discourses produced for the *Mardukite Chamberlains* and compiled into NECRONOMICON: THE COMPLETE ANUNNAKI BIBLE. Then, over the next two years, several key anthologies were added to the *Grade-II* core, including the material found in Joshua Free's GATES OF THE NECRONOMICON and NECRONOMICON: THE ANUNNAKI GRIMOIRE.[‡] Each of these anthologies contain several stand-alone discourses in themselves—all of which were consolidated into a complete *Grade-II* Master Edition mega-anthology titled NECRONOMICON: THE COMPLETE ANUNNAKI LEGACY (with a special *Master Edition* released in early 2020).

The gradation (*Grades*) structure and concept of the *Mardukite Master Course* was announced in August 2019 at THE TABLETS OF DESTINY REV-

---

[‡] *"Gates of the Necronomicon"* anthology includes *"The Sumerian Legacy"* and *"Necronomicon Revelations -or- Crossing to the Abyss"*; *"Necronomicon Grimoire"* anthology includes *"The Complete Book of Marduk by Nabu"* and *"The Maqlu Ritual Book."*

ELATION lectures, as described (from transcripts) in the *Grade-III* text of the same title:—

> "Some of you that have been really following along through the materials over the years already have an understanding, from the *Grades* previously provided... And this is one of the keys or secrets held by the *Master*—an individual who has a complete workable understanding of these various levels and degrees represented in former instruction, but they are not themselves formally attached to any of it—drawing up only those solid examples suitable for citation, example and demonstration. So, that's what a Master is, and we are referring now to this intermediary *Grade-III* 'Mardukite Systemology' material as the *Master Grade*. I expect to also develop a formal instruction course for that, which will solidify the unification of the extant 'Mardukite Core' and NexGen Systemology for this Grade."—*Joshua Free*

The other significant portion of Grade-III material is found within the textbook for the CRYSTAL CLEAR Mardukite Systemology Self-Defragmentation Course Program developed by Joshua Free and officially released in December 2019—so as to make certain that proper introductory tools were available for a 2020's decade of ushering-in the proper NexGen (metahuman) evolution in consciousness. *Grade-III* emphasizes strengthening personal certainty and management of "Reality," employing spiritual philosophies of "Mardukite Systemology." This is our launch point for all further upper-level *Grades*, just as much as it is a capstone representing minimum requirements for our *Mardukite Master Course*—intended to treat *all* material of *Grades I, II* and *III*.

THE MARDUKITE MASTER COURSE MATERIALS
(2022 VERSION)

Since 2009, materials comprising the *Mardukite Research Library* have included all officially published works by Joshua Free to date. From 2008 through 2018, management and responsibility of these materials fell upon the *Mardukite Truth Seeker Press* governed by *Mardukite Ministries* and maintained by the *Mardukite Chamberlains*. As of 2018, a consistent transfer of official responsibility for all materials is increasingly assumed by the *Joshua Free Imprint (JFI Publications)*.

Throughout the years, a continuous development ensued, contributing to the release of many materials—including both those mentioned previously in this introduction, and other supplemental works that have appeared or are reissued for posterity. As the work progressed, goals for refinement and consolidation of the knowledge were repeatedly observed in newer editions and publications. Up until recently, the work was exceptionally "fluid" and required considerable attention over the course of its development. Information and discourses were released as they were discovered or refined for many years before appearing as the newly revised "collected works" anthologies and other "collector's editions" in the past year—making the materials more accessible and comprehensible than ever before possible. Goal attained.

It is of benefit for the *Seeker* (and *Master-in-Training*) to see an outright listing of all available graded materials (and their supplements) considered for inclusion as the *Mardukite Master Course*. Titles given represent the most current editions at the time of preparing this introduction. Some *Seekers* may already be in possession of former editions of these materials; and while the titles may change—and volumes may be collected for various anthologies—any "*Liber*"* designations used to catalogue the *Mardukite Research Library* remain fixed to a particular discourse or release in perpetuity. This means, regardless of whatever "title" may be attached to, for example, *Liber-50* (or whatever anthology it may appear in), the material designated "*Liber-50*" is always *Liber-50*, in any of its formats or revisions. Although some *Seekers* have not taken note of these *liber designations,* this internal consistency has been maintained openly and publicly for over a decade.

Mardukite Master Course supplements are found in each of the "Master Edition" anthologies published for each of the Grades. These may also be

---

* The term *Liber* (meaning *book*) is often used by esoteric organizations to title their individual collections of work.

found in the 'appendix' of *The Complete Mardukite Master Course* anthology along with transcripts for the 48 Mardukite Master Course 'Academy Lectures' given by Joshua Free to the 'Mardukite Academy of Systemology' in October 2020. A four-volume set of these 'Academy Lecture' transcripts is also available as the '*Mardukite Master Course Academy Lecture*' series, including: "*Magick and Mysticism*", "*Druids, Elves and Dragons*", "*Mesopotamian Tradition*" and "*Mardukite Systemology*."

THE COMPLETE MARDUKITE MASTER COURSE
ORIGINAL TRAINING SCHEDULE

|| GRADE-I-A || ROUTE OF MAGICK & METAPHYSICS ||

Primary Textbooks:[∞]
    THE SORCERER'S HANDBOOK
    ARCANUM: GREAT MAGICAL ARACNUM
Supplementary/Optional:
    THE WITCH'S HANDBOOK (newly added in 2021)
Additional: *Route of Druidism & The Dragon Legacy*

|| GRADE-I-D || ROUTE OF DRUIDISM & THE DRAGON LEGACY ||

Primary Textbooks:[*]
    THE DRUID'S HANDBOOK (*Liber-D Series*)
    ELVENOMICON (*Liber-D Series*)
    DRACONOMICON (*Liber-D Series*)
Supplementary:
    THE VAMPYRE'S HANDBOOK
    --The Vampyre's Bible (*Liber-V*)
    --Cybernomicon (*Liber-V2*)
Optional: *Draconomicon Vol.2: The Pheryllt Researches*
Additional: *Route of Mesopotamian Mysteries (Grade-II)*

|| GRADE-II || ROUTE OF MESOPOTAMIAN MYSTERIES ||

Primary Textbooks:[‡]
    NECRONOMICON: THE COMPLETE ANUNNAKI BIBLE
     (-or- THE COMPLETE ANUNNAKI BIBLE)
    --Mardukite Tablet Catalogue (*Liber-N,L,G,9*)
    --The Book of Sajaha-the-Seer (*Liber-S*)
    GATES OF THE NECRONOMICON
    --Sumerian Religion/Sumerian Legacy (*Liber-50*)
    --Babylonian Myth & Magic (*Liber-51+E*)
    --Necronomicon Revelations (*Liber-R*)
    --Crossing to the Abyss (*Liber-555*)
    NECRONOMICON: ANUNNAKI GRIMOIRE
     (-or- PRACTICAL BABYLONIAN MAGIC)
    --Babylonian Magic (*Liber-E*)

[∞] Grade-I, Route-A 'Master Edition' Anthology also available—*"The Great Magickal Arcanum"* (2020 Hardcover) by Joshua Free.

[*] Grade-I, Route-D 'Master Edition' Anthology also available—*"Merlyn's Complete Book of Druidism"* (Hardcover) by Joshua Free.

[‡] Grade-II 'Master Edition' Anthology also available—*"Necronomicon: The Complete Anunnaki Legacy"* (Hardcover) by Joshua Free.

          --The Book of Marduk by Nabu (*Liber-W*)
          --The Maqlu Ritual Book (*Liber-M*)
          --Enochian Magician's Handbook (*Liber-K*)
Supplementary: Optnl: *The Anunnaki Tarot* (*Liber-T*)
          Addnl: *Route of Mardukite Systemology* (*Grade-III*)

|| GRADE-III || ROUTE OF MARDUKITE SYSTEMOLOGY ||

Primary Textbooks:[∞]
        THE TABLETS OF DESTINY REVELATION (*Liber-One*)
        CRYSTAL CLEAR: HANDBOOK FOR SEEKERS (*Liber-2B*)
Supplementary:
        SYSTEMOLOGY: THE ORIGINAL THESIS (*Liber-S-1X*)
        THE POWER OF ZU (*Liber-S-1Z*)
Optional: *Pantheisticon* (300th Anniversary Edition)

SYSTEMOLOGY: BEYOND THE MASTER GRADES
(COMPLETE SYSTEMOLOGY WIZARD COURSE)

|| GRADE-IV || ROUTE OF METAHUMAN SYSTEMOLOGY ||

Primary Textbooks:[‡]
        METAHUMAN DESTINATIONS (2 Volumes) (*Liber-2C,2D,3C*)
        IMAGINOMICON (*Liber-3D*)
        WAY OF THE WIZARD (*Liber-3E*)

|| GRADE-V || ROUTE OF PROFESSIONAL SYSTEMOLOGY ||

Primary Textbooks:
        SYSTEMOLOGY-180 (*Liber-180*)
        SYSTEMOLOGY: BACKTRACK (*Liber-4*)
Supplementary:
        FUNDAMENTALS OF SYSTEMOLOGY (*Basic Course*)
Additional: *Pathway-to-Ascension Professional Course* (*Grade-VI*)

|| GRADE-VI || PATHWAY TO ASCENSION PROFESSIONAL COURSE ||

Primary Textbooks:
        THE PATHWAY TO ASCENSION (2 Volumes)
Additional: *Keys-to-the-Kingdom Advanced Training Course* (*Grade-VII+*)

∞ Grade-III 'Master Edition' Anthology also available—*"The Systemology Handbook"* (Hardcover) by Joshua Free.

‡ Grade-IV 'Master Edition' Anthology also available—*"The Metahuman Systemology Handbook"* (Hardcover) by Joshua Free.

WOULD

YOU

LIKE

TO

KNOW

MORE

? ? ?

AVAILABLE FROM THE **JOSHUA FREE** PUBLISHING IMPRINT

MARDUKITE MASTER COURSE
The Key to Gates of Higher Understanding

Now you can experience the Legendary "Master Course" from anywhere in the Universe, exactly as given in person by Joshua Free to the "Mardukite Academy of Systemology" in September 2020.

800+ pages of materials collected in this volume provide Seekers with full transcripts to all *48 Academy Lectures* of the legendary "*Mardukite Master Course*" combined with all course outlines, supplements and critical handouts from the original "*Instructor's Manual*"—making this the most complete definitive single-source delivery of New Age understanding and spiritual technology.

This book references 25 years of research, development and publishing, including the textbooks "*Necronomicon: The Complete Anunnaki Legacy,*" "*The Great Magickal Arcanum,*" "*The Systemology Handbook*" and "*Merlyn's Complete Book of Druidism.*"

AVAILABLE FROM THE **JOSHUA FREE** PUBLISHING IMPRINT

The Original Mardukite Master Course Lecture Volumes!
Experience the Legendary Course From Anywhere
in the Universe–Available in Four Volumes!

MAGICK & MYSTICISM
The Academy Lectures – Vol. I

DRUIDS, ELVES & DRAGONS
The Academy Lectures – Vol. II

MESOPOTAMIAN TRADITION
The Academy Lectures – Vol. III

MARDUKITE SYSTEMOLOGY
The Academy Lectures – Vol. IV

Based on the lectures by Joshua Free

Transcripts of the Mardukite Master Course Academy Lectures
given at the Mardukite Academy in September 2020.

This is part of a four-part series, each volume providing a serious Seeker with transcripts to 12 of the 48 Academy Lectures previously published in the mega-anthology *"Complete Mardukite Master Course."*

Each volume is designed to match the correlating Master Edition textbook, such as *"Great Magickal Arcanum," "Merlyn's Complete Book of Druidism," "Necronomicon: The Complete Anunnaki Legacy"* and *"Systemology Handbook."*

(Other volumes in this new "Academy Lectures" series are also available.)

AVAILABLE FROM THE **JOSHUA FREE** PUBLISHING IMPRINT

IN A WORLD FULL OF "TENS" BE AN
ELEVEN

THE METAPHYSICS OF STRANGER THINGS

TELEKINESIS, TELEPATHY SYSTEMOLOGY

by Joshua Free

Mardukite Systemology Liber-011

Experimental exploratory edition

Discover the metaphysical truth about the Universe—and maybe even yourself—as we explore what lies beneath the epic saga, *Stranger Things*. You're invited to a world where fantasy, science fiction and horror unite, and games like *Dungeons and Dragons* become reality.

Uncover a world of secret "mind control" projects, just like those at *Hawkins National Laboratory*. Decades of psychedelic experiments among other developmental programs for psychic powers, remote viewing, telekinesis (psychokinesis, PK-power) and more are revealed. Get an inside look at the operations of a real-life underground organization pursuing the truth about rehabilitating spiritual abilities for an actual "metahuman" evolution on planet Earth.

Premiere edition available in paperback and hardcover!

AVAILABLE FROM THE **JOSHUA FREE** PUBLISHING IMPRINT

Commemorating the Mardukite 15th Anniversary!
Deluxe Oversized Revised Hardcover Edition!

NECRONOMICON
THE COMPLETE ANUNNAKI BIBLE

collected works by Joshua Free

The ultimate masterpiece of Mesopotamian magic, spirituality and history, providing a complete collection—a grand symphony—of the most ancient writings on the planet.

The oldest Sumerian and Babylonian records reveal detailed accounts of cosmic history in the Universe and on Earth, the development of human civilization and descriptions of world order.

All of this information has been used, since ancient times, to maintain spiritual and physical control of humanity and its systems. It has proved to be the predecessor and foundation of all global scripture-based religious and mystical traditions thereafter.

These are the raw materials, unearthed from the underground, which have shaped humanity's beliefs, traditions and existence for thousands of years—right from the heart of the Ancient Near East: Sumer, Babylon and even Egypt...

AVAILABLE FROM THE **JOSHUA FREE** PUBLISHING IMPRINT

The dark world of the occult on planet Earth revealed!

NOVEM PORTIS (DELUXE EDITION)
NECRONOMICON REVELATIONS,
NINE GATES OF THE KINGDOM OF SHADOWS
& CROSSING TO THE ABYSS

10th Anniversary—Deluxe Hardcover (*Liber-R,9+555*)
Collected Works by Joshua Free

Commemorating completion of the "Necronomicon Shadows" cycle of research and development by the Mardukite Chamberlains (2009–2012).

Originally intended as a research-companion to "*Necronomicon: The Anunnaki Bible*" and the remaining 'Core', a Mardukite anthology of this cycle of work —known as "*Nine Gates*" or "*Novem Portis*"— eventually developed into an underground bestseller by itself.

In addition to other bonus articles and supplements, a complete collection of material from *Liber-9*, *Liber-R* and *Liber-555* are together in a deluxe hardcover anthology edition for the first time ever!

New Deluxe Oversized Hardcover Edition for 2023!

AVAILABLE FROM THE **JOSHUA FREE** PUBLISHING IMPRINT

The Underground Occult Classic

Collector's Edition Hardcover now available for this 21st Anniversary Commemoration!

SORCERER'S HANDBOOK
A GUIDE TO PRACTICAL MAGICK
by Joshua Free writing as "Merlyn Stone"

The material from "The Sorcerer's Handbook" is also contained within the new Master Edition of the original classic anthology...

THE GREAT MAGICKAL ARCANUM
A Master Course in Magick
for Modern Wizards
(Master Edition)
by Joshua Free

*Oversized Deluxe Hardcover!
Nearly 1000 Pages!*

AVAILABLE FROM THE **JOSHUA FREE** PUBLISHING IMPRINT

*10th Anniversary Hardcover Collector's Edition.
Explore the original religion on Earth.*

SUMERIAN RELIGION
Introducing the Anunnaki Gods
of Mesopotamian Neopaganism
(*Mardukite Liber-50*)
by Joshua Free

*Develop a personal relationship with Anunnaki Gods
—the divine pantheon that launched a thousand
cultures and traditions throughout the world!*

Even if you think you already know all about the Sumerian Anunnaki or Star-Gates of Babylon...

✸ Here you will find a beautifully crafted journey that is unlike anything Humans have had the opportunity to experience for thousands of years...   ✸ Here you will find a truly remarkable tome demonstrating a fresh new approach to modern Mesopotamian Neopaganism and spirituality...   ✸ Here is a Master Key to the ancient mystic arts: true knowledge concerning the powers and entities that these arts are dedicated to...   ✸ A working relationship with these powers directly...   ✸ And the wisdom to exist "alongside" the gods, so as to ever remain in the "favor" of Cosmic Law.

Available in pocket paperback as *"Anunnaki Gods: The Sumerian Religion"*

Sequel title also now available! *"Babylonian Myth & Magic"* (Liber-51+E)

AVAILABLE FROM THE **JOSHUA FREE** PUBLISHING IMPRINT

SYSTEMOLOGY

FUNDAMENTALS OF SYSTEMOLOGY

A New Thought for the 21st Century

The Official
Systemology Society
Basic Course

ALL *Six Lessons* in one
Collector's Edition
hardcover

All *six* lesson-booklets of the first official *Basic Course* on Mardukite Systemology are combined together in *one volume* as "Fundamentals of Systemology."

Also available individually.

"Being More Than Human"

"Realities in Agreement"

"Windows To Experience"

"Ancient Systemology"

"A History of Systemology"

"Systemology Processing"

AVAILABLE FROM THE **JOSHUA FREE** PUBLISHING IMPRINT

SYSTEMOLOGY

THE PATHWAY TO ASCENSION

A New Thought for the 21st Century

New Standard Systemology

ALL *Sixteen Lessons* in *two* Collector's Edition hardcover volumes

All *sixteen* lesson-booklets of the newest *Professional Course* on Mardukite Systemology are combined together in *two volumes* as "*The Pathway to Ascension.*"

Also available individually.

"*Increasing Awareness*"
"*Thought & Emotion*"
"*Clear Communication*"
"*Handling Humanity*"
"*Free Your Spirit*"
"*Escaping Spirit-Traps*"
...and many more!

**THE ORIGINAL TEXTBOOK FOR
MARDUKITE ZUISM AND SYSTEMOLOGY**

Take your first steps on the

SYSTEMOLOGY
Pathway to Self-Honesty

with the book that started it all!

Rediscover the original system of perfecting the Human Condition on a Pathway that leads to Infinity. Here is a way!—a map to chart spiritual potential and redefine the future of what it means to be human.

A landmark public debut of Grade-III Systemology
and foundation stone for reaching higher
and taking back control of your

DESTINY

(Mardukite Systemology Grade-III Research Volume, Liber-One)

AVAILABLE FROM THE **JOSHUA FREE** PUBLISHING IMPRINT

SYSTEMOLOGY
The Pathway to Self-Honesty

CRYSTAL CLEAR
Handbook for Seekers

*Achieving
Self-Actualization
& Spiritual Ascension
in This Lifetime*

by Joshua Free

Mardukite Systemology
Liber-2B

*available in
Paperback and Hardcover*

Take control of your destiny and chart the first steps
toward your own spiritual evolution.
Realize new potentials of the Human Condition with
a Self-guiding handbook for Self-Processing
toward Self-Actualization in Self-Honesty using actual
techniques and training provided for the coveted
"Mardukite Self-Defragmentation Course Program"
—once only available directly and privately from the
underground International Systemology Society.

Discover the amazing power behind the
applied spiritual technology
used for counseling and advisement in
the Mardukite Zuism tradition.

(Mardukite Systemology Grade-III Research Volume, Revised Liber-2B)

AVAILABLE FROM THE **JOSHUA FREE** PUBLISHING IMPRINT

SYSTEMOLOGY
The Gateways to Infinity

IMAGINOMICON
Accessing the Gateway to Higher Universes

A New Grimoire for the Human Spirit

by Joshua Free

Mardukite Systemology Grade-IV, Liber-3D Metahumanism

available in Paperback and Hardcover

The Way Out. Hidden for 6,000 Years.
But now we've found the Key.
A grimore to summon and invoke, command and control,
the most powerful spirit to ever exist.
Your Self.

Access beyond physical existence.
Fly free across all Gateways.
Go back to where it all began and reclaim that
personal universe which the *Spirit* once called *"Home."*

Break free from the Matrix;
control the Mind and command the Body
from outside those systems
— because *You* were never "human" —
fully realize what it means to be a *spiritual being*, then
rise up through the Gateways to Higher Universes and BE.

(Mardukite Systemology Grade-IV Research Volume, Liber-3D)

∞

JOSHUA FREE

A mystic philosopher, world renowned underground occult expert and prolific writer of over 100 books on systemology, ancient history, magic and "esoteric archaeology" since 1995. He founded Mardukite Ministries (Mardukite Zuism) in 2008, is director of Mardukite Research Organization (Mardukite Academy) and its New Thought division "The Systemology Society."

PUBLISHED BY THE **JOSHUA FREE** IMPRINT REPRESENTING

The Founding Church of Mardukite Zuism
& Mardukite Academy of Systemology

mardukite.com

www.ingramcontent.com/pod-product-compliance
Lightning Source LLC
Chambersburg PA
CBHW060412010526
44107CB00006B/663